DANNY

GOODMAN'S WINDOWS 95

HANDBOOK

Danny Goodman's Windows 95 Handbook

Published in the United States by Random House, Inc., New York, and simultaneously in Canada by Random House of Canada, Limited.

Composed by **vivid** studios

Manufactured in the United States of America

First Edition

0 9 8 7 6 5 4 3 2 1

ISBN 0-679-75586-1

Trademarks

New York Toronto London Sydney Auckland

Hardware

Table of Contents cont.

Software

Most chapters are two-page spreads like this one. You can see all related information at a glance.

Each chapter and section starts with a contents spread that explains the information in that chapter or section.

Windows 95-like menubar shows you which chapter and section you are in.

Information in the top level is for beginners.

Special symbols alert you to warnings or other special information.

The warning symbol alerts you to problems or dangerous activities that could harm you or your computer.

Highlighted words alert you to key concepts and help you find your way around a page quickly.

Hypertext-like jumps point you to other pages that contain more information about a particular topic.

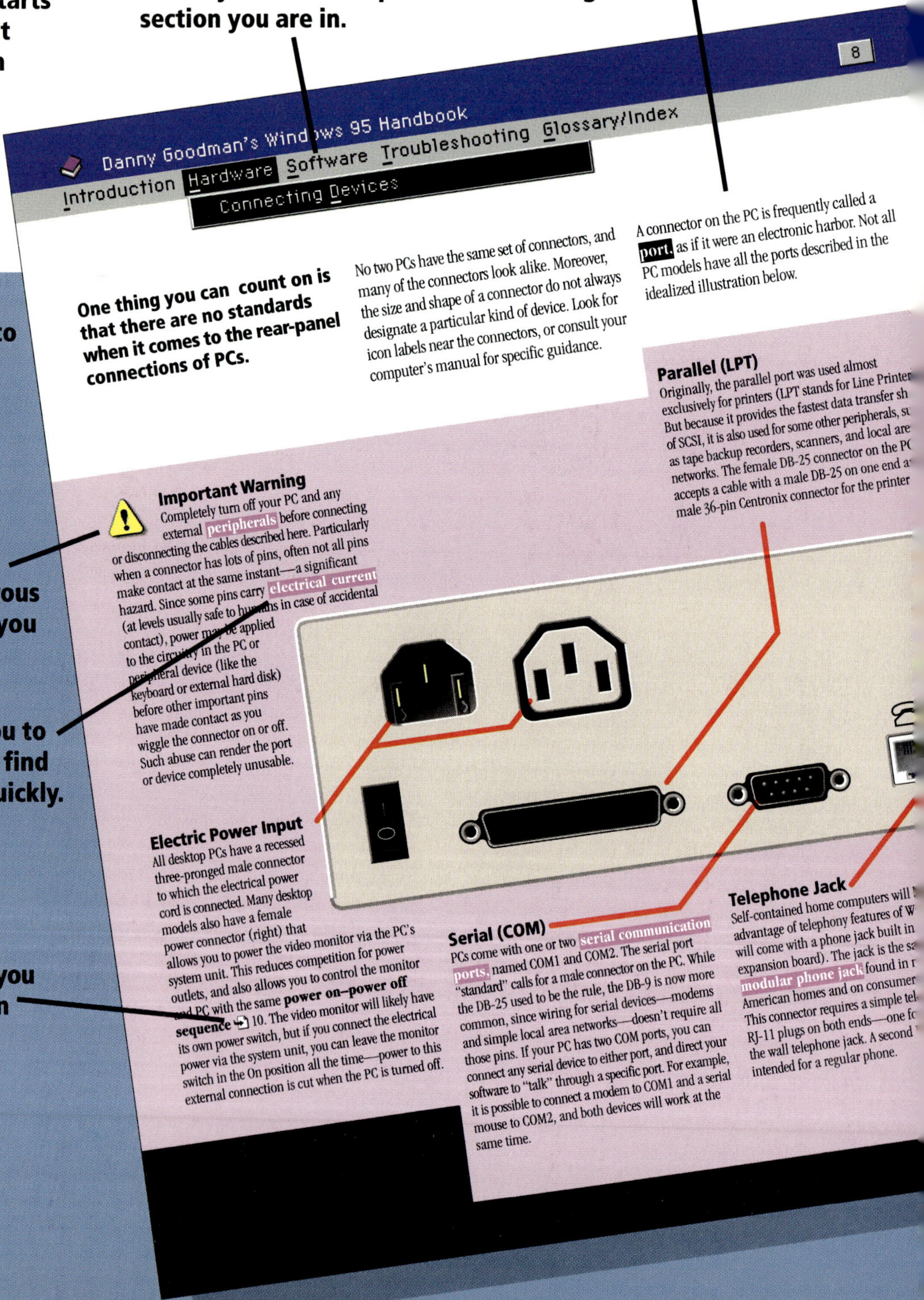

Danny Goodman's Windows 95 Handbook 8

Introduction Hardware Software Troubleshooting Glossary/Index

Connecting Devices

One thing you can count on is that there are no standards when it comes to the rear-panel connections of PCs.

No two PCs have the same set of connectors, and many of the connectors look alike. Moreover, the size and shape of a connector do not always designate a particular kind of device. Look for icon labels near the connectors, or consult your computer's manual for specific guidance.

A connector on the PC is frequently called a **port**, as if it were an electronic harbor. Not all PC models have all the ports described in the idealized illustration below.

Important Warning
Completely turn off your PC and any external peripherals before connecting or disconnecting the cables described here. Particularly when a connector has lots of pins, often not all pins make contact at the same instant—a significant hazard. Since some pins carry electrical current (at levels usually safe to humans in case of accidental contact), power may be applied to the circuitry in the PC or peripheral device (like the keyboard or external hard disk) before other important pins have made contact as you wiggle the connector on or off. Such abuse can render the port or device completely unusable.

Parallel (LPT)
Originally, the parallel port was used almost exclusively for printers (LPT stands for Line Printer ... But because it provides the fastest data transfer ... of SCSI, it is also used for some other peripherals, ... as tape backup recorders, scanners, and local are... networks. The female DB-25 connector on the PC accepts a cable with a male DB-25 on one end a... male 36-pin Centronix connector for the printer

Electric Power Input
All desktop PCs have a recessed three-pronged male connector to which the electrical power cord is connected. Many desktop models also have a female power connector (right) that allows you to power the video monitor via the PC's system unit. This reduces competition for power outlets, and also allows you to control the monitor and PC with the same **power on–power off sequence** 10. The video monitor will likely have its own power switch, but if you connect the electrical power via the system unit, you can leave the monitor switch in the On position all the time—power to this external connection is cut when the PC is turned off.

Serial (COM)
PCs come with one or two serial communication ports, named COM1 and COM2. The serial port "standard" calls for a male connector on the PC. While the DB-25 used to be the rule, the DB-9 is now more common, since wiring for serial devices—modems and simple local area networks—doesn't require all those pins. If your PC has two COM ports, you can connect any serial device to either port, and direct your software to "talk" through a specific port. For example, it is possible to connect a modem to COM1 and a serial mouse to COM2, and both devices will work at the same time.

Telephone Jack
Self-contained home computers will ... advantage of telephony features of W... will come with a phone jack built in ... expansion board). The jack is the sa... modular phone jack found in ... American homes and on consumer ... This connector requires a simple tel... RJ-11 plugs on both ends—one fo... the wall telephone jack. A second ... intended for a regular phone.

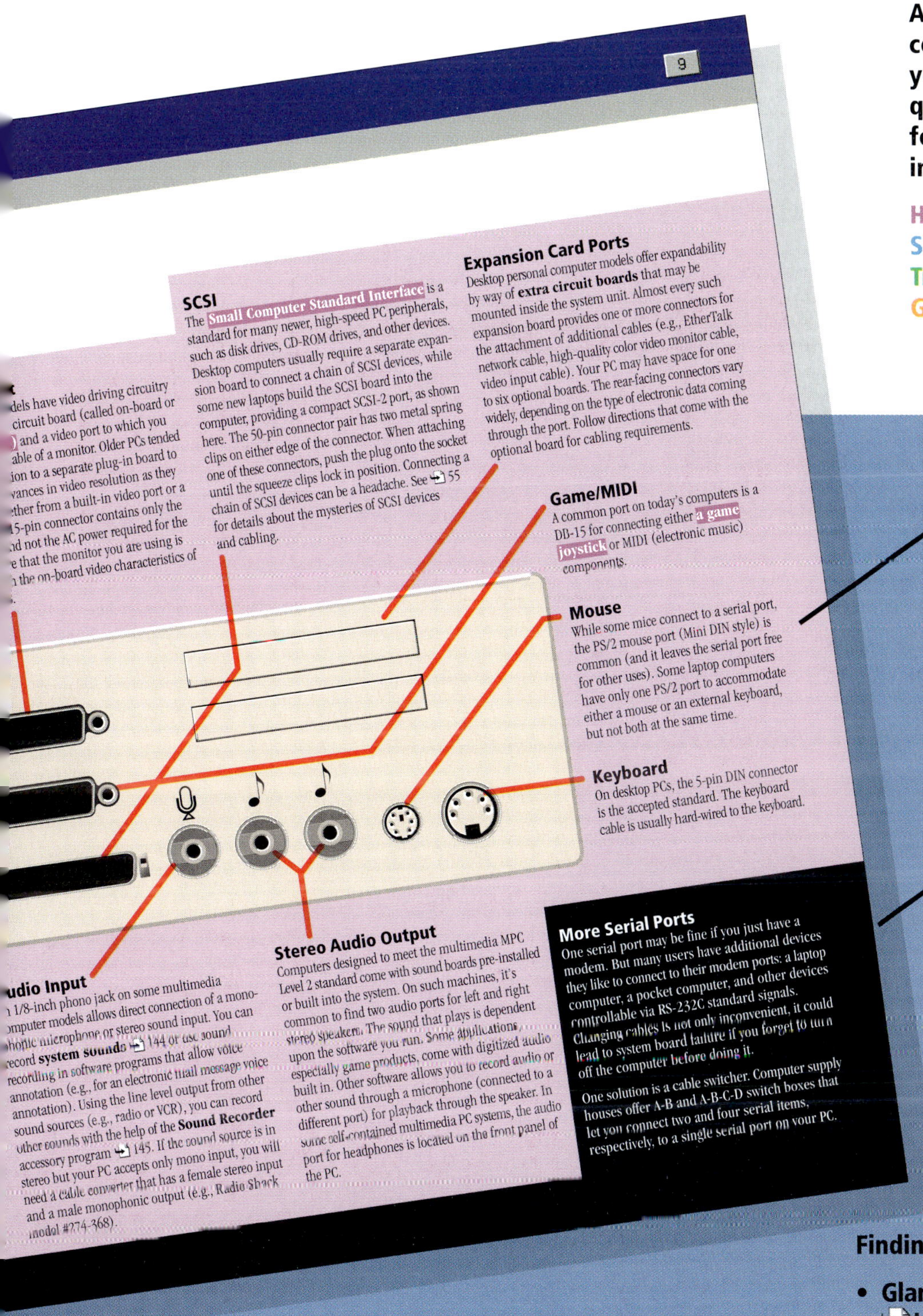

All of the sections are color-coded so that you can find your way through the book quickly and easily. The following sections titles are in their actual colors.

Hardware
Software
Troubleshooting
Glossary/Index

This level of information is for everybody. It contains the most important information for Windows 95 users

This level of information is for more advanced users. Here you'll find information in greater detail.

Finding Information Fast!

- **Glance down the Table of Contents ➔ i-iii, to see if there is a quick match to your question.**
- **Look up any keyword in the Glossary/Index ➔ 186.**

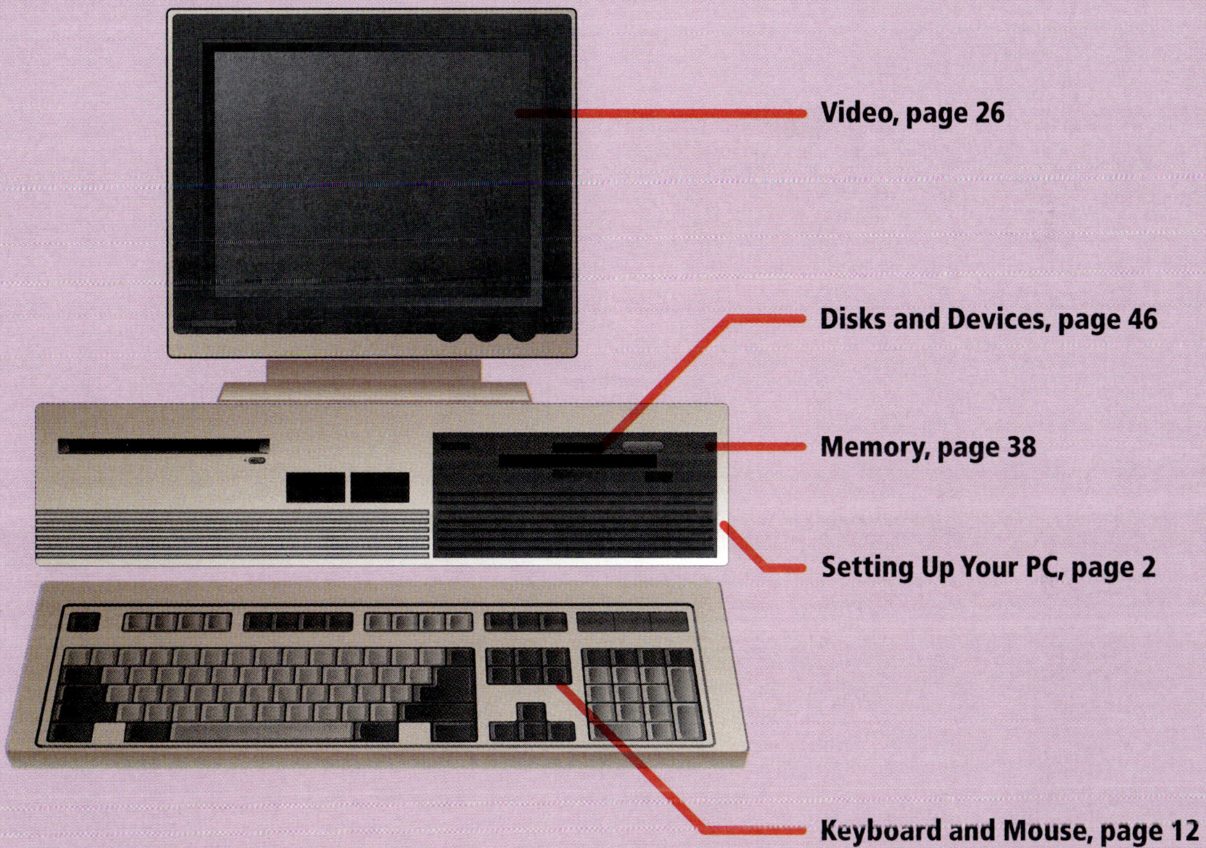
Video, page 26
Disks and Devices, page 46
Memory, page 38
Setting Up Your PC, page 2
Keyboard and Mouse, page 12

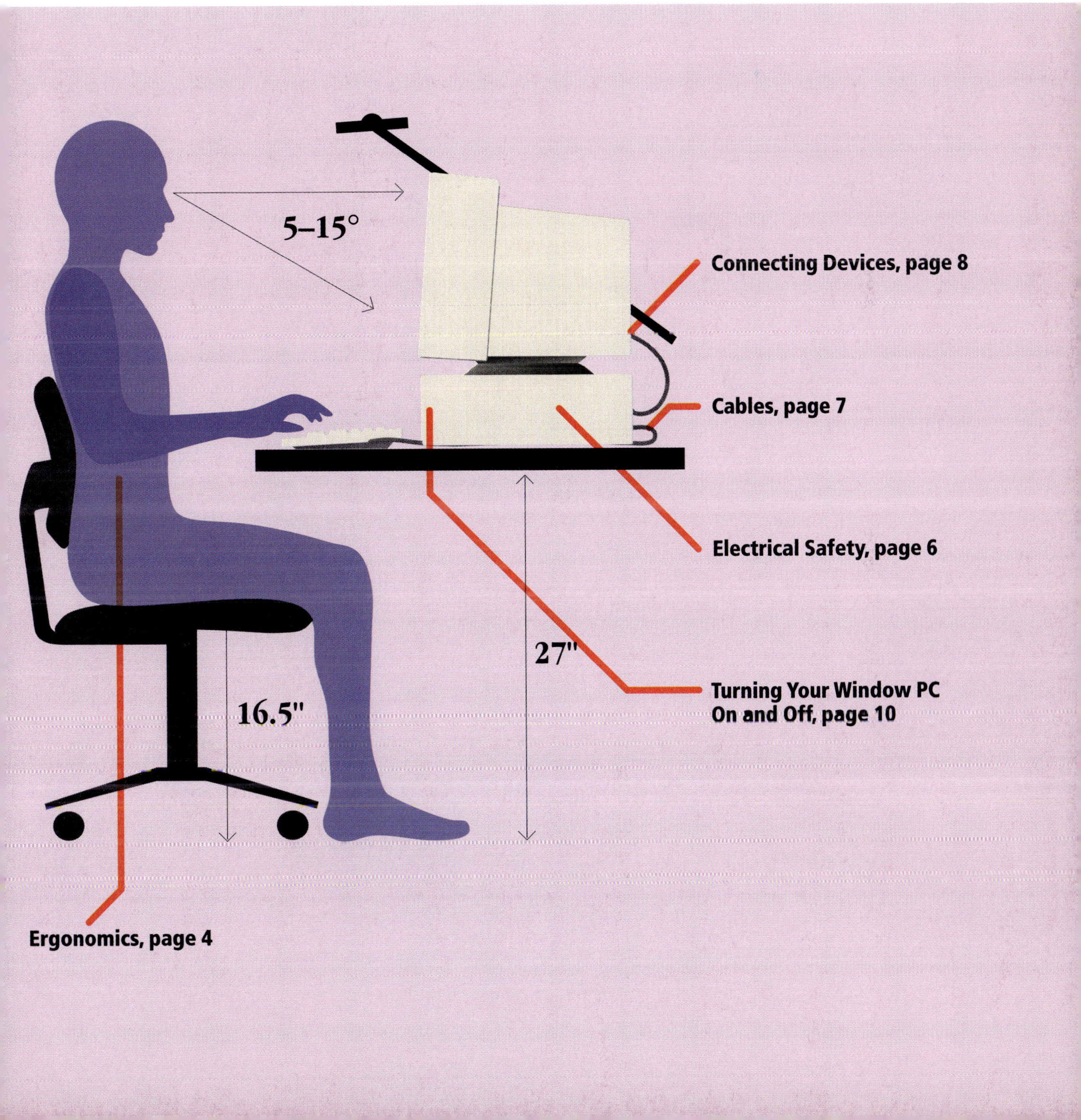
5–15°
Connecting Devices, page 8
Cables, page 7
Electrical Safety, page 6
27"
Turning Your Window PC On and Off, page 10
16.5"
Ergonomics, page 4

Too many personal computer owners overlook the importance of a comfortable work area for their machines and themselves.

Ergonomics, the study of human interaction with work, should play a key role in setting up your work environment. Ignoring these issues can lead to muscular and skeletal health problems if you frequently spend many hours in front of a computer.

In particular, you should pay close attention to the height of the **keyboard** from the floor and the angle between your eyes and the **video monitor.** If typing at the keyboard is a major part of your work, then also investigate wrist supports to reduce the likelihood of contracting a **repetitive strain injury.**

Keyboard Height

Don't confuse **keyboard height** with table height. In both homes and offices (other than at secretarial stations), the tendency is to put the PC and keyboard on the main desk surface. In the United States, a standard office desk surface is 29 inches from the floor. But for most people, a keyboard at that height can become uncomfortable, and may be dangerous during extensive use. If you must use a standard, fixed-height table for your PC, make sure the keyboard is either in a recessed keyboard tray or on a typewriter-height desk return, typically set at 27 inches high.

While the **exact height** of the keyboard is dependent on your height and the height of the chair seat, your forearms (from elbow to keys) should be about parallel with the floor. The chair should offer good back support, be very mobile, and allow your feet to touch the floor fully.

Be most careful with laptop PCs. Hotel room desks are usually too high for comfortable typing. And docking stations that fit beneath the machine place the keyboard even higher. Use **docking stations** only with separate external keyboards.

Viewing Angle

Establishing the proper angle between your eyes and the **video monitor** can make the difference between headaches and painless computing. To impose the least stress on the eyes, the monitor should not be straight ahead (although this is difficult to avoid with 19–21-inch monitors). An angle of 5° to 15° from your eyes down to the center of the screen is considered comfortable for most computer users, especially if you must move your eyes constantly from copy source to keyboard to screen. Try to avoid frequent **focus adjustments** (changes in the distance between your eyes and what you're viewing) by adding a document holder (a device that lets you set papers adjacent to the monitor).

If you are using a separate video monitor, a tilting swivel **monitor stand** is highly recommended. It allows for myriad adjustments to suit your mood or fatigue level, as well as allowing you to adjust the monitor for reduced glare. For more about video monitor safety, ➔36.

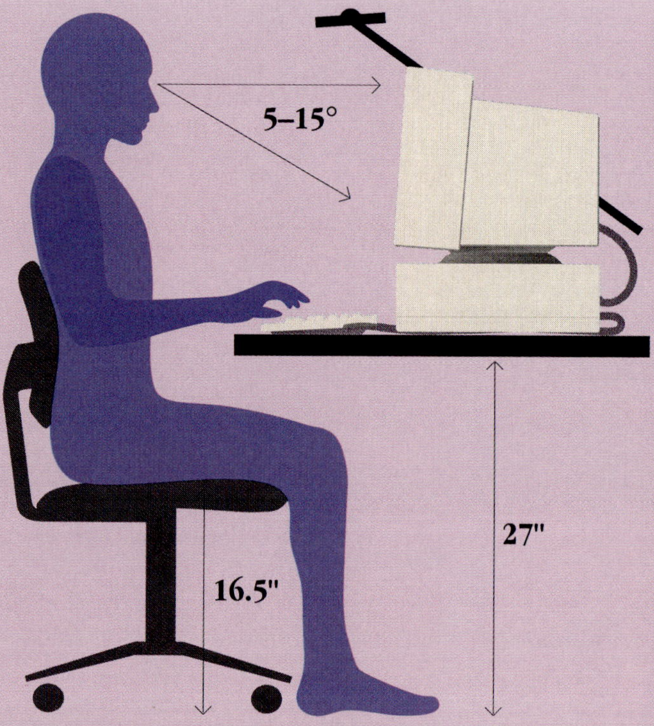

Repetitive Strain Injury

Only within the past few years have the **potential health dangers** of excessive computer keyboard typing been observed and studied. While not everything is understood at this point, it is clear that repetitive hand, wrist, and upper body motions—especially when some level of force is applied—can lead to painful injuries. These can affect virtually anyone in an occupation that requires repetitive motions, from store clerks to assembly line workers. A common cause is straining tendons that can lead to inflammation and swelling, which starts squeezing the nerves.

Among the most common injuries are tendinitis, tensynovitis, and carpal tunnel syndrome (CTS). As a group, these are called repetitive strain injuries (RSIs) or cumulative trauma disorders (CTDs).

No exact measure exists about how much keyboarding is too much, so be aware of these symptoms: pain, numbness, or tingling anywhere from your neck down to your fingers; inability to grasp objects; swelling. If you suspect a problem caused by intensive computing work, consult a physician experienced in RSIs.

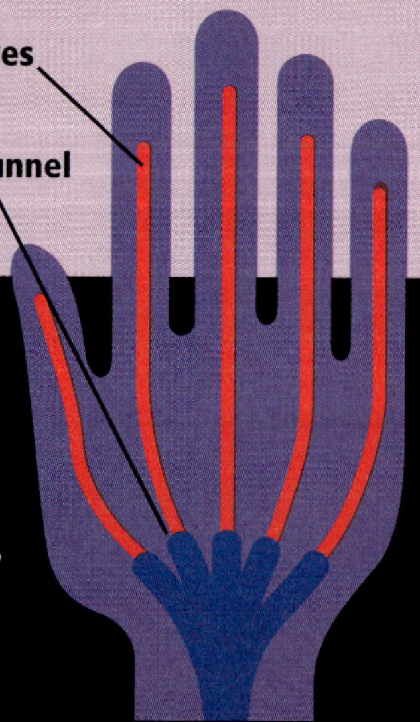

The best way to avoid RSIs is to take frequent rest breaks, maintain good posture, and use wrist supports.

Lighting

In many circumstances lighting conditions are out of your control, especially in an office. Most overhead lighting **glare** (light reflecting off the screen, looking like hot spots) can be reduced with the help of a tilting monitor stand. Light from windows can be especially troublesome because the quantity and direction change during the day. Direct sunlight renders most video screens useless, because the monitors can't deliver enough brightness to overcome the sun's light. If you are near a window, it is best to sit with the window to one side. This reduces glare (when the monitor faces the window) and the strong contrast between outside light and the monitor (when the monitor's back faces the window). Depending on your window's exposure and the time of year, you may still need to shield the monitor from the sun's rays during parts of the day.

Also, be sure to adjust the **monitor brightness** to fit the surrounding light ➔36. During the day, the brightness may need to be turned up full blast. At night, in a darkened room, turn the brightness down to reduce the sharp contrast between surrounding darkness and the illuminated screen.

Keep It Moving

Ergonomic studies of workers who spend their entire workdays at a computer keyboard have discovered that it is important to allow for frequent adjustment of all the surfaces surrounding one's workspace. That includes **chair height, chair angle, keyboard height**, and **viewing angles.** Office and computer supply companies offer self-contained carts that provide almost infinite adjustment of virtually every part of your workstation. In concert with a highly adjustable chair, these carts give each individual the most flexibility in creating a comfortable environment.

Mouse Pads

The mouse is an important element of the Windows 95 environment, but few commercial computer desks take mice into account. The undersides of computer mice have become more durable over time, but running them around a hard desk surface can wear them down after a couple of years. Moreover, many desk surfaces don't give the mouse ball good traction.

A **mouse pad** is a slice of rubber measuring about 6 inches by 8 inches. Pads have various surfaces, such as plain rubber, cloth, or a slightly mottled plastic. Few mouse pads are available that don't have some advertising printed on them. That's good in a way, because it is often possible to get mouse pads for free from hardware and software manufacturers at computer trade shows (you may have to sit through a formal demo of the product to qualify) or as a bonus when you buy goods at computer stores.

Importantly, a mouse pad reserves space on your desk for the mouse. If you leave too little space on your desk for the mouse, you may find the mouse rather inconvenient, since you'll constantly run out of surface to move the pointer where you need it (and then have to pick up the mouse and shift to the other side of the space to continue moving the pointer). Even if you don't use a mouse pad, try to reserve a **10-by-8-inch space** for the mouse next to your keyboard (either on the right or left, depending on your mouse hand of preference).

Breathing Room

No, not for you. For your PC. As a piece of electronic equipment, a desktop PC heats up while in use. The power supply generates heat. Some microchips on the circuit boards get hot. The hard disk motor gets warm. Heat is a personal computer's worst natural enemy. PC hardware designers know that, and have devised various systems to prevent the innards from overheating. Key to those systems are **ventilation holes**, most of which you can't see because they're disguised by aesthetic cabinet designs. Most of the holes are located along the bottom of the cabinet (to allow cool air to come in) and on the top (to allow the heated air to flow out). This kind of convection cooling is a critical part of your PC's hardware. Keep at least a one-inch breathing zone around your system unit's sides. And if you see vents along the top of the machine or monitor, don't block them with other equipment, a notebook, or papers.

Some PC system units may be set on their sides and still maintain proper cooling. Tower-style models are designed this way. Always follow the manufacturer's recommendations about setting up the system unit in any nontraditional orientation.

Earthquake Proofing

You probably won't think about this until after you've lost a PC or monitor to a tremor, but it's important for computer owners in many parts of the world to prepare for an earthquake. In recent experiences around the world, many computer users found that their system units or monitors had crept off the table as the building shook from side to side. Monitors, which typically rest on relatively slippery surfaces, were particularly vulnerable. One of the best defenses is to secure the system unit and monitor to the table. Then, even if the table does a waltz, the PC will go with it.

A few low-cost electrical add-ons can prevent damage to your PC from anomalies in the electrical power delivered to your power outlet.

You should not take the quality of that power—at home or at work—for granted. Fortunately, some offices have specially marked power outlets that should help protect your machine from the vagaries of the electric utility company.

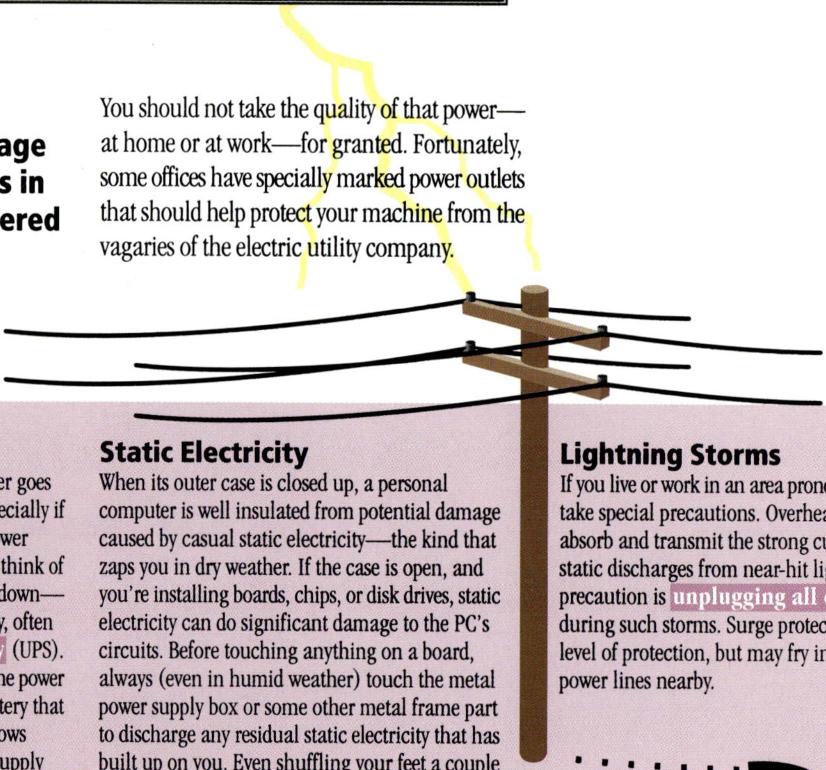

Standby Power Supplies

When you are working on a PC and the power goes out, you can find yourself in big trouble, especially if you haven't saved your work in awhile. If power outages are common—or you can't bear to think of your PC or file server unexpectedly shutting down—then consider adding a standby power supply, often called an **uninterruptible power supply** (UPS). A standby power supply goes in-line between the power outlet and your equipment. It contains a battery that is continually charged while the AC power flows normally. When the power quits, the power supply instantaneously puts its charged batteries to work, usually sounding an audible alert to warn you that you are on emergency power. The purpose of a standby power supply is to give you enough warning and power to save what you're working on and shut down safely. It's an excellent idea for network servers, because other computers on the network may still have power, and you'll want to give remote users a few minutes' warning that the server will be shutting down.

Power Strips

Most homes and offices were not wired for the computer age. While a PC, by itself, doesn't impose that great a threat to the electrical wall socket, additional peripherals begin to fill up outlets at an alarming rate, especially when one of those items has a bulky black transformer that plugs into the outlet.

To **prevent overloading** any circuit into which you plug your computer equipment, a fused power strip is a good addition. Such strips have four to eight electrical outlets, often with a master on-off switch that lets you control the whole collection with a single switch. The advantage of a fuse in the power strip is that it should blow before the main fuse or circuit breaker controlling many other outlets. Some power strips also have surge protectors built in, but the protection can wear out over time.

Static Electricity

When its outer case is closed up, a personal computer is well insulated from potential damage caused by casual static electricity—the kind that zaps you in dry weather. If the case is open, and you're installing boards, chips, or disk drives, static electricity can do significant damage to the PC's circuits. Before touching anything on a board, always (even in humid weather) touch the metal power supply box or some other metal frame part to discharge any residual static electricity that has built up on you. Even shuffling your feet a couple of steps can build up a charge again, so continually discharge yourself. Also try to ground yourself before touching any rear panel connector. Better safe than $orry.

Lightning Storms

If you live or work in an area prone to electrical storms, take special precautions. Overhead power lines can absorb and transmit the strong currents generated by static discharges from near-hit lightning. The best precaution is **unplugging all electronic gear** during such storms. Surge protectors may offer some level of protection, but may fry in a direct hit to the power lines nearby.

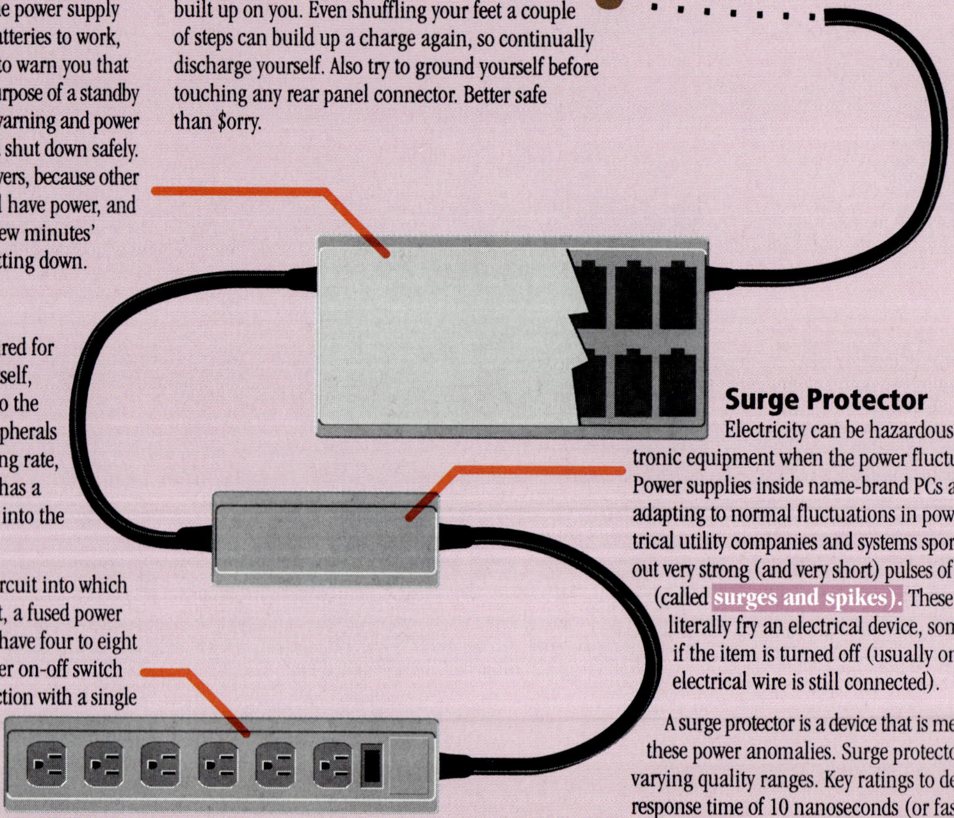

Surge Protector

Electricity can be hazardous even to electronic equipment when the power fluctuates wildly. Power supplies inside name-brand PCs are capable of adapting to normal fluctuations in power. But electrical utility companies and systems sporadically send out very strong (and very short) pulses of varying types (called **surges and spikes**). These are what can literally fry an electrical device, sometimes even if the item is turned off (usually one side of the electrical wire is still connected).

A surge protector is a device that is meant to absorb these power anomalies. Surge protectors come in varying quality ranges. Key ratings to demand are a response time of 10 nanoseconds (or faster) and a clamping voltage in the 350–400 volt range.

Although they are inanimate, connectors have genders—male and female. If you look head-on into the end of a cable connector and see free-standing metal pins (even if the pins are shielded by a metal housing), then it is a male connector or plug.

A connector consisting strictly of holes (into which the pins go) is a female connector (jack or outlet). Cabling is a strictly heterosexual affair, requiring one **male** and one **female** to make a coupling.

When connecting a cable, make sure it is securely fastened to its receptacle. Push plugs until they are firmly seated against jacks. Connectors with screw posts should be screwed into the female connectors to prevent the pair from accidentally coming loose or being kicked apart.

Unmarked (or Almost) Cables

While many cables that come with PCs have appropriate symbols molded into the connectors, most cables do not. Many connectors look alike, yet have different numbers of pins. To make sure you don't exert improper force on connectors that aren't meant to be connected or that are misaligned, look for a top arrow on the molded housing or for matching shapes of the metal shrouds surrounding the pins. Although this is not always convenient, look at the two connectors as you attempt to plug them together.

Connector Types

The array of PC and peripheral connector styles is mind-numbing, especially when you add the many connections required for full-function multimedia computers. Still, you can begin to see families of connector styles.

DB-25

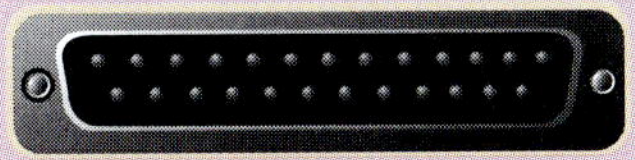

DB-15

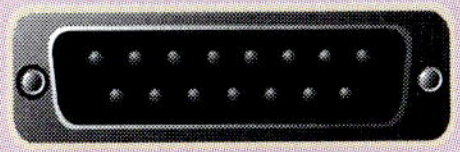

DB-9

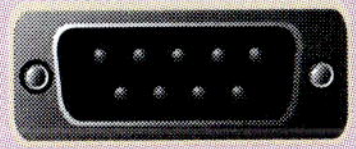

One style is known in the trade by the letters "DB" and the number of pins in the connector. For example, a typical 25-pin serial port connector on the back of a desktop PC is a male DB-25. It requires a cable that has a complementary female DB-25 connector on one end. DB-style connectors in 9-, 15-, and 25-pin varieties are commonly used for serial ports, modems, the PC end of parallel printer cables, and video monitor connections.

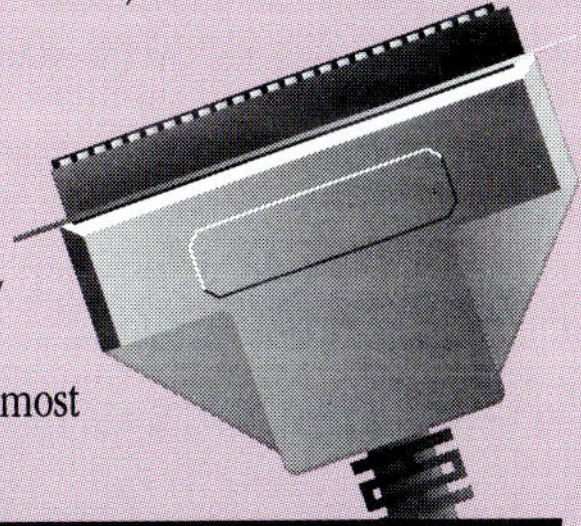

A heftier connector, named after the company that popularized it many years ago, is the Centronics style. Its most common pin counts are 36 (for the printer end of parallel printer cables) and 50 (for some SCSI devices).

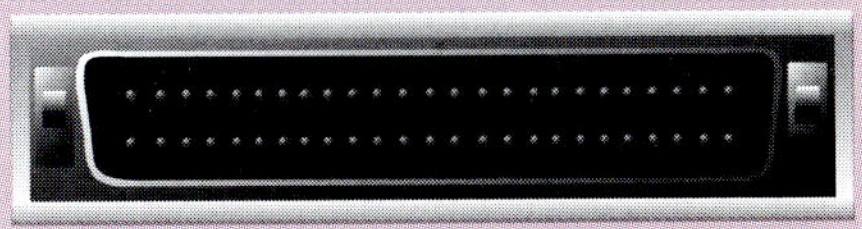

A comparatively new connector for **SCSI-2** ports on laptop and other PCs will likely become more popular with **Plug And Play** computers. This connector is a compact 50-pin style with built-in clips to hold the plug onto its jack.

Two styles of round connectors are based on a European-originated standard, called DIN. Older PC keyboards used a standard 5-pin DIN connector to the rear of the system unit. The **Mini DIN** style (in pin counts ranging up to 8) is used today for PS/2-style keyboards and mice.

Audio jacks (both input and output) use a well-known standard called the RCA phone jack. Typical phone jacks are 1/8 inch in diameter, a common size these days for Walkman-compatible headphones. A full range of adapters are available at places such as Radio Shack for conversion between the 1/8-inch stereo jacks to other plug styles on other audio cables.

Cable Extensions

Setting up a PC workstation in which the system unit is not on the desktop requires **extension cables** for the keyboard, mouse, video, and video monitor power. Major computer supply houses offer cabling kits designed specifically for the various styles of monitors and keyboards. Whenever possible, compare pictures of the cable extension connectors against the connectors on your PC and video monitor.

You may also wish to set up a **SCSI** device or parallel printer at some distance from your system unit. Typical SCSI cables supplied with hardware are notoriously short. Longer cables are available through computer supply houses, but they may affect the installation of multiple SCSI devices ➔ 55. Parallel printer cables should not exceed 25 feet in length.

To prevent interference between a home PC and televisions, stereos, or telephones, always buy **shielded cable** extensions.

Cables for Modems

Not all serial cables are alike. Cables designed to connect a PC to an external modem invert some of the connections inside one of the connectors for the two devices to communicate with each other. Serial cable extensions do not flip these pins.

If you cannot find the desired modem cable, you can use a "straight through" serial cable with a **null modem adapter**. This adapter connects between the cable and the modem. Inside the adapter, the connections are inverted for use with a modem.

Adapters

Computer supply stores and catalogs have a wide range of connector adapters for virtually any legal combination, such as for connecting a DB-25 cable to a DB-9 serial port on a PC. Another kind of adapter, a **gender changer**, can also help you join two connectors of the same gender. For best reliability, however, avoid adapters when a one-piece cable is available.

One thing you can count on is that there are no standards when it comes to the rear-panel connections of PCs.

No two PCs have the same set of connectors, and many of the connectors look alike. Moreover, the size and shape of a connector do not always designate a particular kind of device. Look for icon labels near the connectors, or consult your computer's manual for specific guidance.

A connector on the PC is frequently called a **port,** as if it were an electronic harbor. Not all PC models have all the ports described in the idealized illustration below.

Parallel (LPT)

Originally, the parallel port was used almost exclusively for printers (LPT stands for Line Printer). But because it provides the fastest data transfer short of SCSI, it is also used for some other peripherals, such as tape backup recorders, scanners, and local area networks. The female DB-25 connector on the PC accepts a cable with a male DB-25 on one end and a male 36-pin Centronix connector for the printer end.

Important Warning

Completely turn off your PC and any external **peripherals** before connecting or disconnecting the cables described here. Particularly when a connector has lots of pins, often not all pins make contact at the same instant—a significant hazard. Since some pins carry **electrical current** (at levels usually safe to humans in case of accidental contact), power may be applied to the circuitry in the PC or peripheral device (like the keyboard or external hard disk) before other important pins have made contact as you wiggle the connector on or off. Such abuse can render the port or device completely unusable.

Electric Power Input

All desktop PCs have a recessed three-pronged male connector to which the electrical power cord is connected. Many desktop models also have a female power connector (right) that allows you to power the video monitor via the PC's system unit. This reduces competition for power outlets, and also allows you to control the monitor and PC with the same **power on–power off sequence** 10. The video monitor will likely have its own power switch, but if you connect the electrical power via the system unit, you can leave the monitor switch in the On position all the time—power to this external connection is cut when the PC is turned off.

Serial (COM)

PCs come with one or two **serial communication ports,** named COM1 and COM2. The serial port "standard" calls for a male connector on the PC. While the DB-25 used to be the rule, the DB-9 is now more common, since wiring for serial devices—modems and simple local area networks—doesn't require all those pins. If your PC has two COM ports, you can connect any serial device to either port, and direct your software to "talk" through a specific port. For example, it is possible to connect a modem to COM1 and a serial mouse to COM2, and both devices will work at the same time.

Telephone Jack

Self-contained home computers will be taking advantage of telephony features of Windows 95, and will come with a phone jack built in (or on an expansion board). The jack is the same RJ-11 style **modular phone jack** found in most North American homes and on consumer telephone gear. This connector requires a simple telephone cable with RJ-11 plugs on both ends—one for the PC, one for the wall telephone jack. A second RJ-11, if present, is intended for a regular phone.

Video Output

Some computer models have video driving circuitry built into the main circuit board (called on-board or **local bus video**) and a video port to which you connect the video cable of a monitor. Older PCs tended to leave this function to a separate plug-in board to accommodate advances in video resolution as they came along. Whether from a built-in video port or a video card, this 15-pin connector contains only the video signals, and not the AC power required for the monitor. Be sure that the monitor you are using is compatible with the on-board video characteristics of your PC ➔ 28.

SCSI

The **Small Computer Standard Interface** is a standard for many newer, high-speed PC peripherals, such as disk drives, CD-ROM drives, and other devices. Desktop computers usually require a separate expansion board to connect a chain of SCSI devices, while some new laptops build the SCSI board into the computer, providing a compact SCSI-2 port, as shown here. The 50-pin connector pair has two metal spring clips on either edge of the connector. When attaching one of these connectors, push the plug onto the socket until the squeeze clips lock in position. Connecting a chain of SCSI devices can be a headache. See ➔ 55 for details about the mysteries of SCSI devices and cabling.

Expansion Card Ports

Desktop personal computer models offer expandability by way of **extra circuit boards** that may be mounted inside the system unit. Almost every such expansion board provides one or more connectors for the attachment of additional cables (e.g., EtherTalk network cable, high-quality color video monitor cable, video input cable). Your PC may have space for one to six optional boards. The rear-facing connectors vary widely, depending on the type of electronic data coming through the port. Follow directions that come with the optional board for cabling requirements.

Game/MIDI

A common port on today's computers is a DB-15 for connecting either **a game joystick** or MIDI (electronic music) components.

Mouse

While some mice connect to a serial port, the PS/2 mouse port (Mini DIN style) is common (and it leaves the serial port free for other uses). Some laptop computers have only one PS/2 port to accommodate either a mouse or an external keyboard, but not both at the same time.

Keyboard

On desktop PCs, the 5-pin DIN connector is the accepted standard. The keyboard cable is usually hard-wired to the keyboard.

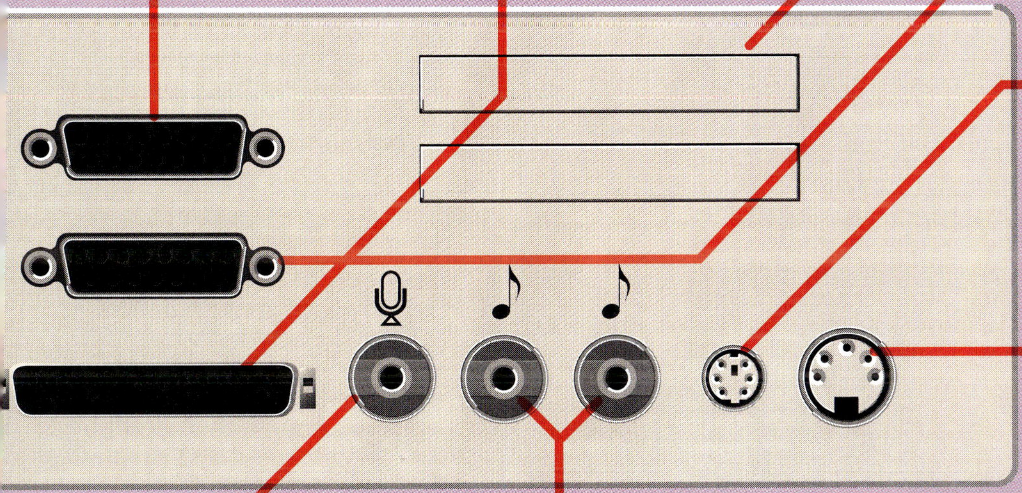

Audio Input

An 1/8-inch phono jack on some multimedia computer models allows direct connection of a monophonic microphone or stereo sound input. You can record **system sounds** ➔ 144 or use sound recording in software programs that allow voice annotation (e.g., for an electronic mail message voice annotation). Using the line level output from other sound sources (e.g., radio or VCR), you can record other sounds with the help of the **Sound Recorder** accessory program ➔ 145. If the sound source is in stereo but your PC accepts only mono input, you will need a cable converter that has a female stereo input and a male monophonic output (e.g., Radio Shack model #274-368).

Stereo Audio Output

Computers designed to meet the multimedia MPC Level 2 standard come with sound boards pre-installed or built into the system. On such machines, it's common to find two audio ports for left and right stereo speakers. The sound that plays is dependent upon the software you run. Some applications, especially game products, come with digitized audio built in. Other software allows you to record audio or other sound through a microphone (connected to a different port) for playback through the speaker. In some self-contained multimedia PC systems, the audio port for headphones is located on the front panel of the PC.

More Serial Ports

One serial port may be fine if you just have a modem. But many users have additional devices they like to connect to their modem ports: a laptop computer, a pocket computer, and other devices controllable via RS-232C standard signals. Changing cables is not only inconvenient, it could lead to system board failure if you forget to turn off the computer before doing it.

One solution is a cable switcher. Computer supply houses offer A-B and A-B-C-D switch boxes that let you connect two and four serial items, respectively, to a single serial port on your PC.

Turning Your Windows PC On and Off

Also called booting or starting the computer, turning on the power is the strongest electrical shock to your PC hardware short of a power company voltage spike.

The power switch is commonly located on the front panel of today's desktop PCs. For older models, look to one of the sides (near the rear) or the rear panel.

While you must eventually flip the same switch to turn off the PC, you should initiate the shut down process from within Windows. Battery-operated PCs may be put to sleep, instead of being shut down entirely. This keeps all documents and applications in suspended animation until you wake up the machine later to pick up where you left off.

Occasionally it is necessary to restart, or reboot, the PC. If at all possible, restart from within Windows (via the Start button). Restarting the PC is much less traumatic to the internal circuits than turning the computer off and back on.

What Happens at Power On

Turning on the PC brings the computer to life with the help of instructions preprogrammed into the **ROM** ➜40. Instructions include checking out the system board and RAM chips, sometimes emitting a startup tone if tests are successful, displaying information about the ROM version installed, and locating a diskette or hard disk containing system software. If no system is found on the first disk the computer sees (it starts with internal floppy drives), the screen displays a message indicating that the disk is a non-system disk or not a boot disk (the message varies from machine to machine). If you believe your PC should find a system disk (floppy or hard) but it thinks otherwise, consult troubleshooting pages 158–162. Worse yet, if you don't even get to the part where the PC looks for a system disk because of other messages, see pages 158–162.

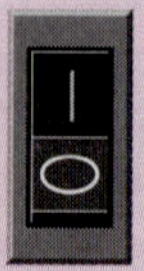

Power On: Desktop PC

Starting a desktop PC couldn't be simpler. Locate the **power switch,** which may be a large rocker type, a slide switch, or a push button. Rocker switches and slide switches may have the international circle and line symbols for On and Off (few people remember which is which). Press or slide the switch fully to the opposite setting. It should snap or lock in place.

Power On: Laptop PCs

Virtually all laptop PCs include a power switch, which must be turned on to get the unit going in the first place (opening the lid for the display is generally not the way to turn on the unit). But laptops can be placed in a **sleep or standby mode.** To awaken a sleeping laptop, press the standby button (if there is one) or any keyboard key.

Shutting Down

Powering off (shutting down) the PC is also a shock to the hardware. More importantly, you should begin the **shutdown process** from Windows before you even think about reaching for the Power switch. Closing Windows first insures that all document files have been saved and closed, all applications have quit naturally, all disk caches have been saved, and the **Desktop** ➜74 is updated with changes to your window layouts.

Brute force powering down (including a power failure) has been known to corrupt files and lose data. Protect yourself and your information: shut down gently.

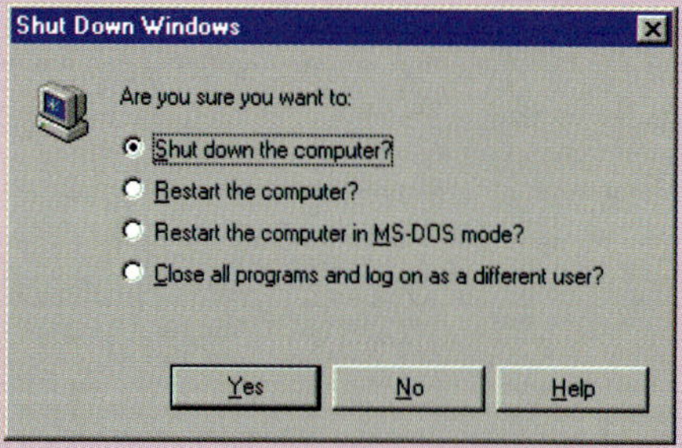

Windows Shutdown

Windows goes through a lengthy procedure internally when it shuts down (or restarts) properly. Follow these steps to shut down Windows safely:

1. Click the Start button in the Taskbar.
2. Choose `Shut Down` from the Start menu.

After the desktop dims, the `Shut down Windows` window appears to ask your confirmation of the menu command. You have three or four options, depending on your Windows security setup. `Shut down the computer?` is the default value.

3. Click the Yes button.

If any applications are open with **unsaved documents,** you will be prompted about whether you wish to save each document. If you don't save the changes, they will be lost. Windows continues closing down all open applications and disconnecting any modem or network connections. Another window asks you to wait while Windows finishes shutting itself down. Eventually, the screen goes blank except for a message that says it is OK to turn off the computer.

4. Now you can flip the big switch.

If your PC seems **frozen,** preventing you from popping up the Start menu, do not rush to pull the Power switch. You can probably get out of this jam by following restart procedures.

Restarting Your PC and Windows

Frequently, after installing new device software, you are instructed to restart Windows or your PC. Restarting (re-booting) the PC from Windows is the **safest way** to allow the Windows to recognize new hardware add-ons. While in Windows, avoid pressing the Control+Alt +Delete keyboard combination to restart your PC.

The procedure for restarting your PC is similar to that for shutting down from within Windows, but in the `Shut down Windows` dialog box, click the `Restart the computer?` radio button. This action properly closes files and shuts down all software before restarting. The restart is performed without powering the machine down and up again—saving wear and tear on the hardware.

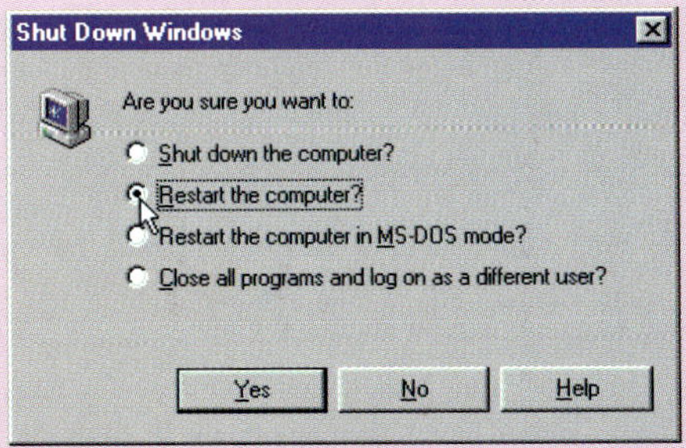

Control+Alt+Delete

The only time you should ever have to press the three-key hardware restart—the Ctrl, Alt, and Del keys simultaneously—is when a program running under Windows freezes. Windows 95 is created in such a way that if one Windows 95-compatible program should freeze, you can usually escape the situation without having to restart all of Windows or your PC. At most, you will lose any unsaved changes in the one program that is causing the trouble.

All running processes—programs, control panels, and desktop windows—that can freeze are called **tasks** in Windows 95. You'll know when a task **freezes** (also called **hanging** or **crashing**) because you will not be able to activate any other task via the Taskbar or by clicking on another window. All window controls in the frontmost task will also not react to clicking or keyboard commands.

When this happens, first wait 30 to 60 seconds. It is possible that the problem will fix itself given a chance to finish on its own. This is particularly true for communications or network tasks. If, after this time, Windows is still unresponsive:

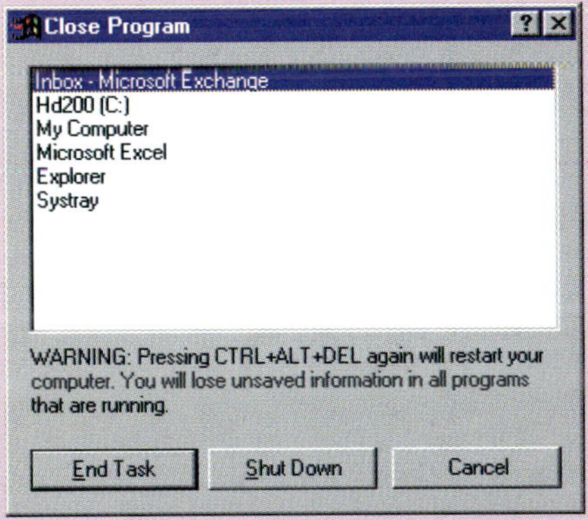

1. Press Ctrl+Alt+Del.

The `Close Program` window appears. All running tasks, which generally mirror the buttons in your Taskbar, appear in a list, with the frontmost, frozen task at the top of the list. The purpose of this window is to allow you to close down the problem task without bothering the others.

2. Click the End Task button.

Wait a few seconds for Windows to close down the selected task. If Windows is still frozen, repeat steps 1 and 2 until you are free. See 160 for more troubleshooting tips.

When Changing Cables...

Prudence calls for **completely powering down** the PC before connecting any cables to or disconnecting them from the system unit. Typically, if any damage were to occur by changing a cable with the PC still turned one, the problem would be local to the circuitry controlling that particular connector port. But the repair shop will replace the whole system board—a very costly proposition if you're not covered by warranty—even if only a two-cent part is blown.

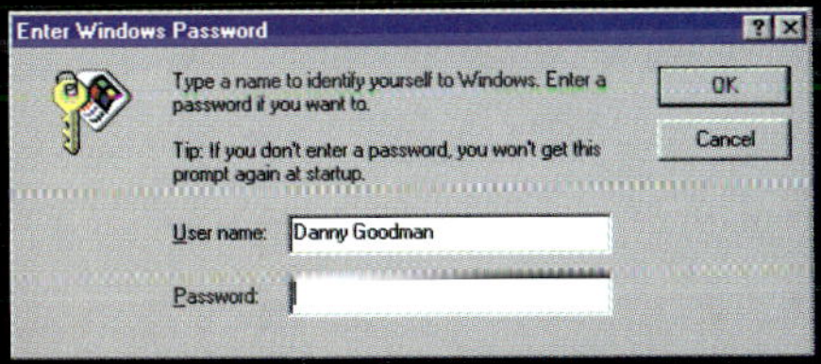

Multiple Users Per PC

Windows 95 simplifies the prospect of multiple users sharing a single computer. Windows can maintain a set of desktop settings and other system-wide preferences—a user profile—for each user

On Windows PCs setup to operate this way, you see the user and password prompt when Windows starts. If a user profile for the name of the person in this dialog exists, then the previous settings for the desktop (and, optionally, the Start menu) are loaded as Windows starts up.

When you leave a PC that you share with others, it is best to return Windows to this user prompt, making the machine ready for the next user. Choose `Shut Down` from the Start menu, and click the bottom radio button, `Close all programs and log on as a different user?` This saves the current desktop settings to your user profile, and prevents other users from modifying your settings.

The process of identifying yourself to the computer is called logging on; returning to the user prompt is called logging off.

To Sleep, Perchance to Dream

A feature of battery-operated personal computers is the ability to put the system (and, separately, the hard disk) to sleep without shutting down the whole machine. In sleep mode, the screen blanks, all disk activity stops, and all processing comes to a halt. The contents of RAM remain intact (drawing minimal power), such that all your open applications and documents stay that way until you wake up the PC later (provided the battery hasn't gone dead). A press of any key or the standby button (depending on your model) brings you back to the exact spot you were working on when the machine put its chewing gum on the bedpost. The software that controls sleep mode is supplied by the maker of your laptop.

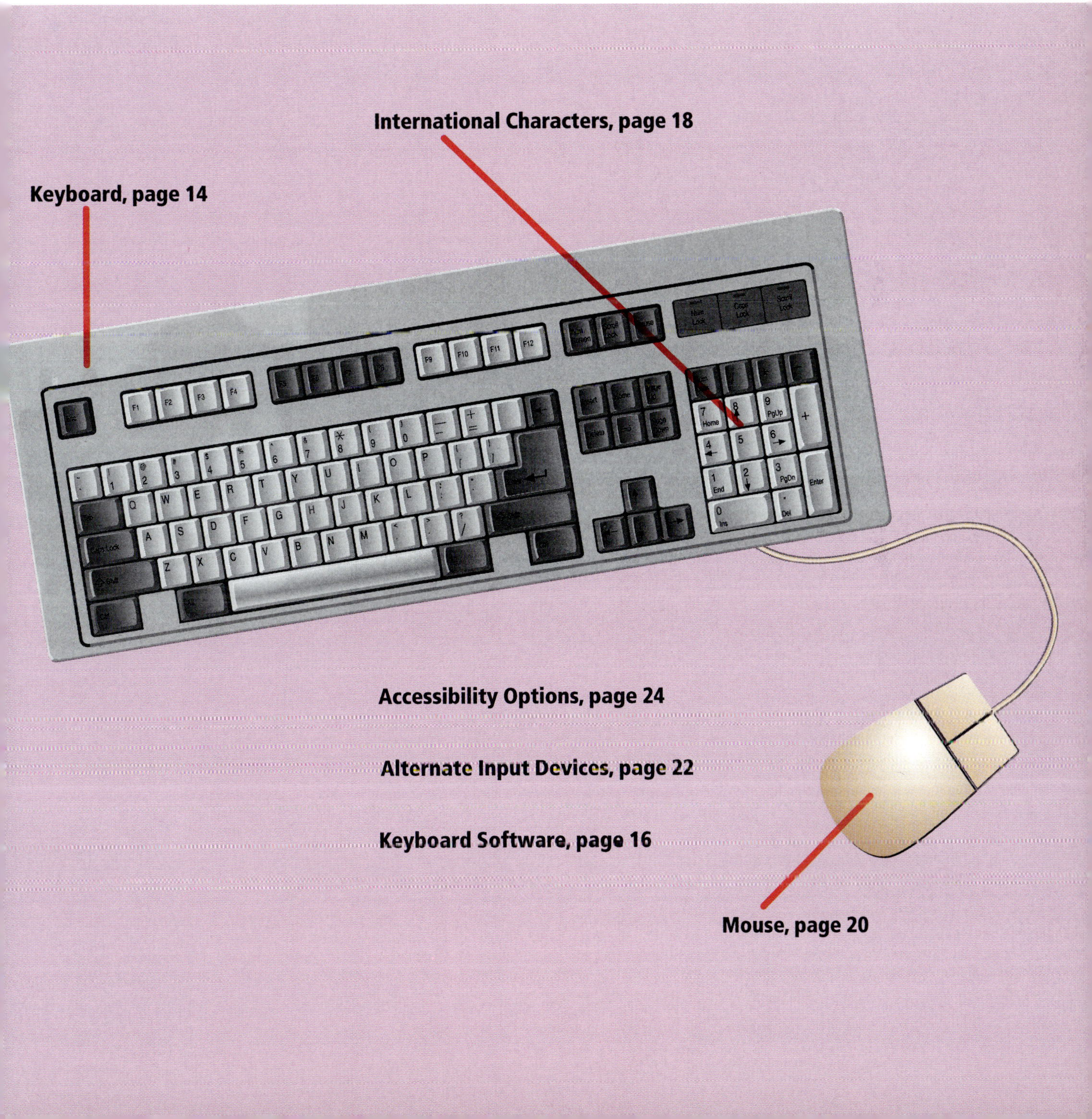
International Characters, page 18
Keyboard, page 14
Accessibility Options, page 24
Alternate Input Devices, page 22
Keyboard Software, page 16
Mouse, page 20

The most common desktop PC keyboard is the 101-key model.

In addition to standard typewriter-like keys, all keyboards have shortcut **function keys** (labeled F1...F12) and special purpose keys for such tasks as navigating through a document, and issuing menu commands. The Escape (Esc) key is generally a way to back your way out of a jam while working with a program.

Multiple-key commands require holding down the Ctrl, Alt, or Shift keys and another key. For example, Ctrl+A means to hold down the Ctrl key, and then press the A key.

Escape

A throwback to the old teletype machines, the Escape (Esc) key frequently lets you cancel from a dialog box or other user-decision state in a program. Typically, no harm comes from pressing the Escape key.

Tab

While this key is used often to align columns in tables and letters, the Tab key also activates successive items from top-left to bottom-right in dialog boxes. Pressing Shift+Tab activates items in the reverse direction.

Control

The Control (Ctrl) key had its start on telecommunications keyboards. While on-line, you press Control and another character as a means of sending a command (instead of sending the character). On communications terminal and DOS screens, the Control character appears as a caret symbol, as in ^C for Control+C. DOS and Windows programs often incorporate the Control key in pull-down menu command equivalents (e.g., Ctrl+X for cutting selected text in **WordPad** 85).

Function Keys

Labeled F1 through F12, the function keys usually provide one-key alternatives to menu commands. Other than the use of the F1 key to summon help, there is no consistency among applications' assignment of function keys to menu commands. Programs that include macro functions often allow you to assign these function keys (or other keyboard combinations) to an otherwise long series of mouse clicks and keystrokes.

Caps Lock

This push-on/push-off key toggles all letter keys between lowercase and capital letters. Numbers and punctuation symbols are not changed to their shifted equivalents, however. Therefore, you can type letters in all capital letters, but still have the period key produce a period, instead of its shifted character, >.

Personal Computer Keyboard Evolution

As the producer of the first popular personal computer (for serious business use), IBM set the standards for keyboard design on compatible machines. The first IBM PC keyboard sported 10 function keys (in two columns to the left of the keyboard) and a combination cursor and numeric keypad. IBM's mainframe terminal keyboards influenced some of these features.

The second standard keyboard arrived with the IBM PC-AT model. The so-called AT-style keyboard is the same one that ships with most Windows desktop PCs today. Modern variations include additional function keys, built-in trackballs 23, and designs for ergonomic comfort.

The Laptop Crunch

Laptop computer designers must find ways to fit the functionality of a 101-key keyboard into a space significantly smaller than a standard keyboard. They use tactics such as slightly decreasing the center-to-center spacing of keys, making non-character keys smaller, and combining functions of keys by requiring a special key to activate alternate functions. Experienced touch typists often have difficulty switching daily between desktop and laptop keyboards.

Print Screen

Despite its name, the **Print Screen** key does not send a copy of the current screen to a printer (as it used to under DOS). Instead, this key copies a picture of the entire screen to the **Clipboard**. **Alt+Prt Scrn** copies a picture of the active window to the Clipboard. You must then copy the picture into a graphics program for printing. Also see ➜ 33 for more on screen capture. The System Request function of this key is not a factor in Windows.

Insert/Help

The need for an **Insert** key is practically nil in Windows 95 software, but it was necessary in early PC software (when inserting text required going into the insert mode). It is still sometimes used in keyboard equivalents to some menu commands.

Pause

Before the days of scrolling windows (for example in plain DOS), a command could flood the screen with data that would immediately scroll off into oblivion. The **Pause** key allowed a user to halt the process. This function and the on-line terminal Break function are not used in Windows.

Indicator Lights

Each of the three indicator lights of the keyboard alerts you to the status of three keyboard toggle settings. The **Caps Lock** light goes on when you push the **Caps Lock** key. **Num Lock** is a carry over from an early PC-style keyboard whose numeric keypad also acted as cursor keypad—**Num Lock** sets the keys to work as a numeric keypad only.

Scroll Lock behaves differently in different programs. When engaged in a spreadsheet program, it means that as you use the **Home**, **Page Up**, **Page Down**, and **End** keys to navigate through a document, the cursor does not follow along with the scroll, but is locked onto the selected cell.

Home, End, Page Up, Page Down

The behavior of these four document navigation keys depends entirely on how a program's designers envision them. **Home** may take you to the beginning of the document, or just move the cursor to the beginning of the first line visible on the screen. Paging also means different things to different programs. Sometimes there is an overlap of a line (or two) when paging in either direction, sometimes not. Programs that fully support these navigation keys usually include multiple possibilities with the help of the **Control** key. Consult your software manuals for how the programs react to these keys.

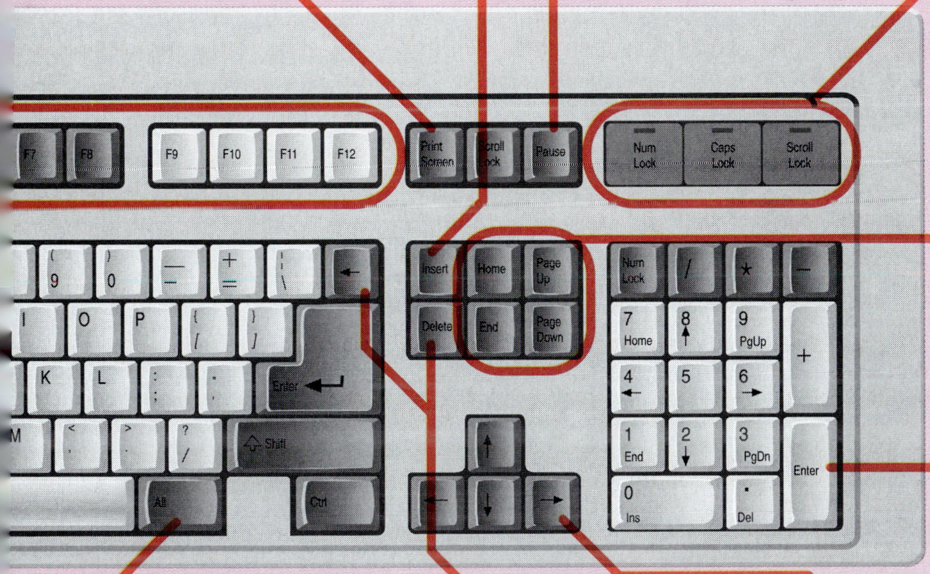

Alt

Like the **Control** key, the **Alt**(ernate) key is a **keyboard modifier.** Used primarily to effect pull-down menu commands from the keyboard, its behavior is governed by both Windows and applications developers. Anytime a window contains a menubar, pressing the **Alt** key highlights the leftmost menu name. Release the **Alt** key, and then use the keyboard to pull down a menu (by typing the underlined character in the menu name) or move around the menu bar and menus with the cursor arrow keys. You can also use the **Alt** key to type additional characters beyond the letters, numbers, and punctuation characters you see on the typewriter keyboard. See the **Character Map** ➜ 17.

Backspace vs. Del

The **Backspace** key on all keyboards deletes the character immediately to the left of the text insertion pointer (or erases an entire selection), as the pointer shifts to the left (this action used to be called **Backspace-Delete**). The **Del** key is a holdover from the old PC days, but one you may find handy. In all Windows 95 text editing, **Del** erases the character or entry to the *right* of the text insertion pointer.

Enter

At the far right of the numeric keypad is a second **Enter** key. In most programs, this key performs the same action as the **Enter** key that is part of the typewriter keys. Since the response to this key is not consistent across applications, check with each program's manual for details on its precise operation.

Cursor Keys

While the mouse is the device that controls the freewheeling pointer on the screen, the **cursor** keys often control the **text insertion pointer** ➜ 79, which shows you where the next character you type will appear on the screen. In a spreadsheet program, the **cursor** keys usually control the movement of the active cell marker. Not all programs respond to the **cursor** keys, nor are their actions consistent across all applications (e.g., some programs allow you to press the **Control** key along with a **left arrow** key to push the text cursor to the left word by word).

Two user-friendly pieces of Windows system software apply directly to the keyboard.

The `Keyboard` control panel lets you select which keyboard version (i.e., the country and language) to use as well as items that reflect the physical response of the keyboard: the key repeat rate and the delay until a key repeats.

Character Map is a small application that both displays all characters associated with a given font style and lets you copy desired characters to the Clipboard for insertion into your documents. Included in the character sets are foreign language characters and symbols.

Keyboard

To access the **Keyboard** control panel, choose `Settings→Control Panels` from the Start menu. This action opens a window showing all the control panels installed in your Windows System directory. Double-click the icon named `Keyboard`. The Keyboard control panel has three screens, the first of which is the one you'll access most.

Character Repeat Delay

This factor controls how long it takes for the character key you press to begin repeating. Setting too short a delay causes slow typists to produce double and triple characters.

Character Repeat Rate

This controls how quickly repeating characters appear at the text pointer once character repeat has started. Most users prefer a fast rate. To turn off character repeat entirely, see the **Accessibility Options** control panel 24.

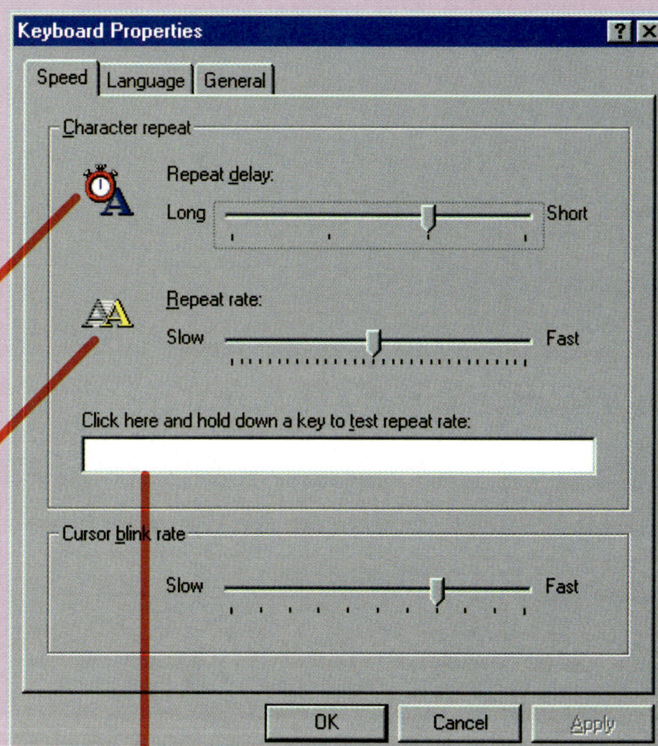

Test Track

Click in the field of the control panel to display a text insertion pointer. Then press and hold one character key to see how the `Repeat delay` and `Repeat rate` settings feel to you.

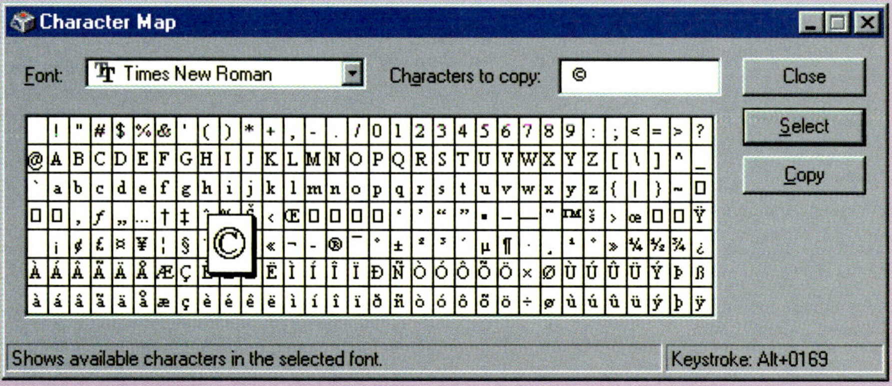

Character Map

The 101 keys of the typical PC keyboard aren't enough to take care of non-English Roman characters, such as those with accent marks and umlauts. But all the text fonts delivered with Windows (and other fonts as well) come with a complete set of characters for almost every eventuality. You can see these characters in the Character Map applet.

Access Character Map by choosing `Programs`→`Accessories`→`Character Map` in the Start menu. Some fonts have slight variations in symbol offerings; choose the selected font from the `Font` pop-up list to view the characters available for a specific font. If you cannot see a character clearly in the table, click and hold on a character until a magnified version appears.

To type a word that contains one or more special characters:

1. Type the English characters on the keyboard. The characters will appear in the upper right field.
2. For a special character, click once on it in the map.
3. Click the Select button. This appends the character to the upper right field.
4. Click the Copy button to copy the field to the Clipboard. You can now paste the text into your document.

A wide variety of symbols are available from fonts such as Wingdings. Character Map is a quick way to see what's available to decorate your documents.

Special Character Codes

When you select a special character in the Character Map, the lower right corner displays an Alt-key combination code that you can also use to enter the character into running text within a program. If you use some characters frequently, you may wish to remember their code numbers.

To enter the codes, hold down the Alt key, and type the four-digit code from the **numeric keypad**—top-row number keys won't work for this. For laptop keyboards with embedded numeric keypads, you may have to hold down an additional function key to keep the numeric keypad active during the entire Alt-key sequence. For a sample of characters and their codes, see 18.

Multiple Keyboards

Windows 95 is a multilingual operating system, recognizing that computer users outside the United States may not use American English. Moreover, not all Roman alphabet keyboards have the same layouts. For example, the Q, W, A, and Z keys of French keyboards are in different locations than a U.S. typist would expect. The variations are due to the frequency of letters in different languages. The `Language` screen of the **Keyboard** control panel allows you to select a keyboard language and layout independently of each other. You can establish pre-set combinations, and choose one from the control panel or from a pop-up indicator on the Taskbar (an option in the control panel's `Language` screen). This system is particularly helpful for users whose documents require a mix of Roman and non-Roman letters (e.g., English and Japanese).

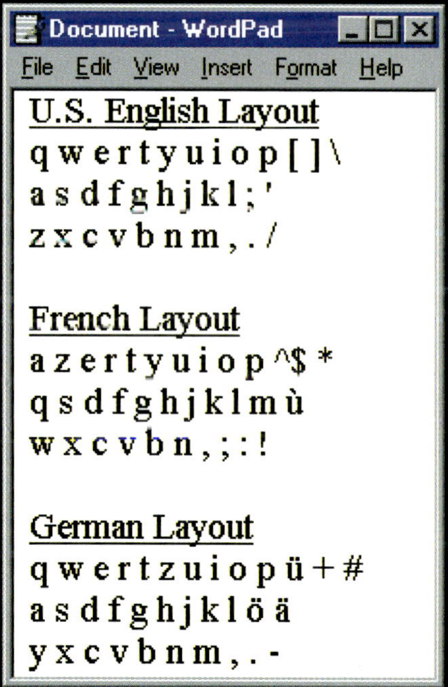

Non-U.S. Roman Characters

The typewriter keys on the typical U.S. PC keyboard are those of the alphabet, numbers, and common punctuation. The character sets of most fonts, however, also include characters from other Roman languages, plus a few useful symbols. To type those characters, use either the **Character Map** applet →17 or the Alt-key combinations listed in the table, below. The numbers following the Alt key must be typed from your keyboard's numeric keypad, not the top row of numbers above the alphabet keys.

Symbol fonts, such as Wingdings, contain characters and font art not normally contained in text fonts.

Character	Key Sequence	Note	Character	Key Sequence	Note	Character	Key Sequence	Note
À	Alt+0192		Õ	Alt+0213		é	Alt+0233	
Á	Alt+0193		Ö	Alt+0214		ê	Alt+0234	
Â	Alt+0194		Ø	Alt+0216		ë	Alt+0235	
Ã	Alt+0195		Œ	Alt+0140		ì	Alt+0236	
Ä	Alt+0196		Š	Alt+0138		í	Alt+0237	
Å	Alt+0197	Usually the tallest letter in a font	Ù	Alt+0217		î	Alt+0238	
Æ	Alt+0198		Ú	Alt+0218		ï	Alt+0239	
Ç	Alt+0199		Û	Alt+0219		ð	Alt+0240	
È	Alt+0200		Ü	Alt+0220		ñ	Alt+0241	
É	Alt+0201		Ý	Alt+0221		ò	Alt+0242	
Ê	Alt+0202		Þ	Alt+0222		ó	Alt+0243	
Ë	Alt+0203		Ÿ	Alt+0159		ô	Alt+0244	
Ì	Alt+0204		à	Alt+0224		õ	Alt+0245	
Í	Alt+0205		á	Alt+0225		ö	Alt+0246	
Î	Alt+0206		â	Alt+0226		ø	Alt+0248	
Ï	Alt+0207		ã	Alt+0227		œ	Alt+0156	
Ð	Alt+0208		ä	Alt+0228		š	Alt+0154	
Ñ	Alt+0209		å	Alt+0229		ß	Alt+0223	
Ò	Alt+0210		æ	Alt+0230		ù	Alt+0249	
Ó	Alt+0211		ç	Alt+0231		ú	Alt+0250	
Ô	Alt+0212		è	Alt+0232		û	Alt+0251	

Character	Key Sequence	Note	Character	Key Sequence	Note	Character	Key Sequence	Note
ü	Alt+0252		©	Alt+0169	Copyright	ƒ	Alt+0131	
ý	Alt+0253		™	Alt+0153	Trademark	«	Alt+0171	
þ	Alt+0254		´	Alt+0180		»	Alt+0187	
ÿ	Alt+0255		¨	Alt+0168			Alt+0160	Hard space
†	Alt+0134		ˆ	Alt+0136		-	Alt+0173	
‡	Alt+0135		˜	Alt+0152		–	Alt+0150	En-dash
§	Alt+0167		¯	Alt+0175		—	Alt+0151	Em-dash
¶	Alt+0182		µ	Alt+0181		^{2}	Alt+0166	
•	Alt+0149	Bullet	ª	Alt+0170		¤	Alt+0164	
×	Alt+0215		º	Alt+0186		‹	Alt+0139	
÷	Alt+0247		…	Alt+0133		›	Alt+0155	
±	Alt+0177	Plus-or-minus	¿	Alt+0191		1	Alt+0185	
¼	Alt+0188		¡	Alt+0161		^{2}	Alt+0178	
½	Alt+0189		“	Alt+0147	Left curly quote	^{3}	Alt+0179	
¾	Alt+0190		”	Alt+0148	Right curly quote	¸	Alt+0184	
‰	Alt+0137		‘	Alt+0145	Left curly apostrophe			
°	Alt+0176	Degree symbol	’	Alt+0146	Right curly apostrophe			
¢	Alt+0162		·	Alt+0183				
£	Alt+0163	British Pound Sterling	‚	Alt+0130				
¥	Alt+0165	Japanese Yen	„	Alt+0132				
®	Alt+0174	Registered Trademark	¬	Alt+0172				

Special Characters on Other Systems

The industry standards in place for the letters, numbers, and punctuation whose legends you see on the PC keyboard do not necessarily extend to the special characters you can view in `Character Map`. Be aware that most on-line mail systems are designed for the lowest common denominator (a dumb ASCII terminal) and do not convey the special characters you may put into messages. Microsoft Network messages do allow these characters because this on-line system is very much Windows-aware.

Also, not all characters from a Windows font map to the same special characters on other computers, such as Macintoshes or palmtop computers. Expect special characters you put into your documents to appear identically only when the document is viewed on other computers running Windows.

Windows-equipped desktop computers usually come with a two-button mouse. You roll (drag) the mouse around the table to control the on-screen pointer.

Pressing (**clicking**) the left mouse button indicates a deliberate action on your part. It may activate an icon or let you pull down a menu. In many places within Windows and applications, a click of the right mouse button produces a pop-up menu of options pertaining to the object or item under the pointer.

With the mouse connected to the serial or mouse port 8, the Windows system software gets into the act. A Mouse control panel lets you adjust how the PC responds to physical action you make with the mouse.

As an important input device, the mouse should be kept in good condition. Regular cleaning is highly recommended.

Inside the Mouse

The lightweight mouse is more complex inside than it may seem. Since you need to access part of the mouse's insides for cleaning, you can remove the mouse ball to get a peek at the internal mechanism. As the **mouse ball** rotates, it drives two metal rollers (a third, plastic roller is also there to stabilize the ball). The metal rollers are connected to two small wheels that have slits in them. As the wheels spin in response to mouse ball motion, optical detectors measure the speed at which light from a tiny lamp flashes through the slits. By calculating those speeds from both wheels at once, the mouse and Windows system software can figure out exactly in what free-flowing direction and at what speed you are moving the mouse along the table.

The mouse tells the PC only in which direction and how fast it's going: it doesn't know anything about the location of the pointer on the screen. It is said to be a **relative-motion device**, independent of the physical screen space. Therefore, you may occasionally run out of desk space before the pointer has reached its destination on the screen. If so, you can pick up the mouse and position it elsewhere on your work table to give you enough space to continue the pointer's journey.

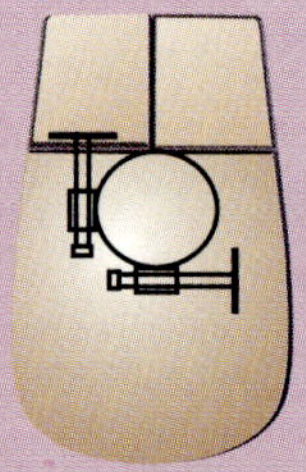

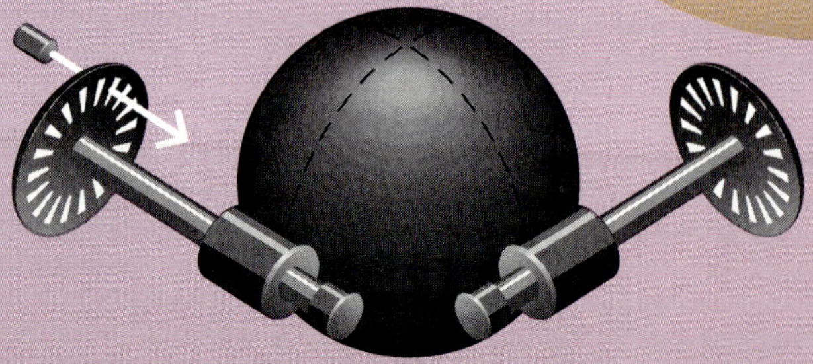

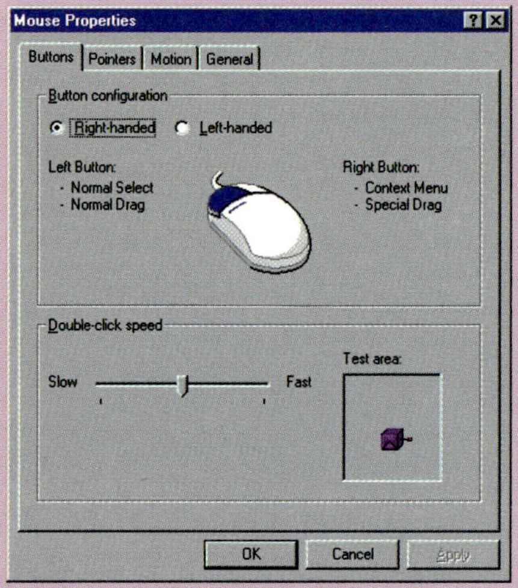

Mouse Control Panel

System software gives you the control over how Windows responds to your mouse motions. Choose `Settings`→`Control Panel` from the Start menu, and double-click the **Mouse** control panel icon. In the Mouse control panel are four screens. Two of these, `Buttons` and `Motion`, let you control the response of the pointer to mouse action. The `Pointers` screen contains settings for the pointer cursor 79, while the `General` screen lets you choose different pointing devices 23.

Left and Right Buttons

Because you should use your index finger on the primary mouse button, the `Buttons` screen of the Mouse control panel lets you swap the behavior of the mouse's two buttons depending on which hand is your dominant one. As you choose between right- and left-handed settings, the graphic displays which button on the mouse is the **primary** (normal) button.

Double-Clicks

Double-click speed controls the time between clicks that Windows recognizes as a double-click → 122 of the primary mouse button. Unless you have a physical disability that prevents rapid double-clicking of the mouse button, a setting of the slider control more than halfway to Fast is desirable. When the double-click speed is set too slow, you can easily click once on an icon and then click again to drag it—but Windows interprets those two clicks as a double-click motion to open the item.

Pointer Motion

The Pointer speed slider in the Motion screen of the Mouse control panel determines how the pointer responds to fast mouse movement. The slowest setting offers linear response: the **speed of the pointer** is directly proportional to the speed you move the mouse around the table. When you choose any of the other settings, the pointer will move faster in response to a faster mouse movement. The faster the setting, the greater the distance the pointer travels as you whisk the mouse around the table. The larger the video monitor you use, the more likely you'll prefer a faster setting. Whichever setting you choose, you still have precise pixel-by-pixel control → 28 when moving the mouse slowly.

To test changes to any setting on this screen without closing the control panel, click the Apply button at the bottom of the window.

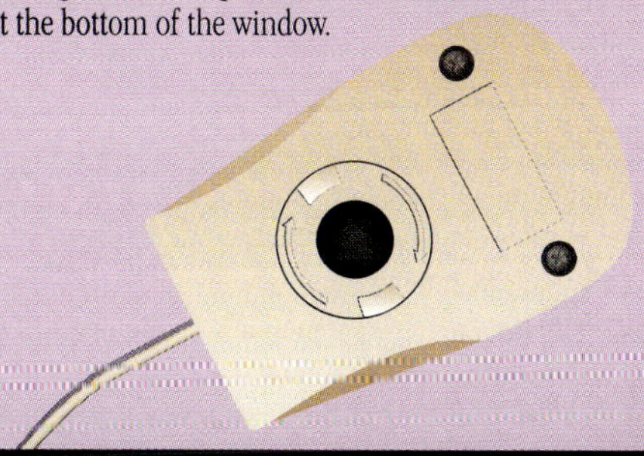

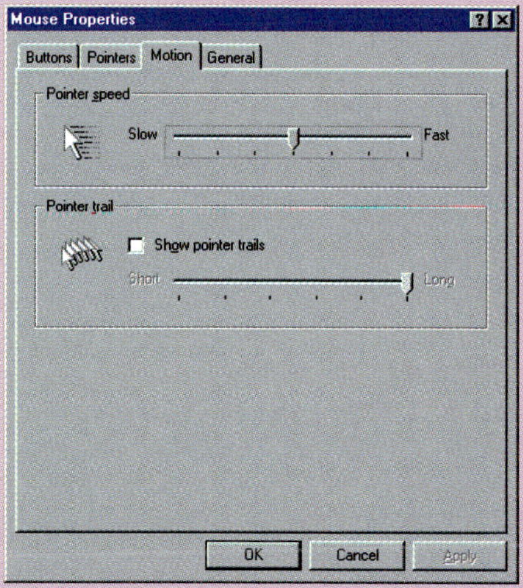

Pointer Trail

With low-cost liquid crystal displays (LCDs) on some laptop computers, a moving pointer seems to disappear from the screen because the display cannot refresh the screen quickly enough to show each instantaneous location of the pointer. For this situation, it is convenient to let the pointer leave ghost trails of its trajectory. The slower the refresh rate of the screen, the longer you should set the pointer trail.

Opening the Typical Mouse

1. Turn the mouse over so that the ball is facing you and the cable runs up and away from you.
2. Notice the plastic washer around the ball. Arrows on or near the washer point in the counter-clockwise direction—the direction in which to turn the washer to release it.
3. With your fingertips or fingernails (depending on how pronounced the grabber wells are), maneuver the washer counter-clockwise about one-eighth turn, until the plastic washer feels loosened.
4. With one hand on the underside of the mouse, turn the mouse over and catch the washer and ball.

To replace the ball later:

1. Drop the ball into the hole.
2. Position the washer so that the tabs slide easily into the slots on the mouse, and the washer falls flush with the bottom of the mouse body.
3. Rotate the washer clockwise until it locks firmly in place.

Cleaning the Mouse

If you're a daily PC user, it's a good idea to clean the mouse every month. In particular you should make sure the rollers are clean and free to roll.

Once you've opened the mouse, examine the three rollers inside. Dip the end of a cotton swab into isopropyl alcohol (or drip some cassette tape cleaning fluid on it) until the swab is moist (not dripping). Wipe the rollers with the swab until they are clean. Use a dry swab to wipe up any leftover liquid.

If dogs or cats share your workspace, it is very important to look for hair that has wound itself around the axles of the rollers. If there is some there, use tweezers to pick it off. Left unchecked, the hair can lock up the rollers.

Before reinserting the ball (which you should wipe with a dry, lint-free cloth), make sure your mouth is dry, and blow strongly into the opening for the mouse ball a couple of times. This will help dislodge dust that has accumulated in the mouse case.

If You Can't Use a Mouse

Windows has a control panel called **Accessibility Options**, which includes settings for those Windows users who cannot use a mouse due to a physical disability (or perhaps because their mouse is broken or missing). The **MouseKeys** utility → 25 lets you work the on-screen pointer by way of the numeric keypad. Even without this utility, you can use the cursor keys and other keystrokes to navigate your way around Windows with any standard keyboard → 84, 88

Mice for Lefties

Even with the help of the **Mouse** control panel, the life of the Southpaw isn't always so grand for Windows users. Many of the mice sold today have been designed with a definite righty's bias. The curvature of the mouse body and relative sizes of left and right mouse buttons favor right-handed users. Some makers offer left-hand versions, available by special order. More readily available are symmetrical designs that provide equal comfort in both hands. In any case, you should insist on using the mouse with your dominant hand, and set up your work space accordingly.

Laptops

Using a laptop computer often precludes the space or surface for using a mouse—and in any case, you won't wish to have wires dangling. A number of mouse alternatives are built into various laptop models → 22 to keep everything self-contained. But when you plan to alight for extended desktop computing with a laptop, you will be far more comfortable with an external mouse. Most laptops have a port built in for an external mouse → 8

The keyboard is not the only way to put information into your PC, nor the mouse the only way to control the cursor.

Existing printed graphics, including color, can be copied to a Windows graphics file by way of a scanner. The same scanner, with the help of **optical character recognition** (OCR) software, can convert printed text into characters you can search for and edit in word processing or page layout documents.

To substitute for the mouse, the trackball and a variety of finger-operated stubs grace many of today's laptop computers. When drawing graphics is the task, a digitizing pad lets you use an electronic pencil as a more natural way to control the cursor on the screen.

Scanners

A scanner is actually one half of a photocopy machine—the part that bounces light off a document and converts the image to a series of very fine dots. Scanners intended for use with personal computers put those dots into a format that can be saved to a disk as a **graphics file.** With a graphics program, you can then open the file and either edit the dots or copy the image (or a section of it) to another document, perhaps to have some text wrap around it on a newsletter page.

The most common style of scanner is the **flat-bed scanner** (although handheld scanners, which cannot scan full pages easily, are attractive for their comparatively low cost). When you lift the hinged lid, you see a glass plate, just like on a photocopy machine. Place the printed material face down on the glass, and then command the scanner software on the PC to scan the page. Software that comes with the scanner gives you many options as to **scanning resolution** (how many dots per inch you want saved in the file), contrast between light and dark areas, and other settings. Trial and error is the primary way to master the software, but you can usually save settings for a particular kind of source material, and reuse those settings later for similar material.

Most scanners come with an interface card (or require a SCSI port 55) for desktop PCs plus driver software.

OCR

In combination with a scanner, **optical character recognition** (OCR) software is a practical alternative to retyping existing printed text into a Windows document. To scan a paper document, lay it face down on the scanner glass, and then instruct the OCR software to scan the page. Each OCR software program treats the next steps differently, but the basic procedure is to select from a miniature representation of the page the area(s) you wish the software to convert to text characters. When the conversion is complete, you see the text in a text editing window; you can then save it to a disk file (often in a word processing program format).

Accuracy of OCR depends largely on the quality of the software and the clarity of the document being scanned. Since OCR software tries to distinguish individual characters (so it can match up each graphical image against internal representations of characters), blurry newsprint, very small print, or very light print may be difficult to decipher. Once the text is in the editing window, however, you can touch it up manually before saving it to a disk file. With crisp source material (e.g., a laser printed business letter), accuracy approaches 100 percent.

Mouse Alternatives for the Desktop

The mouse is not for everyone or for every situation. Users of some graphics programs, for example, prefer a trackball to the mouse. A **trackball** is like an inverted mouse in which the ball faces up. As you roll your hand around the ball, both it and the screen pointer move. Most trackballs for Windows PCs come with a button on both sides of the ball, allowing left- and right-handed people to use the trackball with equal ease.

Some users in the **computer-aided design** (CAD) and graphic arts fields prefer to use a **graphics tablet** (also called a digitizing tablet or just digitizer) rather than a mouse—or in conjunction with a mouse. For many artists, it is more natural to draw with a pen or stylus than with a mouse. A digitizer consists of a large drawing area that has electronic sensors underneath. A stylus, connected by wire to the tablet, controls the screen pointer as it comes into contact with, and is dragged around, the tablet. Buttons on the stylus replaces the mouse buttons for clicking actions.

A variation of the digitizing pad—a small rectangular pad that lets you control the screen pointer by finger touch—is gaining popularity.

Laptop Trackballs and Points

In an effort to keep a Windows laptop self-contained for users on the move, a number of machines provide mouse alternatives built into the units. Trackballs are fairly common, but the **location** of the trackball is anything but standard, with those located on the display panel or at the corner of a keyboard being the most ergonomically awkward—optimum location is below the spacebar. Laptop trackballs tend to be too small for comfortable extended use.

A few laptop models are equipped with a stubby rubber joystick-like device about the size of a pencil eraser. Located amid the keyboard keys or below the spacebar, these point-style devices are operated by nudging them in the direction you wish to move the screen pointer—the more pressure you exert, the faster the pointer moves on the screen.

To equip a laptop with a mouseless controller, you can add a clip-on trackball, such as the Logitech Trackman. You'll still have the cable running from trackball to mouse port, however.

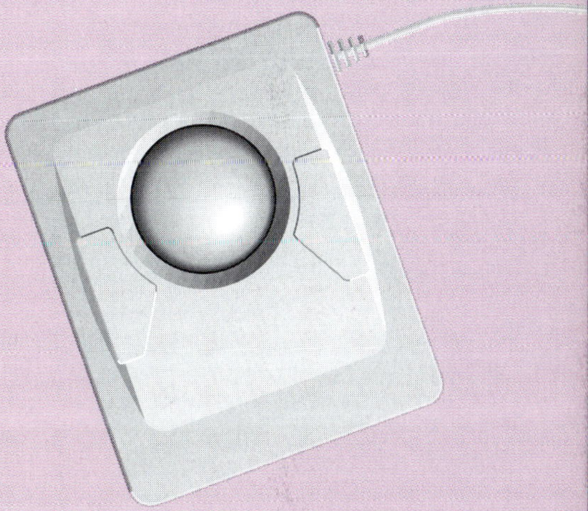

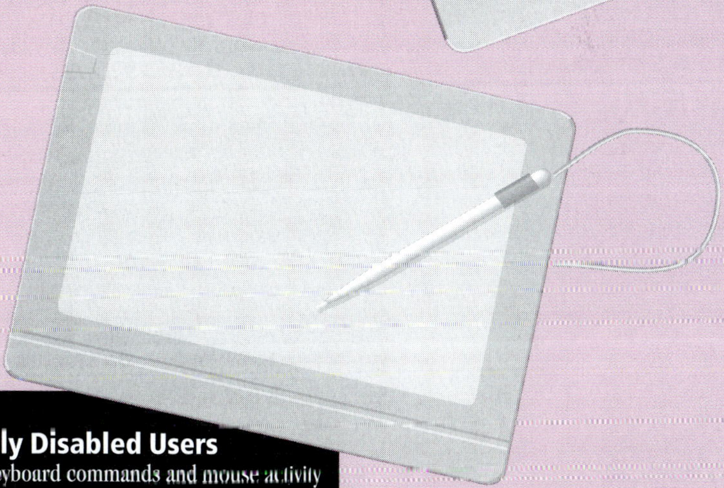

Keyboard Macros

You can reduce the entry of commonly used keyboard commands or mouse-and-keyboard actions to the press of a key or two with the help of **macros.** Built into many programs and also available as a software add-in to Windows, macros let you trigger a sequence of keystrokes and mouse motions with a menu selection or the press of a single function key. Macros are typically used to automate frequent and tedious processes, such as switching printers or typing closing lines of a business letter.

Physically Disabled Users

Multi key keyboard commands and mouse activity aren't easy for users who don't have full use of both hands. But the `Accessibility Options` control panel ➔ 24 leads to many settings that make it possible for users with as little access as a single-key pointer to effect multiple-key commands and mouse actions required by Windows and even by the most graphical applications.

Users with physical disabilities who find certain aspects of using keyboards and mice with Windows challenging can adjust Windows to meet a variety of input needs.

Two of the screens in the `Accessibility Options` control panel lead to many settings for keyboard and mouse use. `Keyboard` options facilitate using a single finger or pointing stylus to effect multi-key combinations and making sure that an unsteady touch of a key produces only the desired single keystroke.

For the mouse, users can turn on a mode that allows complete mouse action via the numeric keypad. Thus, you can even draw in a graphics program without the mouse if necessary.

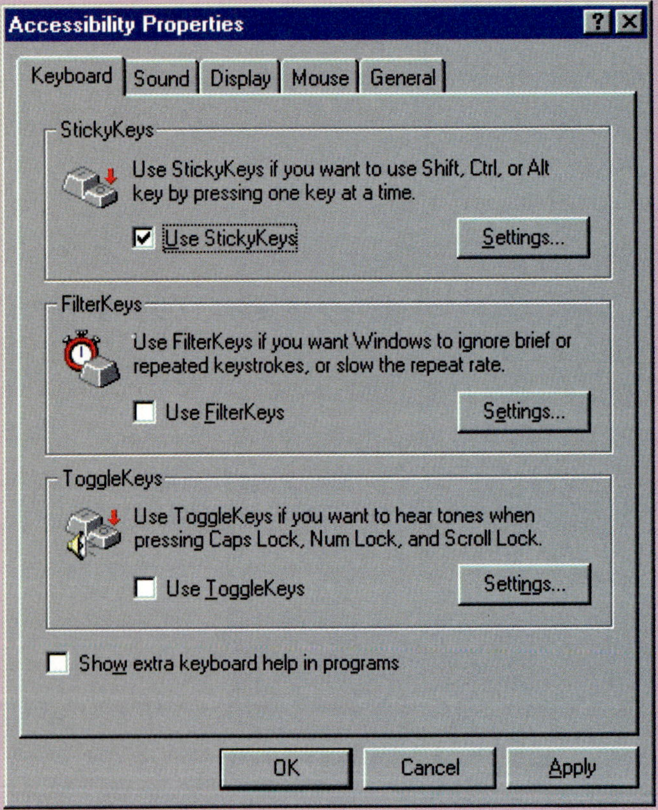

Keyboard Accessibility

Three options in the `Keyboard` screen of the **Accessibility Options** control panel are for `StickyKeys` (to use modifier keys without having to hold them down), `FilterKeys` (to instruct Windows to ignore brief accidental key touches or to interpret long presses of keys as single keystrokes, rather than as repeated keys), and `ToggleKeys` (to hear audible tones when Caps Lock, Num Lock, or Scroll Lock are turned on and off). Each one of these modes leads to a more detailed screen of settings.

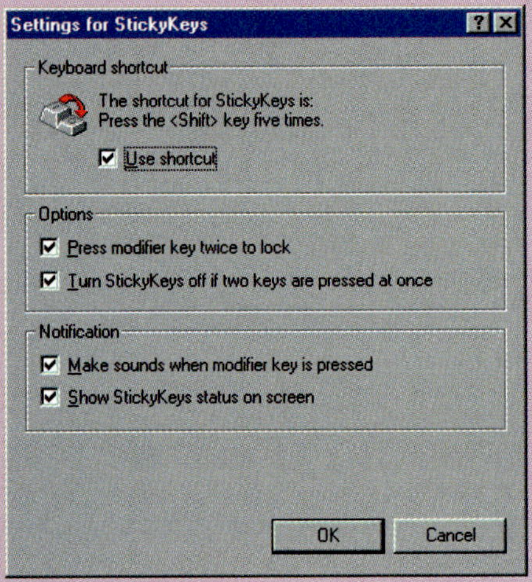

StickyKeys

You can type **multiple-key combinations** without two hands when StickyKeys is on. Turn on StickyKeys either via the Accessibility Options control panel or by pressing the Shift key five times in a row (at no particular speed or interval, but without moving the mouse at all). You may see a window advising that the feature is about to go on and a small icon appears in the Taskbar: The squares in the icon portray, in clockwise order from the top, Shift, Alt, Ctrl.

When you press one of these keys once, you hear a two-tone sound, and its square in the icon turns gray. Press the second key in the sequence to effect a two-key sequence. The modifier key will then be release automatically.

If you instead press a modifier key twice, the icon box stays gray, and you hear an additional tone, indicating that the modifier key is locked down, so you can perform a series of modified key combinations by just typing the final key (e.g., for typing a series of uppercase letters). In the `General` settings for Accessibility Options, the default behavior is for StickyKeys (or any feature) to turn itself off after five idle minutes.

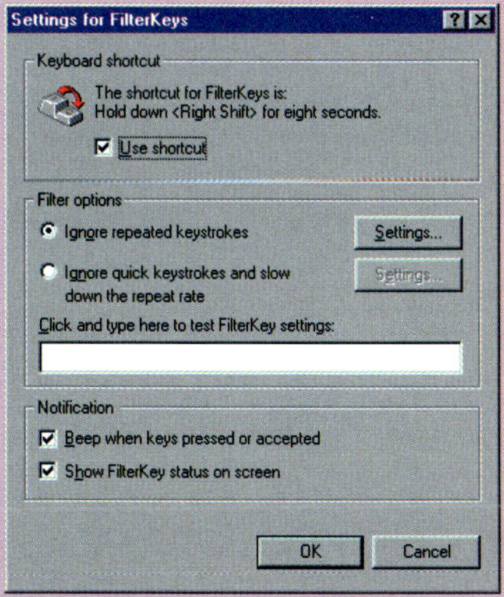

FilterKeys

Designed for those users who may type with an unsteady touch or by way of a stylus, FilterKeys lets you set how long you hold down a key before it registers as a pressed key (`Ignore quick keystrokes`) or how to treat repeated pressing of the same key (`Ignore repeated keystrokes`). For example, if you set FilterKeys to ignore quick keystrokes, when you aim for one key but accidentally touch an adjacent key momentarily, only the key you hold down for a second or two (depending on the keystroke speed adjustment in the `Advanced Settings for FilterKeys` window) registers as a typed key.

ToggleKeys

To supplement the indicator lights for Num Lock, Caps Lock, and Scroll Lock on the keyboard, ToggleKeys lets you have Windows tell you with a tone whenever any of these keys is pressed. While the tones for all three keys are the same, the tone for engaging any of these locks is higher than for turning the locks off.

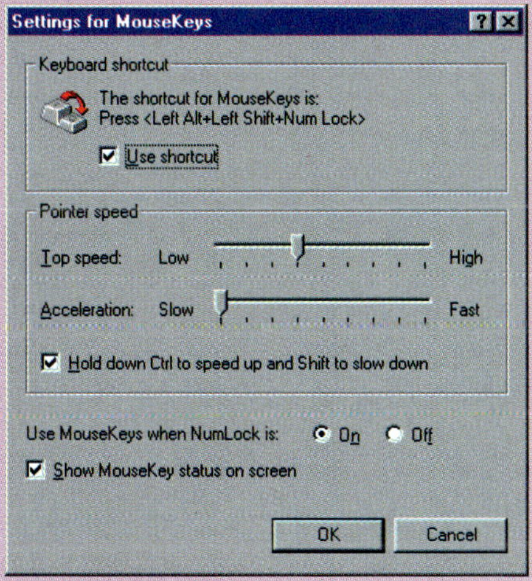

MouseKeys

The MouseKeys option (`Accessibility Options→Mouse`) lets you work the on-screen pointer by way of the numeric keypad.

The control panel settings allow you to adjust how quickly the pointer should start moving after you press one of the numeric keys (acceleration) and how fast the pointer should go the longer you hold down the key (top speed). As you become more familiar with Windows operation, you will probably want to set the acceleration and speed faster.

Refer to the figure to see which way the pointer moves on the screen when you press the numeric keys. For clicking, make sure the desired mouse button is set (/ or - keys). Then press the 5 key to click once, or the + key to perform a double-click. Ordinarily, to make a selection (either along a line of text or a group of icons), you need to click and drag. To replicate this action, move the pointer to the starting position and press the zero key. That plants the mouse button. Then move the pointer with the numeric keys. A press of the period key (next to the zero) releases the mouse button, leaving the selection intact for your next action.

It's easier to use the keyboard shortcuts built into Windows 85, 92 to perform menu and standard dialog box actions (e.g., clicking buttons and activating fields). Use MouseKeys for graphics and other tasks for which no ready keyboard equivalents are available.

General Settings

Default settings in the `General` screen of the `Accessibility Options` control panel may be intrusive if you use these features on a regular basis. You will probably want to uncheck both `Automatic Reset` checkboxes, as well as the warning message checkbox in the `Notification` section. It is, however, a good idea to keep the sound notification turned on as an extra clue about accidentally turning a feature on or off. Also, within the detailed settings for individual accessibility features, always choose to display the feature's status in the Taskbar. Otherwise, you may not know for sure whether a particular feature is active. Right-clicking on any feature's icon in the Taskbar leads to a menu option for also displaying the icons

Accessibility Shortcuts

All keyboard and mouse accessibility features can be turned on from the keyboard via rather unusual shortcuts:

Feature	Shortcut
`StickyKeys`	Press Shift key five times (no intervening mouse movement)
`FilterKeys`	Hold right Shift key for eight seconds
`ToggleKeys`	Hold Num Lock for five seconds
`MouseKeys`	Left Alt+left Shift+Num Lock
High Contrast Display 33	Left Alt+left Shift+Prt Scrn

Video 26

Video Basics, page 28

Color Video Software, page 34

Color Video, page 30

Video System Software, page 32

Video Setup and Care, page 36

Anything you see on a video monitor is the result of a combination of black, white, gray, or color spots on the screen.

Each spot is called a picture element, or **pixel** or pel for short. The inherent crispness of today's Windows-capable monitor is largely due to the use of square pixels. Unlike rounded pixels of earlier PC standards, square pixels fully abut each other, producing clean lines between different colors.

When you are buying a video monitor you are presented with many choices, which are couched in a flurry of jargon. Understanding the terminology is more than half the battle. The rest is up to your own personal taste about the quality of a display.

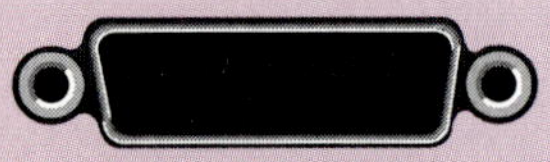

Video Support

Desktop PCs connect to a video monitor by way of a **video port** on the rear panel or a **video card** that plugs into one of the computer's expansion slots ↪9. Video cards are more flexible, because they allow you to upgrade the video quality as your needs change and technology improves. In making changes to the video part of your system, it is important to match the capabilities of your computer's video support and monitor.

Resolution

Often misused, the term resolution simply denotes the density of pixels on the screen. The common measure among PC video monitors is **dot pitch:** the center-to-center distance between individual pixels on the screen. The maximum dot pitch recommended for standard color video monitors is 0.28 millimeters. If the dot pitch is too small, images may appear crisper, but objects will appear smaller than on other screens, and your ability to accurately point to small objects with the cursor will be impaired. This is certainly the case with some laptop displays, which cram pixels into a smaller overall screen area than that of a traditional monitor.

Video Tube Size

PC monitors come in many different video (cathode ray) tube sizes, but because the resolution (pixel density) varies from model to model, there is no definite correlation between the size of the tube and the number of pixels you can see on the screen. Therefore, 14" and 15" tubes may display the same number of pixels, but the pixels (and all images) will be larger on the 15" tube.

Other tube sizes range up to 22" for desktop PCs. Larger monitors are very deep and require a healthy amount of desk space.

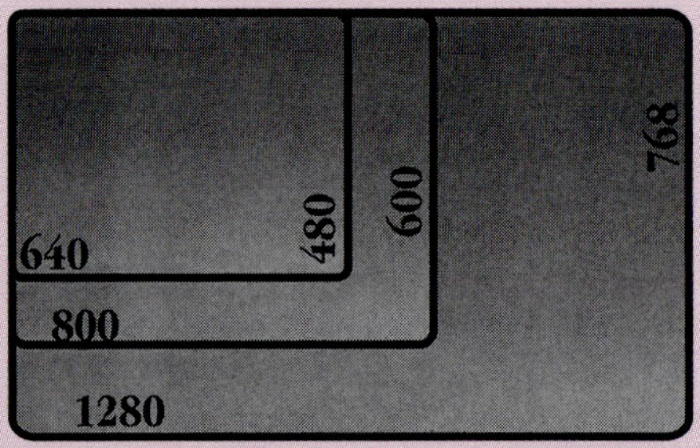

Pixel Grid

The number of screen pixels, measured as the number of pixels horizontally by the number of pixels vertically, is the key factor when matching a monitor to the type of work you do and the video card in your PC. The minimum requirement for Windows is a monitor that displays 640-by-480 pixels. Video cards and monitors capable of this minimum meet the **VGA** (Video Graphics Adapter) standard, originally established by IBM.

Beyond the VGA standard are a variety of pixels grids that let you view more of a document without scrolling. The **Super VGA** (SVGA) name applies to most of the video schemes that display images in an 800-by-600 pixels grid and larger. While standard 14" video monitors can often display up to 1280-by-768 pixels, icons and standard font sizes at this pixel density are difficult to work with. To handle seeing up to two pages of a document at a time (e.g., a desktop publishing spread), upgrade to a monitor no smaller than 17" diagonal, and preferably 21".

Refresh Rate

Video screens are painted—**refreshed**—by an electron beam dozens of times each second. The faster the refresh rate, the less likely your eye will be able to detect the constant refreshing and decay that makes it look like the screen flickers.

The more colors a monitor/video card combo is capable of displaying ↪30 and the larger the screen, the slower the refresh rate is. For each pixel on the screen, more bits of information must course through the video card's veins and arteries. And with more pixels, there is more physical area for the CRT's electron beam to paint.

You must be sure that on larger monitors, the screen's **refresh rate** is faster than surrounding fluorescent lighting, which flickers at 60 times per second (60 hertz). The two refresh rates may also interfere with each other, causing significant screen flicker. **Flicker** is often subtle, but can become mentally tiring and cause eye strain and headaches. Refresh rates of 70 hertz or more on two-page monitors have proven to prevent flicker.

Interlacing

You may not realize that each frame of a standard television picture is actually made up of two "fields." Each field consists of every other line of the frame; first one field is painted on the screen, then the other—all within 1/30th of a second. For close-up computer work, this interlacing of fields causes substantial flicker. Higher quality monitors are capable of non-interlaced video, meaning that they can paint the entire screen in a single pass of the electronic beam. The non-interlaced signal must be generated in the video support circuitry, so, again, the video support and monitor must be matched.

Brightness

A monitor's brightness is a measure of how much light it emits when turned up full blast. The brighter your working environment (e.g., lots of windows or overhead lights), the brighter you'll want your monitor to be. This factor is rarely listed in a monitor's specifications. It is important to try to test out a monitor in your working environment before committing to it.

Contrast

Contrast of a monitor is measured by comparison between the blackest black and the whitest white. Higher contrast makes images stand out much better. As with brightness, no absolute standards of measurement are available in monitor specifications.

Focus

The larger the tube size, the more difficult it is for the monitor's internal circuitry to maintain good focus across the entire screen. On a monochrome monitor, single-pixel-width black lines should be sharp and crisp no matter where you draw them on the screen. Watch out especially for out-of-focus corners and edges. If the entire screen is equally out of focus, this can be adjusted internally by a technician. **Color monitors** ➔ 30 tend to be a bit fuzzier because of the way they display pixels.

Glare

Primarily a function of ambient lighting and the texture of the video tube's front face, glare can be a headache- and fatigue-inducing by-product of working with a video monitor for long stretches. Many monitors have an etched face plate, which helps reduce harsh **reflections** of light sources behind you. The more etching on the tube, however, the fuzzier the picture, since the etching also diffuses the light going from the tube to your eye. A slightly **etched monitor** and an **adjustable monitor stand** ➔ 4 can avoid most glare.

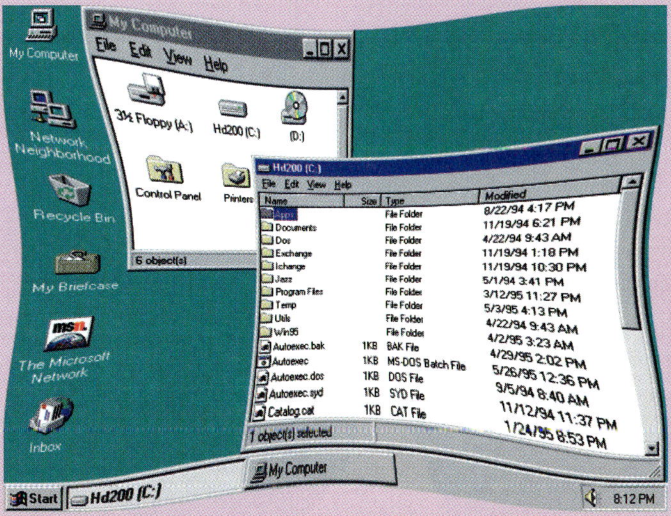

Distortion

Look carefully at the overall rectangle of the active area of the screen. Signs of distortion include a left-to-right narrowing of the rectangle in the middle of the screen (called **pincushioning**). Beware of one or more corners that bow out. The larger the monitor, the more difficult it is to eradicate distortion along the edges. If the entire rectangle is tilted slightly with respect to the plastic bezel of the monitor, it means that the yoke on the neck of the tube is out of adjustment: this can be easily repaired by a technician.

WARNING. There are extremely high voltages and currents running around the back of a video tube, even long after the monitor has been unplugged. Don't poke around there unless you know exactly what you're doing.

Jumpiness

If you see a monitor's picture rapidly jumping vertically or exhibiting a swaying motion, look for a source of electromagnetic radiation coming from a nearby device. The most common source is a black power transformer that is plugged into a power strip near the monitor. The PC system unit fan, a second video monitor, or other peripherals adjacent to the monitor can electrically interfere with the electron beam on its way to the tube's face plate (after all, magnetic fields in the coils around the tube's neck direct the beam in the first place). Try moving the potential source of magnetic field interference farther from the affected monitor (six inches or more). With large monitors, the solution sometimes requires that the monitor be plugged into a separate power outlet from the rest of the computer gear.

Color Specifications

An additional set of criteria plays a role in choosing a color monitor. See ➔ 30 for details.

Eco-Monitors

Many of today's monitors comply with a variety of energy conservation and radiation reduction standards developed by government and industry groups. The **Energy Star** program (U.S. Environmental Protection Agency) sets maximum power consumption for idle monitors. To take fullest advantage of Energy Star, be sure your monitor and system unit work together in reducing power drain (e.g., an Energy Star-compliant computer will automatically control its matching video monitor). If Windows detects that your PC is Energy Star compliant, you can alter the timing for energy savings in the `Display➔Screen Saver` control panel ➔ 36.

Another power management standard is called Display Power Management Signaling (DPMS), which lets software control any DPMS-compliant hardware device.

While health risks of low-frequency radiation emitted by video monitors (and other electrical devices) are not conclusive ➔ 36, a Swedish government standard exists to serve as a guide for concerned users. Look for MPR II compliance in monitor sales literature.

Video Not for Windows

Several video standards pre-date the VGA minimum required for Windows 95. They are all named after the video adapter card used to link a desktop PC with the monitor. MDA and CGA were the first to ship as options for the original IBM Personal Computer.

Standard	Description
MDA	Monochrome Display Adapter
CGA	Color Graphics Adapter
Hercules	Gray-scale graphics on IBM monochrome display
EGA	Enhanced Graphics Adapter

Windows 95 is meant to be seen in color. Many color cues in icons and windows make it easier to find your way around the desktop.

In documents, application of color may range from **spot color** (like a red bar on a chart) to display of an electronically stored photographic image. And with the right multimedia software, you can even watch color **motion video** on the screen.

A key factor in determining the realism of color on your screen is the amount of memory on your video display card or on-board video controller.

Bits vs. Colors

Two fundamental (and often confused) terms in the color video world are **bits** and **colors.**

A bit is also computer terminology for the smallest piece of information that a computer handles. A bit is either on or off, 1 or 0, black or white, or any other method you choose to denote two distinctly different states. The more bits you string together into a unit, the more combinations of ones and zeros can occur within that unit. For example, two bits together offer four possible combinations (00, 01, 10, and 11). If you let each combination of bits in a group represent a color value, then the more bits you can assign to a single pixel, the greater the number of colors a pixel can represent.

Here's a table showing the number of bits used to represent colors in Windows 95 computers, and the resulting number of colors:

Bits	Colors	Comment
4	16	Fine for spot color; uses very little video RAM
8	256	SVGA's increasingly common color mode for Windows PCs; in gray scale, produces photorealistic black-and-white images
16	65,536	Improvements noticeable mostly in color graphics software
24	16,777,216	True color, requires the most video RAM and, often, acceleration for larger monitors

The number of bits per pixel is also known as **bit depth.** The more bits, the greater the bit depth (imagine the bits as being stacked behind each pixel).

How Color Works

Color displays are more expensive than monochrome displays because they are much more complex devices.

It helps to know that each pixel on the screen is comprised of a **mixture of three colors**—red, green, and blue. In a color picture tube, three colorless electron beams representing the three colors are directed to the phosphor inside the video tube's face. There are three colored phosphor spots at each pixel location. The electron beam representing the red color is aimed precisely at the red phosphor spot at each pixel location, while the green and blue beams reach their respective phosphor spots. Our eyes, in turn, see the blending of three color intensities at that spot as a single particular color. The `Color` dialog box 34 allows you to choose from all available colors at your current color setting (in the `Display`→`Settings` control panel, 34) by adjusting the intensity of the red, green, and blue beams.

Video Memory

The image you see on the screen comes from the video adapter's memory. Each bit of each pixel must have a corresponding bit of memory on the **video board** (or built-in video portion of the motherboard). A 640-by-480, 256-color SVGA display card, therefore, must have sufficient memory for 8 bits times the 307,200 pixels on the screen, or roughly 300 kilobytes of RAM. Due to the increments of RAM chips these days, however, manufacturers go to the next highest size, or 512KB. That same 512KB of video memory will accommodate 256 colors at 800-by-600 pixels. But to see true (24-bit) color on a 640-by-480 monitor requires nearly one megabyte of video memory. On two-page monitors, true color requires up to two megabytes.

A color screen takes longer to refresh than a monochrome screen. For each pixel on the screen, more bits of information need to course through the video adapter's veins and arteries. The larger the screen, the longer it takes to refresh, since there is more physical area for the CRT's electron beam to paint. Two-page true color screen refreshing taxes even the fastest PC unless the video card has specially tuned acceleration circuitry.

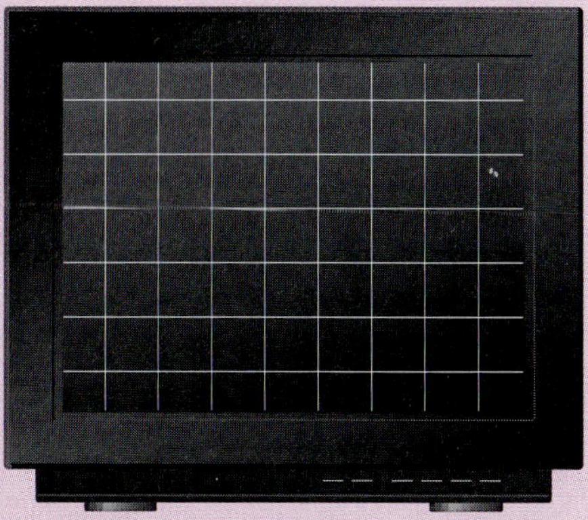

Convergence
In addition to the specifications that apply to all computer video monitors →28, one of the most obvious factors affecting the quality of a color video monitor is convergence—how well the **three electron beams converge** on a single spot. When convergence is perfect, a grid of single-pixel-wide white lines across the entire monitor is, indeed, all white, even upon very close inspection. On larger monitors, good convergence is difficult to achieve, especially at the edges of the screen. Poor convergence results in a distinct colored line appearing on one side of the white line.

Color Monitor Adjustments
Most large color monitors offer user access to a number of control knobs that allow you to **correct misalignments** that may occur when a monitor is jostled. Before making any adjustments, however, write down the settings of the various controls. That way, in case you get everything completely out of whack, you can return to the original settings and start over. More sophisticated monitors include software that lets you adjust numerous settings electronically.

Faster Color
It's rare to find a video board capable of large-screen color that doesn't already have a **built-in accelerator** tuned for Windows. An unaccelerated 24-bit board may be tolerable for a 14-inch color monitor in 640-by-480 mode, but it's definitely a drag on big-screen displays.

If your current hardware setup is too slow when displaying color images, you may be able to speed up the process by choosing a lower bit depth from the `Display→Settings` control panel →32. In the trade-off, however, you lose richness of color.

DRAM vs. VRAM
While all video adapters come preinstalled with memory dedicated for video display, not all memory chip designs are the same. The two styles in use today are **DRAM** (dynamic random access memory) and **VRAM** (video random access memory). DRAM is cheaper, but also slower, because at any given instant it can either fetch information from the computer or refresh the display. VRAM is faster, since it can do both tasks at once. VRAM-equipped video cards are more expensive, but highly recommended for Windows.

CAD Accelerators
Computer-aided design (CAD) programs have special requirements of their own when it comes to displaying objects (color or not) on a large screen. These programs tend to store information about objects as long lists of vectors—lines containing various properties. A Windows accelerator is of little value to this kind of drawing. If you use CAD software, consult with the publisher for guidance on accelerators that work best with the program.

PCs and Television
Strong interest in linking the Windows PC to television pictures has helped produce a wide variety of add-on products. They fall into three categories of tasks you might wish to do with video, with some of the add-in boards capable of more than one of these tasks.

First is **capturing** a frozen video picture—this is like taking a snapshot of a picture so you can store it on your hard disk and display it later (perhaps to work it into a slide-type presentation). Devices that do this, called **frame grabbers** or **video digitizers**, may be standalone boxes (connecting to the SCSI port, →56) or plug-in boards for PCs. Newer electronic still cameras (which store their pictures on small floppy disks) may also be used to capture a shot for conversion into a color graphical file.

Second is the ability to **display live motion** video on the video screen. While you can do this from CD-ROM on multimedia-capable Windows PCs today, it usually requires some extra hardware to capture a live video signal or TV broadcast for display in a window on the screen.

Finally is the desire to view what you see on the PC screen on a television monitor. Perhaps the monitor is a **projection television**, allowing you to show your PC screen to a roomful of people. Or perhaps you just want the video output to go directly to a VCR to capture your screen actions in a software training video. A variety of adapters are readily available to hook up any 640-by-480 VGA video output to a video monitor or VCR. More advanced models include patches for audio between the PC and video device. Picture quality on standard television sets won't be anywhere near that of the typical PC display.

If you try to aim a **video camera** at a computer monitor for the purpose of recording the screen images, beware of two problems. First, the quality will not be good. The fine images of the PC display will be fuzzy on the resulting recording. Second, the differences in refresh rates between your PC monitor and the broadcast video standard will cause the recorded screen to have a recurring line rolling from bottom to top, even though the image is clean when you look at it live. Solving this visual interference requires a video board capable of **genlocking**. The board synchronizes the refresh rates of the PC and recording camera video signals.

Windows comes with an extensive Display control panel that gives you control over your PC's interaction with its video monitor.

Use the `Display→Settings` control panel to adjust the number of colors you view on a monitor, the pixel grid of your monitor, the size of Windows object fonts, and the display driver Windows should be using.

Not so obvious are the built-in commands that let you grab a snapshot of the current screen or window.

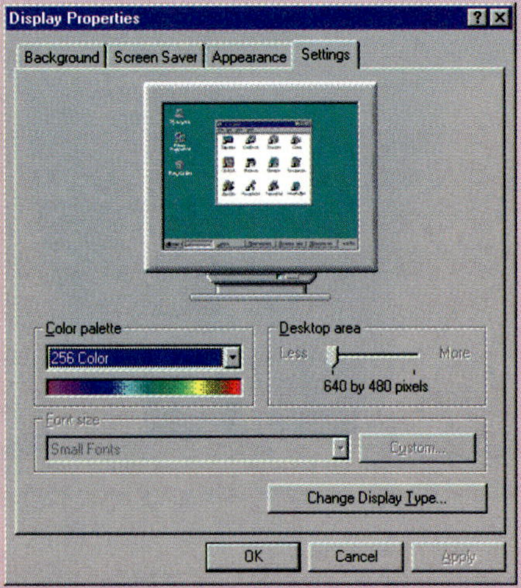

Display Control Panel

Four screens in the `Display` control panel let you modify a variety of **options** affecting the way your video monitor works with Windows and behaves in general. You can adjust the Windows desktop color and pattern 94, an optional screen saver 36, the color scheme for all window objects 34, and settings related to video hardware.

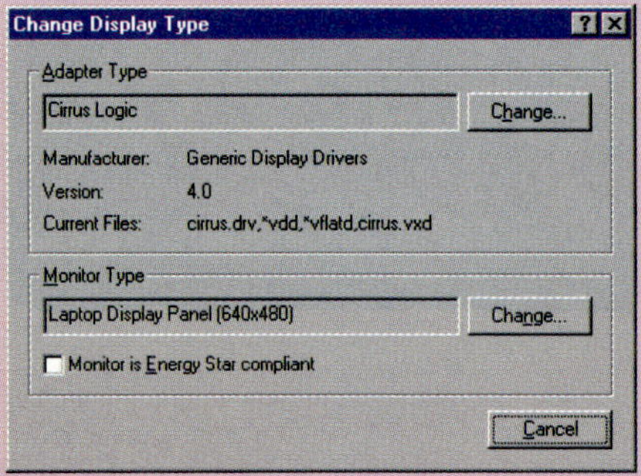

Display Type

A PC display system consists of two hardware elements: a **display adapter** (sometimes built into the motherboard) and a **video monitor.** To Windows, these are distinct items that must be treated separately during the setup process. Under normal conditions, Windows identifies at least the display adapter model, and perhaps the video monitor, during the hardware detection phase of installation.

Before making your first adjustments to the `Display→Settings` control panel, you should be sure Windows has correctly identified both your display adapter and video monitor. Click the [Change Display Type...] button. This leads to a dialog that lists the devices as Windows sees them. If the monitor is listed as "unknown," click the [Change...] button in the `Monitor Type` area to locate your monitor. If your monitor is not listed, then select `Generic` monitors from the `Manufacturers` list, and locate a monitor specification that most closely matches that of your monitor.

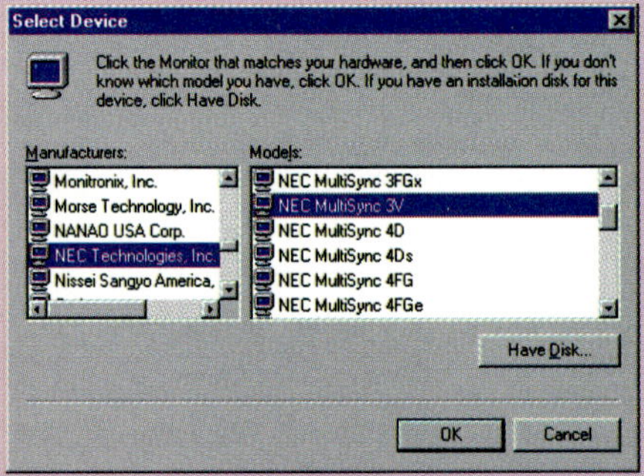

WARNING: When selecting a monitor that is from the Generic group, be sure you match the pixel grid and refresh rate. Selecting an incorrect refresh rate may damage your monitor.

For a new monitor that comes with a Windows 95-compatible installation disk, see 60 about installing devices that have new driver software on disk.

Desktop Area

Choices available in the `Desktop Area` slider control depend on the capabilities of the video hardware selected in the `Display Type` dialog. The smallest pixel grid available for Windows 95 is 640 by 480. As you slide the control toward the `More` setting, available pixel grids appear just below the slider, and the sample in the miniature video monitor shows the sizes of windows, icons, and Taskbar relative to the entire screen. Laptop computers are usually restricted to 640 by 480, so the control will be disabled.

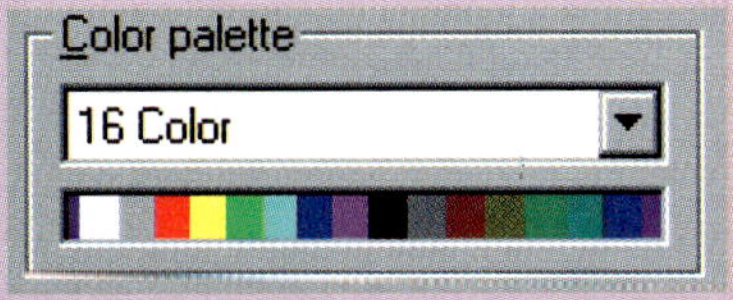

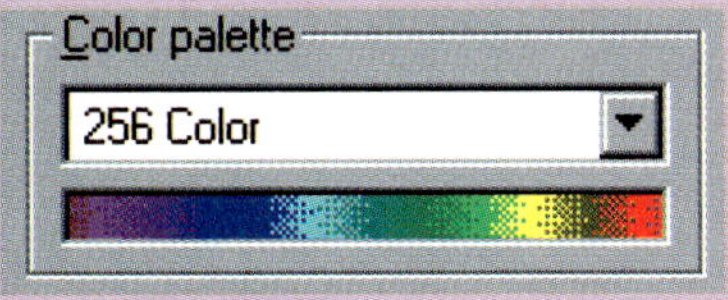

Color Palette

Again, depending on the capabilities of your display adapter ➔30, the `Color Palette` menu lets you choose from the bit depths available at the pixel grid set in the `Desktop Area` control to the right. As you change bit depth values, the sample color swatch changes to give you an idea of how granular the gradations between available colors will be at each setting.

Capturing (Dumping) Screens

You may take a **snapshot** of any Windows screen or window. These snapshots are immediately copied to the **Clipboard.** You can then paste the picture into a graphics program for further editing, or use the Clipboard viewer to save the image as-is. Here are the keystrokes for the two different kinds of images:

Image	Keystroke(s)
Full screen	Prt Scrn
Front window	Alt+Prt Scrn

Snapshots of both types are stored as bitmapped images ➔126, and retain the bit depth at which the snapshots were taken.

Screen dumps do not include the cursor. You can use third-party screen capture programs to help with this, or manually create cursors as separate bitmap files for copying and pasting into screen images in a graphics program (such as Paint).

Printing Screens

Despite the name of the Print Screen key used to capture screens, the key does not send the picture to the printer (as it does in DOS and much earlier versions of Windows). To print, paste the picture from the Clipboard into a program such as Paint, and print from there.

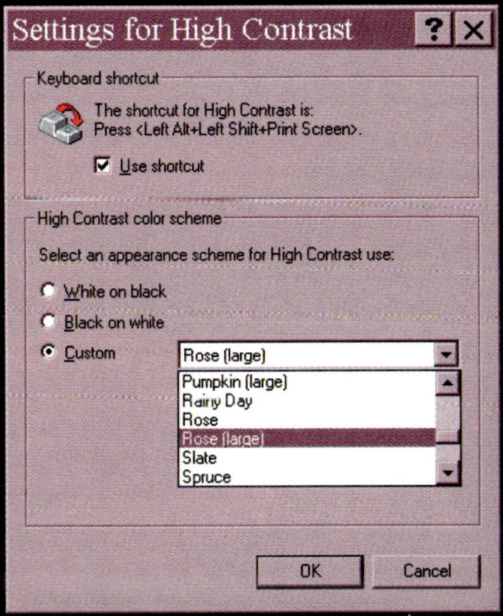

Any group of settings in the `Display➔Appearances` control panel may be saved by name. All named settings are then selectable in the `Accessibility Options➔Display` control panel. The Settings... button there leads to another screen offering the selection of custom color schemes. One benefit of having the schemes available here is that they can be switched on and off via the High Contrast keyboard shortcut (Left Alt+Left Shift+Print Screen). Therefore, if you need a temporary setting with larger window titles or higher contrast colors, the desired set can be toggled into action without having to open any control panel.

Both of these control panels adjust the same system information in Windows. Therefore, if you turn on High Contrast from the Accessibility Options control panel, that color scheme will show up in the `Display➔Appearance` control panel as the one currently selected. But no matter how you change the setting in `Display➔Appearance`, the selected color scheme in `Accessibility Options➔Display` remains in place, ready to be switched on as needed.

Enhancing the View

For some Windows users, text and icons are occasionally too small to see comfortably. For others, the contrasts between colors may not be clear enough.

You can solve some of the font issues (fonts for icon labels and detail listings) by selecting Large Fonts in the `Display➔Settings` control panel.

You can increase the sizes of fonts for window titles and Taskbar items, as well as choose alternate color systems for window objects, from two control panels: `Display➔Appearance` and `Accessibility Options➔Display`. The `Display➔Appearance` control panel ➔34 lets you adjust the size and color of individual elements of windows. For example, if you have a difficult time seeing scrollbars in windows, you can change the colors of the scrollbar and/or its buttons; you can also increase the width of scrollbars. The default setting for window object size and color is `Windows Standard`; larger window titles with the default coloring are available in two sizes: `Windows Standard (large)` and `Windows Standard (extra large)`.

Windows system software provides a great deal of support for setting color and size parameters for screen objects and their component pieces.

You adjust these items in the `Display→Appearance` control panel. Microsoft includes a number of preset color schemes, or you can create and save your own.

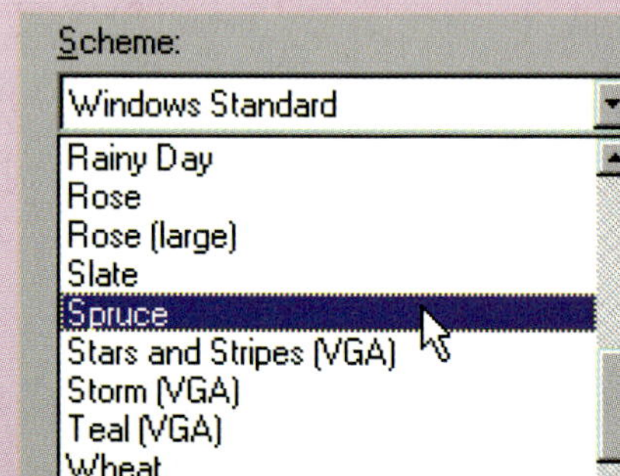

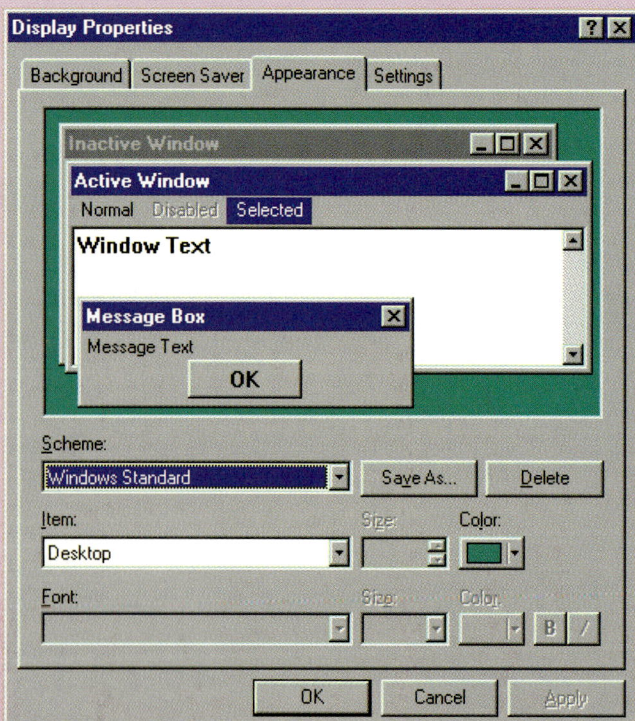

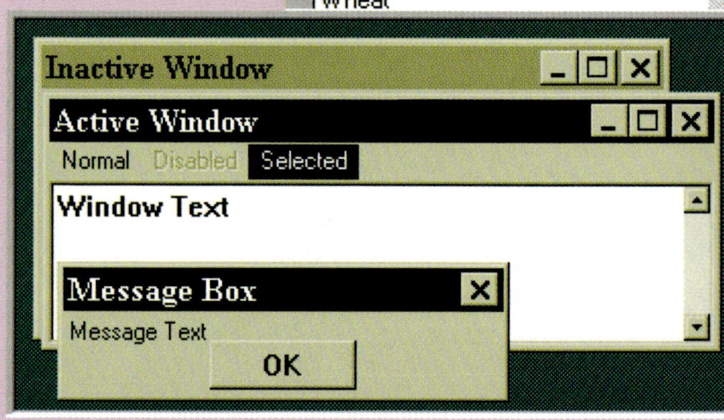

The default appearance scheme is called **Windows Standard.** Of the more than two dozen supplied schemes, some are tuned for optimum display on VGA monitors; some are tuned for video **bit depths** of 16 and 24 (labeled "high color"). The rest can be used at any **bit-depth setting** 30. Several schemes (labeled "large") increase font sizes of text objects, which may make higher resolution screens more readable.

Appearance Schemes

A **sample screen** with a number of Windows objects appears in the `Display→Appearance` control panel. As you select different appearance schemes or adjust individual items, the changes appear in the sample screen so you can see the results without having to check the real Desktop.

More About Custom Color Selector

Instead of dragging the cursor around the color rainbow rectangle, you may directly enter values for **hue, saturation, and luminance.** Hue is a value between 0 and 240 that represents the color. Pure red is 0; pure green is 80; pure blue is 160. As you slowly drag the pointer from left to right across the rainbow, you can see the hue values increasing.

Saturation is a value that designates the absence of white in a particular color. At zero saturation, the color is all white; at 240 (100%) saturation, there is no white, and the color is fully saturated. Luminance, on the other hand, represents the absence of black in a color and is controlled by the vertical slider in the Color selection window. Zero luminance is all black, while 240 (100%) luminance has no black in the color; a luminance

Modifiable Objects

Not all objects or parts modifiable in this control panel are shown in the sample window. As you select an item in the `Item` listbox, controls for all relevant adjustments activate in the control panel.

Item sizes are given in pixels, and the adjustment you can make is usually the **dimension** of the object along one axis (e.g., the height of a window's title bar). When an item has a font associated with it, the font settings also activate, and you can adjust the **font, font size, color, and style** independently of the item's size and color.

Some items have both a foreground and background color. For example, a 3D object, represented in the sample screen by the [OK] button in the Message box, has a background color for the flat surface of the object, and a foreground color for the text on the button. Each color is adjustable independently (the foreground color control is in the row of font controls).

Below is a table of all adjustable items, with associated properties that may also be changed.

	Object			**Associated Font**		
Item Name	Size (Pixels)	Background Color	Foreground Color	Size Points	Ink Color	Style
3D Objects		✗	✗			
Active Title Bar	✗	✗		✗	✗	✗
Active Window Border	✗	✗				
Application Background		✗				
Caption Buttons	✗					
Desktop		✗				
Horizontal Icon Spacing	✗					
Icon Title				✗		✗
Inactive Title Bar	✗	✗		✗	✗	✗
Inactive Window Border	✗	✗				
Menu	✗	✗		✗	✗	✗
Message Box				✗	✗	✗
Palette Title	✗			✗		✗
Scrollbar	✗					
Selected Items	✗	✗		✗	✗	✗
Tool Tip		✗		✗	✗	✗
Vertical Icon Spacing	✗					
Window		✗	✗			

of 120 is the level for primary colors. This HLS (hue, luminance, saturation) model of color representation is an alternate model to the RGB (red, green, blue) model, which determines the intensity of each of those three components in a color. The **Color** selection dialog presents both models, simultaneously displaying values in both systems. RGB values in this dialog range from 0 to 255.

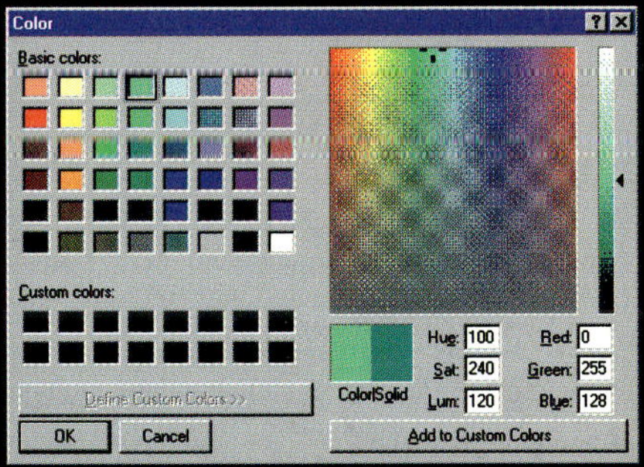

Selecting Colors

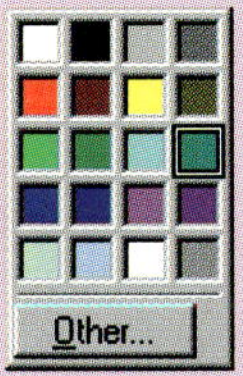

Clicking the down arrow next to an activated color sample produces a small color palette from which you can make quick color choices for the selected item or font. The colors in this palette have been preselected by Microsoft as being recommended for maximum readability and pleasing looks.

The [Other...] button in the palette leads you to the `Color` selection window. This dialog is the Windows standard for choosing a color. A recommended palette of colors appears in the `Basic colors` section, but you can define a color not shown there by clicking [Define Custom Colors >>], which opens the dialog further. From here, you can add your own colors to the palette, which will then appear in the `Custom colors` grouping on the left.

There are several ways to use the **Color** selection dialog. The simplest is to drag the pointer around the rainbow-colored rectangle, watching the color sample rectangle just below. To choose other tones of a selected color, drag the brightness slider control (far right) between total brightness (top) and total black (bottom). You'll need a **high bit depth video adapter** 30 to see finer gradations in color.

When you've selected a color you like, click the [Add to Custom Colors] button. A tiny sample appears in the `Custom colors` section of the dialog. Then click on that custom color and click [OK] to close the dialog. That custom color will be available for many other color settings.

Custom Desktop Color

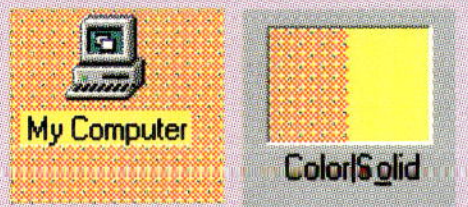

When you access the custom Color selection dialog for setting the Desktop color, the sample swatch is divided into two halves, labeled `Color` and `Solid`. In the Windows Standard color, these two halves are the same color. But as you drag the pointer around the rainbow rectangle, you see that the two halves can diverge significantly.

The `Color` half shows the Desktop background color. The `Solid` half indicates the color surrounding the text of an icon label on the Desktop. You may want to select a combination that produces high contrast of the labels against a hard-to-read background or wallpaper pattern 94.

In addition to ergonomic 4 and cabling considerations 7, setting up a video monitor also means knowing about safety.

Video monitors are highly charged electronic devices and emit **electromagnetic force** (EMF) fields. Research on potential hazards from EMF continues and is controversial. Setting up your monitors correctly, however, can reduce exposure to these fields.

Constant images displayed on the screen, such as the Taskbar, can damage the tube of your video monitor. By using a screen saver, however, you can prevent this damage.

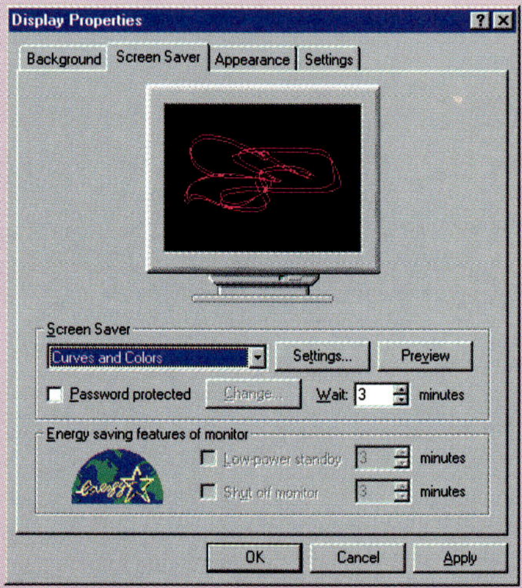

Monitor Distances

Based on testing performed by various laboratories, a **safe distance** between your head or body and the monitor is around **30 inches**. With two-page monitors, this is sometimes difficult to achieve because the monitors are extremely deep, and take up lots of desk space. If that's the case, put the monitor off to one side so that it angles toward you from about an arm's length away. Most of the emissions come from the rear of the monitor, where all the magnetic coils that aim the electron beams are. A distance of about **four feet** from the rear and sides of the cabinet to the nearest person should be adequate. The good news is that monitor makers are more aware of EMF, and are working on monitors with lower radiation emission with each new generation. Monitors meeting the Swedish government's MRP II standard 29 are readily available today.

Adjusting Brightness

Use your **Brightness** control frequently to make your monitor comfortable to view in the surrounding light. If you work where the lighting changes during the day (e.g., windows in your office), the brightness needs to be intensified during bright periods of the day, and turned down as the day darkens. Working at a monitor whose brightness is not compatible with surrounding light can lead to eye strain or headaches.

Preventing Burn-in

The high-power electron beam in the video tube can eventually discolor the phosphor inside the tube. If an area of the screen, such as the Taskbar, is constantly illuminated, you may be able to see the area "burned into" the screen when the PC monitor is turned off. While phosphor degradation is inevitable, it won't be noticed if the screen degrades evenly.

If your monitor is **Energy Star** compliant (or employs another power-saving technology), then the monitor will power down or off after the amount of time you specify in the power management software. The `Display→Screen Saver` control panel includes settings for Energy Star monitors. There, you can specify how soon after idle activity the monitor reduces power (blanking the screen) and/or turns off the monitor entirely. Be aware, however, that when the monitor is completely turned off, it may take a minute or so for it to warm up when you return to the PC. Therefore, you may not want to invoke this choice during the workday, when you may need quick access to the computer.

A burn-in prevention system for all monitor styles is the screen saver that is built into Windows (or third-party screen savers). A screen saver typically removes the normal Windows elements from the screen after a period of no mouse or keyboard activity (you set how long), and displays graphics in random patterns to even the wear. Any movement of the mouse or press of a keyboard key restores the Windows screen.

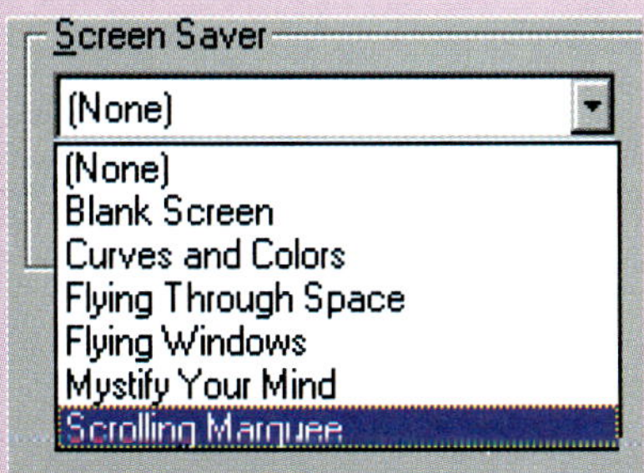

Windows Screen Saver

Windows includes six possible **screen-saving patterns,** ranging from a completely blank screen to your own customizable scrolling marquee. If you choose any screen saver (other than `None`), you can set how many minutes of mouse and keyboard inactivity must elapse before the screen saver kicks in. Moreover, most screen saver patterns have subsidiary options that are accessed by clicking the Settings... button in the control panel. For example, the `Curves and Colors` saver pattern offers choices for the speed of activity, numbers of lines and curves in the display, density of the shapes, and coloration. When a screen saver offers color choices, the most effective in providing even wear of the CRT is random coloration.

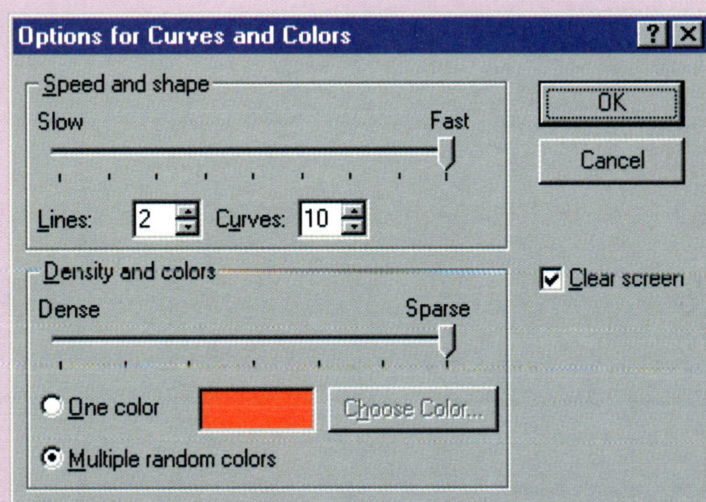

Some screen saver patterns have a checkbox for whether the screen should clear prior to starting the saver. **Clearing the screen** is nothing more than setting the entire screen to black. Screen clearing is recommended, since you want to make sure no long-term images from the Windows Desktop persist in screen saver mode.

Surrounding Space

Video monitors need breathing room around them. Cooling of the video tube is accomplished by **convection cooling:** cool air comes in from the bottom, warm air escapes through the top. Keep this air flow clear. An overheated monitor may automatically shut down as a safeguard against further damage.

LCDs

Most laptop computers feature a liquid crystal display (LCD) instead of a picture tube. LCDs have much lower power requirements and don't emit any radiation. The most common color LCD panels are the STN (single twist nematic) and active matrix style. Active matrix displays tend to have crisper colors and faster overall response. They are also more expensive and more power hungry than STN displays.

The size of a laptop's LCD panel is an important factor in how well its owner likes using the machine for extended periods. Screens under 9.5 inches diagonal scrunch the elements of typical Windows screens so that they appear much smaller and more difficult to control than on a standard video monitor back at the desktop. A number of laptop machines include a built-in video port to connect a full-size VGA or SVGA color monitor—very desirable for extended work at the desktop.

Virtually every color LCD panel is backlit, but some gray-scale panels on subnotebook computers lack any backlighting. A backlight is very important for viewing under a variety of real-world working environments. A backlight insures sufficient contrast between the light and dark areas on the screen, but at the cost of slightly higher power drain.

Memory 38

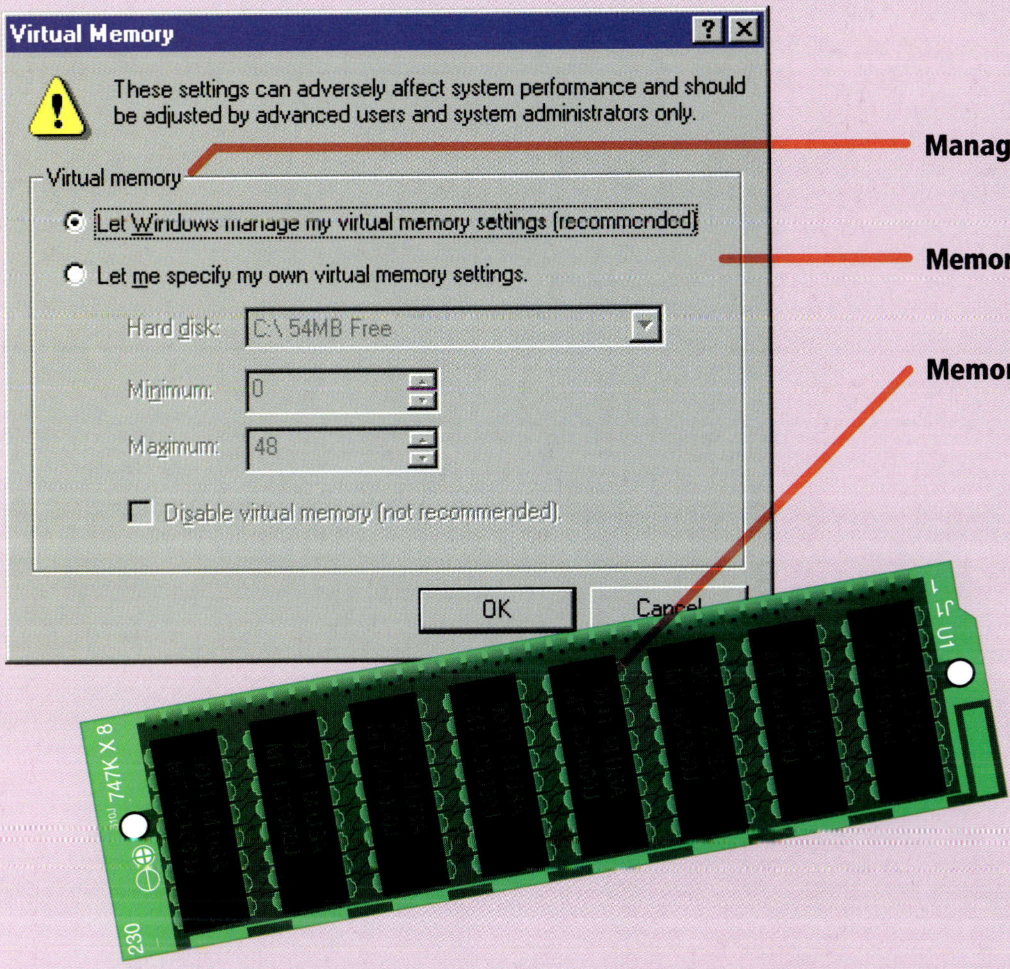
Virtual Memory
These settings can adversely affect system performance and should be adjusted by advanced users and system administrators only.
Virtual memory
Let Windows manage my virtual memory settings (recommended)
Let me specify my own virtual memory settings.
Hard disk:
C:\ 54MB Free
Minimum:
0
Maximum:
48
Disable virtual memory (not recommended).
OK
Cancel
747K X 8
230
U1

There are three types of PC memory: ROM (read-only memory), RAM (random access memory), and disk storage.

ROM contains the most elemental hardware operating system and other software pre-programmed at the factory. It cannot be changed or erased without exchanging the chip(s). RAM, on the other hand, is the temporary storage where Windows, applications, and documents "live" while you use them. The contents of RAM change literally keystroke by keystroke. On all desktop PCs, RAM is completely erased when you turn off the computer. In contrast, disk storage 48–58 is a safe place to store documents, because disks maintain their storage even when the power is turned off. Disk storage is also much larger than RAM in today's PCs, holding hundreds or thousands of documents for retrieval and modification.

In normal parlance, the amount of memory in your PC refers to the amount of RAM installed in your machine. To upgrade your PC to run Windows 95 comfortably, you may need to install more memory than your PC originally came with 42.

Bit, Byte, Kilobyte, Megabyte,...

Memory discussions focus around two primary terms: **bit and byte.** A bit is the smallest amount of information a computer knows about. It is like a switch, either on or off, 1 or 0, white or black. Memory chips consist of large numbers of electron-microscopic, nonmechanical switches that are either in the "on" or "off" position, each switch counting as one bit.

Since human information is more complex than that, it takes groups of bits bundled together to store information we can use. A convention of grouping 8 bits together into a byte gives us a possible combination of 256 arrangements of the ones and zeros in the group (00000001, 00000010, 00000011, etc.). That's enough to assign one combination to each letter and punctuation mark of most Roman languages, like English. Generally speaking, then, one byte equals one Roman alphabet character.

Being a wordy species, we humans work with thousands and millions of characters at a time. A thousand characters is known as a **kilobyte,** abbreviated KB or just K (the binary math of ones and zeros make it more convenient to calculate in base-2 math; a kilobyte is actually 2 to the tenth power (2^{10}), or 1024 characters). The kilobyte is the typical denomination for things like file size.

The developers of application programs need to load perhaps millions of characters (bytes) into RAM for us to use a program. Personal computer RAM is measured by the number of **megabytes** (MB). Each year or so, the amount of RAM installed in basic configuration computers increases. The minimum you'll find on budget systems today is 4MB, with 8 or 16MB more common. Such machines are usually expandable to 128MB or more. Due to power, size, and heat restrictions, few laptop computers are capable of holding more than 20MB of RAM.

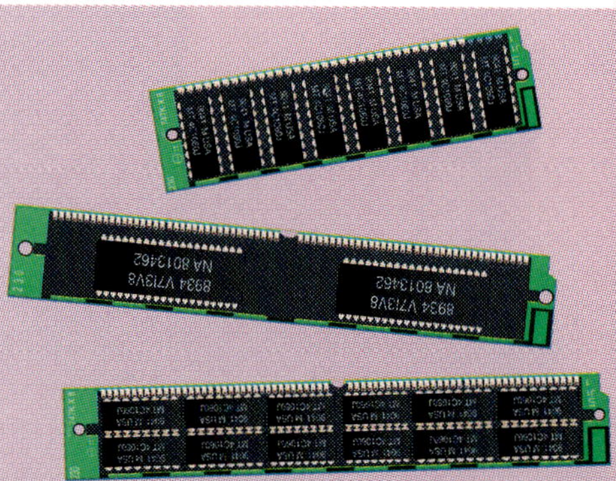

SIMM Memory

Desktop PC RAM is commonly packaged in plug-in circuit modules called **SIMMs** (Single In-Line Memory Modules). A typical SIMM consists of eight or nine memory chips (only eight are used for information storage). The individual chips come in a variety of capacities, usually no smaller than 1,048,576 bits. Multiply that by eight data chips on a module, and you get the byte count of each module. A 1MB ("one-meg") SIMM not much larger than your index finger holds exactly one megabyte of RAM. Newer SIMMs capable of holding 2, 4, and 16 megabytes each are also becoming available, but not all PCs can use them.

SIMMs are much more convenient to work with than individual chips when it comes to installing additional memory. Their construction also allows more memory per square centimeter of space.

SIMMs plug into **special sockets** on the PC system board. The number of SIMM sockets on the motherboard varies from maker to maker. Sometimes the basic memory configuration is manufactured directly on the motherboard; other times, all RAM is installed in SIMM sockets. PC magazines are full of advertisements for mail order SIMMs at discount prices. Be sure to match any expansion SIMMs you buy with the make and model number of your PC.

RAM Speed: The Nanosecond Factor

Individual RAM chips (and by extension, their SIMMs) are rated not only by size but by speed. The speed, measured in **nanoseconds** (ns)—that's billionths of a second—represents the speed at which the PC circuitry reads and writes bits to the chip. The faster the PC's main chip (the central processing unit, or CPU), the faster the RAM required to run inside the machine. Since the access rate is determined by the CPU, adding faster RAM to a slower machine doesn't speed up the RAM access time in any way—but, then, there is no penalty (except perhaps a premium price) for installing faster RAM than needed for your PC, and you may later be able to transfer that fast RAM to a new, faster PC.

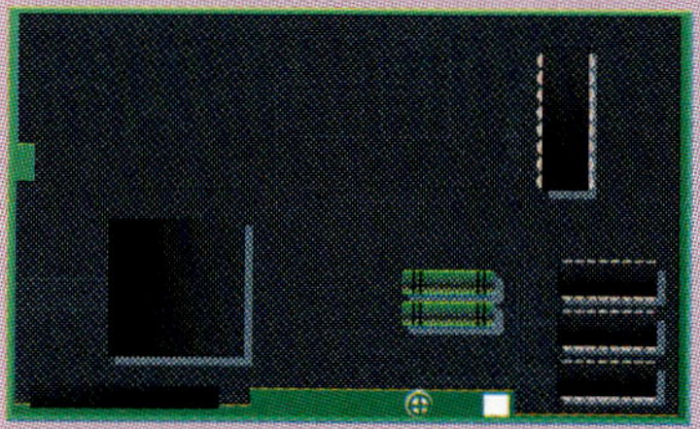

Laptop RAM Modules

The cramped quarters of laptop computers prevents the standard SIMM style of memory. Often, very specialized memory boards or credit-card-sized modules must be installed to increase the memory of a laptop computer. Because the specific design of these modules varies so much, it is vital to buy RAM that is designed for the make and model of the laptop you have. Do not assume that all models of a popular brand use the same memory modules. Because of the comparatively low production runs for these modules, laptop memory tends to be more expensive than desktop PC SIMMs. Still, lower-cost third-party alternatives are often available from memory specialty retailers.

Parity RAM

At the dawn of high-power personal computing, IBM designed its original PC memory with a feature called **parity checking.** Parity is an error detection scheme that uses math to double-check (although not in a foolproof way) the cumulative

Installing Memory

The most common problem in installing SIMMs or memory modules is the failure to seat the memory module securely in the socket. SIMM sockets have clips and pins that should fit squarely around and through the SIMM circuit board. The SIMM will not wobble when installed correctly. After installation, start the computer and see if the new memory is detected in your system ➔ 42.

CAUTION

SIMMs and laptop memory modules are extremely sensitive to **static electricity**, which can blow away expensive chips with less shock than you'd even feel. Always try to hold the SIMM or module like a precious photograph—by the edges that don't have any connectors on them. Before you come near a memory module of any kind, **ground yourself** by touching something metal, like the power supply cabinet or rigid frame of your opened computer (with power off, of course). Electrostatic discharge wrist straps are available, but unless they're connected properly, they don't offer much more protection than frequently touching the grounded metal points of your computer before and after you pick up a SIMM. Even rolling your chair around the floor or sitting down in a chair can build up a static charge on your body. Discharge your static frequently during SIMM installation.

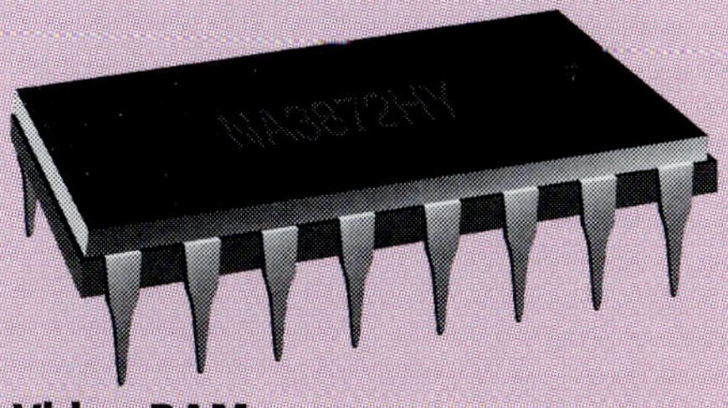

Video RAM

System memory is not used for video RAM. Display adapters provide their own RAM (they still need memory to store the current screen), and can often be expanded to accommodate great amounts of memory-hungry color ➔ 30. Video RAM is primarily of the SIMM variety, but you may still encounter boards that require plugging in individual RAM chips for upgrading. For best performance, your video display adapter should use RAM chips specifically designed for video RAM applications. Known as **VRAM**, these chips or SIMMs are faster than the traditional **DRAM**, the same used for traditional SIMM memory modules ➔ 30.

How Your PC Uses Memory

Before you turn on your PC (except portable machines that may be in sleep mode), all system **RAM** is empty—without power, your PC's RAM can't store a thing. When you turn on the machine, the CPU, following instructions in ROM, performs a number of system tests and then loads Windows and its supporting programs into RAM. Because of the way Windows manages memory ➔ 44, there is no convenient way to measure how much RAM Windows itself occupies.

Each time you open an application, some or all of the program's code is copied from the hard disk into RAM. The RAM copy is what runs when you use an application. The amount of memory used by an application includes space not only for the program, but also for any documents you have open. If necessary, a Windows application can claim additional RAM for itself while it runs—Windows handles all memory assignments automatically.

value of data in a byte of RAM. Parity checking requires one extra bit of RAM for every byte, bringing the total number of RAM chips in a byte-wide bank of memory to 9 instead of 8. Because the IBM PC became so entrenched in government work, parity RAM became a standard requirement for any personal computers considered for government purchase. Apple even responded by offering—for a time—some Macintosh models with a parity RAM option.

Not all desktop or laptop PC systems use parity RAM today, nor is there evidence that non-parity PCs are any less reliable than parity PCs.

Memory Diagrams

If you thumb through the hardware reference section of your PC's user guide or read technical books about PCs or Windows 95, you will surely come upon a variety of diagrams that depict aspects of either a computer's memory or the way Windows 95 treats memory for various tasks.

One kind of diagram is the memory address diagram, typically shown in a column of blocks. Addresses, shown in the engineering-oriented base-16 (hexadecimal) numbering system, are just like house numbers, with each value pointing to a particular byte of RAM. In the days prior to sophisticated memory management schemes of Windows 95 and other operating systems, the map paralleled the actual (physical) RAM space that a machine was capable of handling. Windows 95, however, distributes various pieces of itself and applications throughout its theoretical maximum of four billion addresses. These addresses don't represent physical RAM addresses in your system (unless you have 4GB of RAM!), but rather virtual addresses that Windows assigns to the physical RAM to accommodate growth in the future.

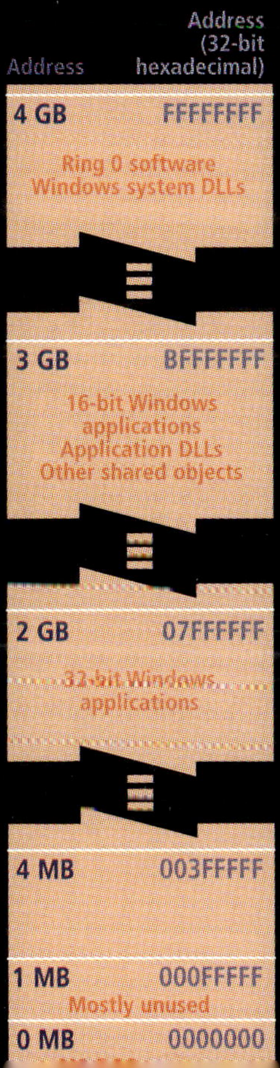

Another type of diagram used often for Windows 95 represents how various running processes occupy segments of RAM. This kind of diagram better illustrates Windows' system architecture ➔ 43. For example, Windows 95 creates what it calls a System Virtual Machine, in which run the following: system services, individual 32-bit Windows applications, and a memory segment in which all 16-bit Windows applications ➔ 43 run. Windows also creates separate MS-DOS virtual machines for each DOS application you start from Windows ➔ 130.

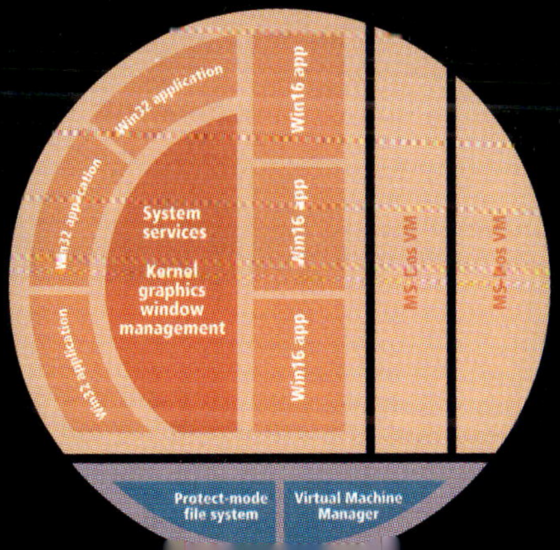

By requiring a PC with at least an 80386 CPU, Windows 95 simplifies the job of configuring your system's memory.

While Windows 95 must still respect the constraints of MS-DOS for users who run DOS-only software, it does so in a way that lets users almost forget about memory once a sufficient quantity is installed in the computer.

Windows 95 operates with 4MB of RAM, but the more memory you have installed, the quicker day-to-day operations will be for you. If you typically keep several applications open at the same time 122, then 16MB of RAM will reduce the time waiting for some operations to complete.

How Much RAM Do I Have?

Windows PCs give you many ways to see how much memory is installed in your computer. For example, upon a cold boot of most PCs, you will see the computer perform a check of the system RAM before doing anything else. The memory figure grows until it reaches the number of installed kilobytes. This is easy to miss, because additional startup items can make this test scroll off the screen quickly.

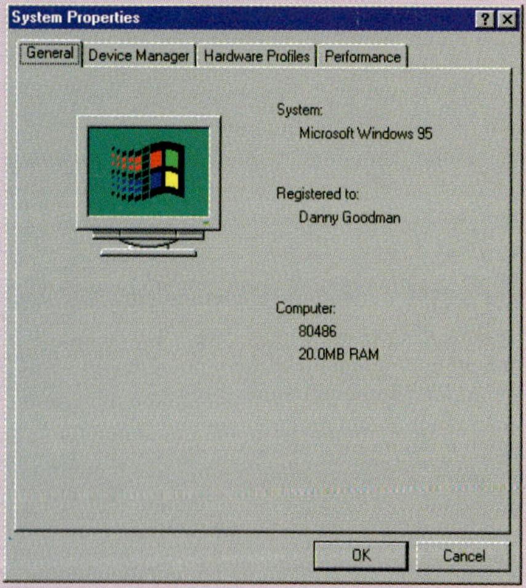

From within Windows, you can open the **System** control panel. In the first screen, Windows details the type of CPU it found, and provides a count of RAM available to Windows.

Additionally, your PC may come with a setup or system utility that reveals complete and accurate details about your system. Advanced users can use the MS-DOS MEM utility from the DOS prompt to learn more about how their memory is being treated (below).

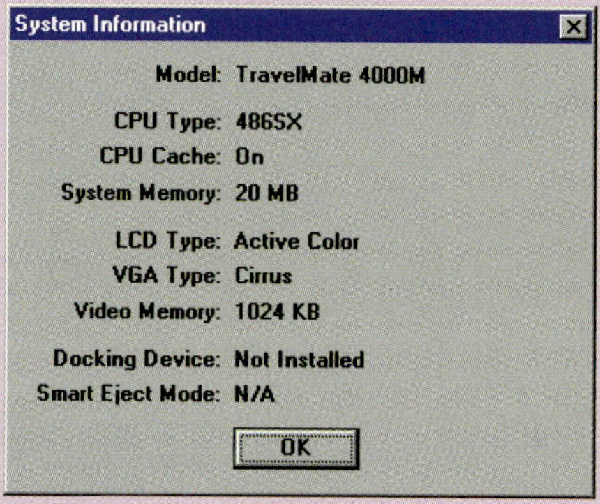

RAM Requirements

While Windows 95 requires a minimum of 4 megabytes of RAM, that may be just a bare minimum for using a single application, especially if you use a large program, such as Excel. The comparatively low cost of SIMMs for desktop PCs makes upgrading to 8 or more megabytes a cost-effective way to improve productivity. Once your PC reaches 16MB, you'll notice a substantial improvement in performance when you keep multiple applications open all the time.

Windows Resources

Because Windows makes up for low memory by sending some in-memory items to a special file on your hard disk (according to default Virtual Memory settings), you cannot get a true picture of how much memory is available for operations. As you open and close applications, Windows constantly massages memory usage to meet the needs of those applications. Instead, Windows supplies you with a readout of what it calls resources. Memory space is only a small part of what makes up resources—the rest consists of items that only programmers tend to worry about. Located in the System→Performance control panel, this value is rated as a percentage remaining. Adding RAM does not necessarily raise the percentage values, but it does increase the ability of Windows to accommodate more programs and tasks at the same time. In general, you can ignore the System Resources value, and wait for Windows to tell you when there aren't enough resources available to load one more program. When you get this message, you'll know that Windows has done everything it knows how to do to make room for the program, but couldn't do it.

RAM Disk

When you have lots of RAM, you may consider assigning part of it to behave like another disk volume. The advantage of this feature, called a RAM disk, is that access to that volume is virtually instantaneous, because there is no physical access required as there is with a floppy or hard disk.

On desktop PCs, a RAM disk is not all that helpful these days. Hard disks tend to be quite fast, so they rarely slow you down unless you are accessing a huge file. Besides, the memory you assign to a RAM disk is then not available to your programs and documents. It is typically more valuable to have RAM available for multiple applications. Also, if you copy a program to the RAM disk, the program must still load it from the RAM disk into the application RAM area for you to use it—the program is then on the hard disk, in the RAM disk,

Virtual Memory

When RAM isn't enough memory for a particular operation, Windows is capable of assigning an unused portion of your hard disk as **temporary RAM** of significant size. This function is called **virtual memory**, because the disk acts just like RAM, albeit at significantly slower transfer rates than RAM chips. All Windows 95–compatible PCs are capable of using virtual memory. See 44 for using virtual memory to manage your PC's memory.

32-Bit (Win32) Applications

Microsoft encourages Windows 95 users to gravitate toward application software that adheres to the Win32 API, which is an internal mechanism that allows program developers to take advantage of modern features of Windows. One supreme advantage of running a Win32 (32-bit) application in Windows 95 is that the application runs in its own protected memory space. If the program should crash, any other program and Windows itself should continue to run, allowing you to save work in all but the crashed application.

Other advantages of Win32 applications include support for long file names 112, more memory available per application, and preemptive **multi-tasking** (multiple programs doing high-performance work at the same time, even though only one is "in front"). Even within an application, multiple processes (threads), such as downloading a file while reading mail in the same communications program, appear to take place simultaneously.

Mixing Old with New

Acknowledging that users who upgrade to Windows 95 on their existing systems will be running **older programs** intended for Windows 3.x and MS-DOS, the Microsoft engineers created a scheme whereby most older programs could run inside the new Windows. How they're treated in memory, however, is quite different. Older Windows applications (called Win16 apps) all run within a single block of memory, just as they did in Windows 3.x. If one should crash, then all other Win16 applications will also go down.

For MS-DOS programs, Windows 95 uses the comparatively vast RAM resources of a Windows PC to make each program believe it's running on its own MS-DOS computer 130. These **virtual machines** can be configured (by way of property sheets) to behave like real machines, including adjustments for conventional, expanded, and extended memory. You probably won't ever have to bother with these memory settings.

and, when running, in your application RAM as well. Most dangerously, when you turn off your PC, anything stored on the RAM disk is immediately erased. If you haven't saved edited documents to a real disk, they'll be gone, probably without notice.

A RAM disk can make sense, however, on a laptop, provided there is sufficient RAM installed. By keeping frequently used programs and documents on the RAM disk, you lower the need for the computer to access the battery-hungry hard disk. Moreover, putting a portable to sleep 11 doesn't erase the RAM—although it's a good idea to back up your documents to the hard disk before putting the machine to sleep, just in case you can't wake up the PC again after a very long, battery-draining nap.

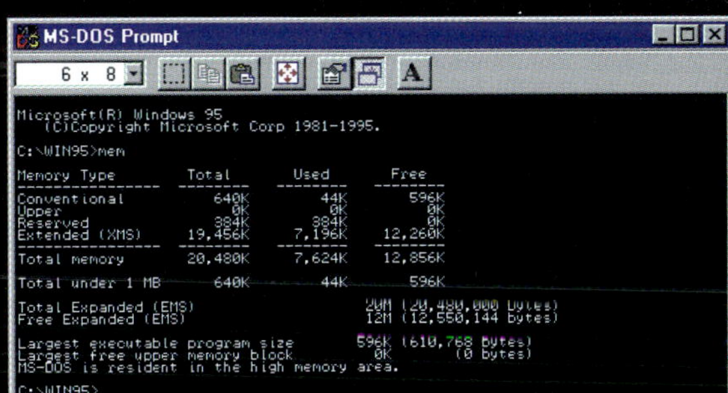

Checking Memory: MEM

If you drop into an MS-DOS prompt and type the command MEM, you'll receive a readout of various memory parameters in your system. If you've just installed some new memory, you should be interested in the Total memory figure at the bottom of the Total column. This represents the physical RAM available on your machine. All but 640KB (conventional) and 384KB (reserved) should be assigned to Extended memory—the kind Windows 95 uses.

Real vs. Protected Modes

The terms real mode and protected mode refer to the way the CPU manages access to memory. The 80286 CPU was the first to offer operating system developers (like Microsoft) a choice between behaving like earlier generation CPUs (real mode) and the more robust protected mode. Unfortunately, the chip made the choice an either/or situation, meaning that if an operating system supported protected mode, it would lose compatibility with programs and devices designed to work in real mode.

With the 80386 chip, however, an operating system could be designed to work in protected mode and as a replica of real mode at the same time (by asking the CPU to create a temporary, virtual 8086 machine for MS-DOS programs and device drivers). That parallel universe of real and protected modes extends to today's 80486 and Pentium CPUs, and Windows 95 milks those capabilities for all they're worth to give users a broad range of compatibility with comparatively ancient software and hardware devices. You'll only really need to be concerned about real mode for certain hardware devices 60.

You can let Windows manage the memory inside your computer, just like you can let a service station attendant fill up your gas tank, check your oil, and do tune-ups.

But Windows users, like car owners, should know something about what's happening under the hood when unexpected things occur. And if you use lots of MS-DOS programs, you may need to tweak some settings for an application to get things working the way you like.

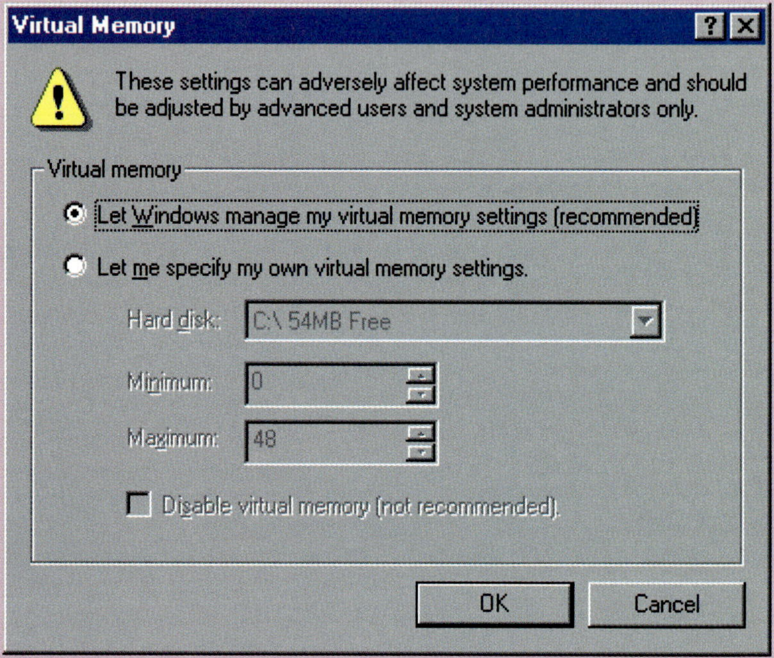

Windows Applications and Memory

Each time you start a Windows application program, Windows loads some or all of that program into **RAM.** That's the copy you use. To use memory efficiently, however, most programs load only portions of themselves when you start. As other portions are needed (e.g., dialog box displays, code that carries out infrequently used menu commands, etc.), the program brings those items into RAM, perhaps flushing other items at the same time if memory is tight. By default, Windows sets itself up to use free space on the hard disk to serve as reserve RAM when your computer's true RAM fills up. This allows you to run more programs in less installed memory.

Memory used by an application is not only for the program, but also for any documents you open. To work with **large documents,** some programs even bring a portion of the document file into RAM, keeping the rest in temporary files on the disk. When you save the document, the program recombines the temporary files and the RAM segment into the saved file.

Memory requirements for a Windows application can change while you use the program, so with Windows, unlike some other operating systems, there is no application memory to adjust or measure.

When Memory Is Tight

If you detect frequent hard disk accesses as you open the same dialog box several times while using a program over a brief period, you may not have enough RAM. If you don't have virtual memory turned on, then you will receive messages that say there is **not enough memory** when you try to open another program. But before you run out to buy more SIMMs, there are some remedies to try.

First, be sure that **virtual memory** is turned on. In the `System→Performance` control panel, click the `Virtual Memory` button. The bottom checkbox (`Disable virtual memory`) should not be checked. Unless you are trying to manage a tight hard disk storage situation as well ➜ 56, choose the option that lets Windows manage virtual memory.

Virtual Memory

Windows 95 usually does its best **memory management** when it controls the details of virtual memory. Microsoft recommends that setting in the `System→Performance→Virtual Memory` control panel, and they mean it. If your PC's RAM is on the low side of Windows 95's desires, the constant disk access you hear as you navigate through your programs and documents is Windows shuttling bits of program or document (in 4K "pages") to and from a normally hidden swap file in the root directory of your boot drive (usually C:). This file can occupy many megabytes, and since it stays in place even when you shut down Windows, low memory can also lower available disk space ➜ 56.

There may be times when you do wish to control the details of virtual memory's behavior on your PC—for example, when you have multiple hard disk drives connected to your PC, and you wish the swap file to be located on a drive other than your boot drive. When you activate the radio button

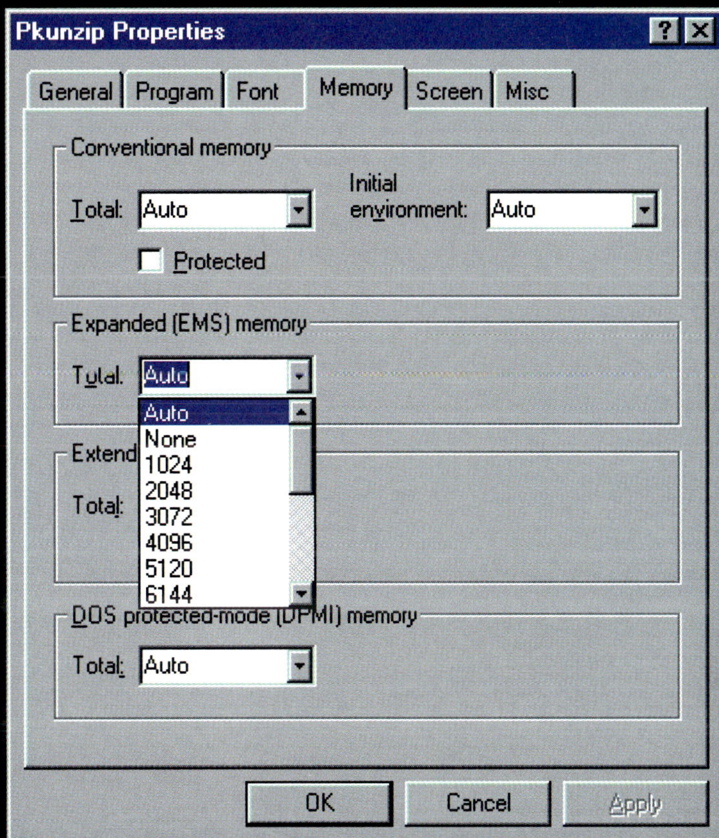

Next, check for any items that load automatically when Windows starts up. These items are in the `Start Menu`➔`Programs`➔`Startup` folder ➔ 107. It is possible that the Windows 95 upgrade process will automatically insert items there from your previous Windows 3.x environment that are no longer needed because the features are built into Windows 95. Remove items from this folder and restart Windows.

As a last resort, close any unneeded open windows on your Desktop. Folder windows with lots of items in them take up RAM.

If, after these efforts, you still notice sustained disk activity once a program or document is opened, or repeated disk activity when popping up the Start menu, then it's time to check the magazine ads and stores for memory upgrades for your machine ➔ 40.

in the control panel to manually adjust virtual memory settings, you see how much free space (to the next lowest whole megabyte) is available on each drive. The default settings for minimum and maximum swap file size are zero and several megabytes smaller than the free space on the selected drive. You should adjust these settings only if you want to reserve disk space for virtual memory (making sure no other files take up the minimum virtual memory space) or if you want to prevent the swap file from expanding beyond a desired size. If you have ample memory installed in your computer when Windows 95 is first installed, you may never see the effects of the swap file on your hard disk capacity.

MS-DOS Program Memory

To provide maximum compatibility with MS-DOS applications, Windows 95 maintains extensive property settings for any DOS program you run. When Windows' automatic memory settings don't work, you can make manual adjustments ➔ 130. These settings are saved in files with the extension `.PIF` and bear an MS-DOS shortcut icon. You can double-click the shortcut to launch its associated program.

Right-click on an MS-DOS application icon (or its .PIF file) and choose Properties from the pop-up menu; then click the Memory tab. The settings here harken back to the days when DOS and Windows 3 users had to be cognizant of the different memory systems: conventional, expanded, and extended. Some programs work only in **conventional memory** (i.e., up to 640KB of RAM); some work with conventional and **expanded memory**; others require **extended memory.**

You should first try to let Windows handle the memory situation. If that fails, consult the documentation for the trouble program and see if it makes any recommendations for memory settings. Anything special will likely be defined in the terminology and values you see in the property sheet's memory screen ➔ 130.

The most common IBM PC-compatible floppy disks come in two capacities: 720KB and 1.44MB. Both use a 3.5" diameter disk (made of material similar to audio tape in a cassette) inside a protective plastic housing. Differences in capacity depend on how information is embedded on the disk.

To insert a disk, slide it into the floppy disk drive slot, with the disk label facing the sky, until the disk snaps into place. The PC won't recognize that you've inserted the disk until you perform some action on it in Windows. When you are finished with the diskette, remove it by pressing the button adjacent to the disk slot firmly until the disk pops out of the drive. Then pull the disk straight out the rest of the way.

Floppy disks have much less capacity than hard disks 51, but they provide a way for software publishers to distribute software, for you to back up important files, and for Windows users to exchange files when the machines are not connected via a network.

Diskette Sizes

For the past several years, the standard floppy disk drive on Windows-capable PCs has been the **high-density drive,** capable of storing up to **1.44MB** of information on a disk (the precise capacity is 1,457,664 bytes of user space, which comes to 1.38MB). Boxes of 3.5" diskettes for this capacity are usually labeled 2HD (two-sided, high-density), or DS/HD (double-sided, high-density). Don't be confused by the 2.0MB rating on these disks: that is its raw capacity, which is not available in full once the disk has been formatted for use on a PC.

A high-density floppy drive can read and write both the older 720KB and current standard 1.44MB disk formats. But an older 720KB drive cannot read a 1.44MB diskette. The 1.44MB disk drive is so common today that virtually every floppy disk program is delivered on 1.44MB disks.

Diskettes are manufactured for each density, and should be used only for their intended capacity to prevent lost data. The outward distinguishing physical characteristic of a 1.44MB disk is a square hole in the plastic case opposite the sliding locking tab. The 1.44MB floppy disk drive mechanism senses that hole, and recognizes the disk as a high density style. High-density disks also feature the stylized letters "HD" on the plastic case next to the spring-loaded metal shutter.

The 3.5" plastic-cased disk has replaced the 5.25" cardboard-sleeved disk as the standard. Although the older disks were larger, they held only 1.2MB of data.

Where Are the Last Few KB?

When you format a diskette, you don't get every byte you may have thought. For example, after initializing what was supposed to be a 1.44MB disk, you see that there is only 1.38MB available. The "missing" space is devoted to the hidden disk directory and control information that the Windows file system uses for a variety of internal disk management tasks.

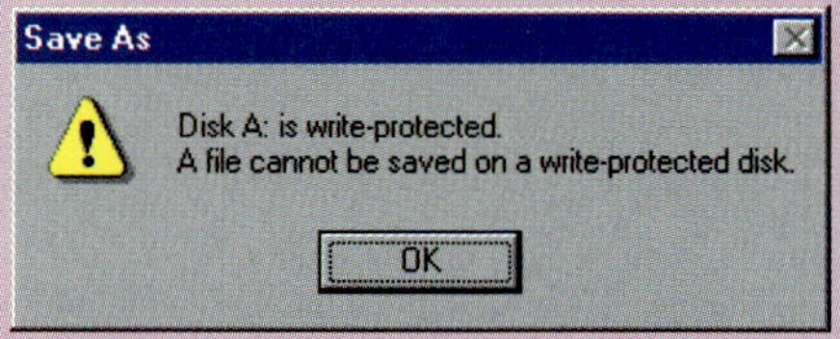

Protecting Diskettes

Unless you intend to save information to a diskette, you should always **lock the disk** before inserting it into a disk drive. This prevents the infection of the disk with a virus 58 as well as accidental erasure. All diskettes have a locking tab. With the round metal disk hub facing you, the locking tab is in the corner opposite the diagonal cut in the disk case. Use your fingernail to slide the locking tab in either direction. When the tab is up and you can see through the hole, the disk is **write-protected.** Your programs may still read files on the disk, and you can run most programs from a locked disk. Unfortunately, when you work with a diskette within Windows there is no visual clue that it is locked or unlocked. Only when you try to save or copy information to a locked disk do you get a message reminding you of the fact.

Inserting a Diskette

PC disk drives are smart enough to prevent you from doing something wrong. You cannot, for example, completely seat a diskette in the drive upside down. If you push the disk into the slot correctly, you can push the disk all the way until it clicks into place. What you don't see is the disk drive sliding the **metal shutter** to one side to reveal the magnetic disk material to the disk drive heads.

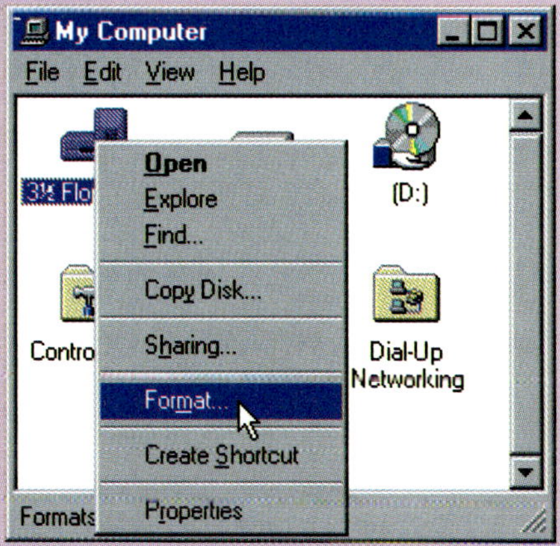

Formatting a Disk

Before information can be saved to a disk, the disk must be prepared to accept the information. DOS and Windows computers call this process formatting the disk. **Formatting** lays down an invisible map of parking places for blocks of information. If Windows tries to read or write a floppy disk, but can't find the necessary hidden items on the disk, you receive a warning that the disk can't be read, with an option to format the disk. You can also insert an unformatted disk (or one that has been used on another type of machine, such as a Macintosh), and right-click on the floppy disk icon in the Explorer ➔76 or in the `My Computer` window ➔74 to locate the `Format` option. This leads to the Format dialog box.

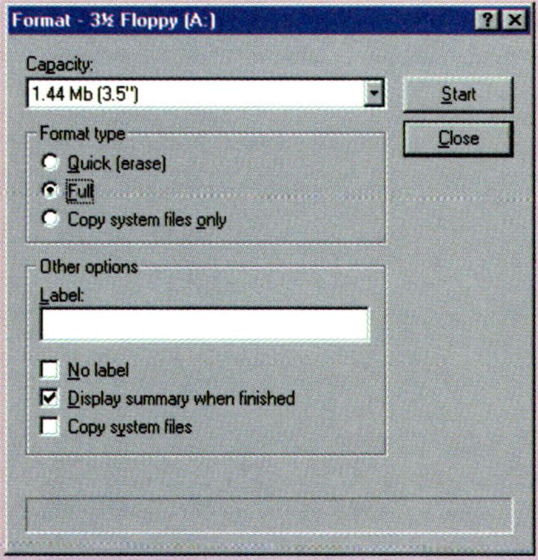

A blank disk or one from another operating system will require the `Full` formatting from the `Format Type` radio button choices. If you also want the diskette to be able to boot your computer ➔70, then check the `Copy system files` box in the `Other Options` area. Finally, select only the capacity of the diskette for which it was designed—1.44MB for a 2HD disk.

Windows will tell you if formatting fails. If you get a **formatting failure** with a new disk, try restarting Windows and reformatting the disk. If initialization fails again, forget the disk. Either return it to the manufacturer for a replacement (if it is so warranted) or toss it. A troublesome disk only gets more so in time.

Erasing a Disk

Dragging files to the `Recycle Bin` ➔93 is not the purest form of cleaning out a disk. In truth, the files are still on the disk, but the **disk directory** has no record of them. A file recovery program may be able to restore those files—something you may not want if the information is sensitive. The `Quick (Erase)` choice in the `Format` dialog simply clears out the disk's hidden directory—the same as dragging all files to the `Recycle Bin`. Therefore, if you want to completely erase a disk, perform a `Full` format of the disk.

A Bootable Disk

When you start your PC, it first looks to the **floppy disk drive(s)** for a disk containing files that can "pull up the PC by its bootstraps," that is, to **boot**, or start the PC under an **operating system**. If one of the drives your PC looks at contains a floppy disk that does not have these start-up files, you will receive a message about an **invalid system disk** being found. At that point, you can eject the diskette, and have the PC continue its search (it next heads for the hard disk).

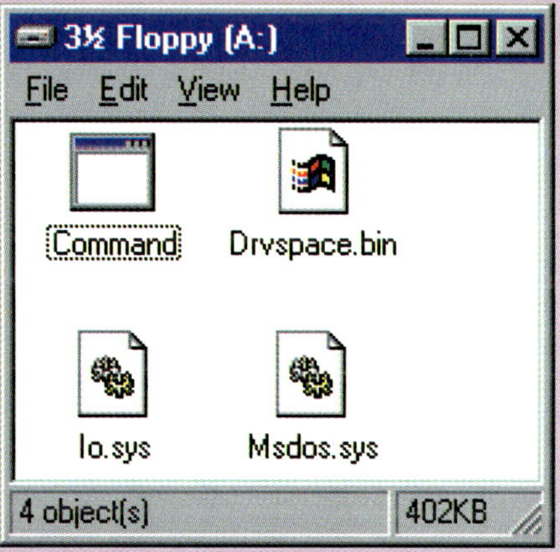

But if you want the PC to boot from a floppy disk rather than the hard disk (this is the case for the **emergency disk** ➔70), then there are four files that the floppy must contain. These files are copied to the disk whenever the `Bootable` options are selected in the Format dialog box. The `Copy system files only` radio button installs the necessary start-up files on an already-formatted disk; the `Copy system files` checkbox instructs Windows to install those files after performing either a `Quick` or `Full` format.

Except for the emergency disk, the need for bootable floppies is limited these days. Back when you could store complete DOS programs on a disk along with boot files, it was possible to boot and run the program entirely from one floppy disk. With an operating system like Windows 95, however, you want to boot from the hard disk so that all your Windows facilities are installed and running for every program you run.

Exchanging Floppies with Macintosh Users

Starting with version 7.5 of the Macintosh system software, Macintosh users can insert, read, and write PC-formatted floppy diskettes. Therefore, you can give a diskette with a Windows file to a Mac user (with System 7.5 or later) with full confidence that the Mac user will be able to access the files on the disk. This is especially helpful when the two of you have the Windows and Macintosh versions of the same application, so you can exchange data files without having to translate the files or disks.

Copying Disks

You can use Windows to duplicate a floppy disk—making backup copies of program disks, for example. Assuming you have one floppy drive with the letter A:, here are the steps to follow to copy one disk to another:

1. Lock (write-protect) the disk you want to copy (source disk), and insert it into the floppy disk drive.
2. In the Desktop/Explorer window, right-click on the floppy drive icon.

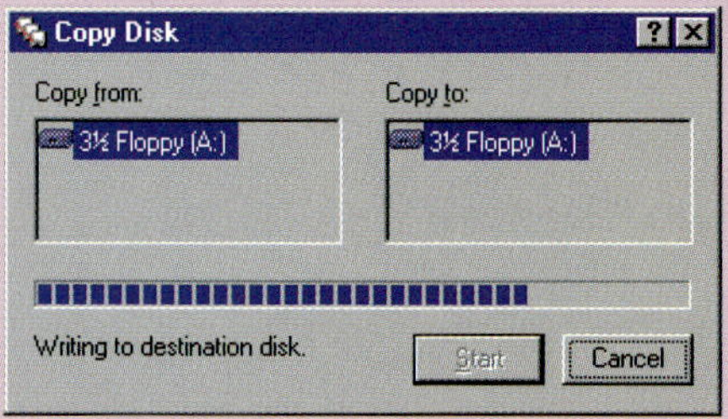

3. Choose `Copy Disk` from the pop-up menu.
4. Click the Start button.

Windows will read all the data from the source disk, and prompt you to swap it with an unlocked destination disk. Click the Cancel button to halt the operation if necessary. There is no damage done if you do this during the reading of the source disk, but interrupting the writing on the destination disk will leave that disk in disarray.

Labeling a Disk

There is an adhesive paper label that you stick on the disk so you can write about what's on the disk, but there is another kind of label, too. It is a name for the diskette, and it is **written to the diskette** and readable by the disk drive. The Format dialog box offers a place for you to assign a label to the disk, but Windows doesn't display it where you can easily see it. The only way you can even find out the label of a diskette is to view its properties (right-click on the floppy drive icon) or open the Format dialog.

Ejecting a Disk

Floppy disk drives on Windows-compatible PCs all require **manual ejection** by firmly pressing the eject button adjacent to the slot where you insert the floppy disk. If you are viewing any information about the disk's contents in Windows (on the Desktop or in Explorer), that information stays on the screen, even after you've ejected the disk. The disk drives on most PCs do not have the capability of detecting a disk insertion or ejection, so they cannot update any views in Windows.

Viewing Diskette Contents

Inspecting the files on a floppy disk involves using either the `My Computer` or Explorer access to open the disk. Changing disks in the drive does not cause any open view of the floppy drive's contents to change. In fact, you can get conflicting views if you open a window to one disk from `My Computer`, change disks, and then start Explorer. The window for `My Computer` shows the contents of the first disk; Explorer shows the contents of the second disk.

Before working with any floppy disk, if you are in `My Computer`, choose `Refresh` from the `View` menu. From Explorer, click once on the floppy drive icon or choose `Refresh` from the `View` menu.

Ejecting a Stuck Disk

If a disk is really stuck—no amount of prodding with the eject button gets it out—then there's probably **something wrong** with the disk. Perhaps the paper label has separated from the disk and is grabbing the disk drive; or maybe the disk's metal shutter is slightly bent and caught on something in the drive. Trying to force it out may damage the disk drive. It will be cheaper in the long run to have a **knowledgeable technician** open the PC and extricate the disk by freeing it from inside.

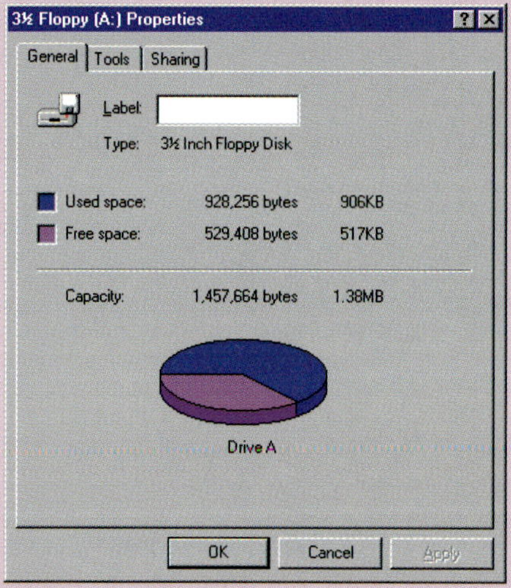

Determining Free Space

Viewing the status bar at the bottom of an Explorer or Desktop window for a floppy disk will not yield the best readout of how much is already on the disk. Folders, for instance, are not counted in the size measurement. Instead, right-click on the floppy drive icon, and choose `Properties`. The property sheet for a floppy (or any disk) reveals details about the amount of space occupied and available on the disk. A **pie chart graphic** gives you an at-a-glance view, as well. Free space on a diskette may be an issue when you need to copy large amounts of data to a disk 112.

Floppy Disk Care

Floppy disks are durable, but not invulnerable. Boxes of diskettes come with standard care guidelines, such as preventing the disks from getting **wet, dusty, or too hot** (the magnetic disk can melt inside an enclosed automobile passenger compartment in the summer sun). Keep the metal shutter closed at all times to keep dirt and lethal fingerprints off the disk medium. When mailing a disk, protect it in a diskette mailer or a bubble pack insulated envelope. Postage canceling machines (which can't read your "Hand Cancel" instructions) can crush unprotected disks enough to make them unreadable. **Magnets** such as those in ringer telephones, motorized gear, power transformers, and audio speakers can cause the most damage to a disk's data. Since the particles on the disk medium are magnetic (disk drive heads use magnetic fields to write data to the disk), anything that generates a magnetic field poses a serious threat.

Practically every personal computer these days has a hard disk installed or connected to it. A hard disk provides mass storage—hundreds or thousands of megabytes in one convenient disk volume. No matter how vast you think a hard disk is when you get it, you'll begin to reach its capacity much sooner than you expected.

The smallest hard disk you should consider for working with Windows 95 and applications is 200 megabytes. Computer stores and mail order companies offer hard disks in varying capacities between 200 and 9000 megabytes (9 gigabytes).

A hard disk may be installed internally inside your PC or connected externally by way of a parallel port or a hard disk interface card (in either IDE or SCSI formats). If you have both an internal and an external hard drive, they appear as separate drive icons (and letters) on your Windows desktop.

Hard Disk Specifications

When evaluating hard disks, the primary factors to consider are **formatted capacity, transfer speed, and sound level.** Hard disk capacities are normally rated in megabytes, but the values can be deceiving. A raw hard disk sometimes has many more megabytes available than what you'll actually be able to use once the disk has been formatted. Control sections on large disks can be huge. Always ask about the formatted capacity. Transfer speed and sound level are difficult to judge from printed specifications, because only with head-to-head comparisons using the same measuring techniques can you be sure of the results. Commonly cited measures, **access** and **seek** times (measured in milliseconds), have become almost meaningless as disk drive makers have reached parity. At current sub-20 millisecond speeds, you probably won't notice a 5 millisecond improvement in day-to-day operation.

The best source of information on disk drives available at the moment are comparative reviews in *PC Magazine* and *PCWorld* magazine. At least once each year they put dozens of disks through their paces in labs under what appear to be controlled situations.

A more difficult to determine—yet more important—consideration is the **reliability** of the disk drive brand you buy. While only a handful of manufacturers make the actual hard disk mechanisms, dozens of companies package those drives with their power supplies and disk maintenance software. You should look not only for a long warranty, but also for a company that has earned a good reputation. Again, the magazines (especially the letters departments) can steer you away from trouble, but there is no guarantee that today's stable company will be around in two years if your disk drive acts up. Also, even a company with a good reputation may have a less than perfect model in its lineup, so in your searches, look for reliability of the specific drives you have in mind.

IDE vs. SCSI Drives

The most common hard disk controller circuitry for PCs is the **IDE** (Integrated Drive Electronics). A majority of the desktop and laptop computers coming from the factory have an IDE interface built into the motherboard, to which the internal hard disk connects. To connect an IDE-style external hard disk to a PC requires an IDE expansion card.

There appears to be a shift, however, to a different standard for external devices. Called **SCSI** (pronounced "scuzzy," and standing for Small Computer Systems Interface), this standard allows up to six devices to be connected in series from a single computer rear panel connector. Therefore, it's possible to have an external hard disk, an external CD-ROM drive, and a backup tape drive all connected to your computer via a single cable chain. Some laptop computers come with SCSI adapters built in, making them ready to accept a wide range of SCSI peripherals. This standard is also called SCSI-2 and SCSI-2 Fast.

Physical Size

Fitting a replacement hard disk into your PC system unit requires knowledge about the physical layout of your PC. Newer desktop units tend to have an internal bay reserved for a 3.5" hard disk drive. That means that there won't be room for a high-capacity drive that is built in the 5.25" form. If your PC has a 5.25" bay, however, there are mounting kits available to accommodate the smaller 3.5" drives. Laptop PCs with internal drives use 2.5" drives, which may explain why laptop PCs trail desktop PCs in the hard disk space derby. You can even buy a plug-in hard disk that disappears into a laptop's PC Card (PCMCIA) slot.

Upgrading a Hard Disk

If you should outgrow your internal drive, you'll be faced with the choice of replacing the internal drive with a larger one or adding a second, external drive. If your PC is an older model (an 80386 or slow 80486), you should consider buying an external SCSI drive, expecting to use it with a newer PC you may acquire in the near future. But if your PC is a fast 486 or Pentium, and you plan to use it for a few years, then get an internal hard disk. Because they don't require a power supply and case, internal drives are cheaper. Also check with your disk vendor to see if they have a kit to turn your old internal drive into an external hard disk.

Using a hard disk brings with it some obligations. Backing up a hard disk is essential to protect yourself against the hard disk's failure (which could wipe out your programs and documents). Also, organizing hundreds or thousands of files takes some effort, especially as the disk fills up.

Formatting a New Hard Disk

Most often an internal hard disk comes from the computer dealer already formatted, usually with Windows 95 installed. Upgrade or external hard drives may be formatted or unformatted. If your hard disk comes with formatting software, you should use that. Otherwise, you can use Window 95's disk formatting program to do the job, provided the disk volume appears in `My Computer`. If it does, then follow these steps:

1. Right-click on the icon for the disk to be formatted.

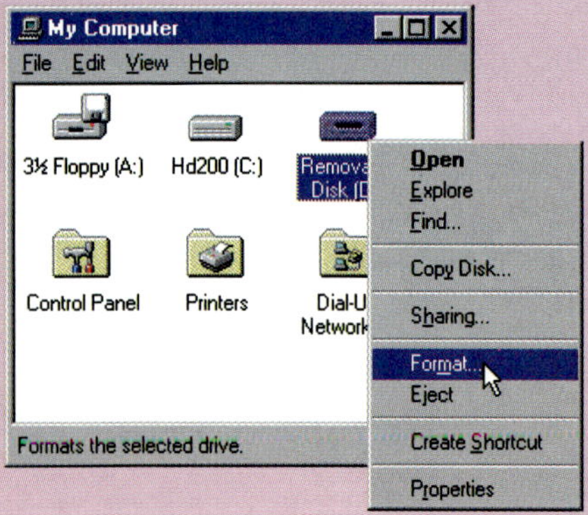

2. Choose `Format` from the menu.
3. Choose the `Full` format type.

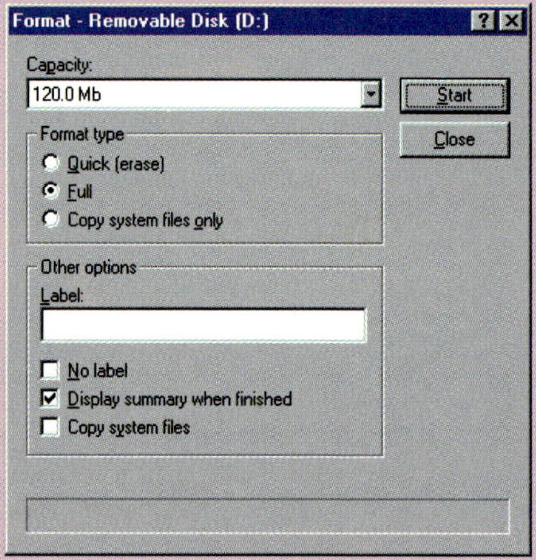

4. Click the Start button in the **Format** dialog.

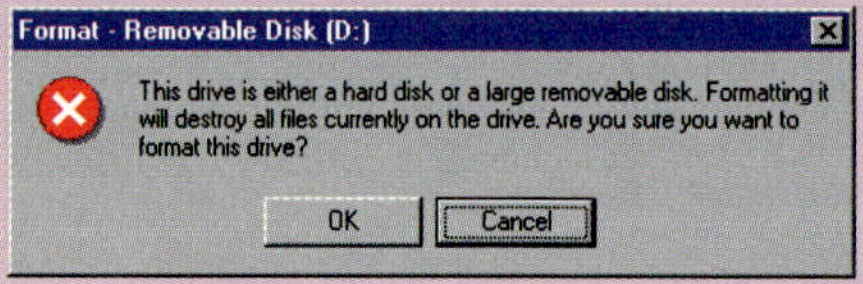

5. In response to the warning prompt, click OK.

Be prepared to wait awhile when formatting a big hard disk. If the format program also has a separate sector verification program or option, run it after the formatting. Not all sectors of a hard disk may format properly—this is not unusual, especially for very large disks. Windows hidden file system software will skip over the bad sectors when writing to the disk.

Reformatting Your C: Drive

In rare cases, it may be necessary to re-format your main hard disk. This would happen only if there appeared to be significant damage to files that is not attributable to a **virus** →58.

Before re-formatting, you should create a **backup set** of all files—system, applications, and data →54. Once you re-format the hard disk, no file recovery program will be able to get your files back, and the only way to get your hard disk back in order is to restore items from a backup.

Use a floppy-disk copy of the formatting software that came with your disk (if any) or your Windows **emergency disk** →70. The program to run from your Windows emergency disk is called `FDISK`. Here's how to run it:

1. Insert the emergency disk, and restart the PC.
2. At the command prompt, type `FDISK`.
3. Follow prompts to create a single MS-DOS partition.

Speeding Up Your Hard Disk

The longer you own a hard disk and the more times your programs save files to it, the more likely that files will be scattered all around your hard disk. In fact, chunks of a single file may be written to several places on the disk (the operating system figures out where all the pieces are with the help of control files hidden on the disk). This allows the computer to save files wherever it can fit pieces, instead of looking (perhaps in vain) for a contiguous part of the disk for the entire file. As files become liberally sprinkled throughout your hard disk, the disk become increasingly fragmented. The downside to fragmentation is that the hard disk has to work harder to read and write a file, increasing mechanical wear and the time it takes to perform disk accesses. You can optimize your hard disk yourself or with the help of a disk optimizer, such as the **Disk Defragmenter** utility supplied with Windows 95 →56.

Internal or External?

Most PC buyers get a machine with a **hard disk inside** the system unit. It's convenient, and usually offered as a package price. Those are the advantages of an internal drive, especially if you have to move the computer around periodically.

An **external drive,** however, has two significant advantages. First, if the drive needs repair, you just bring or ship the drive to the shop, not the entire computer. Second, it is easier to sell an external drive you've outgrown on your way to a larger drive.

Connecting an External Hard Disk

Today's hard disks come in a variety of connection schemes. They include IDE (or IDE-compatible), SCSI, and parallel port. IDE and SCSI drives usually require an **interface card** that adheres to the same standard as the drive. Use a parallel-port drive only as a last resort, because data transfer is not as fast as either IDE or SCSI. While SCSI drives offer the convenience of adding more devices in the cabling chain, getting SCSI devices to work properly can be tough work. See 55 for details on SCSI mysteries.

Powering Up an External Hard Disk

For Windows to recognize a second, external SCSI hard disk, you must turn on the hard disk and let it reach full speed (just a few seconds) before turning on the computer. Occasionally, an external SCSI disk won't show up on the desktop at startup time. This usually happens after changing the SCSI cabling arrangement or adding a disk drive to the SCSI chain. It may take one or two additional restarts to get Windows to recognize the disk (don't turn off the disk between attempts). If a couple of restarts fail to get the disk on the desktop, see troubleshooting suggestions starting on page 159.

Backing Up a Hard Disk

Your most important maintenance chore with a hard disk is backing up important information—if not the entire disk—on a regular basis. Most users do not back up until something disastrous has already happened, and the hard disk is no longer available or is damaged (crashed). One hard disk crash, and a computer user sees backup religion for awhile.

Windows comes with a utility program called **Microsoft Backup** 54, which you can use to copy selected files, folders, or the entire hard disk to other media, such as floppy disks, tape drives, or other mass storage 59. Despite Microsoft Backup's ability to compress backup files on floppy disks, this medium is impractical for the size of today's hard drives, unless you back up only your active data files.

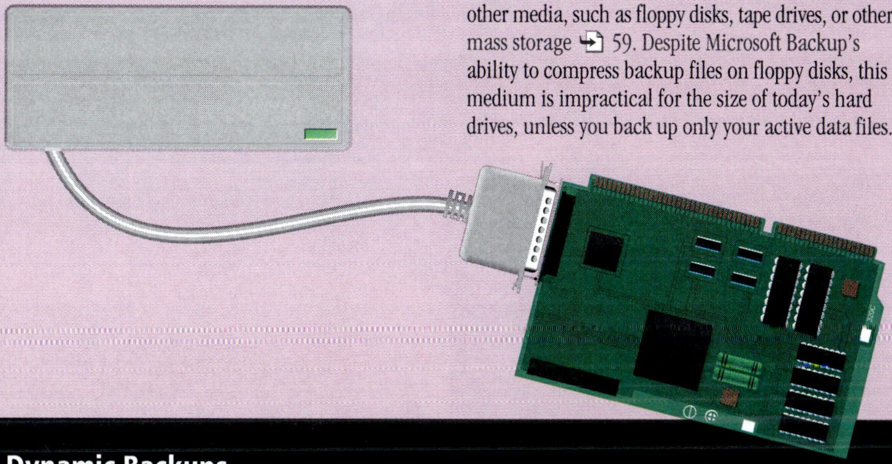

Hard Disk Partitions

Hard disks in excess of about 300 megabytes can be made more manageable by breaking the large disk space into **two or more sections,** called partitions. The MS-DOS FDISK command allows you to divide a large physical hard disk into multiple partitions, in sizes you designate (but if other formatting and partitioning software comes with your computer or hard disk, use it instead of FDISK). Each partition appears on the desktop as a distinct disk volume. See 110 for further ideas about organizing files on a hard disk.

Cautions

Treat your hard disk, especially an external drive, as if it were a **one-of-a-kind fragile egg.** Very possibly, that device has the only copy of your latest work (everything since your last backup). Some might even say that their working lives are on that disk. In truth, today's hard disk drives are pretty durable, but the gentler you can be, the further in the future you put the day when the hard disk fails. Here are few rules to help lengthen the life of an external disk (including one that travels inside a laptop computer):

- Make sure the computer and hard disk are **turned off** before connecting or disconnecting the cable.
- **Do not** move the disk (or a computer with an internal disk) while the disk drive is reading or writing.
- **Hand-carry** a hard disk while traveling, and put it in a protective case if possible.
- Ask airline security checkpoints to **hand-inspect** the disk instead of passing it through the X-ray machine (X-rays don't seem to hurt a hard disk, but the fear is that magnetic fields on the conveyor belt rollers might do some harm).
- Allow a hard disk that has passed through cold or hot air temperatures to return to **room temperature** before turning it on.

Dynamic Backups

Manufacturers of very large hard disks (500MB and up) frequently offer specialized software that automatically saves data not only to the disk you signify in your program, but also, and at the same time, to a backup disk. Techniques for this kind of backup are called mirroring (information is saved to two daisy-chained drives) and duplexing (a second disk is attached by way of a separate interface card). Duplexing is faster than mirroring, because the writing to the two drives is performed almost simultaneously. Both systems give you the comfort of having an up to the minute backup of the primary hard disk. If one drive fails (the software alerts you), you can take it out of service and use the other drive without any data loss. These systems are intended primarily for business network server hard disks, for which backups are critical. An additional backup procedure should be done daily or weekly to another device (cartridge or tape drive) and that backup copy stored in a fireproof location.

Establishing a hard disk backup strategy and sticking to it is a vital task for all personal computer users.

While rare, a hard disk failure caused by virus or physical defect can render your hard disk unusable. You may accidentally delete files that you'd like to have back. Computers can also be stolen or destroyed in a disaster. If you back up your hard disk on a regular basis according to time-tested rules, you will more than likely be able to restore your hard disk or lost files with little difficulty.

Windows 95 comes with a utility program that allows you to back up your hard disk to floppy disks, a tape drive, or another hard disk. Called Microsoft Backup, the program offers many of the features found in third-party backup programs that accompany tape drives.

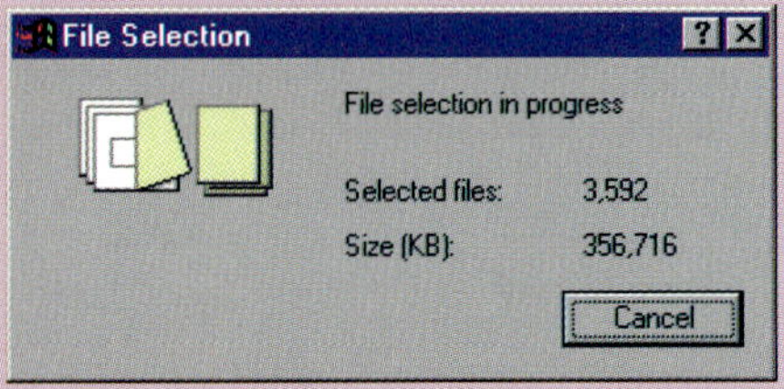

What to Back Up

While everyone's PC usage pattern is different, there is usually a substantial part of the hard disk that doesn't change that much, notably your applications and the Windows operating system. All these items are generally re-installable from the original diskettes. At the other end of the spectrum are **data files** containing information you've created, downloaded, or been entrusted with. For many of these items, the only copies are the ones on your hard disk; re-creation of these files would be difficult or impossible.

You should always maintain a backup copy of your current programs and Windows environment. This part of the backup needs updating only when you add or delete programs. Data files, however, should be backed up more often. For active users, a daily backup of current project files is not unrealistic.

Which Medium?

Due to the size of today's hard disks, backing up the entire disk to 1.44MB floppy disks is extremely impractical, even when the data is compressed. Industry standard QIC-80 **tape drives** 59 are relatively inexpensive, and can store a copy of all your hard drive's files on two or three tapes. Other removable **cartridge media** are also good candidates, since you can expand backup capacity by adding new cartridges. And don't overlook another hard disk. If you use **DriveSpace** 56 to compress the backup files, you can use a smaller drive to back up a slightly larger one. Some corporate sites also encourage backing up to a central or departmental file server.

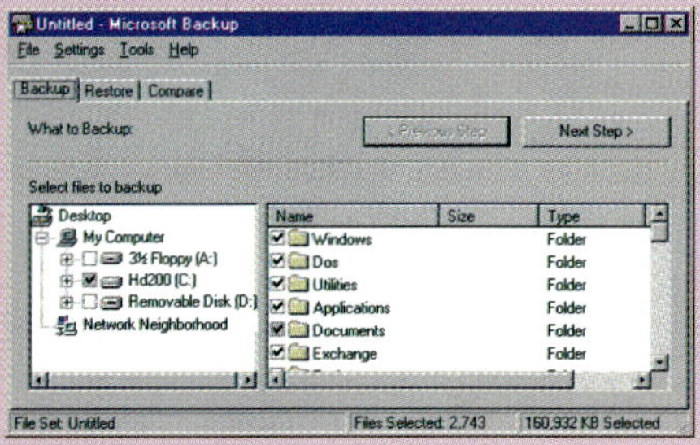

Microsoft Backup Basics

Using Microsoft Backup is essentially a three-step process:

1. Select the drive or folders you want backed up.
2. Select the device used to store the backup.
3. Click the Start Backup button and assign a name to the archive file.

The program copies the files you've chosen to a single file, called a backup set (recognizable by the file name extension .QIC; assigned by Backup). You can use only Microsoft Backup (or a compatible program) to access the individual files of the backup set for file restoration.

An Explorer-like window is the interface from which you can select files to be backed up. An extra feature of this window are the checkboxes that appear to the left of every item. Single-click on a plus icon near a folder to expand the left window pane outline view; single-click on the folder itself to view the contents in the right pane; single-click to check (or uncheck) a folder or file. All items inside any selected (checked) folder will be backed up in the process. If the folder or disk you selected is large, an animated progress dialog shows you what's happening as it builds the list of files to copy. Finally, choose Save from the File menu to save a list of selected items in a file set. You can open the set later to back up the same selected items.

Backup Tips

Prudence suggests maintaining at least two rotating full backups of your system. Make your first backup with Set A of your backup media (tapes or disk cartridges); make your next backup with Set B; for your third backup, use Set A again. This leaves you with two generations of snapshots of your hard disk at any instant.

There are no rules for frequency of full backups, but at least once a month would be wise. This should be accompanied by much more frequent backups of your documents. The closer you are to a project deadline, the more frequently you should back up your data. Back up whenever you reach a point at which loss of data would be unthinkable.

Differential (Incremental) Backup

When Microsoft Backup performs a full backup (as specified in the Backup screen of the Options dialog), it turns off a switch in the file that says the file needs archiving 112. You can then instruct Microsoft Backup the next time to back up only items from the current file set whose archive switch has been set—that is, items that have been changed or added since the last backup.

Storing Backups

Recent backup copies are useless if they're destroyed in the same fire as the computer. Full backups should be stored either in a fireproof box or in another building. It's not uncommon for a user working on valuable projects to carry an incremental daily backup tape or cartridge tucked in a pocket, purse, or briefcase.

The Small Computer Systems Interface (abbreviated SCSI, pronounced "scuzzy") is an increasingly popular standard for connecting add-on hardware that requires fast information transfer: hard disks, scanners, and CD-ROM drives to name a few.

Up to six devices may be connected in a series called a **daisy chain**. Most SCSI devices have two SCSI ports—one to connect to the previous item in the chain (which might be the SCSI adapter on your PC) and one to connect to the next item in the chain. A SCSI device may have the SCSI-2 mini-SCSI connector, or a larger 50-pin Centronics-style ↪7 connector.

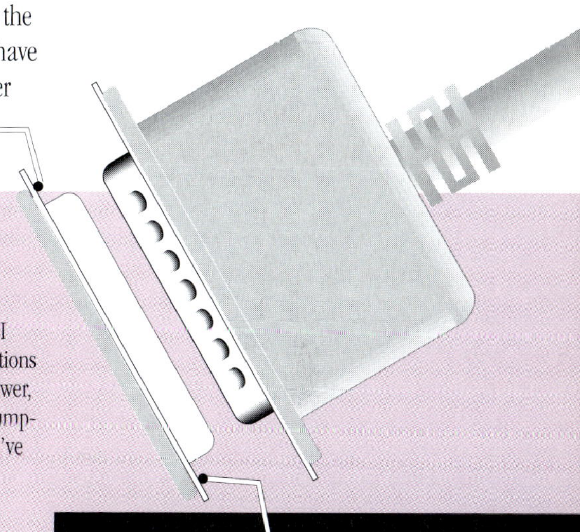

SCSI Device Numbers

Each device in a SCSI chain must have a unique identification number. Most SCSI devices have a small switch on the rear panel that allows you to change the SCSI number. The switch can be any of several designs, including a thumbwheel, push button, or rotary. It generally doesn't matter which number you assign to which device, but remember these rules:

- Number 0 is usually reserved for an internal SCSI device.
- No two devices in a chain should have the same ID number.

If you are about to connect someone else's hard disk to your SCSI chain, check the SCSI ID numbers of all devices before starting up. If two or more hard disks have the same SCSI ID, the disks could become damaged. One more warning: Change a SCSI ID number only when all connected SCSI devices and the PC are turned off.

SCSI Cables

Because there is no universal SCSI connection standard, buy cables only after you know what connectors are on all devices, including the SCSI adapter in your PC. You'll see cables with combinations of DB-25, Centronics 50, SCSI-2, and the still newer, smaller SCSI-3 connectors on them. Make no assumptions about a SCSI device's connectors until you've seen them.

SCSI Termination

Part of the SCSI mystery for users is the SCSI terminator, which normally goes at the end of the SCSI chain. Technically, this device is supposed to absorb the electronic signals that flow through the SCSI cable so that a signal doesn't bounce back through the cable to the sender. Improperly terminated chains have resulted in multiple images of a hard disk on the desktop (and a great deal of dysfunctional behavior as a result).

An external terminator, the easiest to work with, looks like a double SCSI connector (available in Centronics-50 and SCSI-2 formats). The design allows it to be attached by itself to one of the two SCSI connectors on a device or between an incoming cable and the connector it plugs into. Some SCSI devices, especially hard disks, may be internally terminated, meaning that the termination parts are inside the cabinet.

When Things Don't Work

If devices don't appear to work as expected, here are a few items to investigate before fooling with the SCSI chain and configurations:

1. Turn off all equipment, and make sure all SCSI cables are firmly attached to the device connectors. The 50-pin connectors should have the socket's edge clips locked in place, and SCSI-2 clips should be secure.
2. Turn on all SCSI devices before turning on the PC. Occasionally you can leave a device in a SCSI chain turned off, but there is no formula to follow.
3. Be sure that Windows recognizes your SCSI adapter by checking the `System→Device Manager` control panel. For a newly added SCSI adapter, you may have to go through the `Add New Hardware wizard` ↪60.

If fulfilling these obligations still doesn't get your SCSI chain working, it's time to experiment with SCSI cabling and settings. Here are possibilities to explore with the PC and devices turned off:

- Alter the numbering of external SCSI devices so that the devices are in a different order than before.
- Connect the devices in a different physical order if the logistics allow.
- Try cables of different lengths in different positions between devices.
- Remove the terminator from the end of the SCSI chain, especially if you have a long SCSI peripheral cable in the chain.
- Move the terminator from the end of the SCSI chain one step closer to the PC. For example, if the terminator is by itself on one of the sockets on the last device, move it between the other socket and the incoming cable. After each move, start your PC and try it. If the one-step move doesn't work, move it another step toward the adapter card.

If no combination of cabling, termination, or numbering lets all the devices work, try removing the least used item from the chain, and start the process over. You may have to leave a device out of the chain except for the times when you need it, at which time you can put it in the chain without all the other devices. The manufacturer may be of some help, but don't count on SCSI device makers to have a solution to every problem, especially if some of your devices are brand new, obsolete, or out of the ordinary.

Much of a hard disk's performance is determined by its designers, but users do have some control over how well a disk functions on a daily basis.

One area of optimization is in the capacity of the disk drive. The operating system is largely responsible for determining how data is mapped on a hard disk, but it can be tricked into thinking there is more space by disk compression schemes, such as the DriveSpace utility that comes with Windows 95.

The second area of optimization involves making sure that all the component pieces of a file are close to each other on the disk drive, so the drive head doesn't have to move very far to read or write contiguous parts of a file. Moreover, if frequently used files are placed at the start of the physical drive, the drive heads will move less to access those files.

Disk Compression

The disk compression utility program that comes with Windows 95, called **DriveSpace**, prepares a disk for compression by creating a kind of partition on the disk where information is stored in a format that is more compact than normal. DriveSpace tricks Windows into thinking that the new partition is the regular drive. If you have compressed your C: drive and proceed to save a document in a program, Windows believes it is sending the file to the regular C: drive. In truth, DriveSpace intercepts that file, compresses it, and stores it in the compressed partition.

In the process of setting up a disk for compression, DriveSpace assigns the physical drive's regular letter to the partition. Not every bit of the disk drive is given over to this compressed file—a small slice must stay in regular disk format so that a computer without DriveSpace can recognize the disk as a standard Windows or DOS-style disk. This regular part of the disk, called the host drive, is given a different letter than the one you associate with it. If the space dedicated to the host drive is larger than 2MB, you actually see the two images of the compressed drive on your desktop: the compressed partition with the drive letter you recognize, and the host partition, which bears a different drive letter.

Compression Pros and Cons

While a great many professional computer users employ disk compression without any problems, some are more cautious. Compression lovers couldn't live without the extra disk space that compression provides. If a compressed disk can make the current hard disk accommodate needed files for another year or so, then the benefit is clear.

Opponents worry that files are stored in a format that requires the compression software for the files to be opened. In the event of disk problems, they believe, the compression scheme will get in the way of disk recovery utilities. While this is a valid concern, the fear can be overcome to a large degree by maintaining uncompressed backups 54. Copying a file from a compressed disk to a standard floppy disk, for instance, creates a normal copy of the file on the floppy.

Also take comfort in knowing that DriveSpace performs numerous data validity checks during the compression process.

Before Compressing a Drive

As with any disk operation that will be modifying or moving files, always make a full backup of the drive prior to beginning compression. In the event of a catastrophic problem, you will be able to restore your original disk's contents.

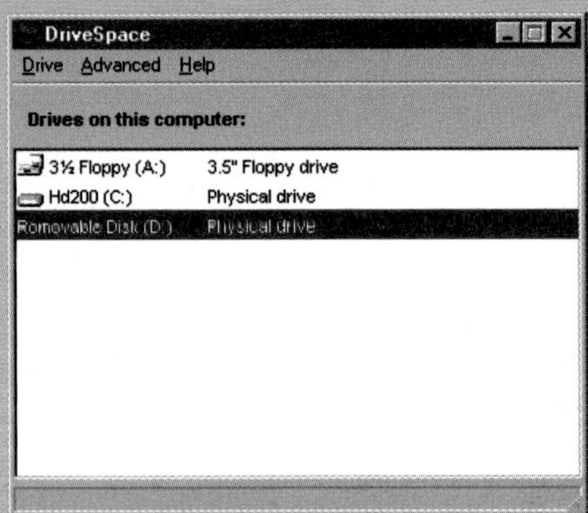

Compressing a Drive

Start `DriveSpace` (located in the `Programs→Accessories→System Tools` list of the Start menu). The program lists all the disk volumes it sees for your computer. If you have connected a new disk drive and it does not appear in this list (even if it does appear in the `My Computer` window), you probably need to assign a drive letter to the drive via the `System→Device Manager` control panel.

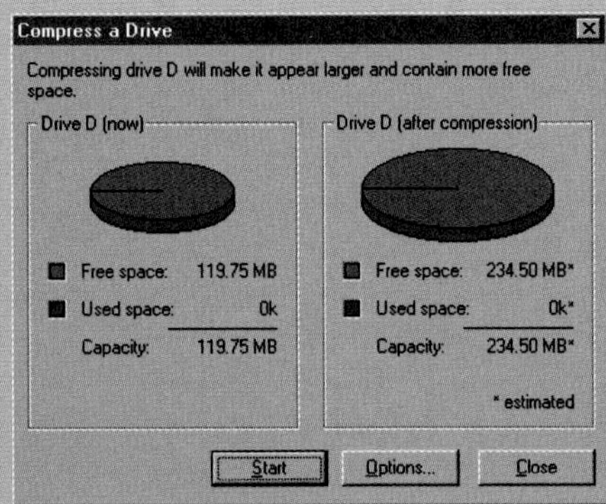

Select the drive to be compressed, and choose `Compress` from the `Drive` menu. DriveSpace looks at the drive to estimate the storage space available after compression. The actual figure will depend on what kinds of files are already on the drive—some files compress better than others.

During the compression process, you will see messages about what tasks DriveSpace is performing. If you are asked to provide a drive letter for the host drive, select the available letter furthest down the list of available device letters to allow other drives you may add (e.g., CD-ROMs) to be in consecutive sequence in `My Computer`. When compression is complete, DriveSpace tells you how large the new drive appears to Windows.

Hiding the Host Drive

When compressing large hard drives, DriveSpace may leave a host drive larger than 2MB, which means that the drive will appear as a separate volume in `My Computer`. There are two ways to hide the host drive on a non-removable disk so it doesn't show up in `My Computer` or the Explorer:

1. In DriveSpace, select the host drive in the main window.
2. Choose `Properties` in the `Drive` menu.
3. Check the `Hide this host drive` box. It will then be marked as hidden in the main window. You can uncheck this box at any later time

or,

1. In DriveSpace, select the compressed drive in the main window.
2. Choose `Adjust Free Space` in the `Drive` menu.
3. Slide the control toward the compressed drive letter, until the free space on the host drive reaches less than 2MB, at which point the `Hide this host drive` box checks itself. If you don't plan to use the host drive for storage, you can reduce host drive free space to just above zero. Override the host drive hiding at any time by unchecking the box.

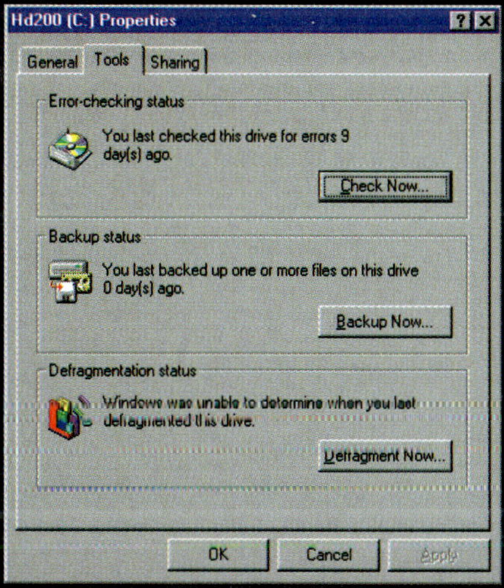

Quick Access to Disk Tools

Right-clicking on a disk volume in `My Computer` or Explorer leads to the property sheets for the disk. You can click on the `Tools` tab to view buttons that lead to **ScanDisk, Microsoft Backup,** and **Disk Defragmenter.** More importantly, the `Tools` screen shows you how long it has been since you have used each of the tools on the selected drive.

Uncompressing a Drive

Before a drive can be uncompressed, enough files must be erased so the data will slightly less than fill the uncompressed capacity of the disk. DriveSpace must have the room on its uncompressed version to restore the contents of the compressed disk.

Disk Fragmentation

Windows writes information to the disk in **sectors** (also called allocation units). On a 200MB disk, for example, each sector is 4 kilobytes. Therefore, saving an 8KB file requires two sectors. Those sectors are not, however, necessarily next to each other on the disk. Hidden files on the disk keep track of which sectors belong to which file, and in what order. But if a file's sectors are scattered all over a disk, it takes a bit longer for the drive's heads to maneuver to all those sectors to retrieve or write the file. Defragmenting a disk sifts through an entire disk, **reorganizing files** into contiguous sectors. It also places most often used system files in locations on the disk requiring the least amount of head movement.

DriveSpace and DoubleSpace

Before there was DriveSpace, Microsoft bundled a different disk compression program, called **DoubleSpace,** with MS-DOS 6.0 through 6.2 (and with the Windows that came with those versions of MS-DOS). Unfortunately for Microsoft, that program too closely resembled another disk compression product, called **Stacker.** Removed in MS-DOS 6.21, compression was again available in version 6.22, under the name of DriveSpace. The DriveSpace that comes with Windows 95 is compatible with drives that were compressed with either DoubleSpace or DriveSpace. You can continue to use DoubleSpace-compressed drives, but any new compression you perform with Windows 95 will be done with DriveSpace.

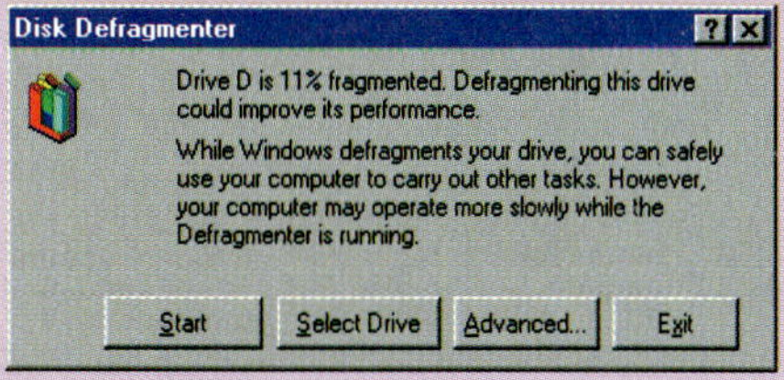

Defragmenting a Disk

Windows comes with **Disk Defragmenter** (Defrag) to handle the job. It works only with uncompressed disks or those compressed with either DoubleSpace or DriveSpace. Start the program from either the `Start→Programs→Accessories→System Tools` menu or from the `Tools` screen of a disk drive's property sheet. The program checks the disk for its level of fragmentation. If the program doesn't recommend defragmenting the disk, then you probably won't gain anything from doing it. Depending on the size and speed of the drive being defragmented, the job can take a few minutes or hours. You'll see progress along the way. It's safest not to do any other file work while defragmentation is underway.

Speedier Defragment

Minimize the progress window during defragmentation. This eliminates the need for the program to update the screen art all the time. In the minimized button on the Taskbar, you can see the percentage completed.

Host Drive Files

If you unhide the host drive of a compressed disk, you will see one a file, with a name such as DRVSPACE.000. This file, known as a compressed volume file (CVF), occupies almost the entire disk. In reality, the file contains the compressed data that you see in Windows as the compressed drive's contents. Do not tamper with this file, or you will likely destroy the integrity of the entire compressed file—in other words, all the programs and data stored on that disk.

Like the biological variety, a computer virus infects quietly until the symptoms start to appear. By then, it's too late—your PC is already infected.

Many viruses have spread throughout the PC community, and more will do so as devious (if not deviant) lone-wolf programmers try to be cute or wreak havoc. If your PC or software begins to exhibit abnormal behavior, a virus may be at the root. Fortunately, **virus detection software** is also available.

A hard disk's medium or key controlling files may become damaged by a virus (or by some other means). The usual symptom is that the disk cannot be read or recognized by Windows. In many cases, the program and data files on the disk are intact. You just need the help of disk repair utility software to bring the disk back to life.

Virus Propagation

The most innocent actions—viewing the contents of a floppy disk or starting a program downloaded from a bulletin board—can begin a virus rampage through your hard disk. Some viruses are of the nuisance variety in that they simply slow down your machine's performance. But other viruses are more deadly: They literally erase files without your knowledge. Floppy disks are the primary carriers of viruses. The strains are in the files on infected floppies, and are copied to your hard disk along with a file, or when you simply look at the disk's contents. If you work in an office full of PCs, the likelihood of your machine becoming infected is very great, especially if there is a free exchange of files and public domain software in and out of the company either by floppy disk or network.

Preventing Virus Infection

Several commercial programs offer virus detection and protection. These programs monitor operating system behavior for the incursion of virus-like activity. Virus creators and detectors are forever in a cops-and-robbers game, with the creators usually one small step ahead of the detectors. Whatever virus protection program you adopt, be sure to keep it up to date—the virus creators are doing their best to do the same.

It is also critical that you don't spread viruses from your hard disk to your application program master disks. Viruses cannot be spread to write-protected floppies. Just in case your hard disk is infected, before installing any software, always write-protect (lock) the floppy disks before inserting them into the disk drive 48.

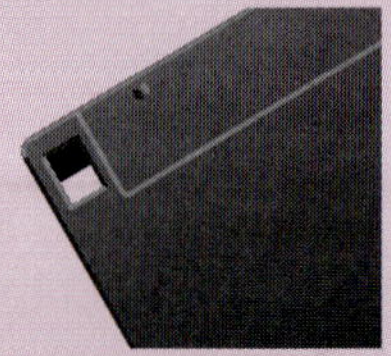

Write-protected

Unprotected

Recovering a Damaged Disk

When a hard disk fails to start or to be recognized by Windows, it is cause for both alarm and a cool head. In virtually all cases, the information is still on the disk. Only the disk's hidden directory is damaged. The directory is like a table of contents to a book. Even if the table of contents is missing, the chapters are still in the book.

The term commonly used for this problem is a disk crash, which came from the early days of disk drives when the heads could literally come into contact with the disk platters and irretrievably scratch the disk. Such hardware disk crashes are extremely rare on PC hard disks. It is more often than not possible to recover from the kinds of crashes that do occur.

Unless you are already using a disk utility program that assists in recovering crashed disks and lost files (products like Symantec's Norton Utilities), start your PC with the Windows **emergency boot disk** 70. At the A:\ prompt, type:

```
dir c:
```

and press Enter to see if your system at least sees your hard disk. If so, then run the ScanDisk program on the emergency floppy by typing

```
scandisk c
```

and press Enter. When the ScanDisk program suggests performing a surface scan, tell it to do so.

If ScanDisk lets your PC recognize the hard disk but not to launch Windows, then reinstall Windows. Go through the entire Installer program on the system disks.

The next step is to buy one of the disk utility programs (e.g., Norton Utilities) to attempt to bring the disk back to life. Each program goes about it in a different way, so you'll have to follow the sometimes cryptic steps in the program's manuals. Try to find a knowledgeable PC friend to help out.

In more severe cases, the disk spins, but neither Windows nor disk utility programs can recognize the disk. Such disasters generally occur to those who have valuable, unbacked-up files on the disk (Murphy strikes!). Call your hard disk supplier to find a service that recovers crashed disks. These services are not cheap. It can cost a few hundred dollars just for the bureau to see if anything is recoverable, and then a charge per file for recovery. On a large disk, the fees could reach $1000.

The last resort is to reformat the disk. If you have been diligent about making backup copies, the loss of work may not be too serious, and you'll have your disk back. Consider installing file recovery software from third-party disk tools programs such as Norton Utilities. They make the task of recovering from a disk crash (or even accidentally erased files) much easier.

In addition to traditional hard disks, other mass storage devices may also be connected to a PC.

They can offer open-ended capacity and alternative methods of backing up your regular hard disk.

Three basic media are worth investigating if you work with large amounts of disk data: **removable magnetic cartridge hard disks, removable optical disk cartridges,** and **tape drives.** All make good backup devices. Mass storage is a very competitive specialty, which helps improve performance, increase capacity, and reduce prices as the months go by.

Huge Hard Disks

While the first hard disk ever available for the PC was a 5-megabyte job, today you can buy a traditional hard disk that holds more than **9 gigabytes** (9000 megabytes). Hard disks in the 300–500MB range that come standard on today's desktop PCs used to be considered cavernous; disk drives in the gigabyte range may seem large today, but could be the norm in a few years. Large disks can get unwieldy (you should **partition** such disks →53), but as file servers or working storage for color graphics, digitized video images, and sound, such sizes become necessary.

Removable Magnetic Disks

Bernoulli and Syquest are the most popular formats in the removable cartridge market. Both brands have expanded their offerings to include cartridges that can store up to 270MB on a **3.5" cartridge** (the disks are thicker than floppies). Drives are available in both brands for internal mounting and external connection (mostly SCSI).

Syquest drive mechanisms are built into many third-party brand drives, which appropriately boast Syquest compatibility. But be aware that Syquest also has an active and popular **5.25" format disk** (in 44, 88, and 200MB capacities), and only the most recent drives can access all capacities of this size disk. In either case, the 5.25" and 3.5" cartridges are incompatible. Access speeds for the newest, high-capacity cartridge drives equal that of traditional hard disks, making hard disk backup quick.

Removable Optical Cartridge Disks

For many years, there were significant distinctions between types of optical drives, some of which could only write once to a platter. Today, however, the **magneto-optical** (MO) disk behaves much like any floppy disk—capable of hundreds of megabytes of **read-write storage.** Common formats today work with 128MB and 230MB cartridges, but access speeds trail those of traditional magnetic media. Optical media are, however, more durable.

CD-ROM

Compact Disc–Read-Only Memory is becoming the method of distributing large quantities of computer information. The discs are physically identical to the single-sided audio compact discs, but they require a special CD-ROM drive, available for internal or external mount, with **IDE** or **SCSI** connections. A CD-ROM disc can store about 550MB of data, but the discs are read-only. You no longer need to spend $1500 at a CD-ROM pressing plant to "press" a CD-ROM; commercial CD-ROM writers are now available for PCs. For monthly updates of reference material or for publishing huge quantities of data, CD-ROM is a cost-effective medium.

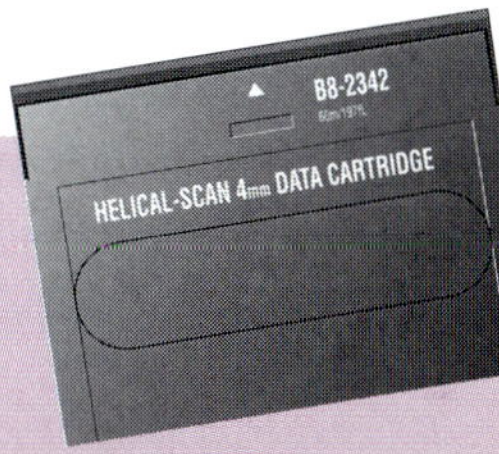

Tape Drives

Because tapes store information in a linear fashion and random access is incredibly slow, tape drives are best suited for batch **backup and restore** operations. Several tape drive hardware standards and capacities are used today, but for now the QIC-80 (quarter-inch cartridge) format is in widest use.

How much a QIC-80 tape can hold depends on the **data compression** used in the backup software and the nature of the files you're backing up (some files compress much better than others). Without compression, a standard-length QIC-80 tape holds up to 120MB; with compression, possibly up to 250MB.

With standard hard drives inching up in capacity, it's no wonder that higher-capacity tape drive formats are emerging to ease the job of backing up an entire disk unattended (like during lunch hour or after hours). Drives compatible with the QIC-3010 format can store up to 340MB uncompressed, and the QIC-3020 format can hold 680MB.

Tape backup drives generally connect via a SCSI adapter, with some also available for parallel port hookup (good for laptops, for instance). The usual connection for an internal drive is to an unused floppy disk controller cable.

Typical backup time for a QIC-80 format tape is less than one-half hour. Although $3 to $5 more expensive per tape, preformatted tapes may be worth the cost, since formatting a single tape can take an hour or more.

One of the most difficult tasks in working with IBM PC-compatible computers has been adding new devices—sound cards, CD-ROM drives, external disk drives, and the like. Windows 95 greatly simplifies the process for many devices.

A lot of help comes from a new hardware standard, called Plug and Play, which helps the operating system identify devices whenever they are connected to a PC. It will take a couple of years, however, for all new PCs to offer complete Plug and Play capability for all kinds of devices.

For other device styles, Windows provides an `Add New Hardware` wizard, which prompts you through the steps of helping Windows identify the device and get it working properly on your PC.

Device Detection

Add New Hardware

When you went through the Windows 95 setup procedure, the setup program took the time to perform a thorough examination of your computer. In the process, it looked for hardware devices that identify themselves, and for various software artifacts (hence the significant disk access during the hardware detection phase). Setup looks for device information files (those with the `.inf` extension) and for device loading statements (device=) in your original CONFIG.SYS, WIN.INI, and SYSTEM.INI files. This information is gathered into the Windows 95 **Registry** file ➔66, where all Windows 95-compatible configuration information is stored.

If you connect a new device to your PC and Windows does not automatically recognize it during a normal start-up, you will have to go through the `Add New Hardware` wizard (accessible via the Add New Hardware control panel) to help Windows do the job.

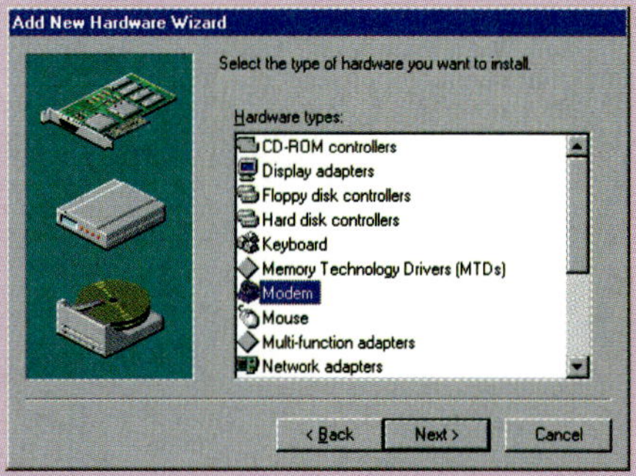

What's a Device?

Hardware devices fall into a number of categories. The most common ones that Windows knows about are: Items referred to as adapters and controllers are usually plug-in expansion cards for desktop PCs, like sound boards or graphics accelerators. For most devices that come with your computer, there is little if anything you need to do until you upgrade or change devices—for instance, if you buy a faster modem.

CD-ROM controllers	Display adapters
Floppy disk controllers	Hard disk controllers
Keyboards	Memory technology drivers
Modems	Mice
Network adapters	PC Card (PCMCIA) sockets
COM and LPT ports	Printers
SCSI controllers	Multimedia controllers

About Drivers

Much of the talk about installing devices revolves around **device driver software.** A device driver is a program that tells Windows how to communicate with the specified device. Not all makes and models of a particular kind of device behave the same or have the same features. Therefore, it's not uncommon for a new device to require driver software that is not built into Windows 95. In such cases, the hardware device comes with a diskette containing the driver. With Windows 95, you install that driver by way of the Add New Hardware wizard.

Add New Hardware Wizard

Your success with the Add New Hardware wizard depends on the make and model of the device you're installing. Each time you use this wizard, you should let Windows try to detect the device on its own (the default choice). If the wizard discovers any devices that Windows doesn't already know about (in the Registry), then it reveals its findings, and offers to install the drivers (from the Windows installation disks) for you.

Device Manager

System

One of the tabs in the System control panel is the **Device Manager,** a powerful tool both for seeing an overview of your computer's devices and for resolving problems. The primary display is the device tree of your PC, as recognized by Windows. Click the plus symbol to view the specific device(s) for a category. By double-clicking any device, you can view the property sheet for that device. The kind of information varies with the type of device, but you can find out if the device is on, whether it's true Plug and Play, and what system resources it uses (helpful for trouble-shooting).

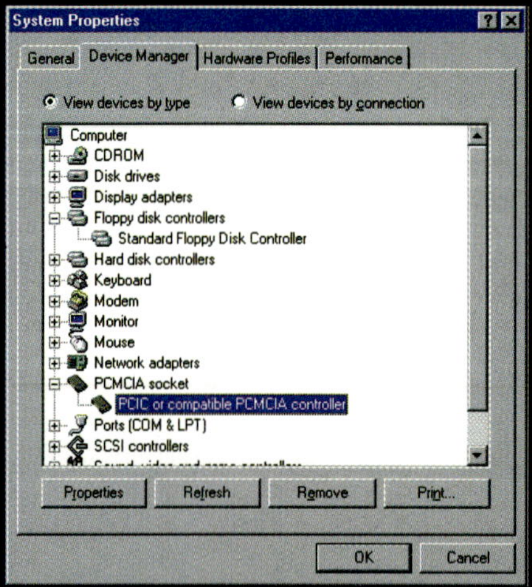

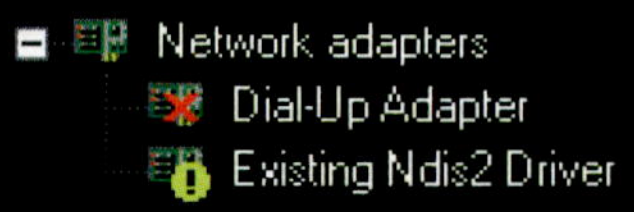

When a device is turned off or isn't being recognized properly (usually due to a system resource conflict), its icon in the Device Manager tree will have a red "X" through it. But if there is a more significant difficulty, then you'll see an alert symbol atop the icon.

But if the wizard doesn't find the device, don't worry. Work your way through the wizard again, this time choosing to install specific hardware. Locate the category of your new device and go onto the next screen. There (or after an intervening screen) are listed all the manufacturers and device model numbers in this device category that Windows knows about. Look for your specific maker and model number. If it's there, then select it, and let the wizard install the drivers for you (have your Windows 95 install disk(s) handy).

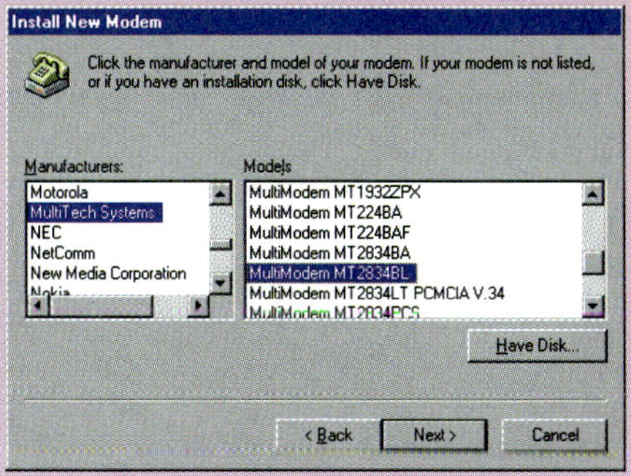

If the model isn't listed there, then prepare to use the driver software disk that came with your device. Click the Have Disk... button in the wizard, and follow the prompt to insert the driver disk. If the wizard doesn't find the kind of driver file that Windows 95 expects, contact the device maker for a Windows 95-compatible driver.

After the wizard installs the driver, it usually asks you to restart Windows. Do this so that Windows will properly recognize your new device.

Occasionally, there may be a hardware conflict, which the wizard will warn you about. The wizard leads you to the Device Manager and troubleshooting.

Plug and Play

The **Plug and Play** hardware standard is a coordinated effort by Microsoft, Intel, and many computer manufacturers to simplify the future of adding devices to PCs. It also applies to the connection of laptop PCs to desktop docking stations, which typically have additional devices and network connections built into them.

There are three kinds of device docking:

cold	Everything must be turned off
warm	A laptop can be in sleep mode
hot	Just connect 'em up

The ultimate goal of Plug and Play is hot docking of virtually any device, but it will take some time for device manufacturers to catch up.

When you connect a Plug and Play device (or when Windows recognizes such a device that has been connected prior to startup), Windows alerts you that it found the new gizmo, and asks whether you want to install the driver for it. If Windows comes with a compatible driver, you can let Windows do that from the installer disk(s); otherwise, you'll have to provide the driver diskette that comes with the device.

PC Card—PCMCIA

PC Card (PCMCIA)

Laptop (and smaller) computers have rallied around an expansion port standard whose name was originally PCMCIA (named after the standards group that devised it: **Personal Computer Memory Card International Association).** As its name implies, the PCMCIA card—about the size of a credit card—was originally designed for memory expansion. But since then, the standard has broadened to accommodate a variety of devices: tiny (in physical size) hard disks, modems, network adapters, multimedia adapters, pagers, and cellular modems. To make this standard more consumer-friendly, it is now simply called PC Card.

Still, you will see plenty of reference to PCMCIA, including in the `Add New Hardware` wizard, and even in the name of a Windows control panel for those computers that have such connectors—or sockets, as they're called in the industry.

PC Cards come in three thicknesses, denoted by Type I, II, and the fattest, III. Most common on today's PC Card-equipped laptops is a dual-purpose slot that can accommodate two Type II cards or one Type III.

Most new PC Cards behave like hot-docking Plug and Play devices. Therefore, assuming the PC Card socket itself is recognized by Windows (i.e., shows up in the Device Manager), you can plug in a modem or network card without having to do anything after the first-time-only driver loading.

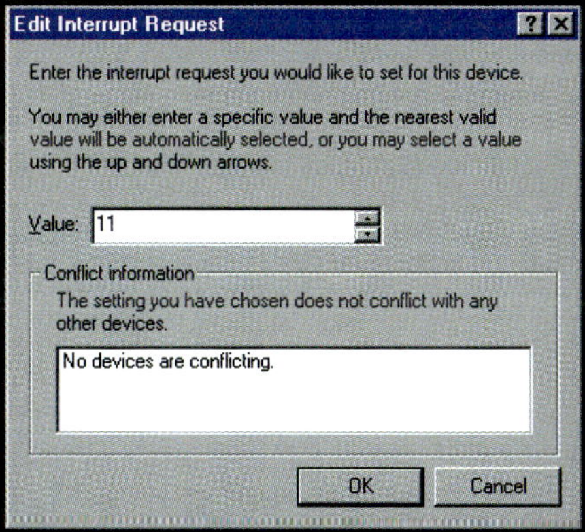

Troubleshooting Device Conflicts

The Device Manager greatly simplifies what traditionally has been the bane of users (of all levels of technical competency) who wish to install new devices. PC systems communicate with devices and their drivers by way of the CPU's interrupt requests (known as IRQs) and input/output (I/O) addresses. Exactly what these do is not important, but what is vital is that no two devices compete for the same IRQ or I/O addresses. Prior to Windows 95, it was very hard to figure out the settings for existing devices that were conflicting with the new device.

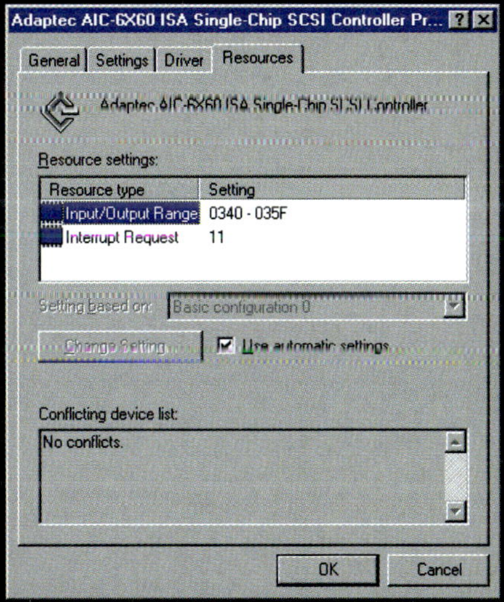

Among the properties associated with almost every device are system resources, which include the IRQ and I/O addresses (the latter in hexadecimal notation, hence the occasional digits A through F). If a new device conflicts with an existing device, the resources screen shows you whether it's an IRQ or addressing problem (or both), and lets you scroll through all possible settings for your PC in search of ones that don't conflict with existing devices. Plug and Play devices can usually figure this out for themselves, but you may have to get involved in this semiautomatic method for older devices (sometimes called legacy devices).

Software, cont.

Installing Windows 95 64

Before You Upgrade to Windows 95, page 66

Installing Windows, page 68

Creating an Emergency System Diskette, page 70

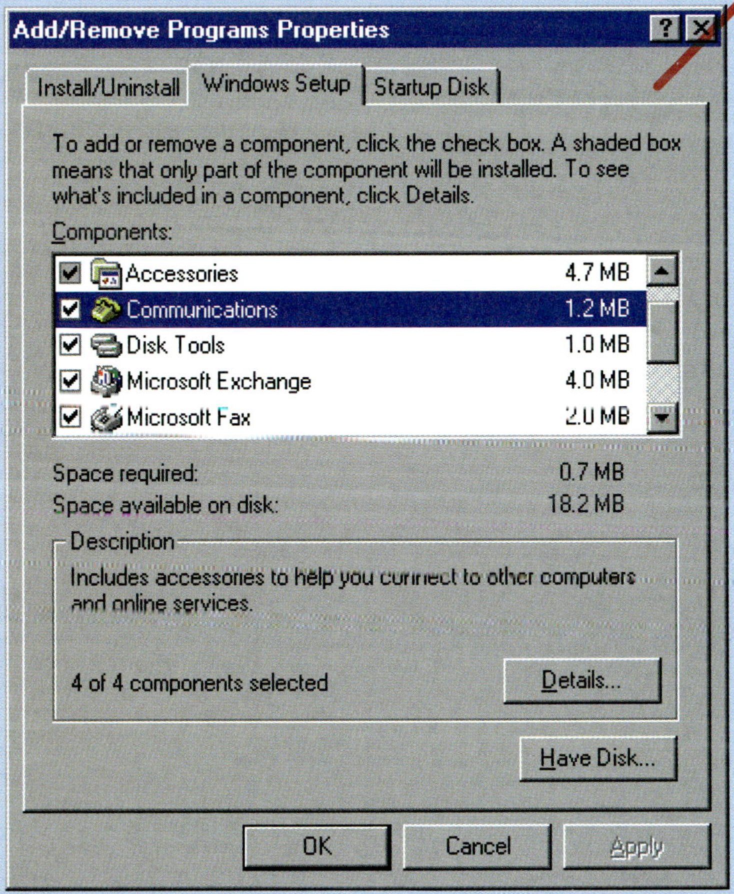

Program Group Conversion, page 48

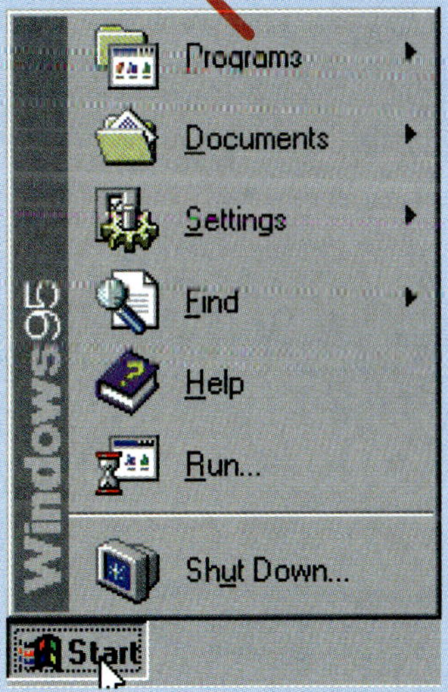

Operating system (OS) software upgrades are a way of life in personal computing. Some upgrades are more painless than others, depending on the level of compatibility between your existing computing setup and the new operating system.

Windows 95 is the most ambitious system software upgrade Microsoft has ever attempted. This means that more user feedback and engineering effort went into this version than into any previous single-user Microsoft operating system. It also means that compatibility with your existing hardware and software is less assured, especially in the first year or so after the release.

While upgrading to Windows 95 is reversible, you should make sure that you and your PC are prepared for Windows 95 before installing it. A basic understanding of Windows 95's new features, compatibility, and hardware requirements will make the transition more enjoyable.

Why Microsoft Upgrades OS Software

What really makes the compilation of components in your computer's cabinet behave like a personal computer is the **operating system software.** The operating system imbues the box with a kind of personality. Despite some outward similarities among popular graphical desktop computer operating systems, such as OS/2, MacOS, and Windows 95, each is quite different, especially the more you get to know them, just as people who look alike are different inside. Despite the highly visible battles between various microprocessor brands and models (Pentium vs. Power PC, for instance), the marketing battle is not truly about the hardware, but about operating system software environments. As competing operating system providers improve performance and ease of use, Microsoft must do the same for Windows, perhaps even leapfrogging competitors with some features. Unlike the more incremental improvements in previous upgrades to MS-DOS and Windows, Windows 95 represents a major leap.

Why Upgrade to Windows 95?

There is no law that says you must upgrade to Windows 95, but as time goes by, more and more applications and hardware add-ons will take advantage of its features. Even without those new products, working with your files more easily, customizing your desktop environment, and better integrating older applications may be reason enough to make the change.

A New Desktop → 74

The first change you notice with Windows 95 is that the background on the screen is a **Desktop**—a place where you can have folders and files lying about, just like a real desk. Microsoft eliminated the duality that was the File Manager and the Program Manager. There is now one Desktop, with a multitude of ways to organize, locate, and open your files and applications. What used to be known as directories are now simply folders.

My Computer → 74

My Computer

A prominent element of the Desktop is an icon called `My Computer`. This icon represents everything that is part of your machine, including all disk drives and their contents. This is one avenue for navigating through and manipulating your files.

Windows Explorer → 76

Explorer

Another way to view and manage your files is with the Windows Explorer window. Its heritage from the Windows 3.x File Manager is evident, but the Explorer's two window panes become a common interface design for hierarchical information in Windows and related products, such as the Microsoft Exchange universal mailbox.

Shortcuts → 114

Current Projects

The flexibility of the Desktop allows you to place icons that represent deeply nested items anywhere you like. A special arrow symbol attached to the icon means that it is a shortcut to a file, application, or folder. Opening the **shortcut** is the same as opening the real item directly.

System Registry → 119

The confusing arrays of WIN.INI and SYSTEM.INI files are gone (except where needed for compatibility with older programs), with the job handled more succinctly and transparently by the **Registry.** If you use recent hardware and all Windows applications, the Registry may even eliminate CONFIG.SYS and AUTOEXEC.BAT file concerns.

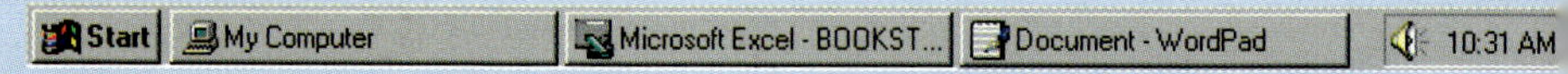

Taskbar → 82

At the bottom of the Desktop screen is a new button bar that serves several purposes. The leftmost button, named Start, has a pop-up menu containing quick **access to programs, control panels, recent documents,** or virtually any desktop item you use regularly. As you open folders and applications, a button for each appears in the Taskbar. Even if an item you want to access should get hidden from view by overlapping windows, a click of its button in the Taskbar brings it to the front. The Taskbar is also where minimized applications collapse.

Long File Names → 112

If you've ever felt hampered by the MS-DOS file naming restrictions, Windows 95 will set you free. Applications designed for Windows 95 let you save documents with names up to 256 characters long.

Memory Management → 44

Except for some cantankerous MS-DOS programs, Windows 95 manages your PC's memory pretty much automatically. It treats memory for Windows applications as **extended memory** → 42, and makes it easy to customize specifics for MS-DOS programs that require more than 640KB of conventional memory.

Windows 95 and Counting...

Software versions are commonly identified by a numbering system denoting the generation of the release. Thus, version 3.0 of Windows was the first release of the third generation. Digits to the right of the decimal usually signify a slightly different release with some new features, rather than an entirely new generation. Thus, Windows 3.1 added new features (and fixed bugs) to version 3.0.

Multitasking and Multithreading

Applications built for Windows 95 can operate in the background while you work on other programs. Moreover, such programs may also carry out some tasks while you work on something else in the same programs, such as reading on-line mail while downloading a file. When you see the hourglass pointer combined with the arrow, it means the current process can be switched to the background by clicking on another task.

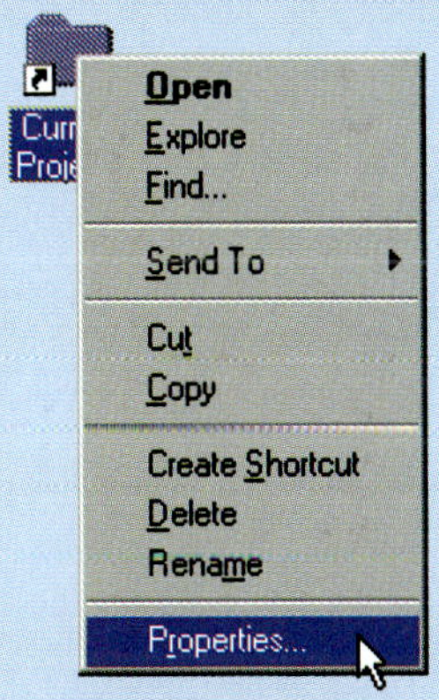

Property Sheets

Right-clicking on most Desktop and Explorer (jointly called Desktop/Explorer in this book) objects presents a pop-up menu of extra commands to carry out on the item. Almost every item includes a property sheet, which lets you view a number of important facts about the file, such as its creation date, size, and type of file.

Quick Views 118

Right-clicking on many kinds of document files produces a pop-up menu with a `Quick View` item in it. By choosing this item, Windows opens a program that is capable of viewing a number of file formats without having to open the application that generated the document.

But Microsoft appears to be veering away from this numbering tradition by making the year a part of the product name. The company does it with some of its multimedia programs (Cinemania '95 and Encarta '95, for example), and now brings this system to Windows. This does not necessarily mean that there will be a new version of Windows every year. It remains to be seen how interim releases for new features or bug fixes are

Plug and Play 61

Windows 95 is the first operating system to take advantage of the Plug and Play hardware standard. Computers that were built for Plug and Play capabilities are virtually self-configuring when you add new devices or set up Windows in the first place.

Hardware Requirements

Windows has a few minimum computer hardware requirements:

- 80386 microprocessor or later
- 1.44MB floppy disk drive (or CD-ROM drive for installation)
- 30MB free space on your hard disk
- 4MB RAM

While Windows 95 performance is on par with earlier versions, experienced users soon discover that a fast CPU makes a great improvement in overall performance. Therefore, a minimum of a 66 MHz 80486 or any speed Pentium CPU is highly recommended.

With 4 or 8MB of RAM, your PC will depend on your hard disk to act as virtual memory 44 a lot of the time. This is slower than real RAM, and detracts from your total available hard disk space. But at 16MB of RAM or more, Windows and a typical set of productivity applications run speedily in RAM, with little reliance on virtual memory.

Software Compatibility

Microsoft supplied software developers with pre-release versions of Windows 95 for a couple of years prior to its release, with two goals in mind: (1) that existing Windows software would run on Windows 95, and (2) to encourage developers to prepare applications that adhere to the Win32 API—standards that let programs take advantage of Windows 95's best user features, such as long file names and multitasking.

Where you may encounter difficulty is in programs that were developed by independent programmers or by companies that no longer support the products. It is possible that an older product will not be compatible with Windows 95, and that there will be no way for you to get a fix for the problem. This is more likely to be true for older MS-DOS programs than for programs written for earlier versions of Windows. The need for some RAM-resident programs (also known as TSRs, for terminate-and-stay-resident) may disappear with features built into Windows. Still, you may have to evaluate the importance of older, incompatible programs and see if there are more modern replacements for critical tasks.

Hardware Compatibility

A potentially thorny issue about upgrading is how well Windows 95 will treat your existing computer hardware and peripherals. For relatively well-established brands and models of all devices, Windows 95 will probably have all necessary driver software built in. Should you anticipate problems with older or more obscure devices, contact the device manufacturer for guidance on compatibility with Windows 95. In some cases, the maker may supply driver software that you can install into Windows 95 60.

Back up. Back up. Back up.

If you cannot back up your entire hard disk (highly recommended), then you should back up at least the following items:

- All personal and business data files
- CONFIG.SYS and AUTOEXEC.BAT from the root directory of your C: drive
- All files in your Windows directory with the following extensions: .INI, .DAT, and .PWL (the last one if you have any network password information on your disk)
- All real-mode device driver files loaded in the CONFIG.SYS and AUTOEXEC.BAT files

Preparing Your Hard Disk

In addition to making sure your hard disk has adequate space for the upgrade (up to 30MB for an upgrade over Windows 3.1), you should also check your disk for media integrity and file fragmentation if you have the programs to do it. From MS-DOS 6.0 or later, type

```
DEFRAG
```

at the DOS prompt. Then, if you have MS-DOS 6.2 or later, type

```
SCANDISK
```

from the DOS prompt, and perform a surface scan of the disk. If everything's OK, then you're ready to install.

Once you've determined that your PC hardware and software are ready for Windows 95 (if it didn't come already installed on your PC) and you've performed the prep work 67, you are ready to install the system software.

Windows 95 installs on your hard disk via the Setup program. For most users, there are only a few bits of interaction required during installation, while Setup performs most of the work automatically. Installation can take up to an hour (or less from a CD-ROM), so allow enough time.

Partway through the installation, Setup restarts your computer to get Windows 95 working. Additional installation continues after this point, as Setup finishes configuring your Desktop.

What Setup Does

Setup's job is divided into four distinct task groups:

- **Gathering information** about you and your PC
- **Copying files** to your hard disk
- **Restarting the computer** to let Windows 95 take over
- **Finishing details** of your Windows 95 environment

At a few points along the way, you must supply information that Windows uses for global settings.

Gathering Information

The first decision you make is the nature of the installation on your PC. Choices are from:

- Typical
- Portable
- Compact
- Custom Setup

Unless you are installing on a laptop, you should choose the Typical setup. Use Compact setup only when you must install Windows 95 but your hard disk is running low on space. Selectable items available in the Custom Setup type are always available for installation later from within Windows 95.

From here, Setup checks that you have enough disk space for the desired installation. If space is sufficient, you are prompted to enter the path 110 to the directory to be used for Windows 95. If you have an earlier version of Windows installed, Setup recommends installing Windows 95 into that directory. Choose the recommended directory unless you plan a dual-boot system.

Next is a prompt window for your name and company name. You must enter information in all fields (even if the company is "(None)").

The next-to-last step in this phase is the hardware detection. In the dialog box, check all device categories that you think are installed in your PC. If the program freezes at some point for more than a minute, consult troubleshooting tips 160.

Finally, you are asked whether Setup should create a start-up diskette 70. This is highly recommended.

Copying Files

All the previous analysis helps Setup determine which files your hard disk will need to run Windows 95 on your PC. Getting all necessary files onto your hard disk is automatic from a CD-ROM installer. If you are installing Windows 95 from floppy disks, you'll be prompted to insert various disks in sequence, as Setup extracts needed files from the `Cabinet` archive files stored on the floppies. Along the way you'll be prompted to insert a blank diskette, which Setup uses to create the emergency start-up disk.

Restart and Finish

Because Windows 95 is no longer a pretty face atop plain old MS-DOS, Setup restarts your PC so that the Windows 95 operating system can take over. Before the job is done, however, you must supply the **time zone** in which you are located. This information is important for networked installations and some on-line communications software. You can also specify a printer at this point (Setup tries to pick out your previous settings), or click the Cancel button to defer this device installation for later (at which point you'll need the installation disk(s) again). The last stages include conversion of old Windows artifacts (especially Program Groups) into Windows 95 objects and folder organization.

Starting Setup

How you start Setup depends on the version of Windows from which you are upgrading. Windows 95 Setup is compatible only with Windows 3.1 and Windows for Workgroups 3.1x. Therefore, you can start Setup from Windows only if you have these versions installed on your PC. From the Windows Program or File Manager, choose `Run` from the `File` menu and type the letter of the drive containing the Setup program (A: for floppy disk; perhaps D: on your machine for CD-ROM), followed by

```
SETUP
```

and press Enter. For Windows 3.0, MS-DOS (5.0 or later), or OS/2, you must start Setup from MS-DOS. From the DOS prompt, type the letter of the floppy disk drive containing the Setup program followed by:

```
SETUP
```

and press Enter. For PCs lacking Windows 3.1 or later, Setup temporarily copies a condensed version of Windows 3.1 to your hard disk so Setup can run properly.

Smart Recovery

All the while Setup is working on your PC, it maintains a log of its activities, successes, and failures. Should Setup cause your PC to freeze because of a device conflict or other problem, it has a record of the problem that caused the freeze. You can then restart your PC and Setup. By reading the log, Setup knows to temporarily bypass the problem device and continue with Setup. Once Windows 95 is installed well enough

Custom Setup

The Custom installation type is intended primarily for people responsible for setting up networked users. Many of the options provided in Custom Setup require extensive knowledge about the nature of the network to which you are connected. In most networked environments managed by a computer support staff, the installation of Windows 95 and network components will be done for you by the support staff or in a preconfigured manner established on a server by the support staff.

to run, you can use the Add New Hardware wizard ➔ 60 to resolve any conflicts that Setup couldn't handle by itself. Therefore, don't panic when Setup freezes. Just restart and carry on until the core of Windows 95 is installed—even if it takes multiple attempts.

Filling in Missed Items

One of the control panels installed in a Typical installation is **Add/Remove Programs.** In the `Add/Remove Programs→Windows Setup` control is a list of component groups that Setup can install. Double-Click each group to see its parts. Checked items are already installed. For non-networked users, be sure the following minimum items are checked:

Accessories
- Character Map
- Clipboard Viewer
- Paint
- Quick View
- WordPad

Communications
- HyperTerminal
- Phone Dialer

Disk Tools
- Backup

Microsoft Exchange

Microsoft FAX

Multimedia
- CD Player
- Media Player
- Sound Recorder
- Volume Control

Microsoft Network

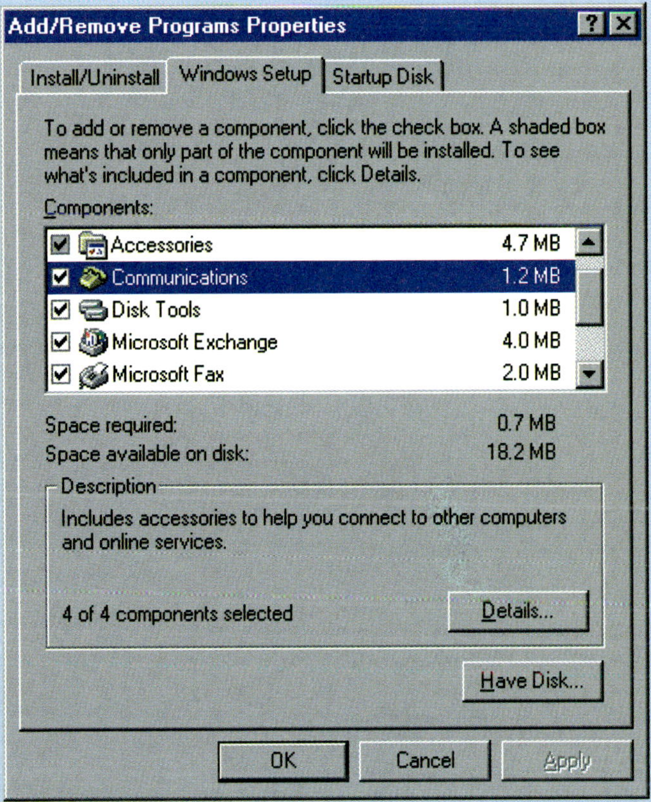

There is no harm in adding all items. After making any changes to this control panel, click the OK or Apply button to install (or de-install) selected items. For installation, you will need your installations disk(s).

Creating a Dual-Boot System

While Microsoft's prescribed installation method recommends replacing Windows 3.x and MS-DOS with the Windows 95 environment, you can elect to maintain the existing world by installing Windows 95 into a new directory, separate from the current Windows directory. You must specify a new directory at the time `Setup` first runs; otherwise `Setup` will delete old Windows 3.x and MS-DOS files. You can set a directory such as WIN95 as the directory for Windows 95 in a dual-boot environment.

A couple of disadvantages attend this method of installation. First, Windows 95 won't have any of your Windows 3.x Program Manager information installed. Therefore, you'll have to manually set up shortcuts to your applications in the appropriate parts of Windows 95 ➔ 114. Second, you will need substantial hard disk space—40MB—for a dual-boot version of Windows 95.

Starting From a Dual-Boot System

Without any user interaction, Windows 95 is the default operating system that boots when you turn on your PC. If you have installed a dual-boot system with MS-DOS and Windows 3.x, you have to stop the booting process and re-direct it to the operating environment of your choice.

When you turn on (or restart) your PC, the instant you see "Starting Windows 95..." on your screen, press the F4 key. From the ensuing menu, choose the environment of your choice.

Internally, this is tricky business, because a number of key root directory files have their names changed so that either MS-DOS or Windows 95 boots successfully. When Windows 95 is installed, Setup preserves key MS-DOS booting files by renaming them:

Original	After Setup
COMMAND.COM	COMMAND.DOS
CONFIG.SYS	CONFIG.DOS
AUTOEXEC.BAT	AUTOEXEC.DOS

In the process of booting DOS, these three .DOS files are restored to their original names, while their Windows 95 versions are renamed with the .W40 extension. This allows your MS-DOS or Windows 3.x programs and drivers to load just as they did prior to installing Windows 95. The next time you restart directly into Windows 95, the files are restored to their Windows 95 file names and extensions.

Trimming Windows

Add/Remove Programs

Once you get to know the innards of Windows 95, you may wish to eliminate some components that you don't need. While you can remove items via the Desktop or Explorer, the `Add/Remove Program→Windows Setup` control panel makes the job for a number of categories easier. For instance, if you do not use **Wallpaper** ➔ 94, you can uninstall the Desktop Wallpaper component (in the Accessories group), which rids your disk of all pertinent items in one action.

It is always advisable to have a startup diskette handy in case of trouble with your hard disk.

Because the core system routines in every PC give startup precedence to a disk in the first floppy drive (A:), you can always start your PC from a floppy, even if your hard disk fails to start normally due to system software conflicts or disk problems.

Using Setup to Make a Startup Disk

Add/Remove Programs

Windows 95 Setup program asks you if you want to create a startup disk during the Windows installation process. You aren't required to do it then, but it's a convenient time, provided you have a spare 1.44MB diskette handy.

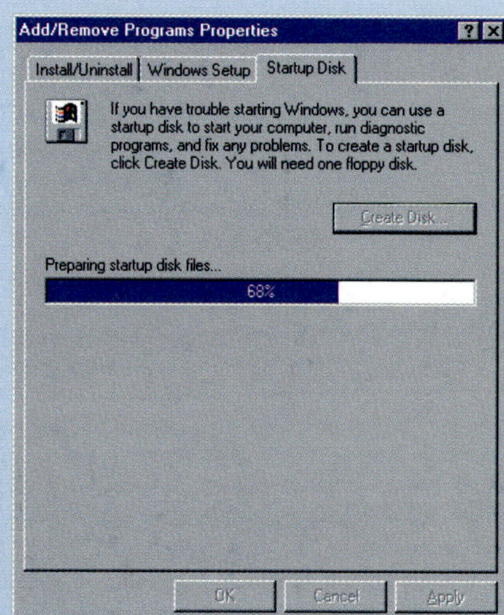

What's On the Startup Disk

A startup disk contains about one megabyte of files that are critical to starting a Windows 95 PC and accessing its hard disk (compressed or uncompressed). Here are the files:

File Name	Description
DRVSPACE.BIN	DriveSpace driver
COMMAND.COM	System software
FORMAT.COM	Disk formatter
SYS.COM	System transfer program
FDISK.EXE	Disk partitioner
ATTRIB.EXE	File attribute editor
EDIT.COM	Simple text editor
REGEDIT.EXE	Registry extractor and importer
SCANDISK.EXE	ScanDisk program
UNINSTAL.EXE	Uninstalls Windows 95
SCANDISK.INI	ScanDisk configuration
IO.SYS	System software (hidden)
MSDOS.SYS	System software (hidden)
EBD.SYS	System software (hidden)

Creating a Startup Disk Later

In case you didn't make the startup disk during installation or want to create another one, you can do so after Windows 95 is installed:

1. Activate the Add/Remove Programs →Startup Disk control panel.
2. Prepare a 1.44MB diskette labeled "Windows 95 Startup Disk."
3. Click the Create Disk button, and follow instructions to insert your installation diskettes (or CD-ROM) and the blank disk.
4. When you see that the process is complete, remove the diskette, and place it in a safe place.

Lock the Startup Disk

Once you have a minimal startup disk, flip the locking tab on the reverse side. This will prevent a **virus** 58 from propagating to it, so that you have at least one clean startup disk for your system.

When to Use a Startup Disk

Most of the time your hard disk will successfully start up as it should. But if you notice some **erratic behavior** when using your PC, you may wish to isolate the problems as being related to a virus or hardware. By starting the PC with a locked, virus-free minimal system disk, you may be able to detect whether the problem is in the motherboard (the problem persists even when starting from the diskette) or on your hard disk (the problem goes away). If the problem is on your hard disk, it may be due to a virus or a **system software conflict** 58.

Using the Startup Disk

When you boot your PC with the startup disk, the description on the screen says that Windows 95 is starting, but you will also see the A:\> DOS prompt. But from here, you can use DOS programs on the diskette to check the hard disk (SCANDISK C:), extract **Registry files** 119 for editing (REGEDIT), edit real-mode entries in CONFIG.SYS and AUTOEXEC.BAT on your hard drive (EDIT), and even reformat you hard disk if absolutely necessary (FDISK). These programs aren't as easy to use as their Windows counterparts, so you may need to find experienced help to get you through the problems. See 160 for further troubleshooting suggestions.

Uninstalling Windows

The Uninstaller program on the boot disk can be used only if you directed Windows 95 Setup to make Windows 95 uninstallable. This action compressed and saved key files that will let you restore your PC to pre-Windows 95 state.

One of the last tasks that Windows 95 Setup performs is the conversion of Windows 3.x program groups to a format compatible with Windows 95.

If you were a religious user of the Windows 3.x Program Manager, you may feel disoriented at first, because you don't see your program groups on the desktop when Windows 95 starts. More troubling, perhaps, is that the concept of program groups has disappeared in Windows 95. Instead, programs are grouped into special folders whose contents are automatically accessible via the Start menu in the Taskbar.

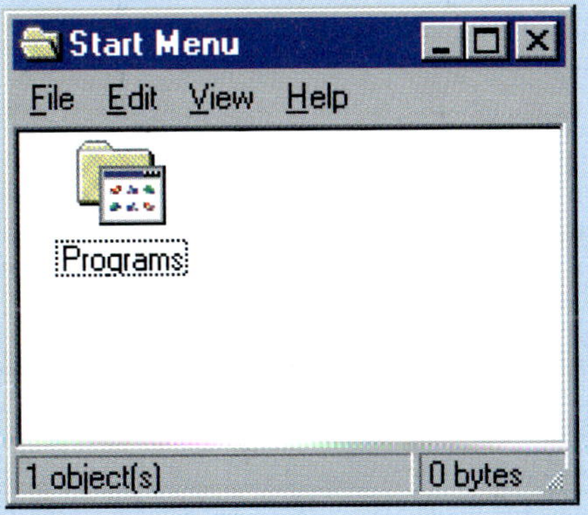

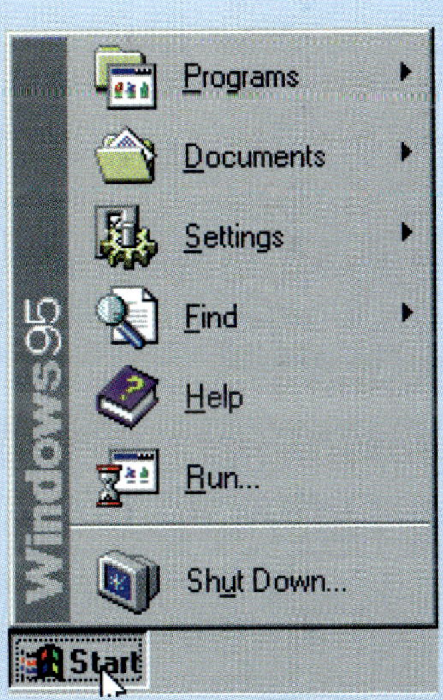

The Start Menu

A new **user interface element** in Windows 95 is the Start menu, located at the lower left corner of the screen (on the Taskbar 82). This menu has a number of properties, including the ability to show the contents of special containers scattered around a Windows 95 hard disk.

The bottom seven items of the Start menu are always there, acting as safety nets for those who may feel overloaded with all the folders and files stored in hundreds of megabytes of Windows 95, applications, and documents. One of the items in the Start menu is a folder icon labeled `Programs`. The Programs folder is a special case in Windows 95 (note its unique program group icon). Any folder nested inside it also becomes one of these program group-style folders. Files, folders, or **shortcuts** 114 placed in one of these program folders will be accessible by way of the Programs item in the Start menu.

Instead of using successive windows to view items in program group folders, you can use the hierarchical nature of the Start menu to drill down through the Programs menu to other groups, such as `Accessories`, `Games` and `Microsoft Office`. You can set up your program organization in any way you wish 110).

Setup's Job

At the end of Windows 95 Setup, the program converts Windows 3.x program **groups** into these Start menu program folders, and **organizes** them closely to the way you had them organized in Windows 3.x. (Unfortunately, that organization probably isn't as convenient via the Start menu as it was in Windows 3.x program groups, so you may have to rethink how you want your programs to be arranged in the Programs folder.) You will also see many new items, which are part of Windows 95.

Modifying the Programs Folder

To change the organization of the program folders in the Startup menu, begin by right-clicking on the Start button. One of the pop-up menu items is `Open`. This action opens the Start Menu folder that contains the program groups (if your PC has user profiles set up, there is a separate Start Menu folder for each profiled user). You can open the program group folders just like any folder in the Desktop/Explorer, and **move** items around. Drag items to the `Recycle Bin` to **remove** them from a program folder; right-click at any blank area in the folder to generate a new shortcut to a different program; **delete** or **add** program subfolders to your heart's content. See 110 for more about managing your applications.

Shortcuts and Windows 3.x Programs

If you were a facile Program Manager user in Windows 3.x, then the concept of shortcuts in Windows 95 will not be foreign to you. In Program Manager, the icons did not really represent the program files that you saw in the File Manager; instead, they pointed to the real files. Double clicking a program icon in Program Manager was the same as double-clicking the program's file icon in the File Manager. You could even have multiple icons in different groups pointing to the same program file. Windows 95 shortcuts behave much the same way 114.

My Computer
Network Neighborhood
Recycle Bin
My Briefcase
The Microsoft Network
Inbox
My Computer
File Edit View Help
3½ Flop
Control
1 object
Control Panel
File Edit View Help
Accessibility Options
Find Fast
Microsoft Mail Postoffice
Passwords
Changes date,
Date/Time Properties
Date & Time
Time Zone
(GMT-08:00) Pacific Time (US & Canada); Tijuana
Automatically adjust clock for daylight saving changes
OK
Cancel
Apply
Start
My Computer
Control Panel
10:36 AM

The concept of the Windows Desktop evolved in the transition from Windows 3.1 to Windows 95.

Strictly speaking, the Desktop is the workspace you see on your video monitor. Think of the background pattern as the top surface of a physical desk. On it rests icons representing your computer, the wastebasket, folders, documents, and so on. Opening a folder window is just like opening a physical file folder and making it the topmost item on what may be a heap of open folders and other papers on the desktop.

Because the Desktop representation of icons and folders is controlled within Windows 95 by the **Explorer shell program** 76, the terms Explorer and Desktop are often used interchangeably. In this book, the Desktop is the graphical backdrop you see when Windows starts, as well as all the windows that open to reveal the contents of your computer; Windows Explorer is a specially designed, two-pane window whose appearance and behavior are reminiscent of the Windows 3.x File Manager. (When writing about features that apply to both, this book joins them together as Desktop/Explorer.)

You can put a document on the Windows Desktop, just as you might on a physical desk's top, instead of inside a folder or storage device. This is a sleight of hand, because all files must really exist on a storage device (in this case, the **boot disk** 110), but in Windows 95, the Desktop appears to be a real place to put stuff.

Just like our real desk and work environment, the Windows Desktop can be tailored to suit our whims. **Control panels** and **window menus** open the Desktop to customization of background colors or patterns, file listings, alert sounds, and many more features 94, 101, 112, 146. The Windows Desktop is where we work—it should be a comfortable place.

While the Windows Desktop certainly gives you more power than any physical desktop, it doesn't include everything you might have on your desk. However, software programs fill most of the gaps (from a card file and calendar to pictures of the family). And, while you don't see a telephone built into the Windows Desktop, some multimedia computers are beginning to bring phone functionality to the Windows environment as well.

The Desktop Metaphor

My Computer

Graphical user interfaces, such as the Windows environment, attract discussion of metaphors. Extending the literary metaphor a bit, screen metaphors present objects or images on the video monitor that remind us of other objects or images from the world outside the screen. Therefore, just like a manila **file folder**, a Windows file folder is a way of grouping documents. By reading the name of the folder, we get a clue about the kinds of documents inside. Fortunately, the computer adds significant power to that folder, including a variety of index listings, search facilities, and almost unlimited size. But because the Windows folder shares its basic properties with the familiar paper folder, we, as users, don't have to conjure some new mental model for the way documents are organized on a PC. **Dragging a document** icon from one folder to another is highly analogous to **moving a paper** document from one folder to another. That's among the things that attracts us to graphical interfaces.

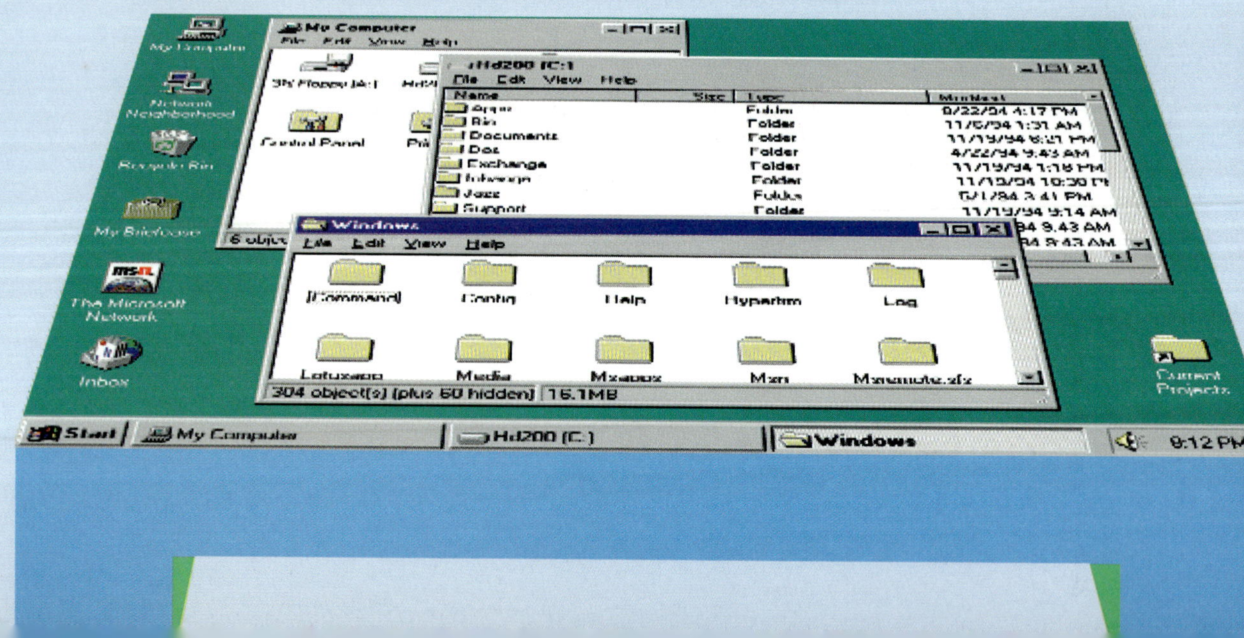

My Computer

Windows installs a few items onto the Desktop automatically. The topmost one, `My Computer`, represents the machine sitting on your desk or in your lap. Opening this icon (double-click on it) reveals a **window** ➔ 86 showing an icon for each storage device that Windows recognizes, and some special folders that store important user-accessed system items, such as fonts, control panels, and printers.

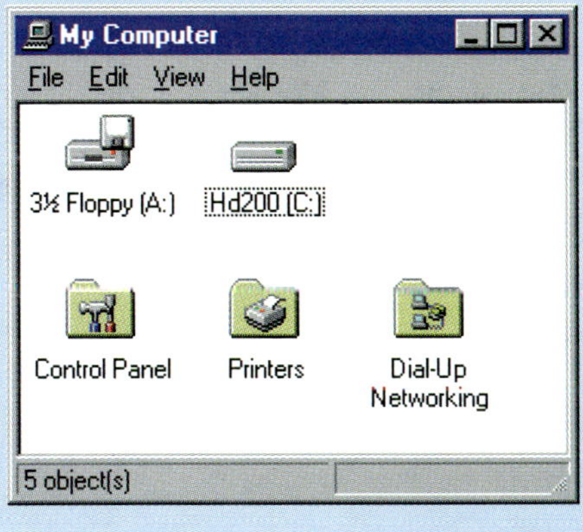

Double-clicking on any of the storage device icons opens a view to their **root directories** (if there is no disk or tape in the drive that you click on, you receive a message that the drive is "not ready"). You will see a variety of document, application, or folder icons ➔ 80, depending on the contents of that directory. If you know where a file is located, you can open subsequent folders to reach the one holding the desired file. The default behavior calls for a new window to open for each folder ➔ 86, and a button for each open window to appear in the **Taskbar** ➔ 82.

Network Neighborhood

Network Neighborhood

If your PC is connected to a network, you may have access to shared folders located on other computers. You can see these by opening the `Network Neighborhood` icon. You can access and move files ➔ 112 as if the folders were located on your computer.

Recycle Bin

Recycle Bin

Windows offers many ways to delete items from your hard disk. The one on the Desktop is the `Recycle Bin` ➔ 93. Dragging ➔ 112 icons to the `Recycle Bin` icon is the same as tossing something into a wastepaper basket (from which items may be retrieved until it is emptied).

Clearing Your Desktop

Because the on-screen Desktop has finite boundaries, it is possible that it will get cluttered from time to time. Right-clicking on the background of the Taskbar reveals a pop-up menu item called `Minimize All Windows`. Clicking on this item removes all Windows from the Desktop (their buttons remain on the Taskbar). Right-click the Taskbar again later to restore opened windows.

Windows opened from `My Computer` have an extra closure shortcut: Hold down the Shift key while clicking the Close(✕)button ➔ 87, and all windows that contain the one you click on close at the same time. Therefore, if you drill down several folders and want to keep only the last folder open on the Desktop, you can Shift-Close the next highest folder in the path ➔ 110 to close all the others.

Right-Clicking the Desktop

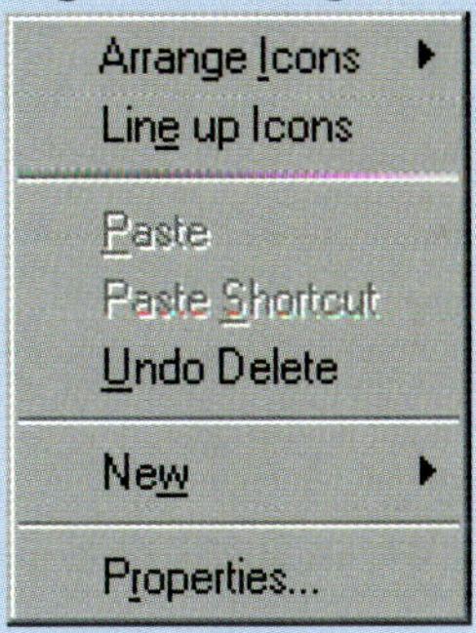

As for any object in Windows, a right-click of the mouse button when the cursor is atop the Desktop background displays a relevant menu—this menu contains choices that pertain to Desktop objects. You can have Windows help you **straighten out icons** strewn about the area ➔ 80, create new documents of various kinds, and access the property sheets pertaining to Desktop display ➔ 32.

Desktop Folder

If you consider that "your computer" rests on the Windows Desktop, you may wonder where items on the Desktop really are. At first glance, they seem to be separate from the computer. In truth, the items are in a special folder inside the Windows folder. Normally hidden unless you change the window view options ➔ 96, the `Windows→Desktop` folder contains the items displayed on the Desktop (except for `My Computer` and, if installed, `Network Neighborhood`). There is little need to access this folder, since it's much easier to work with items directly on the Desktop.

Desktop Strategies

There are as many Desktop strategies as there are serious Windows users. Also, users of monitors capable of displaying more area can put that extra space to good use. Here are some suggestions to start with

- Keep few Desktop windows, if any, open on the Desktop except when you need them. They tend to get covered by application windows anyway, and they clutter up the Taskbar with buttons when you choose to view them in separate windows.
- Right-click on the Taskbar and choose `Cascade` to organize all windows in an easily accessible "stair-stepped" fashion ➔ 87.
- Create shortcuts ➔ 114 on the Desktop to folders containing active documents or projects. If you want to get a **Quick View** ➔ 118 of a document you're working on, it will be easier to find it that way.
- Rather than place shortcuts to frequently accessed applications on the Desktop, consider placing them in the Start menu ➔ 82. They'll be easier to locate when other applications and My Computer windows are open.

For details about organizing files and folders ➔ 111.

An alternative method of navigating through folders and files in Windows is to use the Windows Explorer.

Windows 95 users who upgrade from Windows 3.x may feel more comfortable in the Explorer than in `My Computer`, because the Explorer more closely resembles the old `File Manager`. Not everything is the same, however, so some adjustment may be necessary.

The Explorer presents a single window, divided into two panes. The left pane shows a hierarchical view of each disk volume (and `Network Neighborhood`, if visible on the Desktop). In the right pane are the contents of any item selected (clicked on) in the left pane. Items in the right pane can be dragged to other locations in the Explorer's left pane, to the Desktop, the Start button, and elsewhere.

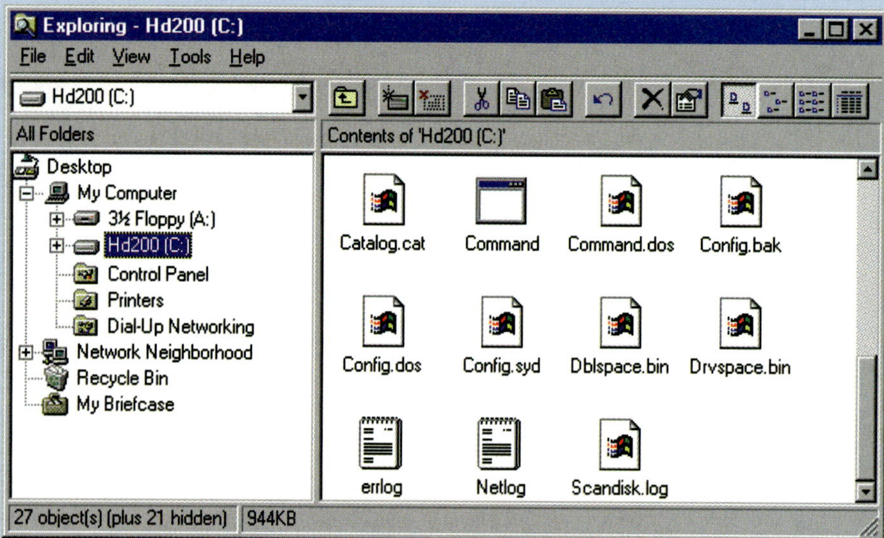

Starting the Explorer

Windows Explorer is the Windows program that presents the **user interface** for managing all storage devices, both on your own computer's disks and in any networked storage areas you may be connected to. Microsoft (and others) use the **two-pane design**—outline overview on the left; detailed view of a selected item on the right—in other contexts where data storage is implied (e.g., the Microsoft Exchange universal mail box).

During setup, a shortcut to Windows Explorer is placed in the Programs folder of the Start button. The shortcut is named Windows Explorer to help insure that it falls to the bottom of the Programs listing, making it easier to locate with the mouse.

Sizing the Panes

In addition to using normal window resizing techniques for the entire window 86, you can move the dividing bar between the two panes of the Explorer window by dragging it. Place the pointer atop the bar until the pointer 79 turns to a double arrow. Then click and drag to the left or right until the panes are at the desired proportions.

All Folders View (Left Pane)

The left pane provides a global, hierarchical view of all containers on disks and other storage areas connected to your computer. The Explorer regards the Desktop as the basis for everything you do in Windows—just as it is the foundation for the Desktop view on your screen. Typical containers on the Desktop include `My Computer`, `Recycle Bin`, and other special-purpose data holders, such as `Network Neighborhood` (if you set up Windows to work with a network) and My Briefcase (if you need to synchronize the contents of desktop and laptop computers). Containers on the Desktop are indented one level from the Desktop icon, just like an outline **(a tree-like hierarchy)**, with dotted lines leading from the next highest item.

To view the contents of any container, click once on its icon. Depending on the `View` menu settings, the right pane then fills with icons or a list of individual items in that container.

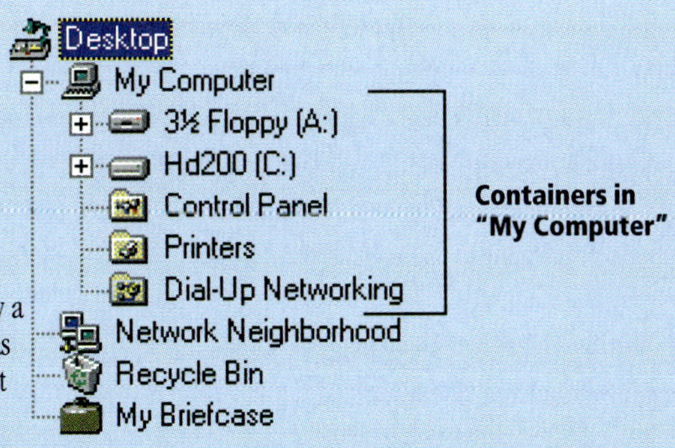

When a container in the hierarchy is preceded by a **plus sign icon**, it means that the container has stuff in it. Clicking on that plus sign icon turns it into a minus sign and expands the view of the contents in the left pane, revealing all containers in the next deepest level. Some of those items may, in turn, have plus icons which may be opened to reveal further nested containers in the tree. When there is no plus sign, there may still be files in the container—click the icon to see what appears in the right pane. To close up the view, click on the minus icon.

Contents View (Right Pane)

The right pane of the Explorer window displays the actual folders, files, and applications that you copy, move, open, delete, rename, and create shortcuts to. Precisely which items appear in this view, and how their names appear, is directed by the items in the `View`→`Options` dialog. Some items may be hidden, and the three-letter file name extension 110 may not be showing, depending on the settings. But icons 80 often give visual clues about the nature of the item, such as which application was used to create a document file.

The `View` menu also controls the visual presentation of items, with choices similar to any Desktop window. How neat or messy you like to keep these views is entirely up to you 111.

Status Bar

At the bottom of the window is the status bar, which reveals information about the contents of any item(s) selected in either pane (only items in one pane can be selected at one time). Select (click once) an item in the left, and its contents appear on the right, along with a readout of how many items are in that container and how large the total items are. If any items are **hidden** 96, the status bar tells you that, but the total size reflects only visible items. When you select one or more folders in the right pane, only the count of folders appears in the status bar, not the total size of their contents (which you can get from the folder's property sheet). Selecting `My Computer` in the left pane and clicking on a disk icon reveals the volume's free space and total capacity.

To hide the status bar, uncheck the `Status Bar` item in the Explorer window's `View` menu.

Toolbar

By checking the `Toolbar` item in the `View` menu, you can insert extra shortcut tools in the window. The pop-up menu presents an abbreviated version of the All Folders view to help you navigate in big jumps when you are viewing a deeply nested folder. A button bearing a folder icon and upward pointing arrow is a one-click shortcut button to shift your view one level toward the top of the hierarchy. Two buttons offer shortcuts for mapping and unmapping networked disk drives 151. The rightmost four buttons provide shortcuts to items in the `View` menu for selecting the type of view for items in the right pane: large icon, small icon, list, or detail view 96.

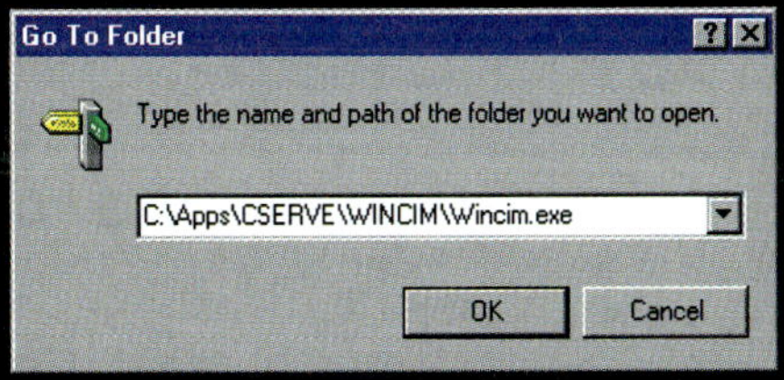

Zip to a Folder

Windows 95 maintains a list of any applications you launch from the Run window (in the **Start Menu** 122). This goes for simulated DOS commands as well 132. You can quickly return to the folder containing most recently run applications by choosing `Go To` in the `Tools` menu. The resulting dialog offers a pop-up list of paths to about the last 25 applications started via the Run dialog. By selecting one of the items from the list, you can instantly navigate to that folder, no matter how deeply nested it is. You may also type the full path to the desired folder if you like, but mousing around the Explorer or using the Find program 116 may be faster.

Comparing Folder Contents

There may be times when you'd like to compare the contents of folders on two different disks, or two folders on the same disk, to see if both have the same items in them. Unlike File Manager of Windows 3.x, which let you open a separate window for each directory, the Explorer has a single set of views. But you can open more than one instance of the Explorer. By tiling the windows (right-click the Taskbar and choose `Tile Windows Vertically` 87) and selecting the same view style in each 96, you can visually compare the two containers line-by-line or icon-by-icon.

Explorer vs. Desktop

Which is more efficient to work with: Explorer or Desktop? There is no absolute answer to that question, because each user adapts to interfaces differently. While there are many similarities in the ways they work, they provide distinctly different ways of thinking about file organization. Some users will find navigation easier in the Explorer, but file management 112 easier in the Desktop.

Still Love File Manager?

For users who simply don't want to part with Program Manager and File Manager of Windows 3.x, yet want to take advantage of other aspects of Windows 95, the software includes a compatible version of both (PROGAM.EXE and WINFILE.EXE) in the Windows folder. You are welcome to use them, but File Manager, for example, does not take full advantage of such Windows 95 features as long file names. Microsoft wants you to switch away from the past.

A graphical user interface, such as Windows, is certainly easier to manage than a command-line interface, such as straight MS-DOS, but the array of choices in pull-down menus and dialog boxes can bewilder a newcomer. Even experienced users may forget how to do tasks they don't do often.

Windows provides a **system-wide on-line help** environment to offer help not only for Windows, but for Windows applications. The purpose of Windows Help is to provide a consistent help environment as you wend your way around Windows and programs. Some help screens are interactive, in that they let you click on buttons to open control panels or other help screens. You can add your own notes to help panels, print out the help, and even change the font size for readability.

Pop-up help windows also abound in many places within Windows and applications. Placing the pointer atop a button or field often reveals a pop-up window that gives a short summary of the item's function—perfect for when you don't remember what an icon means. Additional pop-up help is often available by right-clicking on items to see the What's This? button.

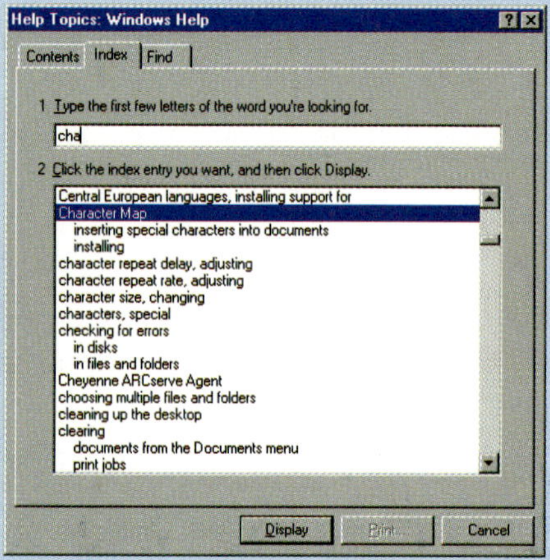

Turning On Windows Help

Whenever you have a Desktop window as the active window ➥86, you can press F1 to display the Windows `Help Topics` window. Similarly, the `Help Topics` item in any window's `Help` menu leads to this window. Of the three screens in the `Help Topics` window (`Contents`, `Index`, and `Find`), the `Index` is the most useful. It lists all the topics alphabetically. To **quickly reach a topic,** begin typing the word in the top field. As you add letters, the scrolling list reaches the entries beginning with the typed characters. Then press Enter (or click Display) to view the actual help window (or sometimes a further selection of related topics, from which you select a single help item). The default behavior is for a help window to float atop all else, allowing you to activate other windows beneath the help window.

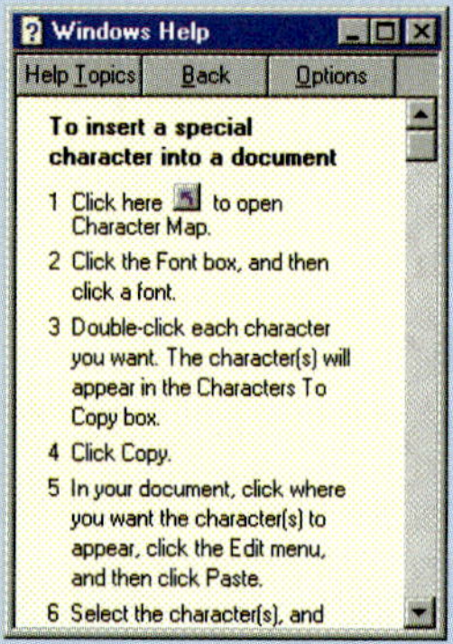

Navigating Windows Help

When you reach a help window, **follow the steps** given on screen. For longer help panels, you may have to scroll down to see everything. Occasionally, small buttons in the text will perform actions for you or lead you to related topics. Beyond that, you have several navigation alternatives available:

- Return to the `Index` (click `Help Topics`)
- Return to the previous help window (click Back)
- Minimize the current window to keep it handy (click the Minimize button ➥86)
- Close help (click the Close button ➥87)

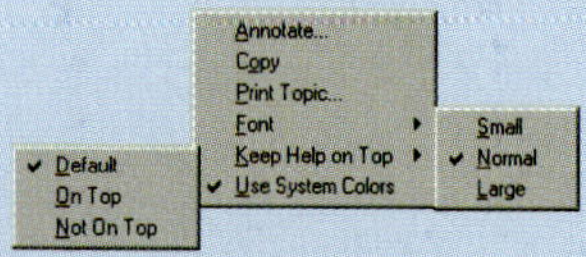

Help Options

The Options button (or right-clicking in the panel) presents a list of options for setting preferences, printing, copying the contents to the Clipboard, or attaching an annotation. Changes you make to visual preferences apply to all subsequent help window views.

Pop-up Help

Two styles of pop-up help are available in a variety of locations (although implemented inconsistently throughout Windows). To use the simplest style, hold the pointer motionless **atop a button** (usually in a toolbar) for a second, and a short description of the button's action appears briefly. In a number of windows, you'll instead see a **question mark icon button** near the top right corner. When you click it, the pointer turns into an arrow plus a question mark. Click on fields and buttons to learn what each item is about. You can usually reach the same pop-up descriptions by right-clicking on these screen items, at which point a single `What's This?` menu item appears. Selecting that menu item leads to the pop-up help description.

Annotate Help

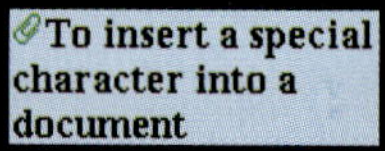

When you annotate a help panel, a small paperclip icon appears at the beginning of the subject title. Click on the clip icon to view, edit, or delete the notation later.

Printing Help

Having a printout of steps for a complex task may be helpful to some, so the help window's menu includes a `Print Topic` option. Any graphics in the panel also print (but with varying quality). Annotations, however, do not print with the panel text.

The terms pointer and cursor are often used interchangeably in the Windows world, but they're not truly the same.

A pointer is the picture you see on the screen that responds to motion of the mouse. The picture changes depending on the kind of action the pointer can carry out when you click the mouse button at that location.

A cursor appears primarily in text fields—a flashing vertical bar that signifies where the next character you type on the keyboard will appear on the screen.

Mouse Pointer

The pointer that tracks along with the mouse on screen changes its shape, depending on where the pointer is and what the system is doing. To confuse the terminology issue, the shapes are often called cursors (custom ones have the file name extension of .CUR). The most common pointer shape is the angled upward arrow. The arrow is what appears when you drag the pointer onto a menubar or atop an icon.

All pointers have a **hot spot**, a single pixel on the pointer that must be atop an object or menu item to perform whatever action you intend. On the arrow pointer, the hot spot is at the very tip of the arrow. Other pointer shapes place their hot spots in different locations, but generally in a place that is logical for the pointer art—the tip of a drawing pencil, the spout of a paint bucket, the center of a crosshair.

Microsoft defines a number of pointer actions in the `Mouse→Pointers` control panel. Here are the ones that apply to keyboard-centric PCs:

Normal Select	**Unavailable**
Help Select	**Vertical Resize**
Working in Background	**Horizontal Resize**
Busy	**Diagonal Resize**
Precision Select	**Diagonal Resize**
Text Select	**Move Resize**

If you open a text editing program, like a WordPad, almost the entire document window is for typing text. As you slowly drag the pointer from outside the window into the window, the pointer changes first from the Normal Select arrow to one of the resize double arrows (used to resize a window ➜86). Then the pointer shape changes to the Text Select pointer. The design of this shape allows you to place the vertical line between characters when you need to insert additional characters. When you click the text pointer inside a text editing area, a text insertion cursor flashes in that spot. The mouse pointer is free to move. The flashing text insertion cursor indicates where the next keyboard character or item pasted from the Clipboard will appear (the cursor blink rate is adjustable in the `Keyboard→Speed` control panel ➜16).

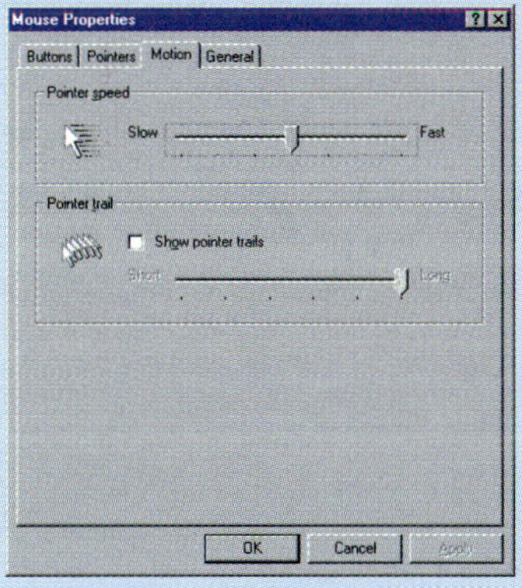

How the pointer tracks the motion of the mouse is controlled by the `Mouse→Motion` control panel ➜20. For most users, the efficient setting of the `Pointer speed` control is a medium setting. For very large screens, however, faster settings allow you to whisk the pointer from edge to edge on the screen using the smallest desk real estate under the mouse.

Changing Windows Pointers

The `Mouse→Pointers` control panel allows you to assign pointer shapes to each of the pointers that Windows defines. Windows comes with a few alternate sets of pointers, and numerous collections of third-party static and animated pointers can be found in on-line service libraries, in public-domain software collections, and on user group diskettes. To assign a new shape to a pointer:

1. Double-click on the pointer in the control panel.
2. Locate the file containing the desired shape (usually in the `Cursors` folder), and open it.
3. A sample of the pointer appears in the control panel. Click OK or Apply to make the change(s) take effect.

Windows' own pointer shapes are not separate files, but are built into Windows itself. To restore an original pointer shape, select it in the control panel, and then click the Use Default button.

If you want to use different collections of pointer shapes for different occasions, you can save any set as a pointer scheme in the control panel. Later, you can select any saved scheme from the pop-up list.

Application Pointers

In addition to the pointer shapes that Windows provides, applications are free to supply pointer shapes that make sense for the kinds of pointing their users need to do. For example, in the Microsoft Paint applet that comes with Windows, the pointer shape is determined by the tool you choose. Click the rectangle tool, for instance, and the pointer turns into a variation of the precision select pointer, with a small circle and dot at the center. Notice that the pointer is in that shape only when in the drawing area—elsewhere the pointer is the Normal Select style, to let you choose menu items, colors, and tools.

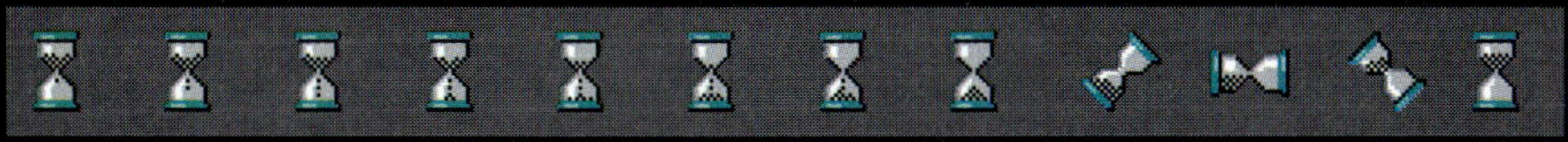

Animated Cursors

Third-party commercial and shareware software collections for Windows often include sets of animated pointers—sequences of shapes that appear to move. For instance, there is one showing tapping fingers, which, as a substitute for the Busy pointer, is more entertaining than the hourglass. The `Mouse→Pointers` control panel lets you assign an animated cursor (file extension .ANI) to any of the pointers. To see the animation, select the pointer in the control panel, and view the result in the sample panel at the upper left.

In both the Desktop and Explorer, icons represent files or places to store files.

The pictographic nature of icons allows them to convey a meaning. A folder icon, for instance, represents a collecting place for items. Those items may be documents, applications, or other folders.

Elsewhere in the Windows user interface, icons are often used to illustrate the purpose of a clickable button. Desktop icons, on the other hand, represent objects. You can move them, open up most of them to see what's inside, and select more than one at a time before carrying out actions on those items.

Container Icons

Several items on the Windows Desktop can hold other items. `My Computer` represents all the hardware sitting on your desk (or in your lap). Inside `My Computer` are icons representing each disk drive volume and some system-wide folders (Control Panel, Printers, and one for accessing your desktop computer from a remote location). In addition to the text labels below the icons, the icons themselves give you **visual clues** about the identity of the device (e.g., floppy drive and CD-ROM player) by indicating the device's appearance or function.

Windows has a few folder icons reserved for itself. These icons have additional art on them (e.g., a hammer and nutdriver on the Control Panel folder). But folders you can use for organizing other items are plain folder icons.

Application and Document Icons

Each Windows application program has a distinctive icon for the main application file (the .EXE or .COM file). But if the application produces any documents or has any support files (like an on-line help system), several icons may appear in your Desktop and Explorer windows. Recent programs use a **document icon** that **looks like a piece of paper** with the top right corner turned down, combined with elements from the application's icon art. Other supporting files have icons associated with on their file type (below).

Unselected Icon **Selected Icon** **Arrow Key Selected Icon**

Selecting an Icon

For several operations in the Desktop/Explorer, it is necessary to select an icon. To select a single icon, position the tip of the arrow pointer atop the icon, and click the mouse button once. The icon label's reverse color and the icon's shaded tone indicates that it is selected. To de-select an icon, click anywhere except on the selected icon or its label. You cannot tell by looking at an icon, however, whether the container it represents is open or its document is in use.

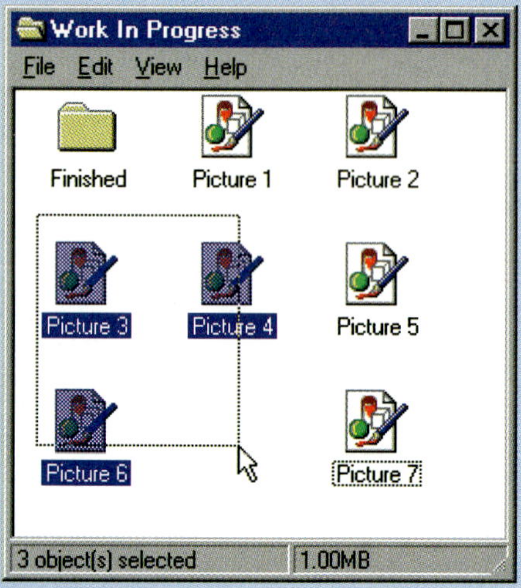

Selecting Multiple Icons

You may select more than one icon within the same window for various operations, such as copying to another disk, dragging to the `Recycle Bin`, or moving into a folder. There are many ways to select multiple icons, depending on the geography of the selection.

When the icons you wish to select are in widely different locations in a window, hold down the Control key while clicking once on each icon you wish to gather into the group.

For adjacent icons, there are two methods: **dragging** and **Shift-clicking.** To perform the dragging method, click and hold the mouse button at one corner of the rectangular area you intend to select (not on an icon), and drag the mouse until the selection rectangle (the dotted-line rectangle) encompasses the

Associations and Custom Icons

You can also setup more detailed associations via any Desktop window's `View` menu (`Options→File Types`). In this dialog (via the Edit button), you can even set a file with a particular extension to open with one program and print with another when activated from the Desktop/Explorer. If you don't like an icon for a particular file type, you can change it by choosing a new one from an application or other file that contains icons (.DLL files can contain icons, but you'll have to set Desktop views to show all files first). Any icon you choose affects all files with the same extension (but see about shortcut icons 115).

desired files—drag outside the window to **auto-scroll** the window while selecting more icons. As the selection rectangle encompasses at least one-half of the icon-plus-label area in the window, the enclosed icons highlight, indicating that you have successfully selected them in the grouping. Release the mouse button when all are selected. As an alternative, you can click once directly on the icon of one corner of the rectangular selection area, and Shift-click on the opposite corner.

Once multiple icons are selected, you can expand the current selection by Control-clicking on individual items or Shift-clicking to extend the current rectangle. Control-click on a single selected item to remove it from the group.

To select all icons in the frontmost window, simply choose `Select All` from the `Edit` menu, or type Control+A. The `Invert Selection` menu item applies to the entire window, selecting unselected items, and de-selecting currently selected items. To de-select an entire icon grouping, click anywhere except on one of the selected icons.

Dragging Icons

Once one or more icons are selected, you can click on and drag any of the highlighted icons to grab them all, even if some of the selected icons are not in view in the window. The **methods for dragging** a single icon apply to a group of selected icons as well. The basic actions you probably want to accomplish are:

- Moving the icon to another location in the same window (icon views only 86)
- Dragging the icon to another folder, disk, or `Recycle Bin` icon
- Dragging the icon to the Desktop

Each action has its own behavior associated with it, and much also depends on the type of item the icon represents.

Dragging a selection around its own window is simplified with auto-scrolling. If the window's scrollbar is active 96, then you can drag the icon into the area of the window to which you would normally scroll manually (**Auto-arrange** 96 must be turned off). For example, if an icon is at the bottom of the window and you wish to reposition it at the very top, drag the icon such that the arrow pointer is just above the active area of the window and keep holding the mouse button down. The window will scroll to bring the top into view. You cannot auto-scroll beyond the manual scrolling limits of the window.

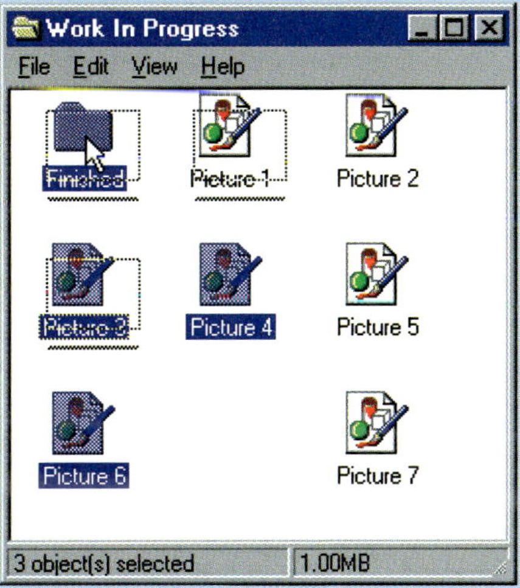

To move a selection into another folder, disk, or `Recycle Bin` icon, drag the selection and carefully position the arrow cursor atop the destination object. The destination object must highlight before you release the mouse button, and the pointer must not display as the **Unavailable** style 79. Only when the object highlights does it mean that it is selected as the destination. If you miss, the dragged icon will overlap the destination icon without going into it. You can combine the actions of auto-scrolling inside a window to reach a folder and dropping the icon into it. If you change your mind about the move, choose `Undo Move` from the `Edit` menu of any Desktop/Explorer window.

Finally, you may drag an icon to the Desktop layer. The Desktop's storage is only on the **boot disk** 74, so any items you drag there from other disks will become **shortcuts** 114 to the original items.

Renaming Icons

Every Windows Desktop/Explorer icon has a name attached to it. If `Long File Names` is turned on for your system 110, then a name can be up to 256 characters long.

Warning: Altering the names of existing folders and program items can cause shortcuts 114 to stop working and other program activities to be interrupted because you have disturbed path names 110.

The quickest editing of an icon's name is accomplished by clicking twice slowly (slower than a double-click) on the name. The icon's name becomes an **editable text field** 124, in which you can type a new name or make changes to the existing one. Press the Enter key or click outside the field to make the change stick.

Generic Document Icon

When Windows doesn't know what program to link to a document, it displays a generic document icon. You see a lot of these Windows icons in your root directory and nested all over the place. If you think a document should be associated with a particular program on you hard disk, you should establish that association. Windows will then assign that icon to all documents of the same type.

Establishing Icon Associations

The **Windows Registry** **maintains the links** between file name extensions and applications. If, for example, you have Excel installed, the Registry knows that all files with the .XLS extension belong to Excel and should bear the appropriate document icon. When there is no entry in the Registry for a particular extension, that item's icon reverts to the default Windows file icon (and the extension appears in the file name). To learn about associating an extension with a program 119.

Icons in Programs

You don't have to go far when working in Windows programs to see a host of icons within toolbars, palettes, or document windows. In many cases, these icons are merely buttons, which are activated by a single click of the pointer. Other times, as in many icons you see while cruising through Microsoft Network, you must double-click to initiate any action.

If you are unsure about a single- or double-click, you should be safe double-clicking any icon. No icon performs different actions with different numbers of clicks.

More disturbing, however, is double-clicking an icon in a communications program and nothing appears to happen right away. Sometimes there is a lag of a second or two before the Busy pointer appears. Be patient.

One of the most recognizable elements of the Windows 95 Desktop view is the Taskbar, which extends across the bottom of the screen.

The **Taskbar** has many purposes, but perhaps the most important of them is contained in the Start button, at the left edge of the bar. Clicking the Start button reveals a pop-up menu of programs and other actions you can begin without having to navigate through other folders and windows.

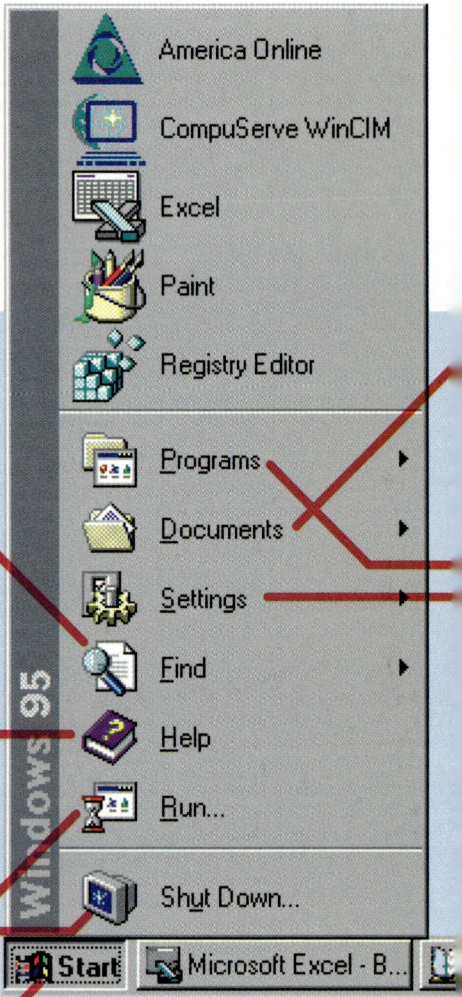

Taskbar Topography

Windows initially installs the Taskbar along the bottom of the Desktop, but you can drag it to **any screen edge** (nothing happens when you click and drag until the pointer nears an edge, when you see an outline of the destination). For some users, having the Start button at the top left of the screen may seem more natural. You may also **resize** the height (or width) of the bar by clicking and dragging the edge adjacent to the Desktop. While this gives you more space for buttons, it also means that the bar intrudes on Desktop area.

As items are added to the Taskbar, the buttons get smaller so that they can all fit on the bar. With a loaded Taskbar, you may see little more than the icon of the item.

The space at the far right can be reserved for various indicators, such as the current time, access to audio volume, and other items in various programs. These are controlled by switches in the programs and control panels, rather than by Taskbar settings.

Multiple User Profiles

When a Windows PC is set up to be available to more than one user, Windows stores many user preferences for each individual in a separate folder inside the Profiles folder. All of the Start menu's contents (Recent, Start Menu, Programs, Startup folder, etc.) are stored individually for each user. Paths to each of the user-specific items are stored in the Registry under `HKEY_CURRENT_USER→Software→Microsoft→WINDOWS→CurrentVersion→Explorer→Shell Folders`. All paths should begin the same way, pointing to items either in your Windows directory or in the directory of a particular user's profile. Do not let these paths point only to an important directory, such as the Windows directory: Windows will try to hide the entire contents of that window in the Desktop/Explorer.

Find

The `Find` menu item gives you a hierarchical menu, producing a further choice between searching for a computer on the network or looking for items (files and folders) on a disk connected to your PC. Windows' **file searching program** ➪116 is a valuable tool in **locating a file** on a large hard disk when you don't remember which folder the item is stored in. The program offers many choices to narrow the search and to display the search results.

Help

In case you don't know about the nearly universal `F1` function key that summons on-line help, the `Help` item in the Start menu leads you to the `Help Topics` window ➪78. This menu item is for **Windows help;** for help with an application, choose `Help Topics` from the `Help` menu in the program's window.

Shut Down

Before you turn off or reboot your PC, always choose `Shut Down` in the Start menu ➪10. This action makes sure that all **changed documents are saved,** and that Windows will open to the same arrangement of Desktop windows you have at that point.

Taskbar Properties

Aside from deciding which screen edge works best for your Taskbar, you can also choose between keeping the Taskbar as the **topmost layer** of all windows on the Desktop or letting other **windows overlap** the bar. On a 640-by-480 VGA screen, those 28 pixels are valuable real estate for document windows, so an overlap setting may be best. Or, you can elect to have the bar shrink to a mere two pixels in height whenever you work in a window. To redisplay the Taskbar when you need it, simply bring the pointer atop the two-pixel bar and drag upward. This setting (with the `Always On Top` also engaged) is a good compromise, unless you rely constantly on the clock or other controls at the right edge of the Taskbar.

Start Button

For many users, the Start button is like **home base** for working with programs and active documents. When in doubt about what to do next on the Desktop, click the Start button. At least you'll be able to access the **Windows Help** system if nothing else makes sense to you.

Run

There are many ways to start up a program in Windows ➪122. One that has a heritage going back to earlier versions of Windows is the Run dialog—the dialog now displayed when you choose `Run...` in the Start menu. The Windows 95 Run dialog also remembers the 25 **programs most recently started** from this window, available as a selection from the pop-up list in the entry field. Click the Browse... button to navigate through **folders** ➪110 to find other programs.

As you open windows and applications in Windows, buttons for those items are added to the Taskbar. Should a window or program you need be hidden by others, you can quickly find the desired item in the Taskbar. Clicking that item's button brings its window to the front.

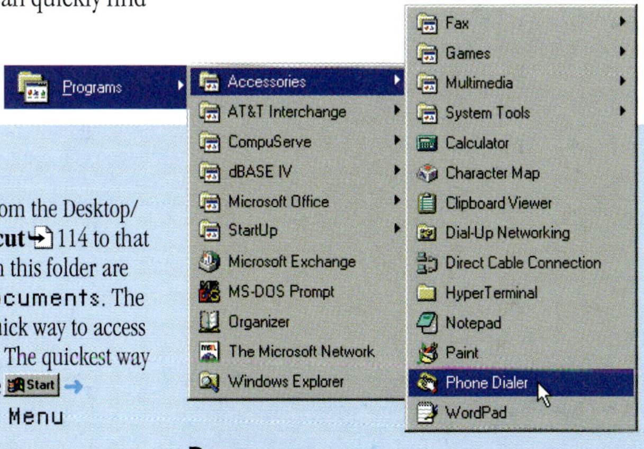

Documents

Each time you open a document from the Desktop/Explorer, Windows creates a **shortcut** 114 to that file in the `Recent` folder. Items in this folder are what appear in the submenu of `Documents`. The `Recent` folder is intended as a quick way to access files that you have recently opened. The quickest way to empty this list is to clear it via the Start → `Settings` → `Taskbar` → `Start Menu Programs` dialog box.

Programs

The submenu(s) to the `Programs` menu item are intended to act like a **table of contents** to the applications on your PC. During the Windows 95 upgrade installation, any Windows 3.x Program Manager groups are converted to entries in this menu, and Windows 95 includes some new items of its own at various levels. This menu gives you yet another way to organize and open your applications, independent of the Desktop/Explorer 76. As you install new Windows programs, they will likely make their own entries, which you will want to customize for the way you work.

Settings

Items in the `Settings` submenu lead to windows that let you adjust numerous **preferences** about the way Windows behaves and works. `Control Panel` and `Printers` items are the same as the like-named folders in `My Computer`. `Taskbar...` leads to a two-screen property sheet with many customizable settings for both the Taskbar and Start menu.

Shortcuts

Chances are that of all the programs on your hard disk, you use a handful of them regularly, if not daily. For convenience, you can install them in the Start menu, just above the `Programs` menu item. Although the icons don't look like it, the items are created by shortcuts 114 in the Start Menu folder. Here are the ways to get items there:

- Drag a Desktop/Explorer item icon to the Start button.
- Create a shortcut to a Desktop/Explorer item in the Start Menu folder.
- Use the wizard in the Start → `Settings` → `Taskbar` → `Start Menu Programs` screen.

You aren't limited to programs here: document files and folders to which you need constant access can also be placed here.

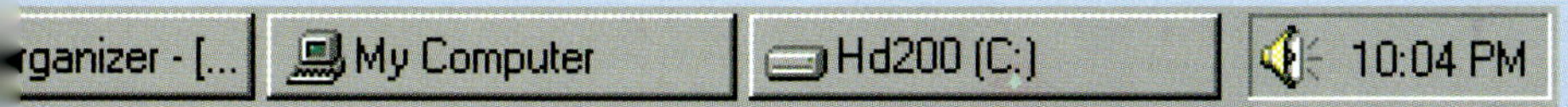

Customizing the Start Menu

If you feel that the large icons and Windows 95 advertising banner are more than necessary, you can **shrink the size** of the Start menu by opting to show only small icons in the Start menu (Start → `Settings` → `Taskbar` → `Taskbar Options`).

More importantly, the Start → `Settings` → `Taskbar` → `Start Menu Programs` screen provides wizards to help add and remove programs or files (but not folders) from the top of the Start menu or any of the Programs folders. The wizard is a version of the `Create Shortcut` wizard 114, with an added screen that lets you place the new shortcut in any allowable part of the Start menu.

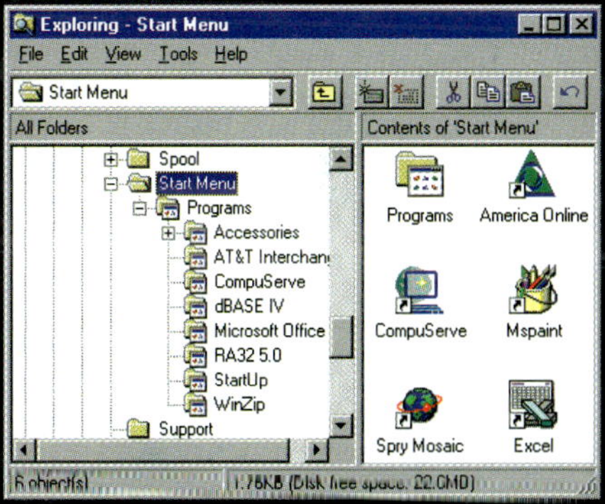

Where Is This Stuff?

Contents of the Start menu are scattered in a few places on your hard disk. The shortcuts listed in the `Documents` submenu are in a normally hidden folder (`Windows` → `Recent` for a single-user installation). Shortcuts to programs and contents of all the Programs folders are located in the Start Menu folder (in the Windows folder). You can massage their contents manually via the Desktop/Explorer. In fact, the advanced options button in the Start → `Settings` → `Taskbar` → `Start Menu Programs` screen leads to an Explorer window that is automatically opened to the Start Menu folder.

You will encounter three different types of menus in Windows 95: drop-down window menus, pop-up menus, and list menus. All three types require that you take an initial mouse button action to display the menu, move the pointer to the desired object, and then click the primary mouse button.

Drop-down menus are in the menubar of many types of windows. These menus let you control actions in the Desktop/Explorer or an application. Several elements of the menubar—the `File`, `Edit`, and `Help` menus—are consistent across virtually all applications, including the Desktop/Explorer. Yet, while most applications sport `File` and `Edit` menus, the contents of the menus vary from program to program.

Some programs also feature a variation of the drop-down menu called the **hierarchical menu**. A hierarchical menu item displays a right-pointing arrow at the right edge of the displayed menu. As you drag the mouse pointer atop this item, an additional submenu appears to the right.

Pop-up menus are most often displayed by **right-clicking** on objects. The menu pops onto the screen wherever the pointer is at the moment, and the items usually represent shortcuts to drop-down menu items.

Desktop/Explorer Menubar Anatomy

Many of the actions you perform in Desktop-type windows and the Explorer are the same, so it's no accident that the menubars of the two window styles have a lot in common. The Explorer window has one special menu, `Tools`, which brings together items available when using the Desktop. Unlike the Taskbar, a window's menubar pertains only to the contents of the window, and does not extend beyond the context of that window.

Accessing Standard Menus

To pull down a menu, use the mouse to position the arrow cursor atop the icon or text menu title in the menubar. Then click the left mouse button. A menu of choices—menu items—drops down from the menubar and stays down until you click somewhere outside the menu or touch another menu title in the same window with the pointer. You may drag the pointer left and right along the menubar to see what items are under each menu title.

With the mouse button either up or down, drag the pointer down so that the arrow stays within the area of the menu. As you position the pointer anywhere on a line containing a menu item, the item highlights, showing you what command or selection applies when you click or release the mouse button. Inactive dividing lines help the program author to group related menu items. To close the menu without making any menu selection, simply move the pointer outside the drop-down menu, and click or release the mouse button.

An **ellipsis** (...) at the end of a menu item means that the selection leads to a **dialog box** 88. It is common practice to explore a new program's depth by choosing these menu items to see what dialog box options are available. You can almost always cancel a dialog box, so you won't make any unexpected changes to a program or document by choosing ellipsis menu items.

When a menu item is preceded by a checkmark, it means that the item controls an on-off switch for some setting, and that the switch is on (e.g., a toolbar is visible in the window). Choosing the checked menu item will turn off the item.

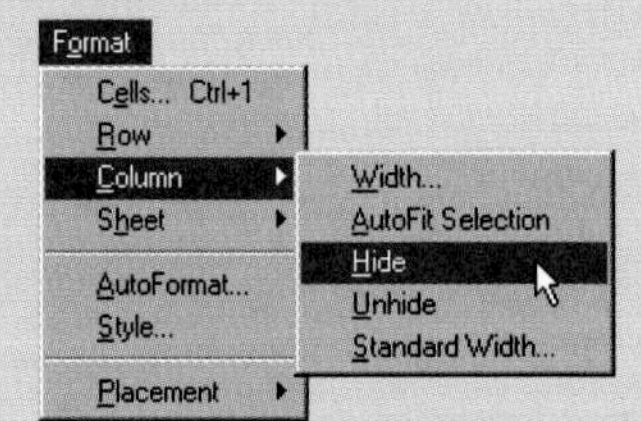

Hierarchical Menus

Some programs feature hierarchical menus, also called submenus. A menu item that displays a right-facing arrow at the right margin of the drop-down menu has a submenu connected to it. When you select the main menu item, its submenu appears to the side of the drop-down menu (to the right if space is available on screen; otherwise to the left). To access one of the submenu items, click on the main item to hold the submenu open; then click on the submenu item. Hierarchical menus are difficult for some users to access comfortably because of the steps required to make the submenu appear.

Keyboard Menu Activation

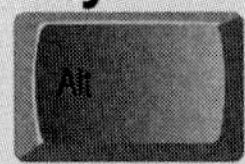

Pressing the Alt key always activates the menubar of the active window, providing you with keyboard access to any drop-down menu and menu item. In every menubar, a unique letter is underlined, signifying the letter you can type to display that menu. For example, in any Desktop window, pressing the Alt key (you can then release it) and the E key causes the `Edit` menu to drop down. Once a menu appears, you may then activate a menu item by typing its underlined letter. Once the menubar is activated by the Alt key (the `File` menu title highlights), you may also use the cursor keys to move the selection in any available direction. Pressing the Alt key a second time deactivates the menubar.

This method of keyboard activation is different from keyboard equivalents for specific menu items. You do not have to rely on the program's author to provide shortcuts to your frequent menu commands, nor do you have to remember the shortcuts (the underlined characters serve as ready legends). And, should you lose your mouse or need quick access to a laptop without a mouse, you can initiate any menu command from the keyboard.

Finally, in many toolbars ➔86 and dialog boxes ➔88 are **list menus**. They appear as text entry fields, but with a distinctive down arrow button at the right edge of the field. Clicking that button presents a list of items that can fill in the blank.

Keyboard Equivalents

The right margin of a drop-down menu is reserved for display of **keyboard function keys** or **key combinations** that perform the same action as choosing particular menu items with the mouse. These keyboard equivalents are often more efficient for frequently used commands if you are working primarily at the keyboard instead of with the mouse.

In addition to the clearly labeled function key equivalents (e.g., F3), you will see many items that require two or more keys being pressed at the same time, designated by the plus symbol between them. The first key to press is always a **modifier** key ➔14, such as the Control key (Ctrl). To issue the menu command Ctrl+N, for example, hold down the Control key and press N (while letters are shown as capital letters, the unshifted character is what you type). Control key equivalents common to many Windows 95 programs are:

File Menu		Edit Menu	
Ctrl+N	New	Ctrl+Z	Undo
Ctrl+O	Open	Ctrl+X	Cut
Ctrl+S	Save	Ctrl+C	Copy
Ctrl+P	Print	Ctrl+V	Paste
Alt+F4	Exit	Ctrl+A	Select All

If two modifier keys are shown, then hold both keys and type the remaining character.

The Window Menu

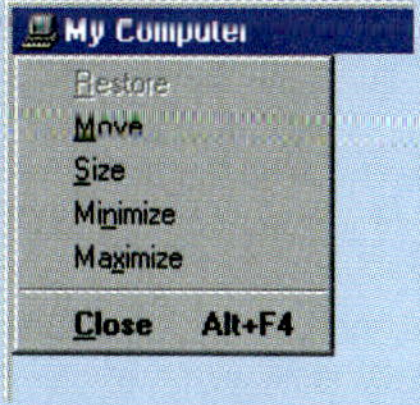

Hidden from view in every Windows 95 window is a menu for controlling various physical aspects of the window ➔86. A holdover from Windows 3.x, the window menu is accessible by mouse only in windows that have icons in their upper left corners. Click the icon to view the window's options, most of which are there for the convenience of non-mouse users. Dialog windows also have these hidden menus, but with options only for moving and closing. The quickest way to access this menu from the keyboard in any window style is Alt+Spacebar.

Right-click Pop-up Menus

Whenever in doubt about what choices are available

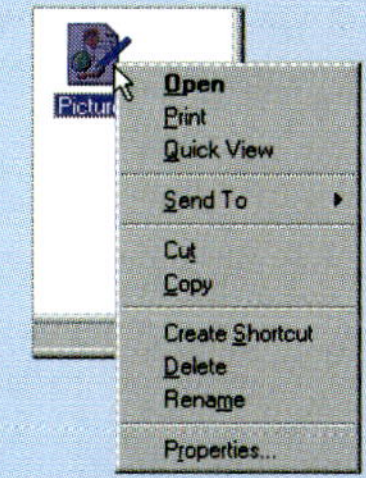

for any object or surface you see on the screen (especially in Desktop/Explorer areas), right-click on the object. A menu appears adjacent to the pointer. These menus can contain submenus, just like menubar menus, and you choose items the same way. To hide a pop-up menu without taking any action, click anywhere outside the area of the menu.

List Menus

Another style of menu that appears inside dialog boxes and program windows is most often used as a way to let you choose from a list of settings or possible entries for a text field. Such fields are identified by the down arrow button at the right edge of the field. Clicking that arrow button makes the list menu appear. The current setting is highlighted in the menu (and the list scrolled to the selected item, if scrolling is necessary). The field is usually editable, so you can type in the information if you like, but selecting from the list is usually easier.

Desktop/Explorer File Menu

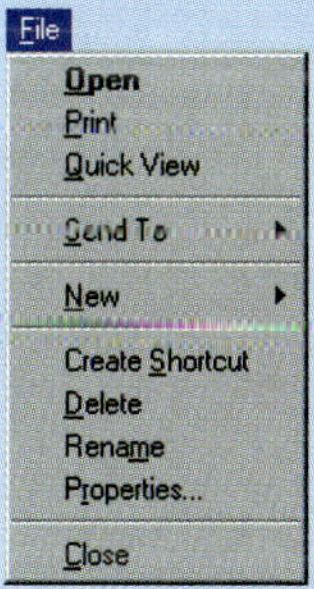

Items in the Desktop/Explorer's `File` menu relate to organizing files and folders stored on your disk. The precise contents of the menu changes depending on the type of item (if any) selected in the window. Registered document file types ➔119 have more options for opening, viewing, and printing than unregistered file types, folders, and program files. Because some menu items require selections of files or folders, those items may be dimmed when no selections are made.

Desktop/Explorer Edit Menu

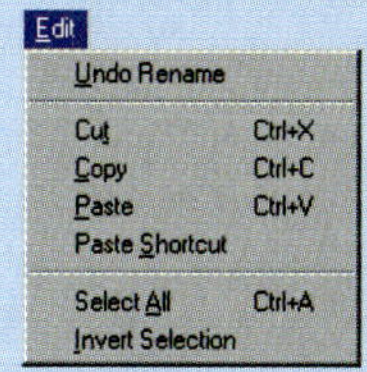

Actions of the Desktop/Explorer's `Edit` menu items assist in selecting items and manipulating selected items for duplication or moving to other folder windows (there are other, non-menu ways of accomplishing the same tasks). `Cut`, `Copy`, and `Paste` work on actual file and folder objects you see in the windows. `Undo`'s exact name changes depending on the most recent action that Windows can take back for you (e.g., `Undo Move`) ➔113.

Desktop/Explorer View Menu

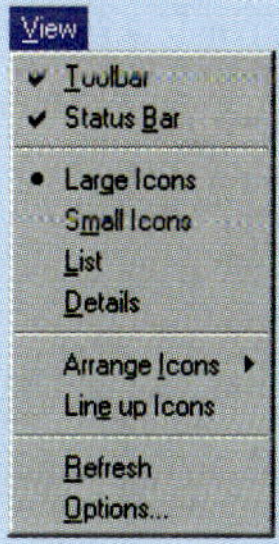

The `View` menu is the way for you to control the way the current Desktop/Explorer window is to display file and folder items. Some items affect all windows, while others apply only to the current window. See ➔96 for guidance on file views.

Explorer Tools Menu

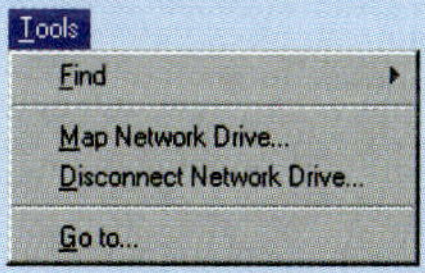

Available only in the Explorer, the `Tools` menu contains navigation shortcuts and network server connectivity control. For Desktop window users, most of these menu items are available in other places, such as the Start menu and the right-click menu of `My Computer`.

Desktop/Explorer Help Menu

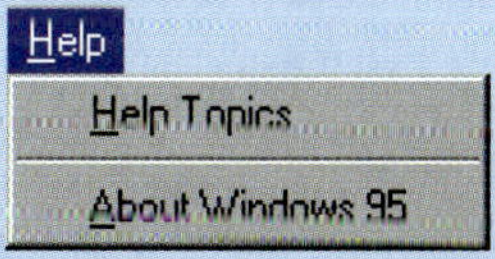

The first item in the `Help` menu leads directly to the Windows Help system ➔78. You are brought to the top of the Help system (in either Contents or Index view, whichever you used last), so the help is not context-sensitive. The last item in all `Help` menus displays the About window for the application. From the Desktop/Explorer, the information is about Windows, revealing version number, copyright, license information, and available resources.

A computer window is much like a real-life window—you look through an opening to see some or all of another space.

For example, when viewing a text document in a window, you essentially look through the window to see as much of the entire document as fits in the opening on the screen. To see other parts of the document, you manipulate **scrollbars** or other devices to shift the item "behind" the window.

Windows 95 windows come in a variety of styles, and may overlap one another on the screen. In most circumstances, only one window—the window nearest to you—can be active at any instant. Clicking anywhere on a window brings that window to the foreground, making it the **active window.** To reduce window clutter when many applications are open at the same time, you can **minimize** any window. The window will disappear, but its corresponding button remains in the Taskbar; click the button once to see the window at its previous size.

Desktop Window Anatomy

Because Desktop windows have much in common with windows you often find in application programs, most of the details here apply to both.

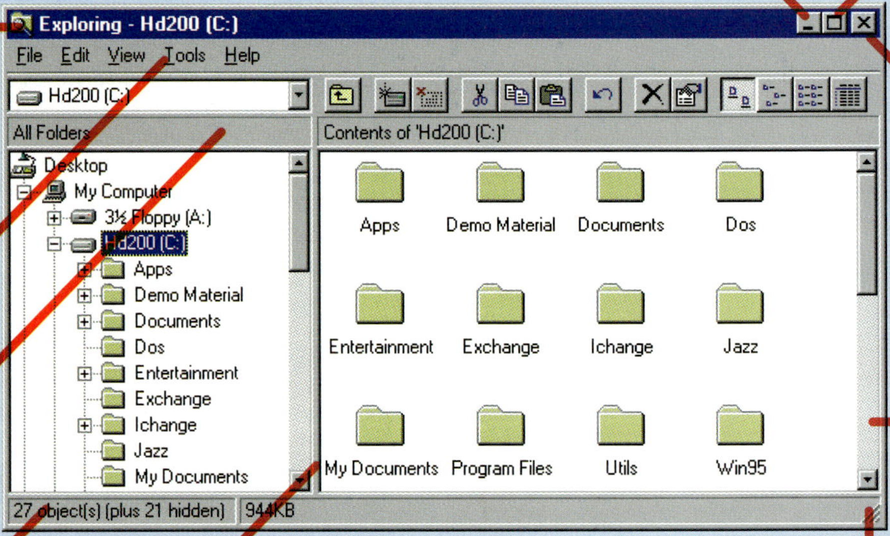

Title Bar

A window's title bar displays the name of the item whose contents you see in the window. In the Desktop, that may be a **disk volume or folder name;** in an application, the name is of the file containing the document (Untitled for a new file that has not yet been named and saved) plus the name of the application. **Drag** the title bar to move an entire window. Double-clicking the title bar is the same as clicking the maximize button.

Menubar

Desktop/Explorer and application windows have menus 84 that pertain to the window contents.

Description Bar

Explorer windows and some other programs provide labels for multiple window panes. To turn off Explorer's description bar, choose View→Options→View, and uncheck the last checkbox.

Status Bar

An optional strip along the bottom of Desktop/Explorer windows provides information about the **contents of the window** or selected objects. The left side always shows the number of objects (or selected objects); the right side displays the item sizes in bytes (but folder contents are not counted).

Moving Windows

In addition to resizing a window by dragging its corners or borders, you may move a window around the screen by clicking on its title bar and dragging. An outline of the window follows the cursor. When you release the mouse button, the window is redrawn at the position of the outline.

Tool Bar

Many windows let you show an area that provides **shortcut buttons** to frequently accessed menu and dialog box items.

Pane Divider

In multi-paned windows, dividing bars are usually draggable to let you adjust the relative sizes of the panes 76.

Horizontal Scroll Bar

When there is more in the horizontal plane than can appear in the window, the elements of a horizontal scroll bar appear at the bottom of the screen.

Minimize Button

Clicking here **hides the window** in the corresponding button on the Taskbar. To restore the window to its former size, click the button in the Taskbar.

Resize Edges and Corners

↔ ↕ ⤡ ⤢

All four edges and corners may be dragged to resize the window. Look for the pointer to change to a double-arrow showing the possible directions you can drag an edge or corner. Release the mouse button to let the window redraw itself at the new size.

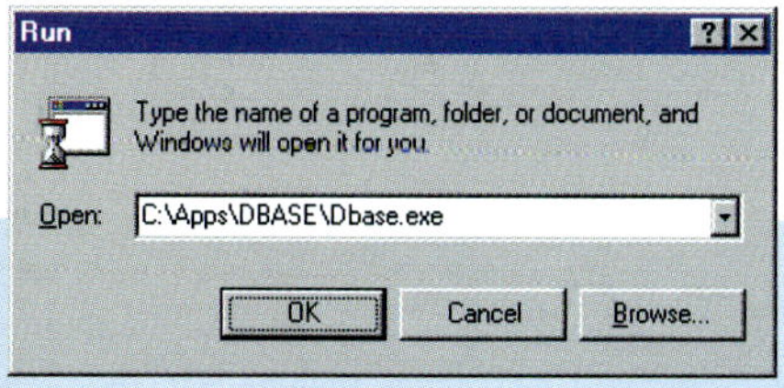

Dialog Window Style

In addition to the Desktop/`Explorer` type of window, you will often see a fixed-size window: a dialog window ➜88. Corners and borders are not draggable, nor can the window be minimized (or accessed via the Taskbar). A help button ➜89 lets you query the function or operation of individual items in the window. Dialog boxes of older programs may not let you activate other windows while they display, forcing you to take action or cancel the dialog.

Maximize Button

If you want the window to occupy the **entire screen**, click this button when it looks like a single window icon. In **full-screen mode**, the button icon shows two overlapping windows. Clicking on that style of button restores the window to its previous resizable, draggable smaller window.

Close Button

Clicking the upper right button closes the window. In Desktop windows, this is the same as activating a window and choosing `Close` from the `File` menu. Windows remember their own sizes when they close, so when you reopen them later, they appear at the same location and size as before. Holding down the Shift key while clicking this button closes all Desktop windows up the hierarchy to `My Computer`.

Vertical Scroll Bar

When there is more in the window than can be seen through it, the scroll bar becomes active. Consisting of five parts—up arrow, down arrow, page up area, page down area, and the scroll box—the vertical scroll bar allows you to **shift the contents** of the window vertically to see items not currently visible. Clicking the arrows scrolls the view in small increments; clicking the page areas causes larger jumps. You may click and hold arrows and page areas to get repeat action scrolling.

The scroll box represents the relative location of the current view within the entire vertical distance of the window's contents, as well as the relative size of the view compared to the entire document: a small scroll box means the view is of a small portion of a large document; a large scroll box indicates that you are seeing most of the document in a single view. Drag the scroll box in either direction to jump to an approximate location in the window's contents, watching the contents shift as you drag.

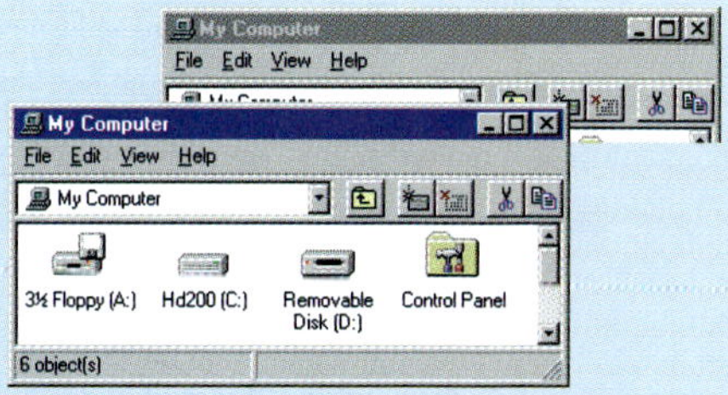

Active vs. Inactive Windows

On the Desktop, only one window may be active at a time. **Activate a window** by clicking anywhere within its visible rectangle, or clicking its Taskbar button. You can recognize an active window (in default color schemes ➜34) by the dark color band in the title bar and white lettering of the window name. An inactive window lacks the color bar, and the window name is in black.

Keeping Windows Clean

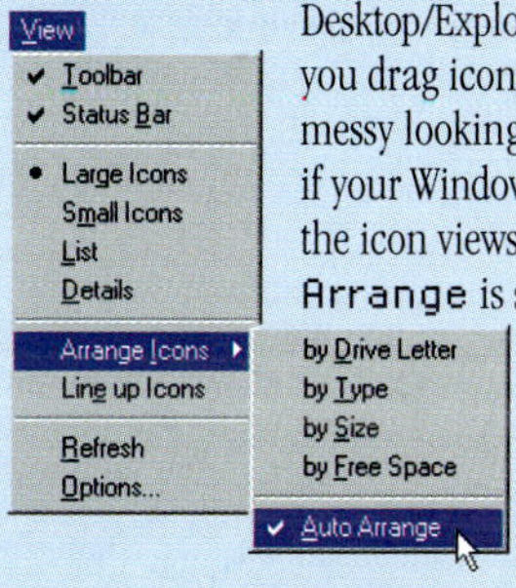

Desktop/Explorer windows that let you drag icons around can get messy looking from time to time if your Windows 95 is set to one of the icon views ➜96 and `Auto Arrange` is switched off. With these settings, you are free to group and organize icons (large and small) around the window as you see fit. If you want a free-form organization to clean itself just enough so that all items are aligned to the nearest point of an invisible grid, then choose Line up Icons from the `View` menu. This action may shift some icons a few pixels, but leaves empty spaces if that's the way you want it.

To cinch up all icons just one time, choose any of the first four items in the `View`→`Arrange Icons` submenu. You determine whether the items should be sorted by name, type, size, or modification date (but all folders come before files in any case). If you want Windows to keep your icons cinched up toward the top left corner of the window, then switch on `Auto Arrange` in the `View`→`Arrange Icons` submenu. When this item is checked, no matter how you drag an icon around the window, it will fly back into formation. The order isn't automatic for icon-only views ➜96: you must choose from the Arrange Icons submenu after the drag to make sure everything is in the desired order. All settings for the `Arrange Icons` submenu affect only the current window—it will open to these specifications next time.

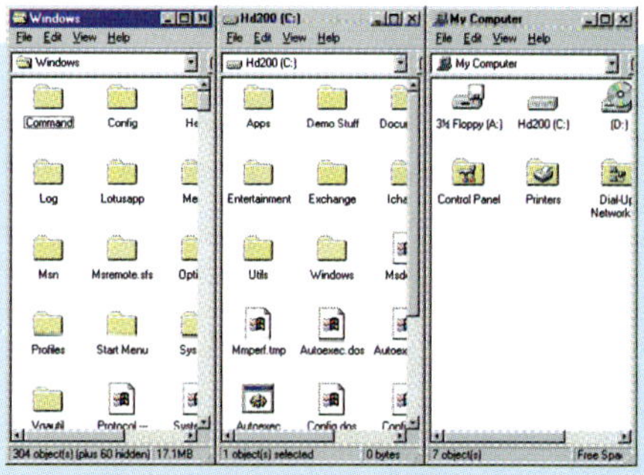

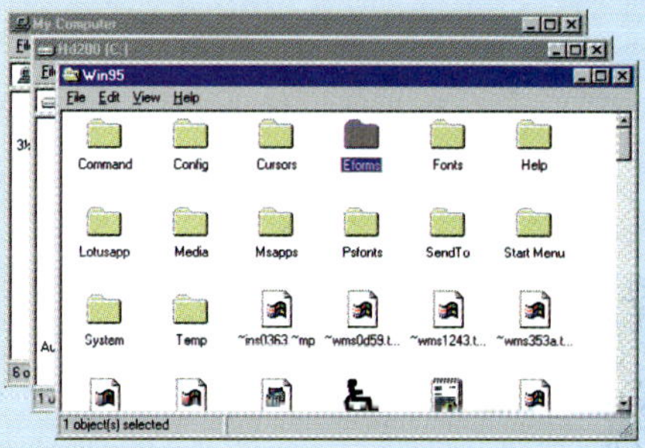

Organizing Window Layers

Most Windows programs, including the Desktop/Explorer, remember the size and location of a window just before it last closed. Depending on the size of your screen and the number and sizes of open windows, you can choose from two primary methods of organizing windows: **cascading** (overlapping) and **tiling**. Cascading windows resemble pieces of paper on a desk, where one item might cover some or all of other items, with one item definitely on the topmost layer. Tiled windows are adjacent to each other, such that you can see the entire window opening of all windows at once (although only one window is active).

Windows will automatically cascade or tile windows for you if you like. Right-click on the Taskbar (between buttons if the bar is full) to display the pop-up menu. Choose the desired organization method. This choice affects all visible windows, including programs, and Windows resizes the windows to equal rectangles. Unfortunately, these actions cover the left column of Desktop icons, so you may want to organize your windows manually.

Remember, too, that you can reduce the number of open Desktop windows. In the `View`→`Options`→`Folder` property sheet, select the choice for browsing folders in only one window whose view changes as you open or close folders. In this window form, the Toolbar is highly recommended to assist in navigating through your folder organization ➜111.

A window that appears on the screen but doesn't have a menubar in it is called a dialog box—as in a dialog between the user and computer.

Some dialog boxes (or just "dialogs") do little more than alert you to an important step you're about to take or perhaps signal an error message. A friendly alert is a dialog that tells you that an action has been completed (e.g., transferring a file to another computer). Clicking the lone OK button in the alert indicates to the program that you acknowledge the message—and the dialog box goes away. A more helpful dialog is one that warns you of impending danger (e.g., you are about to overwrite an existing file on your disk). With this kind of alert, a choice of two buttons (usually OK and Cancel) lets you tell the program whether it should go ahead or cancel the request.

A more complex dialog box, on the other hand, usually offers many choices in the form of buttons, list menus, and text entry fields. In these dialogs, you choose from various settings or preferences that are to apply to a selected chunk of text, the current window, or the entire document, depending on the nature of the dialog box. You can usually predict when this type of dialog box will appear, because it comes in

Cancel/No Buttons

A Cancel option generally means that nothing has yet changed (e.g., no installation has taken place), so that a click of the button returns you to the state before the alert appeared. When you see both Cancel a and a No button, consider the question in the message carefully: Cancel returns you to the previous state, while No usually means that a process will continue, but with some setting based on the No selection. Whenever a dialog box indicates progress (e.g., copying a folderful of documents), clicking the Cancel button interrupts the process, leaving the task only partially completed.

The Alert Message

This may be in the form of a **question or a simple statement.** If there are no buttons in the alert, then the box will go away by itself (e.g., the **"splash screen"** you see when you start a program) or else requires a mouse click to clear.

OK/Yes/Continue/Retry Button

This button responds in the **affirmative** to any question presented in the alert. If this button is the only one showing, then the alert is generally telling you that something has already happened. A dialog with a Retry button gives you a chance to rectify some problem (e.g., a missing disk or an empty printer paper tray) before trying the action again.

Tabs

Many dialog boxes include tabs that lead to different screens within the same window. Click on the tab of the category of the desired setting. When two or more rows of tabs appear, the row you click becomes the front row.

Item Grouping

A labeled border around items is another way to help you understand which **settings are related** within a complex dialog box.

Checkbox Button Grouping

Checkbox buttons allow you to select or deselect any **combination of items** in the group. Occasionally, checkbox items in a group will be mutually exclusive or inclusive, meaning that a click of one item automatically affects the setting of another item in the - same group.

List Menu

The down-pointing black arrow indicates that a **pop-up list** contains applicable items for the field. Click on the arrow to show the list. The currently chosen item is highlighted in the list. If the list is a long one, scrollbars may appear at the right edge of the list. Click once on any item in the list to insert it into the field.

Modal vs. Modeless Dialogs

The majority of dialog boxes you encounter in Windows 95 are **modeless** meaning that while they are displayed, you may switch to other programs or other windows within the same program without any harm. Some dialogs, however, take over control, causing the **Critical Stop** sound 146 to play if you click anywhere but in the dialog. You must close these dialogs before continuing.

Keyboard Shortcuts

The keyboard usually gives you great control in an active dialog window. Pressing the Tab key advances the focus through individual items within the dialog: field text highlights, the first button of a button grouping highlights (with a shaded rectangle around or inside it), and pop-up lists highlight. With the first item of a button grouping highlighted, press the down or right arrow keys to advance to other buttons within the group. A button that has focus responds to the Spacebar as if clicked with the pointer; a slider can be adjusted with the arrow keys. When a list is activated, you may press the up and down arrow keys to advance through the possible selections. Also, you can often jump to your selection in the list by typing the first letter of item (if there are multiple items beginning with the same letter, continue typing the letter until the desired selection appears).

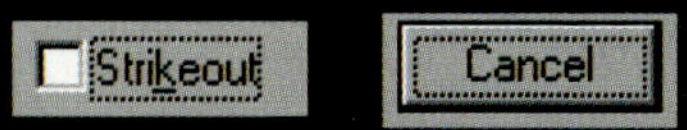

In some field and button labels, an underline marks a unique character; holding the Alt key while typing the marked character activates that item.

response to a click of a button (with text on the button) or a menu choice ending in an ellipsis (three periods). In fact, if you want to explore the depth of a new program, choose all menu items with ellipses, and study the resulting dialog boxes for choices they offer.

Button Leading to Another Dialog

Settings... Just like the button or menu item that led you to the current dialog, the **ellipsis** at the end of this button's name means that a click of it will take you to another level of dialog box, usually overlaying the current one. Depending on the design, closing the subdialog may either bring you back to the previous dialog or close them both. Don't be surprised to find yourself three or four dialog windows deep in some areas.

Help Button

When you click this button, the pointer turns into a **help pointer.** Click the pointer on any item in the dialog to see **pop-up help** info about its function or action.

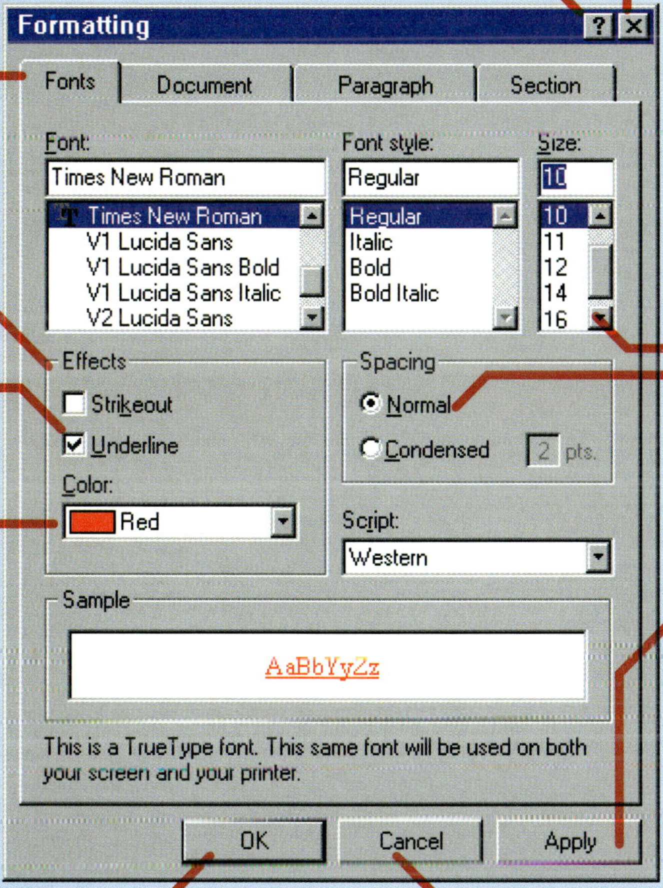

OK Button

A click of this button tells the program you wish the **current settings** in the dialog to take effect. When a **black border** surrounds this button (or any button in a dialog or alert), it means that pressing the Enter key is a keyboard shortcut to clicking the button with the pointer.

Close Button

This is the same button as appears in other windows. Its action is the same as clicking the dialog's Cancel button.

Dimmed Item

Buttons and fields that don't apply to the current settings may be **dimmed** or **"grayed out"** to indicate that they are **not available.** Clicking on or tabbing to a dimmed item has no effect.

Radio Button Grouping

Radio buttons are always **mutually exclusive** within a group—only one may be selected (and usually one **must** be selected).

Apply Button

In some programs, this button lets you apply the current settings to the selection or document underneath the dialog. Thus, you can **experiment** with variations in settings without repeatedly opening and closing the dialog box.

Cancel Button

None of the changes to settings in the dialog box will take effect when you cancel the dialog. This lets you change your mind before clicking the OK button. In many dialog boxes, pressing the Escape key is the same as clicking the Cancel button.

Editable Field

Enter requested text into entry fields. Entry fields may already contain information when the dialog opens. Because these fields can be longer than what shows in the field rectangle (they can be scrolled horizontally), the text already in the field may contain more than you realize. It is always best to select the text in the entire field and type new text to replace it. The safest way to do this is to press the Tab key to advance the **focus** of the dialog from object to object. When focus reaches a field that has text in it, the entire text is automatically selected. Whatever you type next replaces all of the selected text (no need to delete first).

Scrolling Text Field

Scrolling text fields may be editable, but in dialog boxes they are most often used to present **lists of choices.** Clicking once on an item selects it (perhaps marking with a checkmark or inserting the text into an associated one-line field). A double-click on a single selection in some dialogs is the same as choosing the item and clicking the OK button. Where applicable, you may also be able to Shift-click to select a contiguous range of items in a list or Control-click to select individual items scattered throughout the list—these actions fall under the term **multiple selections.**

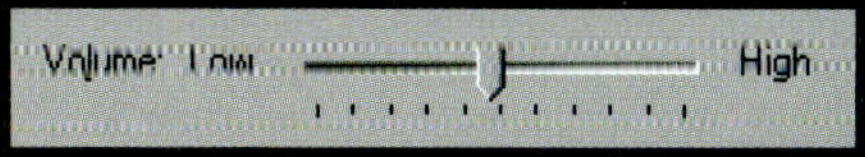

Other Dialog Controls

Slider controls (like the volume settings in the Multimedia control panel) are relatively common in Windows. Advanced graphics programs may provide controls for spinning graphical objects along three-dimensional axes or adjusting their perspective.

The more specialized the requirement, the less standardized the control. Since you're not likely to read a program's manual at first, experiment by clicking and dragging on anything you see in a dialog. With a well-designed program, you should be able to figure out most of what's going on.

A special kind of dialog box—the file dialog box—assists you in opening and saving documents while you are in applications.

Opening and saving actions display two variations on the file dialog box theme. In the Open file dialog, you simply select a document; in the Save As file dialog, you must enter a name for a file before it is stored on the disk.

Both types of file dialogs, however, share hard disk navigation procedures so you can open or save a document in a specific folder on any disk or network server volume normally visible from the Desktop. In fact, the view of all volumes in file dialogs starts at the Desktop—the most global view of volumes connected to your PC and mounted.

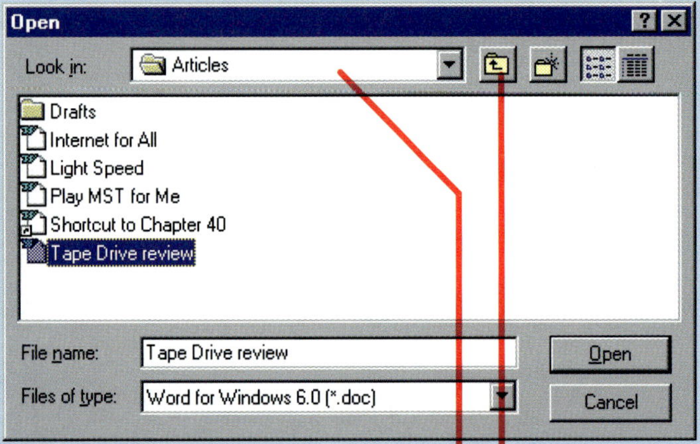

Open File Dialog

Whenever you choose `Open` from a Windows 95 application's `File` menu, you see the Open file dialog box. The most basic version consists of a scrolling field beneath a pop-up list, several buttons, and a pop-up list of file formats ➔ 126. Open file dialogs tend to show files at the disk or folder level of either the application or the last file opened or saved.

Older Windows applications will show the Windows 3.x style of Open file dialog, which is more cumbersome to work with and displays only MS-DOS short file names for documents and folders (directories).

List of Files

This large field displays a list of **openable items** inside the container named in the field just above it. Containers (e.g., disk drives and folders) always appear in the list when available, but files are usually filtered according to their file type, as chosen in the file type pop-up list (below).

If you open a container (double-clicking on its line in the scrolling list is the fastest way), you will see icons for folders and document files in that container. Open folders as needed to wend your way to a document. Some graphics applications allow you to see a miniature preview of a file's contents in the Open dialog by selecting the document in this list.

The keyboard offers a shortcut to locating a file in a long list. Press the Tab key until the first item activates (a dotted line appears around its name). Then type the first character of the document name you want, and Windows scrolls the list to the first item that starts with that letter. Type the letter again to advance to the next item starting with that letter.

Next Higher Level Button

Clicking this button changes the current container to the folder one level closer to the Desktop (the **parent** of the current folder). You may continue clicking this button until you reach the Desktop.

Current Container

The name of the container (e.g., disk, folder) that holds the items in the list of files appears in this field. If you want to navigate quickly to a different disk volume (or network container), display the pop-up list, and click on the desired item.

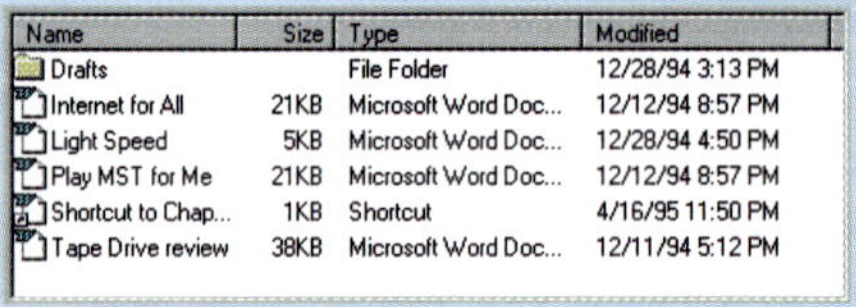

List/Details Views Buttons

These buttons let you alter the way items are displayed in the list of files. In List view, Windows displays item names with small icons such that you typically see as many as 28 items at one glance. As in the Desktop/Explorer, the Details view provides a columnar listing so you can see each item's name, size (if it's a file), file type, and modification date. Clicking on any of the four column headers, you can change the sorted order of items to help you locate the one you want.

File Name Field

As you select a document file from the list of files, its name appears in this field. If you like, you may type the name of an existing item in the current folder, although pointing and clicking is usually faster.

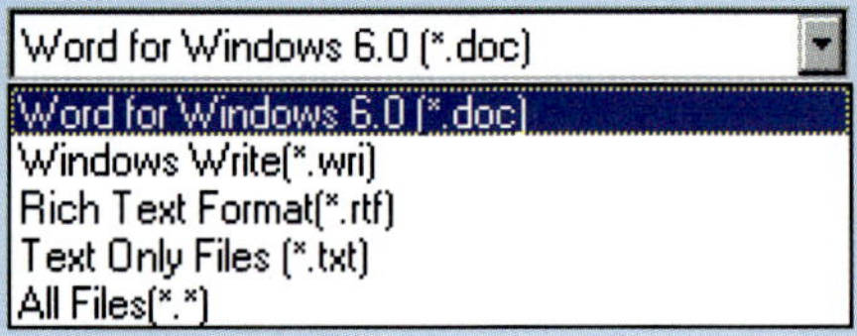

File Type List

Windows applications can open only those documents saved by the program or those that the program knows how to convert. The mechanism for accomplishing this—**file name extension**—is the same as that used for managing file associations ➔ 119. Therefore, when an application can convert files of other formats, those formats are listed here both in plain English and by the extension (with the asterisk wildcard placeholder for the file name). When you choose a format, only files of that format appear in the list, no matter where you navigate around your hard disk.

The pop-up list of formats usually includes one called `All Files`. This will show all visible files in the selected container. Just because a file is listed doesn't mean that the program will be able to open it. For example, a word processing file may not know what to do with a spreadsheet file (but see ➔ 128 about embedding OLE objects of other types in documents).

Not all open and save dialogs are alike, however. Programmers have extraordinary latitude in adding elements that make the most sense for their programs. Microsoft Office programs, for example, let you search for a desired file from within the Open file dialog.

Open Button

You may either double-click an item in the file listing to open it, or click it once to select the item and click the Open button.

Cancel Button

To close the Open File dialog without opening a document, click the Cancel button. In most programs, the original path is restored as the default path for the next time you try to open a document. The X button (upper right corner) performs the same action as the Cancel button.

File Name Field

A program may insert a default document name for a new document (e.g., "Document"), but you can type anything you want up, to 256 characters long, in Windows 95 (32-bit) applications. Do not enter the file name extension into this field—the program does that automatically based on the file type selected in the pop-up list below.

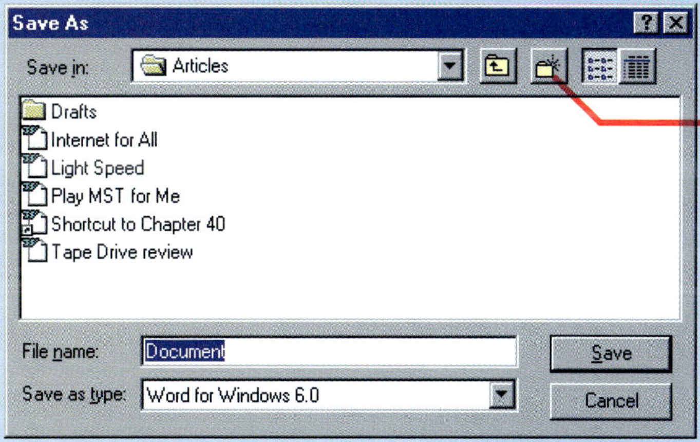

New Folder Button

When you need to save a document to a folder not yet in existence, click this button. The new folder goes into the folder level showing in the file list, ready for its name to be entered.

Save File Types

Don't be surprised if the list of file type conversions for saving documents is different from the one for opening documents. Many programs like to accept documents from other programs, but save them only in their own format or some universal format, such as Rich Text Format, Bitmap, or SYLK.

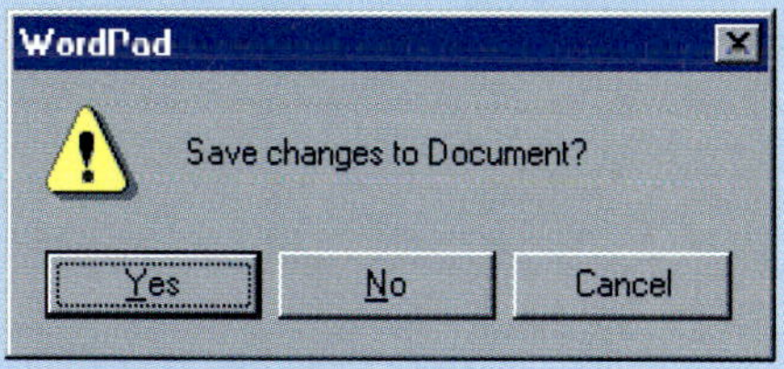

Save Changes Dialog

If you try to **close a document** or quit an application without saving your last changes, you will likely see a three-button alert box asking you about what to do with those changes. Yes is the default button. Press Enter to save the file to disk. Cancel stops everything, returning you to the document without closing it. The No button closes the document without saving the changes. This action cannot be undone, so consider wisely before

Save As File Dialog Box

All navigation possibilities of the `Open` file dialog box apply to the `Save As` file dialog box. In this case, you navigate through levels to find a folder into which the current document is to be saved.

Save Button

This button's label changes to Open if you select a folder in the file list. It reverts to Save when you enter a name for the file.

List of Files

For file saving, you normally access this list only to open a folder to reach another level for the new document. But if you select an existing item, its name is inserted into the `File name` field, and you will be asked about overwriting the existing file. If that's your intent, then proceed; but read the alert message carefully so that you fully understand what you're about to replace.

Advanced File List Items

While the Open and Save File dialogs are modal within the program that generates them, you still have the same control over the listed files and folders as you do in the Desktop/Explorer.

Provided the Recycle Bin is visible, you can drag individual items there. Moreover, the complete complement of right-click options are available here as well, including getting a Quick View and printing.

Effective use of the Clipboard can boost your productivity with Windows 95→103. After a while, the Clipboard will become second nature, especially when used with the convenient keyboard equivalents of the Cut, Copy, and Paste commands from the Edit menu.

The Clipboard is constructed to meet requirements of new programs and types of information. Demands today have far outstripped the text and graphic information of early PC applications. In some programs, you can cut, copy, and paste sounds, animation, and even video movies. **It's still important to remember that the Clipboard is erased upon shutdown.**

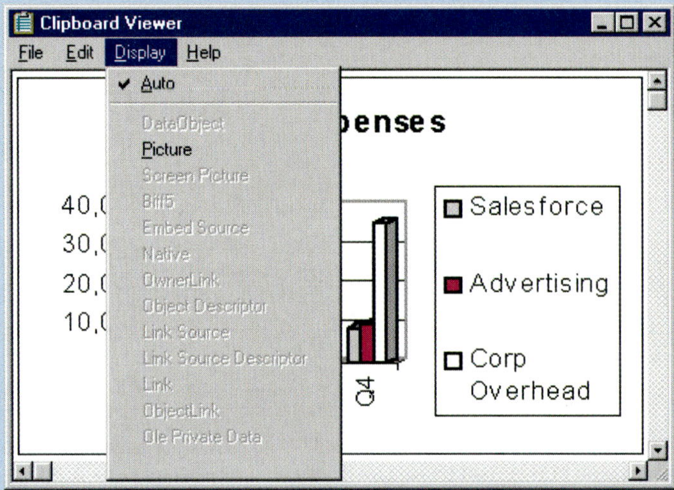

Efficient Keyboarding

A vital component of using the Clipboard efficiently is mastery of the keyboard equivalents of the Cut, Copy, and Paste items in the Edit menu. While their keyboard letters, X, C, and V, may not make mnemonic sense, notice that the letters are all in a row at the bottom left of the U.S. keyboard. Common manipulation of information is to select an item from a document with the mouse in the right hand, and then perform the cut or copy on the keyboard with the left hand (bias for righties, to be sure). Similarly, for pasting, position the pointer where needed and then press Control+V with the left hand. In the same vicinity is Control+Z for undoing an erroneous cut or paste.

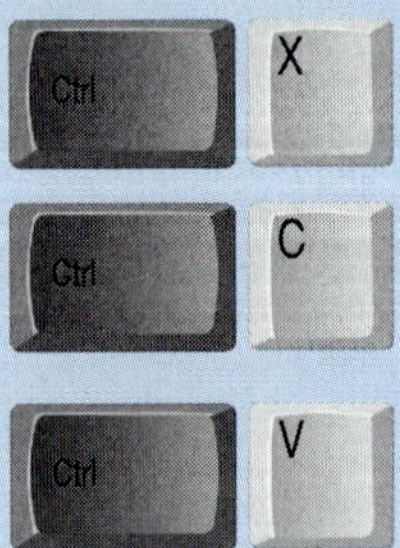

Cut

Copy

Paste

Pasting Special

Some programs have an extr Paste command in their Edit menus: Paste Special. Exactly what this does depends on the contents of the **Clipboard**, but it highlights a point about the Clipboard: When you copy a selected chunk of data into the Clipboard, the Clipboard can contain a lot of information about that chunk. The Paste Special typically allows you to paste certain aspects of that chunk. For example, in a spreadsheet program, if you copy a cell into the Clipboard, you can choose to paste any combination of the plain value, the formula, and the format of the original cell. This is also how to **link** or **embed** information from other programs→128.

Viewing Clipboard Contents

While the Clipboard can hold only one item at a time, you may forget what's in there if you've been copying and pasting a lot. Only a few programs let you view the Clipboard from within the program. Fortunately, one Windows 95 accessory program is the Clipboard Viewer, which displays a window showing the contents of the Clipboard.

Preserving Clipboard Contents

Via the Clipboard Viewer, you may save the current Clipboard contents to a file (.CLP extension). This will allow you to open the file and stuff its contents back into Clipboard memory at a later time (use the Open File menu item in the Clipboard Viewer).

Clipboard Data Types

The Clipboard Viewer window tends to show the simplest representation of Clipboard data (Auto Format). But if you open the Display menu, you will often see a number of other formats in which to view this data (active items in the menu). The data types available in the list depend on the program from which the data was copied into the Clipboard in the first place. A saved Clipboard file retains all the data types associated with the Clipboard data.

Recycle Bin

Recycle Bin

Living up to the desktop-as-metaphor guideline of the Windows 95 interface, one way to erase a file from a disk is to drag it to an iconic waste-basket, called the Recycle Bin.

Just as in the real world, if you change your mind about something you throw in the wastebasket, you can rummage through the discarded items to retrieve it—as long as you haven't emptied the bin. Once you empty the `Recycle Bin`, the file is gone (although third-party file recovery programs may be able to rescue it from the city dump).

The `Recycle Bin` does not automatically empty itself when you shut down or restart. On the one hand, this means that you have to think about your garbage more often; on the other hand, it means that you can change your mind about a discarded item many days later.

Getting Items into the Bin

Windows offers numerous ways to dump an item (file or folder) into the `Recycle Bin`. You are free to use any combination of methods that meets your needs.

From any Desktop/Explorer window, you can drag one or more selected items to the `Recycle Bin` icon on the Desktop—provided you can see it. Windows is smart enough to recognize that some files are either applications or potentially important operating system files, and will ask you to confirm that you want to delete the item.

When the `Recycle Bin` icon is not visible, you can also select items to delete and then choose `Delete` from either the `File` menu or the right-click pop-up menu. With this method, Windows inserts a dialog box asking you to confirm the deletion of the items.

As more programs are designed to work specifically with Windows 95, you will be able to drag more document objects directly to the `Recycle Bin` icon, rather than dealing with the `Cut` or `Clear` items in the `Edit` menu.

Emptying the Bin

Whenever something is in the bin, the icon shows crumpled paper bulging out the top. To empty the bin, choose `Empty Recycle Bin` from the right-click pop-up menu on the `Recycle Bin` icon. The default behavior of this menu item is to remind you of how many items are about to be dumped.

Retrieving from the Bin

Recycle Bin

Before an item is emptied from the bin, you can **restore** it. Double-click the `Recycle Bin` icon to open a Desktop window showing its contents. Select the desired item, and choose `Restore` from the `File` menu (or from the right-click pop-up menu). This puts the item back in its previous folder.

Recycling Options

Right-clicking on the `Recycle Bin` icon presents a menu that includes access to a property sheet. If you have multiple fixed disk drives connected to your PC, you can assign different settings to each drive. Click the top radio button, and then the tabs for each drive. Whether for all (global) drives or individual ones, a checkbox lets you set whether items you delete (either by dragging to the icon or deleting via menu) should be stashed in the bin until it is emptied or immediately discarded. If you choose the latter, a dialog alerts you just prior to deletion that the item won't be put into the `Recycle Bin`.

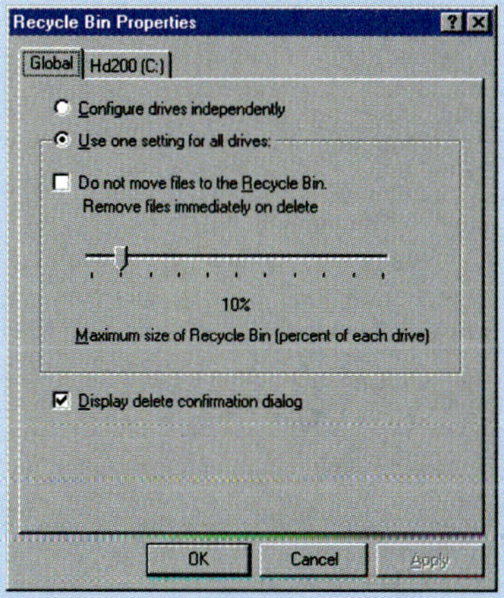

Since items in your `Recycle Bin` are still on your hard disk, they occupy space there. If you don't want the bin to get too big, you can adjust the slider control to a lower value. For example, if you have a 200MB hard disk and the control is set to 10%, the `Recycle Bin` will begin automatically removing items once the bin "contains" 20MB of deleted files. It removes items you deleted earliest, leaving the most recently deleted items in the bin for possible restoration. A setting of 0% is the same as checking the `Remove Files Immediately` checkbox.

Bypassing the Bin

If you normally want deleted items to stick around in the `Recycle Bin`, but definitely want to delete a certain file, use the Shift key to bypass the `Recycle Bin`. Hold Shift when choosing Delete from an item's pop-up menu or when dragging an item to the Bin icon.

Sounds of Empty

Emptying the `Recycle Bin` is one of the events to which you can attach a sound. If your PC is multimedia equipped, you can use the `Sound` control panel 146 to assign an existing sound file to that event. With a microphone attached to your multimedia PC, you can use the `Sound Recorder` program to record your own sound 144—perhaps the word "Empty" with an echo effect.

What Gets Recycled?

Emptying the `Recycle Bin` really doesn't remove its contents from the disk. The items are still there until something else writes over the same space on the disk. Gone, however, are the entries in disk directory (a hidden file) that helps Windows locate files on the disk. Therefore, third-party file recovery programs can help you restore a file that has been deleted, provided it hasn't been

Removable Media

Items deleted from removable media such as floppy disks and cartridge disk drives do not go into the `Recycle Bin`. A dialog alerts you that

Windows 95 provides a number of ways for you to customize the appearance and behavior of the Desktop.

You may change the underlying desktop pattern, the way files are listed in folder or Explorer windows, sounds in response to your actions on the Desktop, and a variety of color elements if you use a color monitor. Most of the customization is performed in the Display control panel, and is retained from session to session.

Reaching the Display Control Panel

Display

Access to the **Display** control panel is possible through many routes. Besides the obvious route via the Control Panel window, you can also right-click anywhere on the Desktop background. In the pop-up menu, choose `Properties`.

Desktop Patterns and Wallpaper

The `Display→Background` control panel is where you can choose from several desktop background patterns and/or wallpaper designs, as well as create your own. A pattern uses the current **Desktop color** 35 and black to establish a repeating sequence of 8-by-8-pixel panes. Wallpaper, on the other hand, is full-color art that can be set to overlay the entire background (hiding the pattern).

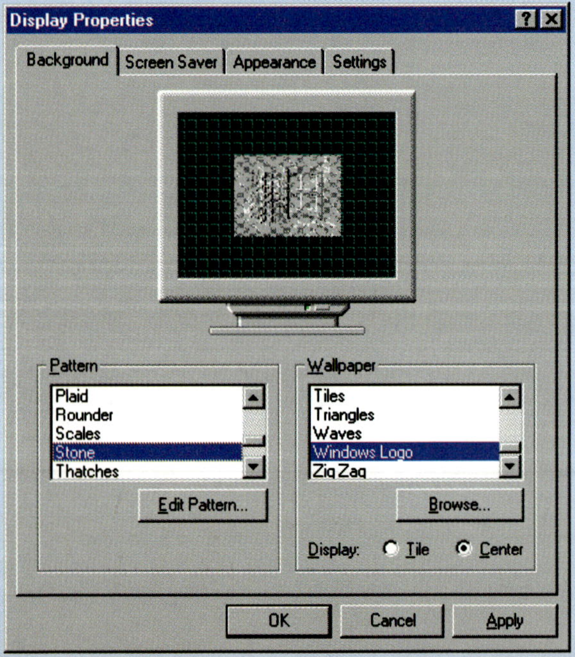

Pattern Anatomy

A Windows pattern is defined by the pixel layout of an 8-by-8 grid. This endows the desktop pattern with a regularity that befits a background. That 64-pixel pattern is repeated to fill the entire screen.

Default Patterns

From the factory, Windows is set to display no pattern (or wallpaper)—just the solid background Desktop color. But Windows comes with a number of predesigned patterns, which you can choose in the `Display→Background` control panel. As you select patterns from the left scrolling list, a life-size example of the pattern appears in the video monitor above. To accept a pattern for your Desktop, click either the Apply button (to keep the control panel window open) or OK.

Changing Desktop Pattern Color

The Desktop pattern color is governed by the Desktop color as set in the `Display→Appearance` control panel 34. Select `Desktop` in the `Item` pop-up list, and then click the `Color` pop-up list. Choose from the recommended colors, or click Other... to reach the color selection dialog 35. Patterns consist of black plus the Desktop color.

Wallpaper Art

Windows comes with more than a dozen wallpaper art files (bitmap files, .BMP extension). Unlike Desktop patterns, wallpaper art can be any size, including full-screen. The scrolling list in the control panel displays all bitmap files located in the Windows folder. Click Browse... the button to locate other bitmap files elsewhere on your disk to set as wallpaper.

Tiled vs. Centered

Whether you choose to tile or center wallpaper art depends on the nature of the art file as well as your personal taste. Small bits of art, such as the Argyle and Cars files, are designed for repeated deployment (pattern-style) in a tiled arrangement—filling the entire screen. When displayed centered, a single instance of the art appears at the center of the screen, which can look pretty strange if the art is small.

A large bit of art makes more sense being displayed centered, since it can provide an interesting-looking Desktop background, without interfering with Desktop icons (which tend to gravitate around the edges, where windows don't cover them). A full-screen wallpaper image will appear the same in both tiled and centered format.

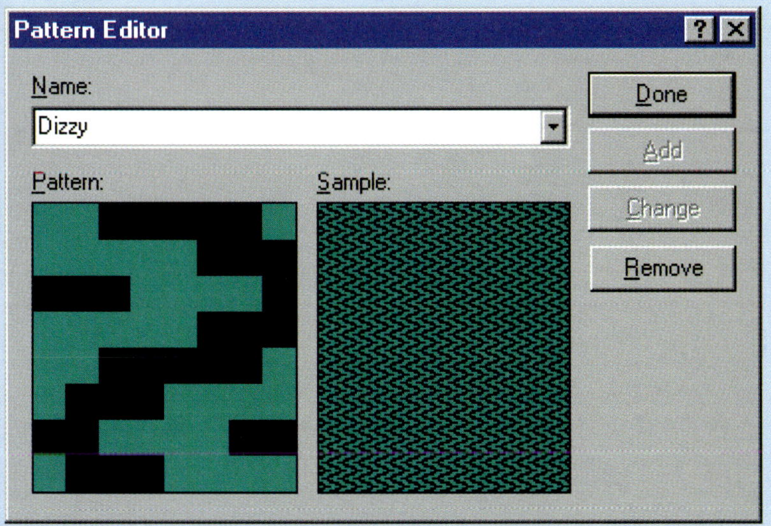

Editing Pattern Pixels

Select any pattern, and click the Edit Pattern... button of the `Display→Background` control panel to reach the `Pattern Editor`. The magnified view on the left is also a pixel editing area. Clicking the arrow pointer in the area toggles each pixel between black and the Desktop color. As you change each pixel, the result will be displayed in the sample area to the right. You may alter any existing pattern and click the Change button; but to save a pattern you created with its own name, enter the new name—at which point the Add button activates. Click Add and Done to return to the control panel. Click Apply or OK to put your creation on the Desktop.

Editing Wallpaper Art

Because wallpaper art files are **bitmap files**, you can use Microsoft Paint or any other bitmap graphics program to inspect and modify them. It's important to realize that the size of a wallpaper "tile" is the total image size of the bitmap file. Therefore, when you open a small wallpaper file, such as Cars, you see that the image size is 32 pixels square. If the image space were larger than the automobile art, that extra white space would appear in the wallpaper tile. To adjust the image size in Microsoft Paint, choose `Attributes` from the `Image` menu, and enter the desired pixel dimensions for your art "tile."

Microsoft Paint includes a shortcut for assigning a saved bitmap file to your Desktop's wallpaper. Regardless of the folder in which the image is saved, choose one of the `Set As Wallpaper` items in the `File` menu. The art is immediately applied to the Desktop (but is not copied to the Windows folder, so it won't show up in the scrolling list in the `Display→Background` control panel).

Desktop Pictures

Don't forget that any art you can get into your PC as a bitmap file can be used as wallpaper. That includes a scanned photo of a loved one or a vacation snapshot →22.

Pattern and Wallpaper Strategies

If you use both a desktop and a laptop computer, a different Desktop pattern for each machine serves as visual reinforcement to remind you which PC you're using. The Desktop pattern and wallpaper settings are part of the information stored in user profiles when a PC is shared by two or more users. Therefore, it's possible for each user to have a completely different visual environment.

Desktop Pattern Details

All Desktop patterns are stored in a configuration file called Control (CONTROL.INI). While you can view this file with a text editor such as Notepad, the data won't be of much help to you. Each pattern is defined by a series of eight numbers (0 to 255). Each number represents the decimal equivalent of the bit pattern of a horizontal line of pixels in the pattern. For example, a line that has all color pixels except for a single black pixel at the right edge has a binary value of 00000001, which translates to decimal 1. A line with alternating black and color pixels would be 10101010, or 170 to you and me. As such, patterns you don't use don't take up a lot of disk space. To remove entries, you should do so via the Pattern Editor, rather than risking damaging your Control file.

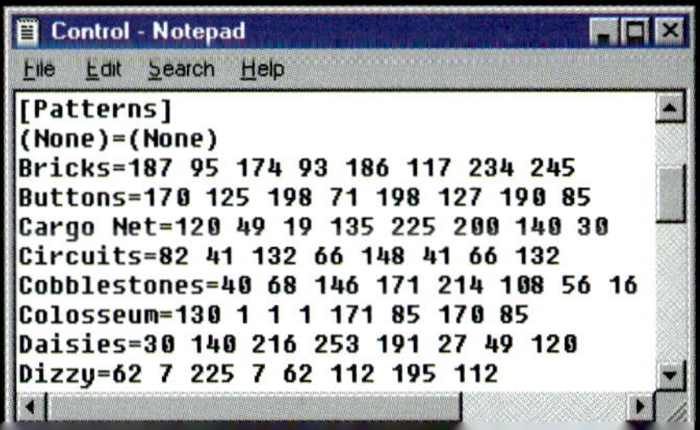
Control - Notepad
File Edit Search Help

```
[Patterns]
(None)=(None)
Bricks=187 95 174 93 186 117 234 245
Buttons=170 125 198 71 198 127 190 85
Cargo Net=120 49 19 135 225 200 140 30
Circuits=82 41 132 66 148 41 66 132
Cobblestones=40 68 146 171 214 108 56 16
Colosseum=130 1 1 1 171 85 170 85
Daisies=30 140 216 253 191 27 49 120
Dizzy=62 7 225 7 62 112 195 112
```

Deleting Wallpaper

Wallpaper files, on the other hand, can consume a fair amount of disk space. Tiny tiles, such as Cars, are only about 1 kilobyte, but several others are much larger. And when you add up the total, it could be a few hundred kilobytes. If you aren't using wallpaper or are likely to stick with a single scheme, delete all unnecessary bitmap files from the Windows folder. To delete all of them, you can also use the `Add/Remove Programs→Windows Setup` control panel. The component to uninstall is the one named Desktop Wallpaper in the Accessories group.

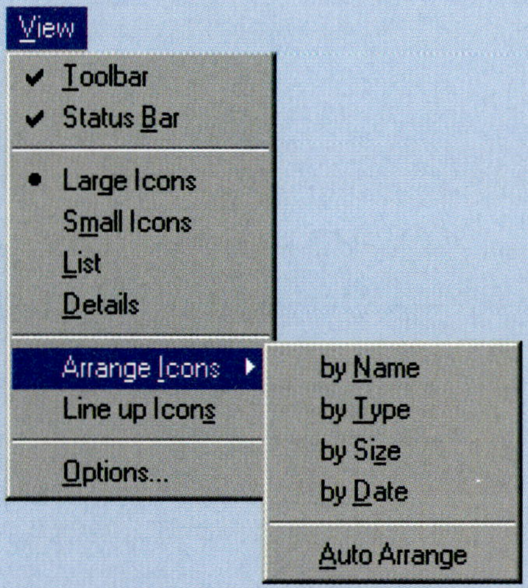

View Menu

Each window's `View` menu lets you set the view and sorting order for files in the window. The same `View` menu items are available by right-clicking inside the window on anything but an icon or file/folder name.

Three of the `View` menu options show files as icons in the window—large or small free-form icons, or small icons in a rigid list format. In Large Icon mode (the default mode for Windows), icons have the file names beneath them; in Small Icon mode, each file is represented by a miniature icon with the file name to its right; List mode may appear to be the same as Small Icon mode at first glance, but you cannot drag items around this window. Given a window of a particular size, you can display more than twice as many files in Small Icon and List modes as in large icon mode. Still, the larger icons are more visually appealing and distinctive—a plus for visually oriented users.

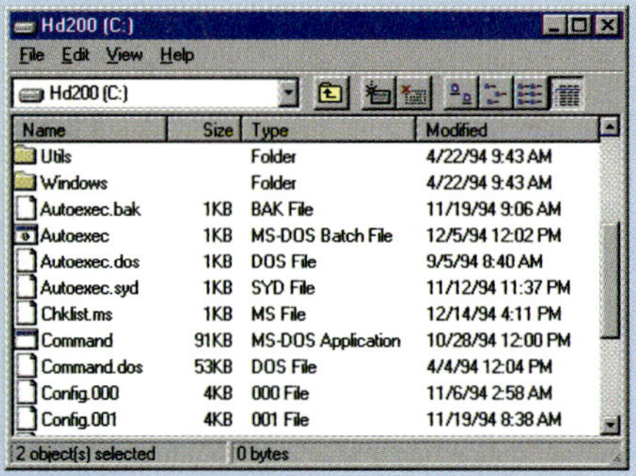

The `Details View` menu choices list files as text in the window. Four columns of information appear—spreadsheet-like—to reveal data about each item. The column headers—`Name`, `Size`, `Type`, and `Modified` (date)—are also buttons, which you can click as shortcuts to sort the items in the view (similar choices are available in the `View→Arrange Icons` submenu). These buttons toggle between forward and backward order; each time you click one, the items are sorted in the opposite direction by that column's data. For example, one click of the `Size` button sorts items with the smallest items first (preceded by the unsized folders); a second click inverts the sort, placing the largest items at the top. The width of each column is adjustable by dragging the dividing bars between column headers.

If you find that you change view formats frequently, you should turn on the tool bar in the `View` menu (this setting affects all Desktop windows). Four buttons in the tool bar provide the simplest shortcuts to changing views.

Tidy Icon Views

With the `Large Icon` or `Small Icon` view in force, the default behavior is to let you drag items around willy-nilly. The `Line Up Icons` item in the `View` menu will perform a quick **alignment of icons** so that they zip to their nearest location in an invisible grid in the window. But if you always want Windows to help you keep icons tidy and available near the top left corner of the window, turn on `Auto Arrange` in the `View→Arrange Icons` submenu. No matter where you drag an icon in the window, it will always snap back to the group. With Auto Arrange turned on, Windows displays as many columns of icons as fit neatly within the current window size. You can move items around to place them in order, but the order tends to go from left to right, top to bottom.

Folder Browsing

Unless directed otherwise, Windows opens a new Desktop window each time you open a folder or other container. If you are wending your way down a long **path** 110, you can end up with numerous windows open, none of which are of interest to you. In `Views→Options→Folder`, however, you can instruct Windows to open only one window (starting from any currently visible container icon), and use that window for further excursions deeper into your hard disk. Because all items open in only one window, the `View` menu settings apply to every folder you open; also, the window remains the same size with different folders. If you choose this single window format, be sure the tool bar is turned on, because it contains a navigation button that lets you click your way back up the path 110.

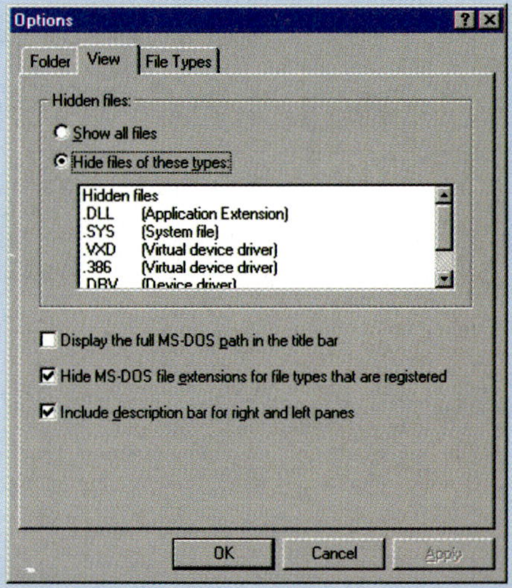

View Options

One area on the `View→Options→View` panel concerns itself with the display of normally **hidden files.** The files Windows prefers to hide are those that are used silently by Windows and various applications. You can't open most of them (although you may want to delete them sometime when you know for sure you don't need them). By leaving these files hidden, you reduce the file clutter in crowded folders such as those of Windows and your applications.

The first of the two remaining checkboxes applies only to Desktop windows. Normally turned off, it displays the MS-DOS-style path name for the current window's folder in the titlebar. Such paths can get pretty long, especially with long file names, so don't be surprised if deeply nested paths don't appear in their entirety.

In another step toward weaning experienced users away from concern about file extensions, you can elect to hide file name extensions for files whose types are registered with your copy of Windows ➜119. Again, it's a way to reduce clutter, although it may be hard for old hands to trust Windows to manage the extensions properly when they're not displayed. The fact is, there is less chance of mangling a file by leaving extensions hidden: renaming a file without the proper extension will cause the file to lose its association with its application; if you don't display the extension, Windows manages the hidden extension and application association perfectly.

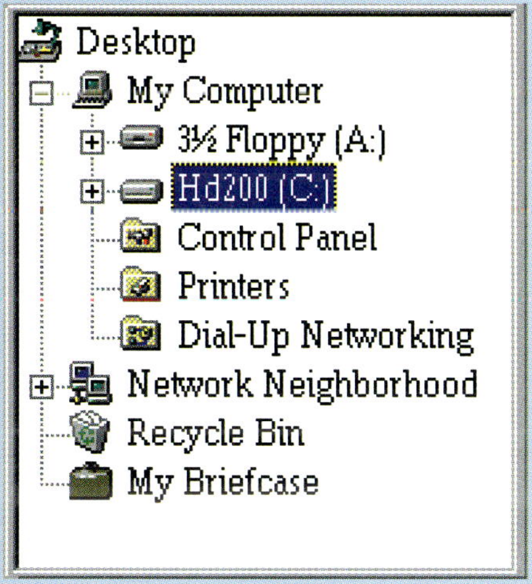

Explorer Window in MS Serif 10

Icon Label Fonts

Should the default font for text in Desktop/Explorer windows not be to your liking, you can adjust the font, font size, and font style in the `Display→ Appearance` control panel ➜34. No example of this text appears in the sample area of this control panel for you to click on, so you must select `Icon Title` from the `Item` pop-up list. The **default font** is **8-point MS Sans Serif.** You don't see what the font looks like in the control panel window, so be sure you can see a portion of a Desktop/Explorer window behind the control panel for tests of the Apply button. Exercise care with larger font sizes for `Large Icon` displays: icon spacing does not adjust for the increased height of multilined icon labels, resulting in possible overlap with icons above and below.

Very Long File Names

While Windows 95 offers facilities for file and folder names **up to 256 characters** long ➜110, using a lot of very long names can inconveniently affect the views of items in Desktop/Explorer windows. In `Large Icon` view, long names wrap to multiple lines beneath the icon. Windows' large icon grid leaves room for three lines for an icon name; if there are more lines, it is possible that the name will cover other icons in the same window or be partially obscured by other icons. In `Small Icon` and `List` view, a long name extends to the right, so you will always be able to read the entire name. A downside, however, is that very long names reduce the number of columns of items that can display in the window. Detail views handle very long names most elegantly, because Windows truncates (with an ellipsis) the names within the Name column of the display. Except in unusual circumstances, you should try to restrict names to a **maximum of about 40 characters** (the exact measure will vary depending on the number of wide and narrow letters used).

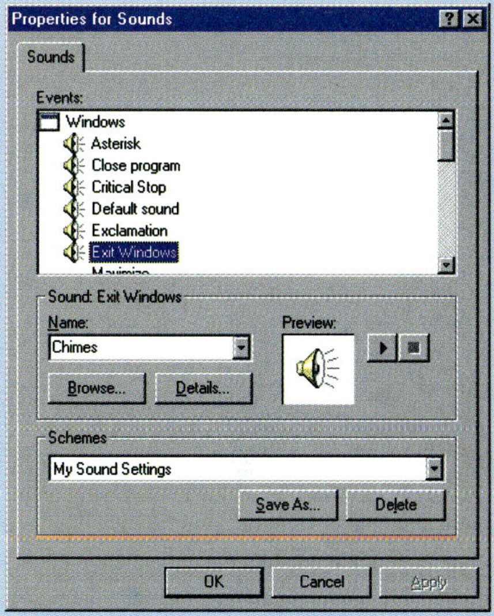

Sounds

The `Sounds` control panel lists many Desktop-related events that can have sounds attached to them. To attach a sound, select an action from the list of events. The `Sound` area in the panel activates. Next, select from the sounds Windows knows about in the `Windows→ Media` folder, or click the Browse... button to locate other sounds. You're looking for sound files with file extension .WAV, some of which may be tucked away in application folders. To hear what a file sounds like, click the `Preview:` button.

You can save sets of sounds as separate **sound schemes.** Click the Save As... button to assign a name to the current set. It will appear in the `Schemes` pop-up list so you can recreate a unique set at any time.

Windows 95 comes with a few sound schemes to try out. You are free to mix and match individual sounds from these sets to create custom schemes of your own.

Additional sound files are readily available in public domain software collections and from on-line services. You can also record your own sounds with the **Sound Recorder** program (Soundrec) that comes with Windows. Windows Setup places it in the Startup menu at Start `→Programs→Accessories→ Multimedia`. If you have a microphone and multimedia hardware (sound card) installed in your PC, you can use this program to generate sound files ➜144.

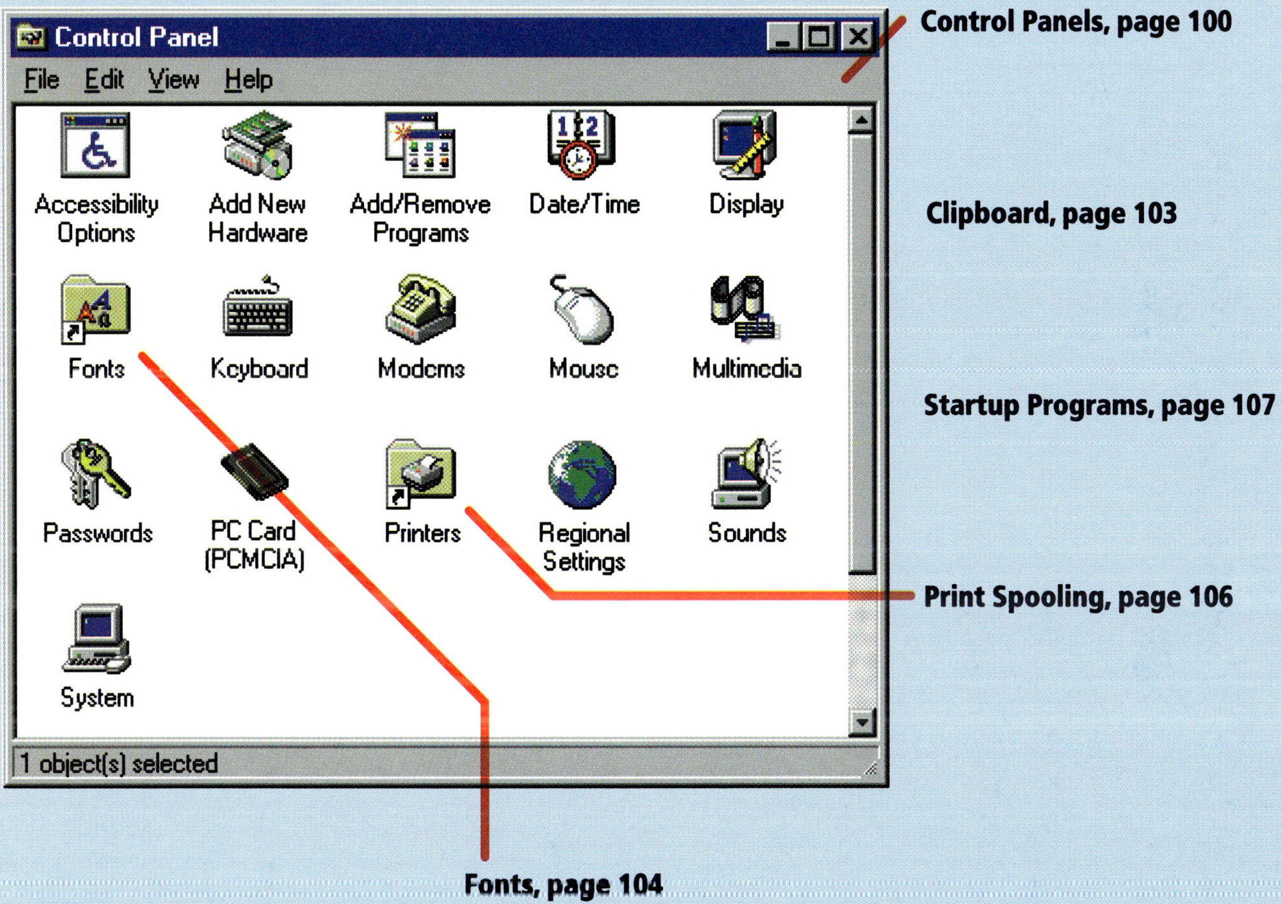
Control Panel
File Edit View Help
Accessibility Options
Add New Hardware
Add/Remove Programs
Date/Time
Display
Fonts
Keyboard
Modems
Mouse
Multimedia
Passwords
PC Card (PCMCIA)
Printers
Regional Settings
Sounds
System
1 object(s) selected
Control Panels, page 100
Clipboard, page 103
Startup Programs, page 107
Print Spooling, page 106
Fonts, page 104

Control Panel

Windows 95 control panels generally consist of system-level preferences that you adjust once or infrequently.

Windows Setup installs more than a dozen control panels, the exact number depending on capabilities of your PC hardware and network setup. Third-party hardware and software products also occasionally provide control panels as ways of letting you set user preferences.

A control panel is a small file that appears to open like an application. You may open multiple control panels at the same time. Settings in some control panels don't take effect until you restart your PC. You will usually see an alert message to that effect upon closing such a control panel.

Add New Hardware

The `Add New Hardware` wizard helps Windows recognize any kind of hardware device and install drivers for devices that Windows is not familiar with. In the event of hardware conflicts, the wizard helps you locate the conflict and fix the problem by making various dialog box selections → 60.

Accessibility Options

Windows 95 provides numerous adjustments that allow those with physical disabilities to use Windows more easily. The keyboard can be set to be used with a single pointing device or stylus. Or you can turn the keyboard into a complete pointer control system. Additional settings make the screen easier to read or turn alert sounds into on-screen messages → 24.

Keyboard

Adjustments to the speed of key repeating and the length of time you have to hold a key before it starts repeating are made in the `Keyboard` control panel → 16. If you have multiple language keyboards connected (or their software installed), this control panel is also where you choose the keyboard to be recognized by Windows at the moment → 16.

Add/Remove Programs

This control panel performs three distinct functions. First, it assists in installing third-party programs by looking for a `Setup` or `Install` file on a floppy or CD-ROM drive. More recent software registers itself with Windows so that this same control panel can assist in removing (uninstalling) all component files of a program if you later wish to eliminate a program from your hard disk.

The second function allows you to select various Windows components for installation or removal → 69. Many of these items are automatically installed for you during the initial Windows setup.

The third function in this control panel is the facility to generate an emergency Windows startup disk. If you didn't do this during initial setup, you should make a disk now to keep handy at your workstation or with your laptop → 70.

Date/Time

Your PC's internal clock should be set to the correct time and date to assist in backing up files and helping you track document file revisions. The `Date/Time` control panel has two screens. The first shows a calendar and clock. To set the date, select the month and year from the lists in the calendar, and click on the current date. To set the time against a time standard, you must first stop the ticking clock by clicking the up or down arrow in the digital time display. Select the hour figures and type the current hour; tab to the minutes and seconds, setting them to the time you'll wait to hear from your time standard. Be sure the AM/PM indication is correct. At the sound of the tone from the time standard, click the Apply button.

Setting the time zone on the other screen of this control panel is optional. Either click on the map in the general vicinity of your location, or choose the time zone from the pop-up list. This setting might affect some network and remote access activities.

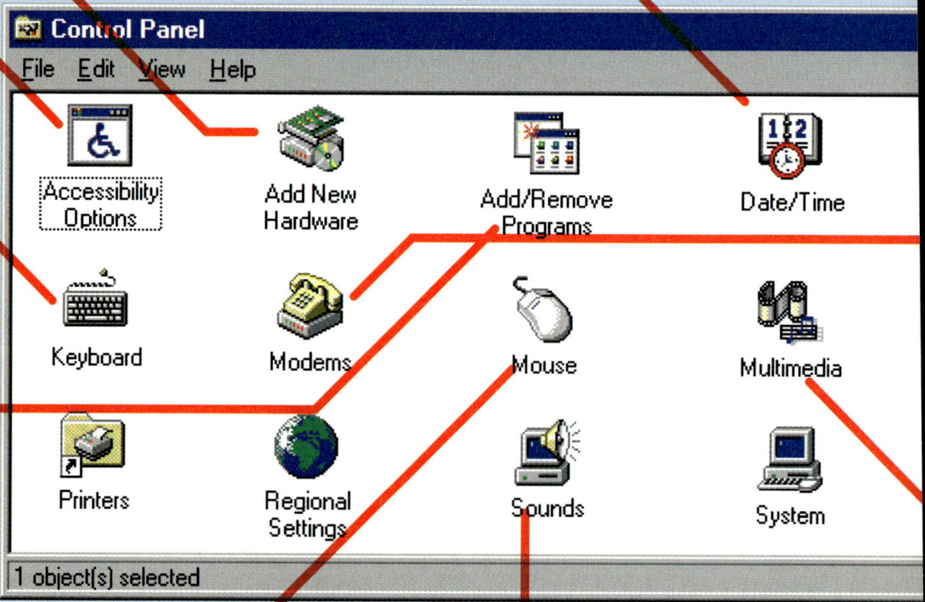

Mouse

Many aspects of the mouse—left and right button orientation, the speed of a recognizable double-click, and how fast the screen pointer tracks actual mouse movement—are set in the `Mouse` control panel → 20. Here, too, is where you select alternate pointer icons for many mouse functions → 79. Custom mouse drivers can also be installed here (or via the `Add New Hardware` control panel).

Sounds

The sole purpose of the `Sounds` control panel is to let you assign existing sound files (.WAV files) to any of 18 different actions you take in Windows. If your PC is equipped with a microphone port and microphone, you can record your own sounds to attach to these actions → 144, and then save sets of sounds for different moods or computing environments → 146.

All control panel files are located in the **Control Panel** folder, which you access via Start →`Settings` or the `My Computer` window. When you open the Control Panel folder, you will see the icons or text listing of the control panels installed in your Windows system. To open a control panel, double-click on its icon or name. You may drag the control panel window around the screen, and leave it open as you click on another window to activate a different program.

Display

Four screens-full of data adorn the `Display` control panel. This is where you select background art or wallpaper 94, screen savers 36, window object color combinations 34, and monitor settings, such as the pixel grid and color palette 34. A shortcut to reaching this control panel is to right-click on the Desktop and choose `Properties`.

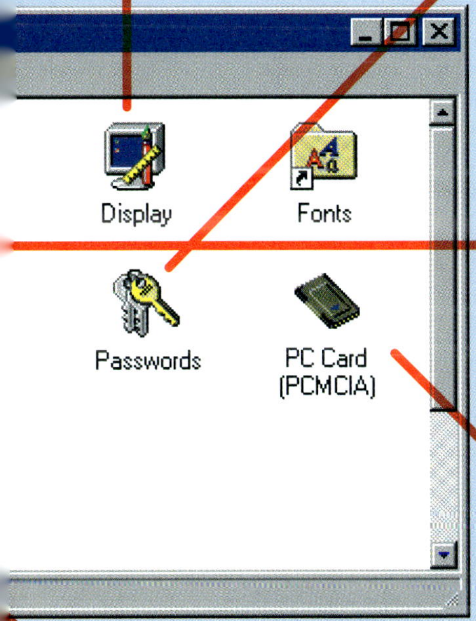

Passwords

Three screens in the `Passwords` control panel encompass various privacy settings for your PC and Windows. Single, non-networked users can ignore this panel, but those in networked environments will probably have to pay close attention to setting a personal password for access to the local computer and remote computers. In the second screen, networked users can use this control panel to grant others on the network (or via dial-in connections) access to their files 152. The password you assign here is the password others must enter to gain that access. The third screen of this control panel tells the copy of Windows on your PC whether it should save desktop settings and other preferences in user profiles 82 for each user of this machine.

Multimedia

The `Multimedia` control panel encompasses settings for sound recording 144 and playback 146, MIDI musical instrument interfaces, playback volume for compact audio discs (when the CD-ROM drive is built to be so controlled by Windows), and driver information for all multimedia (sound, video, and game controller) devices. Some or all of these parts of the control panel may be disabled if your PC is not equipped as a multimedia machine with sound playback and recording card, MIDI interface, or CD-ROM drive.

PC Card (PCMCIA)

Available on PCs equipped with PC Card (also known as PCMCIA) slots, this control panel lets you adjust memory settings for the card "socket." Normally this can be left in automatic mode, but another checkbox lets you turn off sound effects for PC cards that produce them (e.g., a modem's dialing and connection sounds). Theoretically, you should be able to pop out a card without ill effects 61. But if some software is accessing the card at that instant, or the card contains a hard disk, things could go awry. Use this control panel to safely turn off a card before removing it from the socket.

Modems

Modem communications are now an integral part of Windows. This control panel gives you direct access to settings that apply to whatever modem is connected to your PC. One screen of this control panel (`General`) lists the modem drivers installed at any given moment. Selecting a modem and clicking the Properties button displays the property sheet for that modem. A second screen (`Diagnostics`) displays information about all serial ports that Windows 95 recognizes on your PC. This includes dedicated serial mouse ports as well as COM ports.

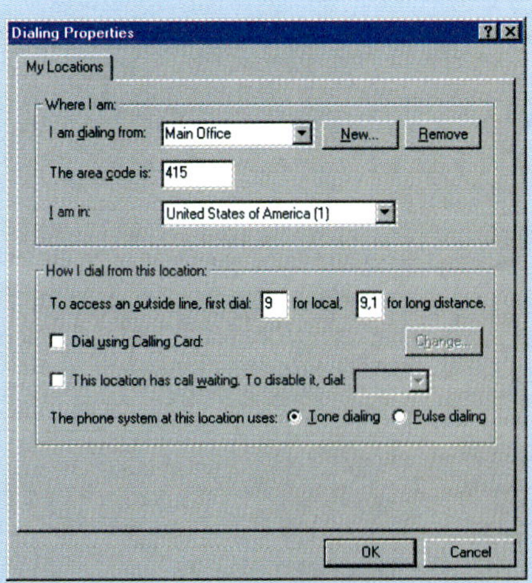

Many aspects of using a computer with a telephone have been built into the Windows 95 operating system. Thus, the `Dialing Properties` button in the `Modems` control panel leads to a `Dialing Properties` screen. Here you save settings for each location from which you intend to use telephony software, specifying the local area code (so dialing programs can ignore the code for a local number), any access codes necessary for local or long distance lines, the code to disable call waiting, and even a telephone credit card number. Of course, your software must be written to work with these features, as the HyperTerminal communications program, Microsoft Network, and the Phone Dialer applet 122 are.

Regional Settings

Regional Settings

To prove that Windows 95 is intended for the world's computer users, the Regional Settings control panel provides adjustments for hundreds of combinations of number, currency, time, and date formats in use around the world.

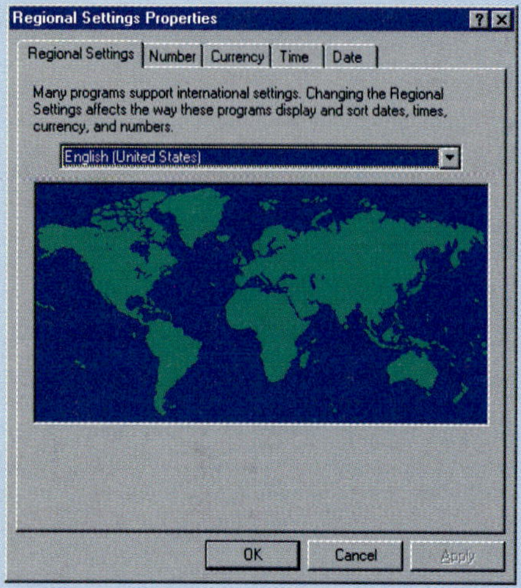

The opening screen of the control panel is a world map. Some language choices have multiple possibilities (e.g., German has a standard version, plus others for Austria, Switzerland, Luxembourg, and Liechtenstein). Click the Apply button to make your choice.

In the other four screens of this panel, you can make fine adjustments to a variety of settings for numbers, currency (symbols, decimal characters, groupings for large numbers), time (AM/PM symbols, hours/minutes separator character), and date (order of items in short and long date formats). Windows makes the most common selections for each region you select, but you can choose other individual settings if you like. Adhering to local custom can be very important. For example, in many countries outside of North America, the convention for short date format is dd/mm/yy, where the numbers for date and month are the reverse of the U.S. convention. Thus, 3/4/95 means March 4th in the United States, but April 3rd in many other countries.

System

System

No other control panel reveals more about how Windows is utilizing your PC's hardware than the System control panel. Its four screens provide a comparatively friendly face for some aspects of your system stored more cryptically in the **Registry** 119.

The first screen is like an About dialog for Windows running on your system. It shows the name of the registered user, and displays the type of processor (CPU) in your PC plus the amount of memory available to Windows (i.e., other than what is reserved for DOS compatibility).

In the second screen is the **Device Manager**. It presents a hierarchical listing of all devices that Windows recognizes on your computer. Click the plus symbol next to a device category listing to view all devices in that category. The Device Manager visually alerts (with overlaying icons) you to any devices that are either currently turned off or are experiencing hardware conflicts 60.

By opening the property sheets for a device (select the specific device and click the Properties button), you can instruct Windows to engage or ignore the device on the next start-up, adjust settings and driver files that are unique to the selected device, and make changes, if needed, to low-level settings—I/O Ranges, Interrupt Request lines, and DMA addresses 60.

Third-Party Control Panels

The more utility software and external devices you connect to your PC, the more control panels you'll accumulate. It's not uncommon to have several third-party control panels installed. Your PC may even have come with one or more custom control panels to handle special hardware attributes of your PC.

Control Panel Strategies

It is an excellent idea to place shortcuts 114 to frequently accessed control panels into the Start button or on the Desktop. This will let you access them quickly and directly, instead of by way of the Control Panel folder first. Remember that the Control Panel folder itself is also available from the Start button: Start→Settings→Control Panel.

You may leave most control panel windows open as you work on other applications. Look for an active Apply button on control panels. If you make a change, click the Apply button for the changes to take effect without closing the control panel.

Where Control Panels Really Are

The Control Panel folder is a special system folder in Windows 95. It has its own unique icon, and is accessible in places that normal folders are not (ostensibly at the same level as a disk volume when viewed in the Explorer hierarchy). Windows constructs the contents of this folder out of Control Panel extension files (filename extension .CPL), which are all located in the Windows→System folder. These files are hidden unless you choose Show All Files in the View→Options window in the Explorer or Desktop window. You must use the Windows→System folder to delete or duplicate a control panel.

In the following table are some of the most common control panels and their corresponding file names:

Control Panel	Filename
Accessibility Options	Access
Add/Remove Programs	Appwiz
Date/Time	Timedate
Display	Desk
Joystick	Joy
Mail and FAX	Mlcfg32
MS Mail Postoffice	Wgpocpl
Modems	Modem
Mouse	Main
Multimedia	Mmsys
Network	Netcpl
Passwords	Password
Regional Settings	Intl
System	Sysdm

The Clipboard stores one piece of information at a time, and its contents disappear the instant you turn off or restart your PC or Windows. There is one Clipboard that serves all applications.

Versatility is a hallmark of the Clipboard. Anything you can copy and paste in a document—text, painted graphics, a graphic object, a sound, an icon, an animation sequence—can be stored in the Clipboard. You can even copy and paste files and folders via the Clipboard.

Each time you choose `Copy` or `Cut` from the `Edit` menu, the content of the Clipboard is replaced by the current selection. If no information is selected, then either the `Cut` and `Copy` menu items will be disabled (grayed out) or choosing the menu items won't disturb the Clipboard.

Use the Clipboard as the means of moving information from place to place during a single Windows session. If you need the information to survive the next shutdown of the Windows, save it to a file via the **Clipboard Viewer** 92.

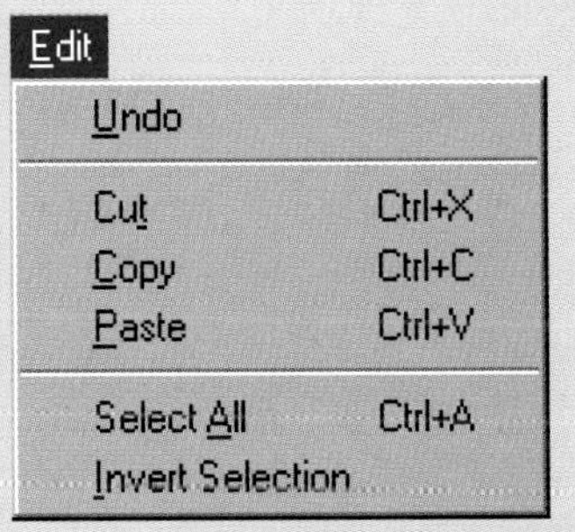

How the Clipboard Works

The Clipboard works almost invisibly. Virtually every Windows program, including Explorer and the Desktop, contains a menu and tool bar buttons with the `Cut`, `Copy`, and `Paste` items, which control access to the **Clipboard**. Some programs also let you view what is in the Clipboard. If they don't, you can use the **Clipboard Viewer** program 92 to see what's there.

To copy to the Clipboard, you select something—a range of text, a graphic, a file icon—and choose `Copy` from the `Edit` menu (or type Control+C). To put the contents of the Clipboard in another place on the document or in another document (even in another program), click the mouse at an insertion point (this may not be necessary in graphics programs), and choose `Paste` from the `Edit` menu. After pasting, the Clipboard still contains the item, so you can paste another copy of it in another spot if you like.

Choosing `Cut` from the `Edit` menu both clears the selection from the current document and places the information into the Clipboard. If the program has a `Clear` menu item, this simply deletes the selection without placing it into the Clipboard.

Clearing the Clipboard

The Clipboard takes up memory, so the larger the amount of information in the Clipboard, the less is available for you to open other programs. Pages of text or complex color pictures in the Clipboard can absorb many kilobytes of RAM without your knowledge. While you cannot completely clear the Clipboard, you can reduce it to a negligible size by selecting a single character of text and copying it into the Clipboard. That single byte shouldn't get in the way of any other operation.

Mixing Data Types—Paste Special

An application program determines what types of information it can accept from the Clipboard. Not all programs accept all information types directly (you can't paste a picture into a spreadsheet formula, for example), but Windows does accommodate wide ranging data elements. For instance, WordPad's primary data type is text, but that doesn't stop it from letting you insert data of other types into its documents. In addition to pasting graphics into a text document, you can even paste a "live" icon from a Desktop window. In both cases, the foreign data is treated as an object with properties dependent upon the kind of object it is. In the case of a file icon, you can double-click it in the WordPad document to launch another application.

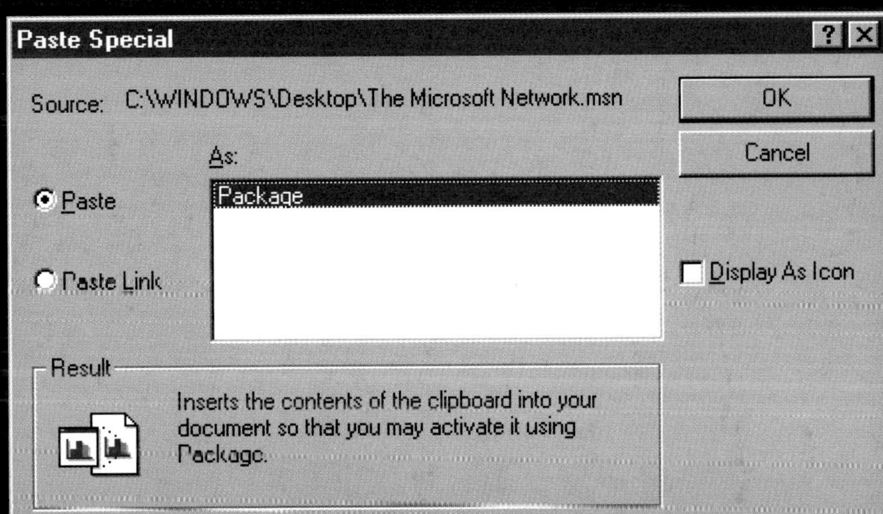

While Windows will perform this kind of pasting with the normal `Paste` command, some programs offer a `Paste Special` menu item. Choosing this item presents choices about how the foreign object should be treated in the destination document. Some items can be embedded, others linked to react to changes made to the source document 128.

In Windows, a font is the typeface style for any text character displayed on the screen or produced on a printer.

In the typesetting world, a font is a particular style and size of a typeface, but the electronic nature of Windows character generation makes it much easier to consider a font as a typestyle in any size and, in some cases, more than one style (e.g., bold, italic, etc.). A Windows font is software that appears in the **Fonts** folder (although some other fonts may reside elsewhere). While some printers have fonts built into them, your Windows system also needs font files to display those fonts on the screen.

Raster Font | **TrueType Font (on screen)** | **TrueType Font (printed)**

Of Points, Leading, and Serifs

Font sizes are measured in points. A point is a typesetter's unit of measure equaling 1/72 of an inch. **Character size** is measured as the distance between the highest and lowest part of the space that characters can occupy. Characters line up along a **baseline**, and the distance between baselines in adjacent lines of text is called **leading** (pronounced LEDD-ing), also measured in points. Windows software tends to call this measure Line Spacing. It is common practice to refer to the combined font size and line spacing in a specification of so many points "over" so many points, as in "10 over 12," meaning a 10-point font with 12-point leading.

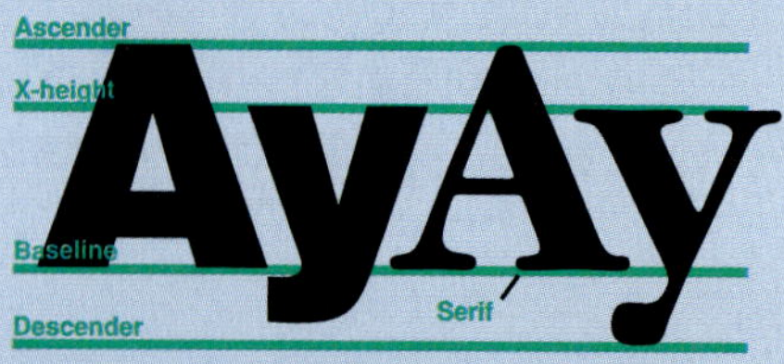

Fonts with alphanumeric characters fall into two broad styles: serif and sans serif. A **serif** is an ornamental stroke appended to any location on a character, usually at some free end of a line. Times New Roman is a serif font. When characters lack these serifs, they are said to be **sans serif** (French for "without serif"). Arial is a sans serif font.

Fonts Folder Fonts

Fonts

When you open a freshly installed Windows 95 Fonts folder, you notice two styles of icons representing fonts. One style, with an icon showing a double-T, is a TrueType font. This kind of font (called a **scalable font**) allows a Windows program to display and print that font in any size, including fractional point sizes and sizes well beyond the capabilities of most page printers. The other font file style (called a fixed-size or **raster** font) contains a font in fixed-point sizes. Windows uses raster fonts that have been optimized for readability on the screen for its display of window titles, menus, and alert messages. But for documents you intend to print, the **best results** will come from scalable (TrueType) fonts.

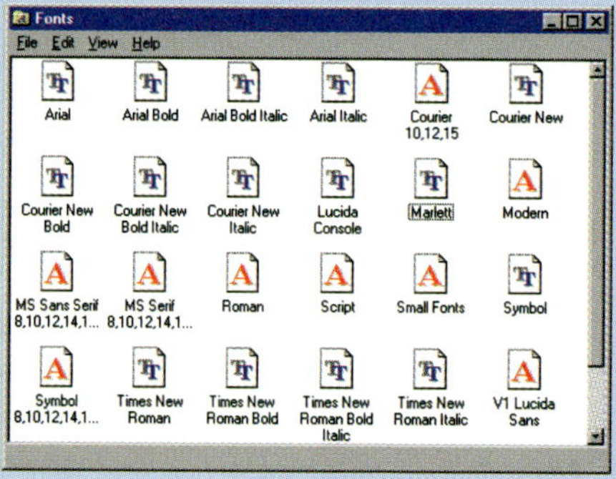

Raster Font

TrueType Font

To see the difference between a scalable and fixed-size font, double-click one of each in the Fonts folder. Scroll down the window to see the larger sizes. Scalable fonts maintain their shapes up to 72 points; fixed-size fonts display lots of jagged edges and giant pixel-like dots.

Not all programs give you access to raster fonts. Most word processing programs display lists of TrueType and other scalable font types. Paint, on the other hand, is a bitmapped graphics program that is well suited to the pixels of fixed-size fonts.

Font History

The fonts for the earliest versions of Windows were raster fonts—fonts whose dot patterns were optimized for screen display. Such fonts were printable on dot-matrix printers, which could replicate the dot pattern of the screen. The font file actually contained the location of dots for each character in a few common sizes—a map of the on and off bits for each character. Bold, italic, and other derivative styles were modified from the basic font, so separate font files weren't needed for those styles.

On the Apple Macintosh side of personal computing, **PostScript** (by Adobe Systems) emerged as a standard for high-quality printed output on personal laser printers and professional typesetting machines. Among PostScript's characteristics was its ability to define characters by mathematical descriptions, essentially describing the outline of a character's design. This outline font methodology allowed printing devices to use the same font software to print at a variety of resolutions, up to thousands of dots per inch. Fixed-size fonts were still needed to display the characters from the outline printer fonts on the screen. If you purchased an outline font, you also received a set of screen fonts in several standard sizes. Even today, if you purchase a printer that has PostScript fonts built in, you usually receive a set of screen fonts for those built-in fonts (i.e., the printer doesn't supply its font data back to Windows)

Adobe Type Manager (ATM), an add-on software program, eliminated the need for separate screen fonts by allowing a PostScript outline font file to also display the font in many sizes on the screen. You can use ATM with Windows 95.

TrueType fonts in Windows (available since Windows 3.0) also utilize outline font technology (with a font definition algorithm quite different from that of PostScript), and allow a single outline font file to control both screen and printer font representations. Many typeface producers have created libraries of TrueType fonts for sale to PC owners.

The built-in font display and printing system is called TrueType, although Windows 95 still works with another font system called PostScript (developed by Adobe Systems). With TrueType, the distinction between printer fonts and screen fonts disappears.

Windows allows a single TrueType font file (in the Fonts folder) to display and print characters of that type style in any size on any Windows-compatible printer (including dot-matrix, ink-jet, and laser printers). You may copy a huge number of fonts to the Fonts folder.

Installing Fonts

TrueType and raster fonts are installed in your Windows system by copying the font files to the **Fonts** folder. Any fonts in this folder automatically appear in font menus and pop-up lists in applications. TrueType fonts often come in **font families**, with separate font files for plain, bold, italic, and bold italic versions (the Arial font consists of four font files). These separate files indicate that the font has been finely tuned for the particular style, and it doesn't rely on Windows to approximate the style variant.

PostScript fonts require **ATM** to perform the font installation into a separate PostScript fonts folder. Each PostScript font has two files associated with it: the .PFM version contains the outline data; the .PFB version downloads the font into a PostScript printer when a document needs that font.

When purchasing fonts, be sure they are versions specifically for Windows. PostScript and TrueType are available for Macintosh as well, but the fonts are not compatible with Windows.

Choosing Fonts

Your choice of fonts for your text depends a lot on the kind of printer you use. Non-PostScript printers print dot-for-dot what Windows tells them to. For these printers, you can use any TrueType font. Avoid raster fonts, because they are not optimized for high-resolution printed output.

TrueType Document Fonts
Arial
Courier New
Times New Roman

Raster System Fonts
Courier
MS Sans Serif
MS Serif
System
Terminal

TrueType Symbol Fonts
Symbol θωερτψυιοπασδφγηφκλζξχϖβνμ
WingDings

For PostScript printers, however, your font choice may be influenced by the extent of your PostScript and TrueType font libraries. Because some printers have several PostScript fonts already built into them, compare sample printouts of built-in PostScript fonts against similar TrueType fonts. You may, for example, prefer the built-in Times font over the TrueType Times New Roman. Be aware, too, that when you print a TrueType font on a PostScript printer, Windows must send additional software to the printer before the printer can handle the TrueType font. Mixing PostScript and TrueType fonts in a document slows the process.

Printer Fonts

If your printer has fonts built in, Windows displays those font names in pop-up font lists within text-oriented programs (a small printer icon appears to the left of the font name in the list). Choosing such fonts causes Windows to substitute one of its installed fonts for the screen display. The displayed font may bear no resemblance to the real font, but the printout should look just fine.

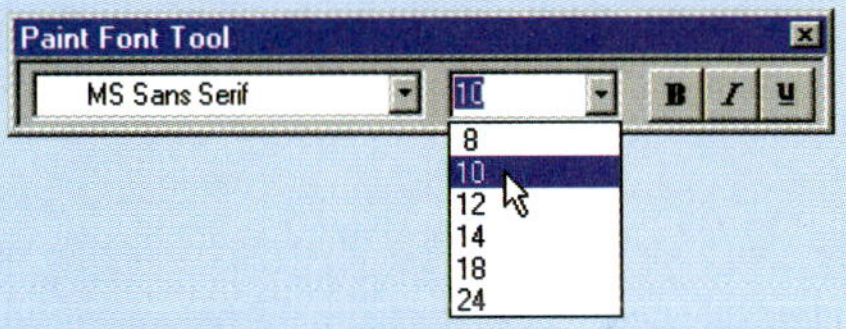

Choosing Font Sizes

Modern Windows programs are intelligent about the font sizes shown in the `Size` or `Style` menu. When you choose a font, the list of available sizes reflects likely selections you can make. A TrueType font lists small sizes (8 through 12 points) in increments of one point, but you can type in half-point font sizes, like 9.5. If the font is a fixed-size font, then only those sizes installed in the Fonts folder are listed. For a fixed-size font, if the application lets you enter any unlisted size, the resulting font characters will probably be distorted on the screen and in printouts.

Slimming Down the Fonts Folder

You might be able to remove some of the font files in your Fonts folder if you know how you want fonts to be handled. If you upgraded an older version of Windows to Windows 95, you may have many old versions of fonts that are replaced by more up-to-date versions with slightly different names.

Font Substitution for Printer Fonts

When a printer has built-in fonts, the output will generally look best with those fonts, rather than with a TrueType equivalent. The Fonts property sheet for some printers allows you to adjust entries in a **Font Substitution Table**. The left column lists all the TrueType fonts installed in your Fonts folder; the right column contains the instructions about substitutions (if any) Windows should make when a TrueType font is specified for text in a document. Select a TrueType font and then click the pop-up list below, which lists all printer fonts in your printer and installed with ATM. When there is no equivalent, choose Send As Outlines, which forces your printer to use the TrueType font. A hazard with font substitution is that minuscule differences between the TrueType display on the screen and printed output could result in unexpected character and word spacing, or different line wrapping.

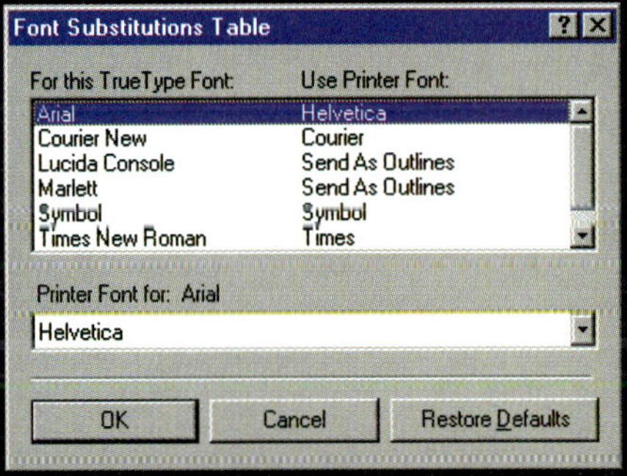

If you are preparing a document for high-resolution typesetting by a service bureau, be aware that most bureaus prefer PostScript fonts. Prepare your documents with screen fonts corresponding to the exact imagesetter (e.g., Linotronic) fonts used by that service bureau.

Print Spooling

Windows provides a printing service that quickly prepares a printable version of a document as a file, and hands control of the program back to you. In the background, Windows then begins parceling out characters or pages from the file to the printer at whatever speed the printer can accept instructions.

Printers

That file, called a **spool file,** is automatically placed in a special folder (spool). In the meantime, Windows quietly and continually checks the contents of the Printers folder. If it finds spool files, then it starts sending them to the printer selected in the Print dialog 141.

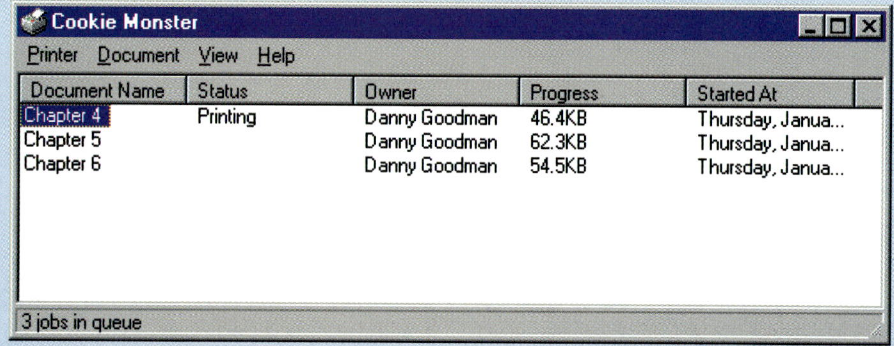

Print Spooling at Work

You can watch the queue of items fill and empty for your printer.

1. Open the Printers folder, and double-click the icon representing your printer.
2. Prepare a document of about three pages in any word processing program.
3. Issue the `Print` command four times, and then activate the window for your printer.

Each time you send the (or any) document to the printer, the document is saved as a **spool file** in the Printers folder, with its own serial number (you must open the `Windows`→`spool`→`Printers` folder to see these serial numbers). The documents queued for your printer will be listed with document name and other information about the spool file. As Windows finishes sending the top document in the list to the printer, the item disappears from the list. Windows continues working its way through the files (in the order in which they were sent from applications) until the list is empty.

Print Queue Control

The window to your printer lets you control the overall printing process. For instance, if there is a mechanical problem with the printer that Windows doesn't detect, choose `Pause Printing` from the `Printer` menu. To clear the entire queue, choose `Purge Print Jobs`.

When you select a document in the Printers window's list, you can choose to pause its printing (if it's first in the queue) or remove it entirely with choices in the `Document` menu (or by right-clicking on a document name). Thus, even after the printing progress dialog goes away in your application program, you have another chance to halt printing in your printer's window. The `Progress` column indicates how much data is left to be sent to the printer.

Spool Trivia

While you may be able to conjure up a physical metaphor for the action of "spooling" a print file, the name is actually an acronym: Simultaneous Peripheral Operations On Line. Spooling can apply to actions other than printing, but in the personal computing world, the term is used primarily for printing.

You can direct Windows to start one or more applications (including stand-alone programs, applets, and control panels) or load a particular document each time the system starts up or restarts.

Startup

Therefore, if you typically work with a particular set of applications all the time, you can let Windows prepare your work environment for you. The way you teach Windows what to load is to put a file (or preferably a shortcut to the file) in the Windows→Start Menu→Programs→Startup folder. If you place a document file in the Startup folder, Windows both launches the application for that document and loads the document.

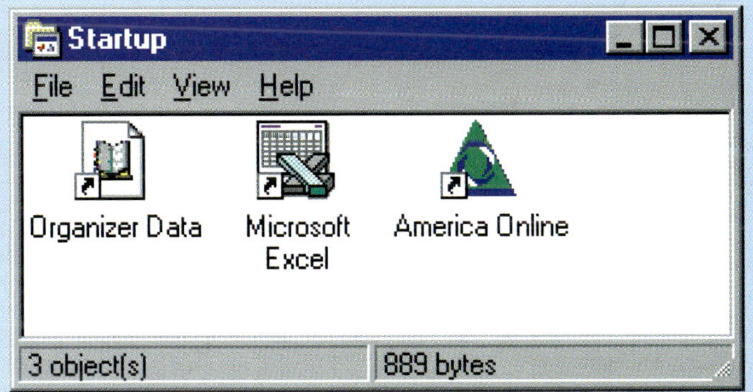

Adding Applications

You should add only as many applications, desk accessories, and control panels to the **Startup Items** folder as your PC has RAM (physical and virtual) to load.

When you copy a combination of items into the Startup Items folder, you have a measure of influence over their startup order. While items open in alphabetical order of the shortcuts in the folder, some programs take longer to launch (and therefore appear in the **Taskbar**) than others.

Adding Documents

As you drag multiple document files or their shortcuts to the **Startup** folder, be aware of how the associated programs treat multiple documents. Applications that allow multiple documents to be open at the same time will open Startup folder documents as separate document windows within one instance of the application. But single-document applications (e.g., WordPad) will open an instance of the program for each associated document in the folder. In limited memory PCs, this could lead to performance problems.

Preventing Startups from Opening

Having programs start up for you is handy under normal circumstances, but the additional launching time may get in the way if you just want to start your PC for a single task. You can bypass the items in the Startup folder by holding down the Shift key while Windows starts up. You can begin holding the key down after the initial startup menu appears, and continue until the Desktop and Taskbar appear on the screen. The "Click here to begin" sign will appear in the Taskbar. This bypass works only for the current session of Windows. The next time you start up without holding the Shift key down, items in the Startup folder will launch.

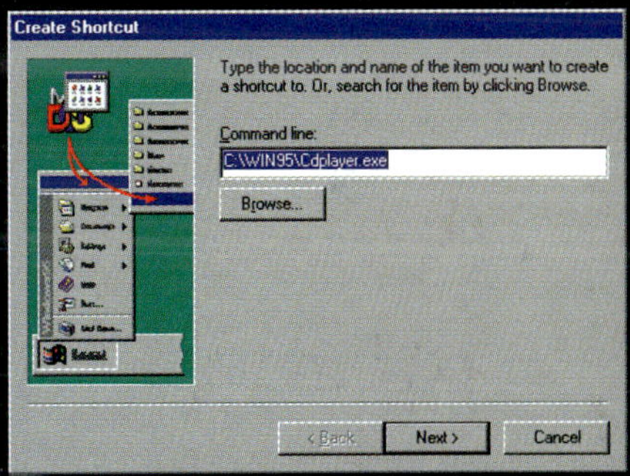

Startup Strategies

It is rare that you would store actual files in the Startup folder. More likely, you will keep applications, applets, control panels, and documents in other folders that are more natural repositories for those files. Instead, create **shortcuts** for any file you want to have in the Startup folder. The most efficient way to load your Startup folder is to right-click in the folder's window and choose New→Shortcut. In the ensuing dialog, click the Browse... button to locate the file you'd like to launch at start-up. For folders, however, you'll have to use the Desktop/Explorer to right-click-and-drag them into the Startup folder.

File Management 108

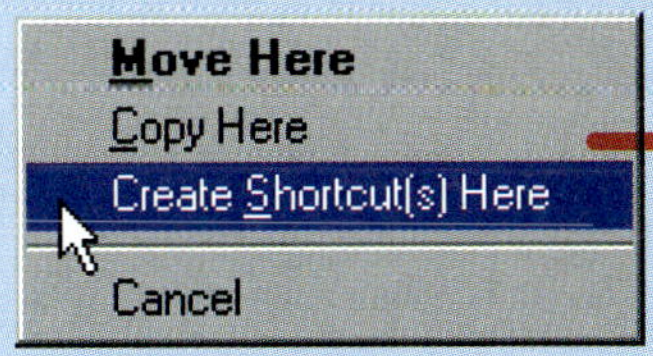

Move Here
Copy Here
Create Shortcut(s) Here
Cancel

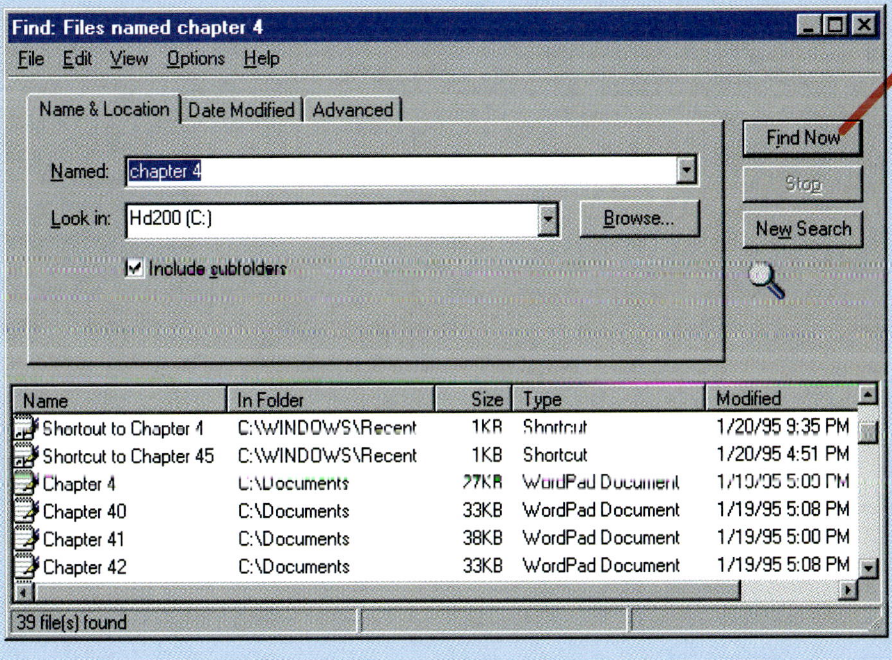

Find: Files named chapter 4
File Edit View Options Help
Name & Location
Date Modified
Advanced
Named:
chapter 4
Look in:
Hd200 (C:)
Browse...
Include subfolders
Find Now
Stop
New Search
Name
In Folder
Size
Type
Modified
Shortcut to Chapter 45
C:\WINDOWS\Recent
1KB
Shortcut
1/20/95 4:51 PM
Chapter 40
C:\Documents
33KB
WordPad Document
1/19/95 5:08 PM
Chapter 41
C:\Documents
38KB
WordPad Document
1/19/95 5:00 PM
Chapter 42
C:\Documents
33KB
WordPad Document
1/19/95 5:08 PM
39 file(s) found

Windows 95 provides a folder structure that you can use to store and organize any files on a disk. This structure is a virtually unlimited electronic version of file drawers and folders. You may nest folders to depths unheard of in the physical file folder world.

Regardless of how many levels below the top level of any disk drive, each file has a kind of address, called its **path.** The path consists of a sequential list of folders you'd have to open to reach that file. Fortunately, Windows gives you many ways to transcend and navigate a complex path.

The manner in which you organize application and document files in folders is a personal affair, but it helps to give it some thought based on your work methods. And while you can change your mind at any time, some processes in Windows depend heavily on the path *not* changing.

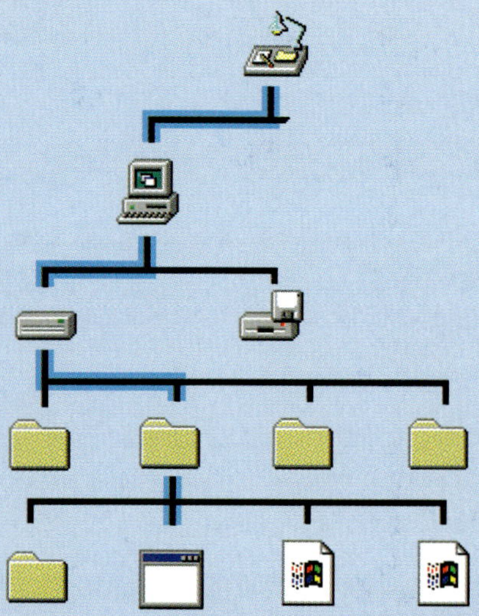

Folder Hierarchy

The Windows file system is said to be hierarchical, because you can organize files according to a **structure** that resembles a corporate organizational chart, with each horizontal slice representing a rank within the entire scheme. The most global view is at the top, with each lower ranking nested inside a folder just above it in rank. At the top of the file structure is the Desktop, which gives you an overview of all the computers you can reach from where you're sitting. The primary machine is `My Computer`, where live the **volumes** (disk drives, tape drives, etc.) mounted on your machine. Next comes the contents of each volume. When you open a volume's window, that window is said to be at the **root** of that volume. From the root grow the folders and documents further nested within. At any level starting at the root, you may park any combination of individual files and folders.

Navigating the Hierarchy

Your methodology of working your way through the hierarchy depends on whether you use Desktop folder windows or the Explorer. With Desktop windows, you may open successive folders by double-clicking on their **icons** 74. In the Explorer, you see two views side by side: a graphical, expandable hierarchy of disk drives and folders, and the immediate contents of any disk drive or folder selected on the left side 76.

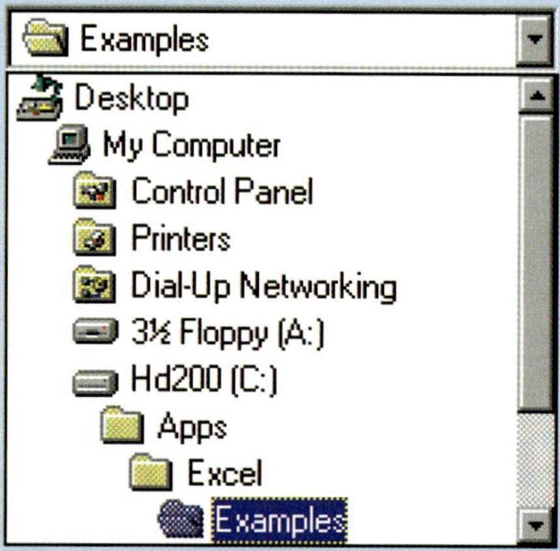

Path Notation

Far less prominent in Windows 95 than in earlier versions is the textual way of referring to a folder or file based on its path name—the trail of folders you would traverse to reach the target item. Windows path names always start with a disk drive letter, colon, and backslash. Delimiting each folder name in the path name is the backslash character. Here's an example of a pathname to a file on the C: hard drive:

```
C:\Documents\Books\Beethoven
Biography\Text\Chapter 14
```

While viewing any Desktop folder window that has the **Toolbar** turned on (`View` menu), you may find where that folder exists in the hierarchy by displaying the pop-up list in the Toolbar. Select any item in the list to open that folder's window.

Within a file dialog box 90, a similar pop-up list of the path to the current folder appears above the listing of file names. Navigate to any level between the current folder and the root by selecting it from the list.

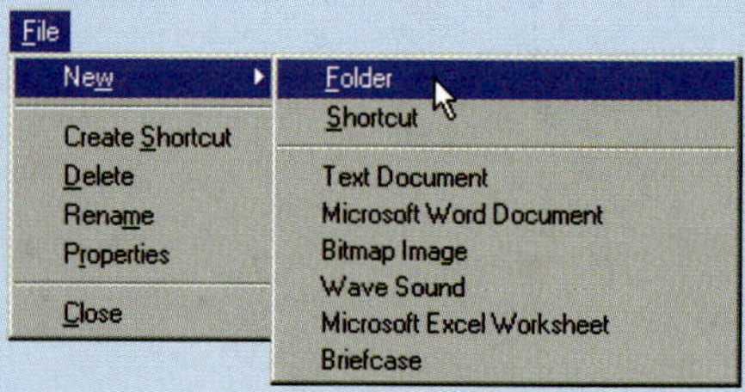

Creating New Folders

In any folder or Explorer window, you can create a folder very easily. While viewing the contents of the disk drive or folder in which you want to add the new folder, choose `New`→`Folder` from the `File` menu (or from the right-click pop-up menu in the window). A folder named "New Folder" appears in the first available location in the window (or, in list view, at the bottom of the list). "New Folder" is highlighted, ready for you to rename it.

In almost every instance in which Windows requires a pathname to fill a field in a dialog box, there is a Browse... button located nearby. Clicking this button brings up a file dialog box that lets you select the item by clicking with the mouse: Windows then fills in the path name of the item you clicked. To avoid potential typing errors (causing "invalid pathname" errors), take advantage of these mouse shortcuts to fill in path names.

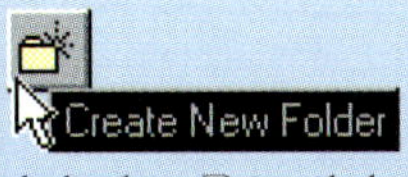

Within applications, you may also create a new folder from the **Save File** dialog box ➥91. Clicking the Create New Folder button places a "New Folder" at the end of the list of files appearing in the dialog.

Naming Folders

You may rename a folder at any time, but doing so may cause a shortcut linked to a file in that folder to fail to locate the target file. In the Explorer, only folders displayed in the right-hand pane may be renamed.

There are two ways to prepare a folder name for renaming. In the menu method:

1. Click once anywhere on the folder to select it.
2. Choose `Rename` from the `File` menu.

A quicker way is to click twice slowly on the folder name in the window. As a result of both methods, the folder name becomes an editable field. Use standard text editing techniques to delete or edit some or all of the name. Press **Enter** to apply the new name.

A folder must have a name, even if it is one character. Maximum length is 256 characters, with any character allowed except:

/\ : , * ? " < > |

A folder name may contain spaces, but it may not begin with a space.

Be sure the folder's name in some way identifies the nature of its contents.

While all viewing methods display a folder icon along with the name, some users also add the word "Folder" or a lowercase script *f* (**Alt+031**) to designate a folder object. This seems redundant.

Longish Filenames

The 256-character limit to file and folder names is a bit misleading. A more significant limitation is the Windows 95 maximum of 260 characters for an item's path name. Because many file manipulation commands invisibly refer to full path names while they execute, you'll have to avoid very long names for individual items that may get deeply nested.

How Many Levels?

Each user's approach to the depth vs. breadth issue is different. Some users prefer to limit each folder window to a small number of items that can be viewed all at once in a relatively small window, even if it means that a document may be deeply nested many levels away from the root. Others prefer fewer levels, and don't mind lots of items at each level. One rule of thumb says that if you have to mix depth and breadth, then keep windows clutter-free closer to the root, but allow deeper folders to contain many files or other folders. For example, a hierarchy for a writer of a biography might look like this:

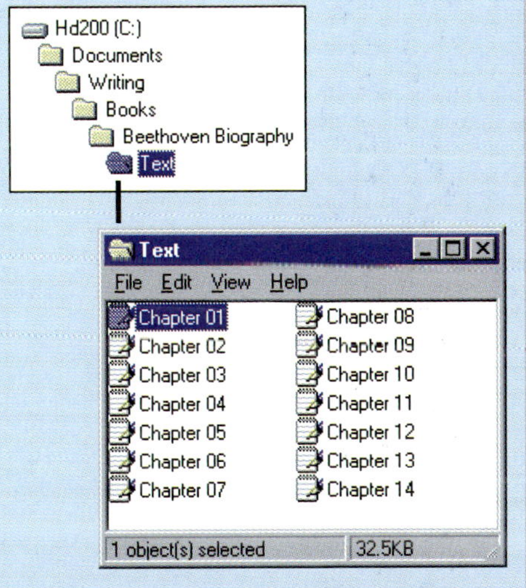

Quick Access to Nested Folders

When a deeply nested folder is one you need to access all the time, you have two choices for easy access. One is to leave the folder window showing on the Desktop all the time. The other, more efficient method is to create a shortcut for that folder, and place the shortcut either on the Desktop or in the Start menu ➥83. Choosing that item in the menu activates the Desktop, and opens that folder.

Folder Views

Use the settings in the Desktop/Explorer `View` menu ➥96 to establish the way you want items to appear in a disk or folder window. Icon views can provide a spatial organization that works well for frequently accessed items—you get to know where an item is, and go to it without even looking closely at the icon or name. You may also drag icons around a window and resize a window so that only some items show when the window opens, thus reducing visual clutter.

Text views, on the other hand, make it easier to find items when there are many in the folder. Choose the sorting scheme that makes the most sense for your viewing pleasure—for example, alphabetical when looking for a file name, chronological when looking for recent files to back up.

Organizational Schemes

Hundreds of megabytes of files can become unwieldy very quickly. To be most efficient with your disk storage, you should be aware of a few organizational techniques that you can adapt to the specific way you work with your applications and documents. For very large hard disks (in excess of 300 megabytes), it is helpful to make your first organizational layer in the form of multiple hard disk partitions ➥ 53. Each partition becomes a separate volume in `My Computer`.

DOS Organization

A remnant of the MS-DOS structure is the one in which you create a separate root-level folder for each application. Into each folder goes the application and all documents created with that application. This is a computer-centered organization, because it makes you think about files by path rather than by content or context.

Work Type Organization

You may divide your work into the typical software categories, with root folders for Word Processing, Spreadsheets, Telecommunications, and so on. Within each folder are the relevant applications (e.g., a word processor, outliner, and spelling checker in the Word Processing folder) plus all documents created by those applications.

Applications/Data Organization

At the root level, you can create one folder that holds all applications. Since you can launch an application by opening one of its documents or by opening a shortcut in the Start menu ➥ 83, you may not need to open this folder very often. Other root folders are for documents, and can be organized around context. For example, a Finance folder might contain spreadsheets, relevant memos, charts, and presentations—all created from numerous applications, but all pertaining to the Finance department.

Contextual Folder Organization

Document organization can be radically different in different folders, depending on the context for a group of documents. In some instances, grouping by project may be appropriate; in others, grouping by the nature of the documents (e.g., all correspondence) is best. In all likelihood, you'll find a need for a combination of techniques.

The Windows Desktop and Explorer simplify basic file operations to little more than clicking, dragging, and making menu selections.

Right-clicking on icons in windows is the surest way to find out what you can do with a folder, file, or application. A right-click pop-up menu of the most common operations for the selected item makes it easy to know what to do next.

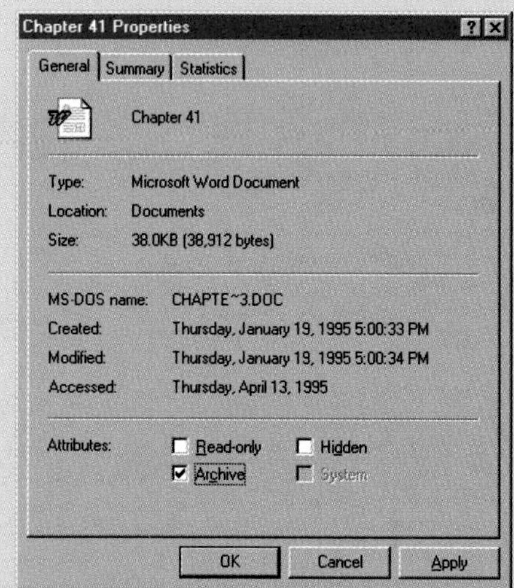

File Properties

Select any icon in a Desktop/Explorer window, and choose Properties from the File menu (or right-click on the item and choose Properties from the pop-up menu). Depending on the kind of object you select, Windows presents relevant information about that file, including what type it is, the name of its enclosing folder, its size, its short file name (i.e., as it would appear in a straight MS-DOS listing), creation and last modification dates, and other pertinent info. Some files include additional panels in the Property sheet, as follows:

Icon Type	Additional Property Data
Windows application	Version, copyright info
DOS application	DOS partition settings 45
Folder	Sharing status 152
Document	Depends on originating application
Shortcut	Path to original copy 114

The two measures of file size indicate the amount of disk space (in KB) being occupied by the file and the actual byte count of the file 51. On large hard disks, the disk space may sometimes be a few kilobytes larger than the actual byte count.

Naming Files

A file's name is usually entered when you save a document in an application 91. The name may be up to 256 characters long, and be any combination of letters, numbers, and symbols except the following characters:

/ \ : , * ? " < > |

A name cannot begin with a space, and the name must be at least one character long.

The shorter and more succinct your file names, the more you will be able to tell about a file when viewing its name in a **file dialog** 90. Since file dialogs and text listings by file name are sorted alphabetically, you can influence how files are arranged in the list. Be aware, too, that numbers sort by their character value left to right, and not by total numeric value. Thus, the file name Chapter 12 sorts before Chapter 2, because character sorting places the "1" of the "12" before the "2." Therefore, consider numbering items with leading zeros (e.g., Chapter 02).

No two files may have the same name in the same folder level, but the same file name may exist in each of your folders.

Renaming Files

As for folders, there are two ways to prepare a file name for renaming. In the menu method:

1. Click once anywhere on the file icon to select it.
2. Choose Rename from the File menu.

A quicker way is to click twice slowly on the file name in the window. As a result of both methods, the file name becomes an editable field. Use standard text editing techniques to delete or edit some or all of the name. Press Enter to apply the new name.

If you rename a file that has a shortcut pointing to it, the shortcut will usually find the file anyway, but renaming enclosing folders closer to the root may cause problems for **shortcuts** 114.

Moving Files

You have many choices in moving files and folders in the Desktop view. The kind of item you drag, however, influences the default results of the drag. For example, **dragging a file** to another window ordinarily moves the file; **dragging an application** to another window creates a shortcut to the original. To prevent the confusion, drag while holding the **right** mouse button rather than the left. When you release the button at the destination, a pop-up menu of all possible options appears (usually to move, copy, or create a shortcut); you can choose the desired action with confidence.

You may move a single file, a selection of files, or a folder (including all items in the folder). Possible destinations include other windows, folder icons, disk icons, the Desktop, the Recycle Bin, and the Start menu button. As you drag an icon to various places, the pointer often changes to indicate what will happen when you release the mouse button. Pay close attention to these signals, because they may help you undo a mistake.

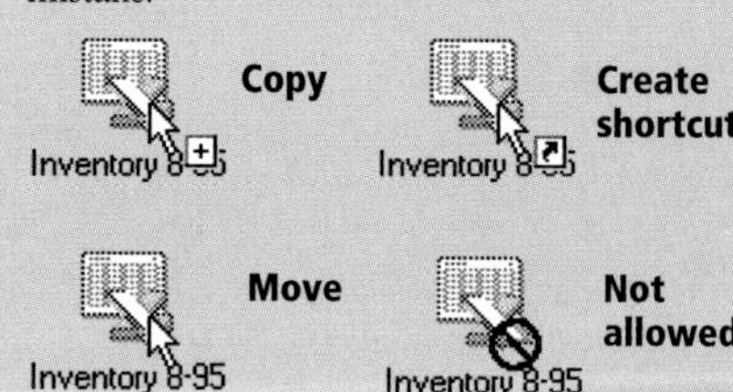

To move the file to any container icon (folder, disk, Microsoft Exchange, etc.), you must drag the file icon until the destination's icon has highlighted. Release the mouse button (and make your pop-up menu choice if you right-dragged), and the file icon disappears, meaning that the move was successful. If the file icon is still visible atop the destination icon, the move didn't take—you just missed the icon. Try again, making sure the destination icon is highlighted before releasing the mouse button.

If you move several files all at once, you may see the Move progress dialog box, showing you the files making the journey one by one.

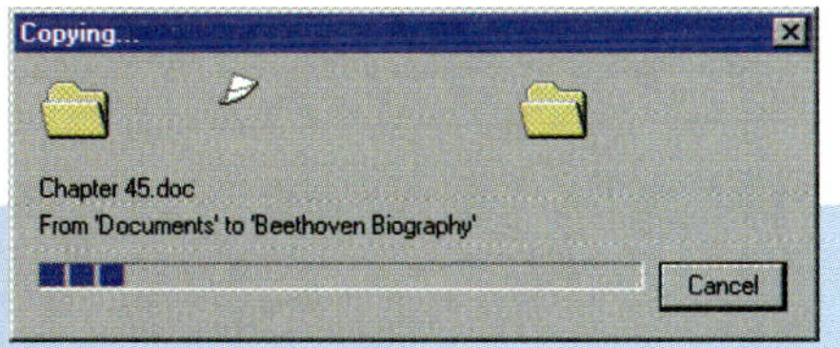

Copying Files

Dragging any icon to a destination that represents another disk volume automatically copies the item to the destination. But **right-dragging** (recommended) always gives you the option of copying, moving, or creating a shortcut. Another shortcut for copying within the same volume is to hold down the Control key while clicking and dragging the icon to its destination. The copy maintains its original name, unless it is copied within the same folder, in which case Windows appends "Copy #1 of" to the beginning of the name of the copy. If there are many selected items, a copy progress box shows you how many files are still to be copied (remember, a single folder icon may represent dozens of individual files).

Deleting a File

One way to delete a file from the Desktop/Explorer is to drag it to the Recycle Bin 93. You can also select an item, and choose Delete from the Edit or right-click pop-up menu. This moves the item to the Recycle Bin. Neither method removes it entirely from the disk, however. You'll still have to empty the bin to free up space on your hard disk taken by that file. Holding the Shift key before initiating any Delete action causes Windows to delete without stopping at the Recycle Bin.

Undoing Changes

Windows remembers many of the steps you take when moving, copying, deleting, and renaming files or folders in Desktop/Explorer windows. If you make a change by accident, you can undo it. In the Explorer window, the first item of the Edit menu indicates what you can undo; in Desktop windows, right-click on any empty space to display the pop-up menu that offers the same undo option.

Locking a File

Application and document files may be marked as "read only" in their property sheets. A read-only file cannot be modified by a program, nor can it inadvertently be renamed in the Desktop/Explorer (an alert asks you to confirm the renaming). Copies of read-only files maintain the read-only property. Marking a file as "read only" does not keep it from being deleted.

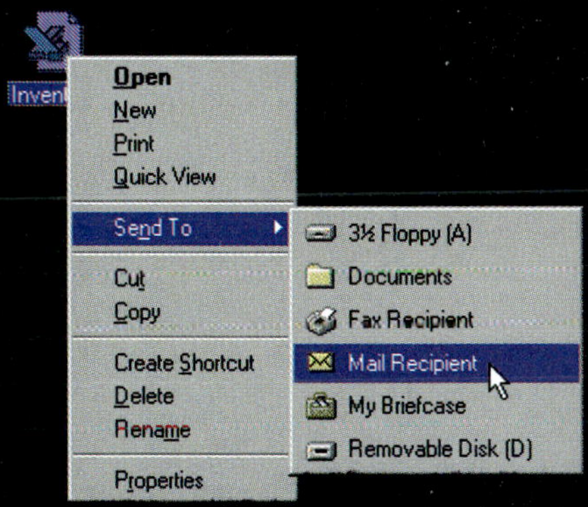

Long and Short File Names

The default behavior of Windows 95 is to allow the use of long file names, meaning you have up to 256 characters to name files and folders. But programs that predate Windows 95 are not capable of using long file names in their file dialogs 90. Moreover, you may want to send a file to another user who still uses Windows 3.x and MS-DOS. To maintain compatibility with older applications and systems, Windows 95 generates an MS-DOS-compatible file name ("8 dot 3") for each long name you or your programs create. Here are the steps Windows 95 follows to generate the short file names:

1. Remove all spaces.
2. Try first eight characters (maintain original extension).
3. If file name already exists in the folder, replace characters 7 and 8 with "~1".
4. If XXXXXX~1.XXX already exists, increase final number by one, up to 9.
5. If XXXXXX~9.XXX already exists, replace characters 6 through 8 with "~11".
6. Continue increasing number (and robbing from name characters) until there is a unique file name in this folder.

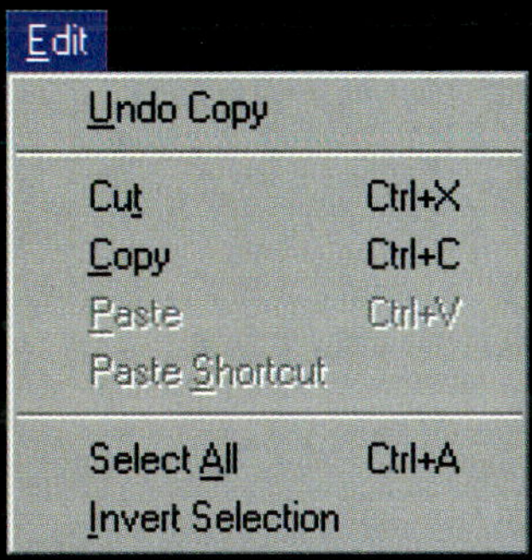

Cut, Copy, and Paste

Desktop/Explorer Edit menus (as well as right-click pop-up menus) contain standard Cut, Copy, and Paste commands (Paste only when there's something to paste), which work with files and folders. These commands are very handy when the source file and destination (including the Recycle Bin) are hidden by other windows or aren't immediately available when you need them. An extra option, Paste Shortcut, pastes only a shortcut to the Clipboard item.

Select an item (or items) to copy, and choose Copy from the Edit menu or right-click pop-up menu. Next, navigate to the open window or Desktop where you'd like the copy to go (you can close the original), and choose Paste from the Edit menu or right-click pop-up menu. Using Cut and Paste in the same manner replicates the action of moving an item. When you select an item and choose Cut from the menu, the original icon is

Sending Files

The Send To item in Desktop/Explorer File menus (and right-click pop-up menus) is another way to move items to places on your hard disk (or other disk volume) where you frequently store items. For instance, if a communications program always downloads files in a folder you don't use often, you can open that folder after a session and send the items to more convenient destinations, such as a Documents or Games folder.

Windows automatically installs the floppy disk A:, other mounted volumes, and the FAX wizard in the Send To list. But you can add to the list. To do so:

1. In any Desktop/Explorer window, choose Options from the View menu.
2. In the View panel, engage the Show All Files radio button and click Apply.
3. Locate the Send To folder inside the Windows folder.
4. Create shortcuts 114 to your favorite destinations, and copy them into the Send To folder.
5. Restore the original setting in the View→Options→View panel, and close the Options window.

One of the biggest boosts to efficient hard disk management in Windows 95 software is the shortcut.

A new concept for Windows 95, the shortcut allows you to create a tiny file (only a few hundred bytes) that can stand in for any file, folder, or disk. In other words, you can have one folder or file appear in many locations on your hard disk with only one true copy of the item.

Shortcut Overview

When you create a shortcut, you create a **small file** that behaves exactly like the original file. It has the **same icon** as the original plus a small square showing an angle arrow, indicating that this icon points to something else. That's how you can readily tell if an icon is the real thing or its shortcut.

Shortcut to Current Projects

The **shortcut is** actually nothing more than **a pointer** to the original file, passing along any action sent to the shortcut. All the action—reading and saving data, changing preferences, editing a document—really takes place only in the original file. The shortcut is merely an extra set of eyes, ears, and mouth for the original file.

Folder shortcuts sometimes seem even more like magic. Double-click a folder shortcut, and the original folder opens. Drag an item to the shortcut, and the item goes into the original folder.

Multiple Shortcuts

An object may have more than one shortcut. In fact, it may be worthwhile in some cases to have multiple shortcuts. For example, you may want a shortcut to a file in the Start menu as well as in some other document folders, convenient to other related documents.

Semi-Permanent Link

The link between shortcut and original is **one-way**—the shortcut knows about the original (also called the **target**), but the original doesn't know about shortcuts created from it. Therefore, if you delete the original file, you won't be alerted about the shortcuts out there that still point to the original. You will get an alert, however, when you try to access a shortcut and it can't find the original.

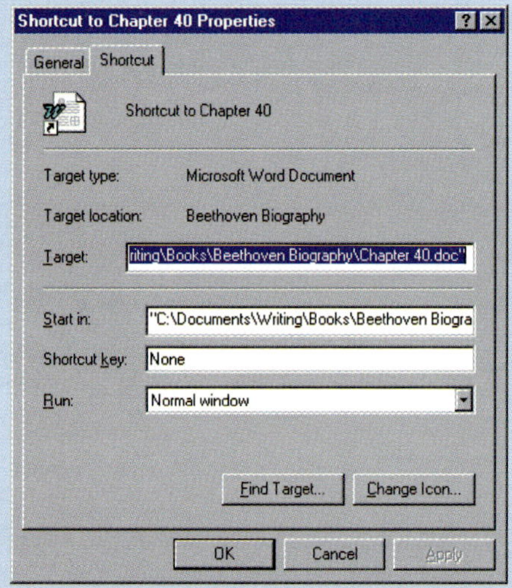

Shortcuts **maintain their links** based largely on a **path name** to the original item. There's more to it than that, because you can rename the original file and the shortcut will still locate the correct item (even if another item in the same folder now has the original name). But if you also change the names of folders in the path name containing the target, there is a chance that the shortcut will not be able to locate the original, even after Windows tries to locate it by other searching methods (based on the original file's previous path name). This potential disconnection occurs more frequently if you change the names of folders closer to the root directory, because Windows will not know where to begin the search for the target item. Therefore, it is a good idea to **establish a solid organizational approach** for your hard disk early on → 111 and stick to it, if you plan to use shortcuts in the Start menu and elsewhere.

Creating a Shortcut

To create a shortcut from the Finder, you have many options, depending on the window landscape on your monitor. Here's one method:

1. Display the original file or folder item and the destination for the shortcut (e.g., Desktop background, other folder window, Start menu).
2. Right-drag the original item to the destination.
3. In the pop-up menu, choose `Create Shortcut(s) Here`.

When you cannot readily see the original item and the destination at the same time:

1. Display the original file or folder item, and click once to select it.
2. Choose `Copy` in the Desktop/Explorer window's `File` menu (alternatively, right-click the item, and choose `Copy` from the pop-up menu).

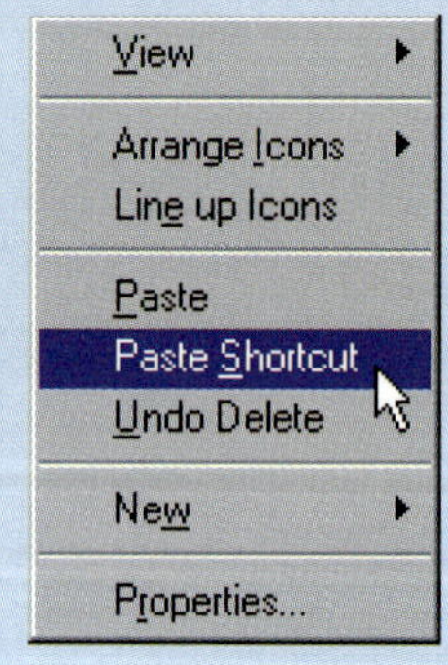

3. Navigate to the destination, and choose `Paste Shortcut` from the `Edit` menu (or the right-click pop-up menu).

When you create a shortcut, Windows assigns an icon very similar to the original, but with the addition of an upward angled arrow inside a tiny box. Windows also appends the words "Shortcut to" to the beginning of the original item's name.

Renaming a Shortcut

What you name a shortcut can depend on how you plan to use it. Of course, you don't have to rename the shortcut file, although the identifiable arrow in the icon makes the "shortcut" part of the name redundant. Since a shortcut file is a file like any other, you rename it just like any other file 112.

A significant advantage of a shortcut is that its name **does not have to resemble its original item's name**. As an example, you could create shortcuts to a series of forms that need to be filled out in a particular sequence. Group the shortcuts in a folder, and rename them with sequence numbers to help the user know which is which.

Changing a Shortcut's Icon

While Windows automatically generates a shortcut-style icon for any item's shortcut, you can assign any other available icon to the shortcut. In the Shortcut screen of a shortcut file's property sheet is a button that leads to an icon selection dialog. You immediately see icons supplied by Windows, but you can also browse to locate other icons from applications or other icon collections. Still, Windows puts the identifiable shortcut arrow atop whatever icon you choose so there will be no confusion between a shortcut and a genuine item.

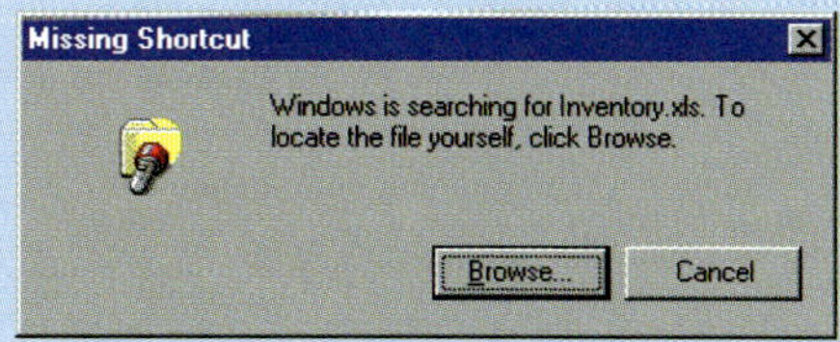

Finding the Original File

Because a shortcut may bear no resemblance to its original file (it can have an entirely different name and icon), you may need help finding the original file. Select the shortcut file in a Desktop/Explorer window, and choose `Properties` from the `File` menu (or right-click on a shortcut and choose `Properties` from the pop-up menu). In the `Shortcut` panel of the property sheet window is a button (Find Target...) that finds the original item, opens its window, and selects it for you.

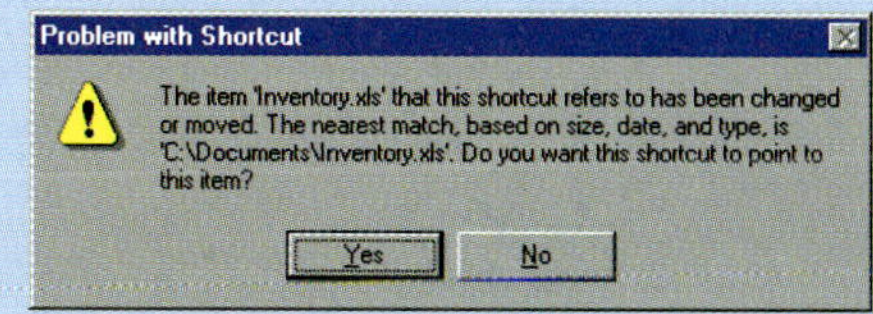

If the original file has been deleted or there have been substantial changes to the names of folders comprising its path, Windows may not be able to locate the item. You may see an animated pointer showing a flashlight scanning for items. If there is low confidence about the original item, you will receive an alert message that the original cannot be found (the path or working directory is invalid) or, occasionally, a message that there is a near match, offering you a chance to go there instead.

Shortcut Strategies

Here are several productive ways to use shortcuts:

- **Start Menu.** Determine which applications, documents, folders, or disks you'd like to have ready access to from the Start menu. Create shortcuts for those items, and drag them to the Start button. Right-click on the Start button and open the Start Menu folder's contents. Rename the shortcuts as you like, with the knowledge that the Start Menu displays these shortcuts alphabetically by their shortcut name. While the shortcuts in the Start Menu folder display shortcut-style icons, the icons that appear in the actual Start menu don't have the shortcut arrow on them.
- **Startup Folder.** Copy shortcuts of your all-day applications or documents to the `Windows➜Start Menu➜Programs➜Startup` folder. Those programs will launch when you start your machine, without disturbing your file organization.
- **Desktop Icons.** If you prefer to emulate the workstation scenario that displays icons to frequently accessed programs and documents on the Desktop, do so with shortcuts. Copy each file, and paste the shortcut into the Desktop Rename the shortcuts for easy identification.
- **Folder Shortcuts.** Because a folder shortcut behaves like its original, if you drag a file to a shortcut folder, the item actually goes into the original folder (a shortcut never stores any of your data). While working with the contents of a deeply nested folder, create a shortcut and place it on the Desktop, making it much easier to access or modify the folder's contents without opening up a series of nested folder windows.

Shortcut Files

The shortcut file name extension is .LNK, but the extension appears only in its MS-DOS file name. A shortcut long name displays an extension if the original file name displays an extension.

No Shortcuts of Shortcuts

Windows does not allow you to create a shortcut of a shortcut file. If you attempt to create a shortcut of a shortcut, the result is a second shortcut to the original item. This is just as well, because otherwise you'd establish a potentially fragile chain that could go awry with the slightest folder renaming along the path to the original or first shortcut.

With hard disk storage of hundreds of megabytes, it is vital to have a quick way of searching through thousands of files and folders to locate an item whose path you're unsure of. The Windows 95 Find utility does a great job.

Your searches can be as broad or as narrow as you like. You can search on a **partial file name** as well as limit searches to **particular kinds of items**, items modified within a **certain date range**, and items of a **certain size range**. The results of the search appear in a window similar to any Desktop/Explorer window, with your choice of view type. You can then act directly on found items—opening, deleting, moving, and so on.

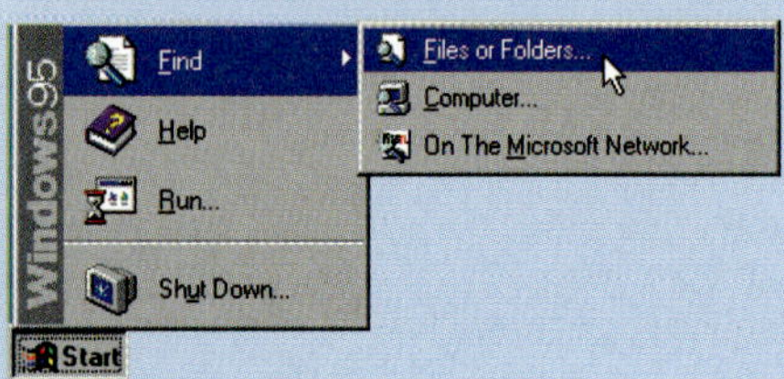

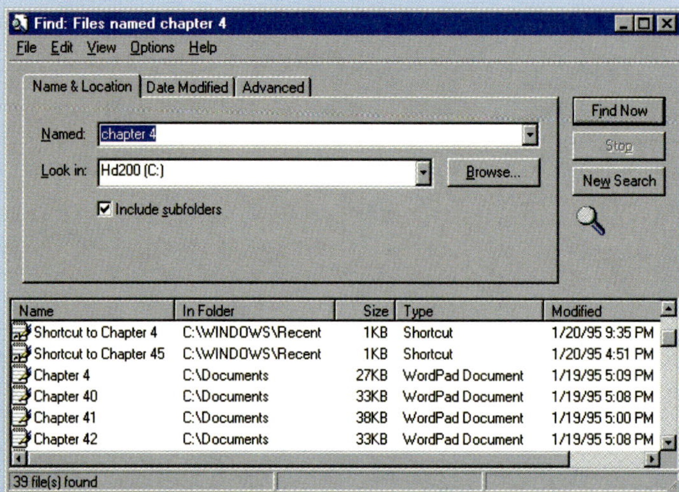

Starting a New Search

Your access to the **Find** utility is via the Start menu. Choose Find→Files or Folders from the Start menu. The Find window appears on the screen. In the window are three panels, each providing places to enter search criteria for **name** and **location**, **modified date of items**, and **advanced criteria** (e.g., files of just a certain type or minimum size). All three of these panels work together in every search you perform.

Simple Name Search

Without making any changes to other screens of the Find window, you can perform a **quick search** through the entire C: drive on a complete or partial item name. Enter the search text into the Named field and click the Find Now button. During the search, the magnifying glass icon animates to indicate that Windows is searching. As items whose names contain the typed text are found, they appear in a file list at the bottom of the Find window. Click the Stop button at any time to halt the operation.

Windows treats text you enter into the Named field as **raw characters** to compare against entire names of files and folders on your disk(s). If the text you typed is only a portion of a file name, all file names containing that string of characters appear in the list of found items. The good news is that if you remember only a portion of the file name, you can still search for it, and then scan the list of found items to locate the desired file. The more information you supply in the Named field, the fewer "hits" Windows will find, slimming the list of found items.

Hidden files will not be found unless you first set the Desktop/Explorer's View menu Options→View settings to show all files.

Saving Search Criteria

Files of type Microsoft Excel Worksheet named Inventory

If you notice that you frequently perform searches with the same criteria, you can save a lot of time by saving a search criteria set (and the results). Turn on Save Results in the Options menu, then choose Save Search from the File menu. Windows places an icon representing the search criteria and results of the most recent search on the Desktop. The name of the saved search can grow pretty long, since it attempts to fully label what the search does. When you re-open one of these saved searches, you should click the Find Now button to locate any new additions to your hard disk that may meet the criteria (the saved search itself may also appear in the list of found files, since its name might include the name you searched for earlier).

Periodic Maintenance

One of the byproducts of the ease with which Windows lets you create shortcuts and new folders or files at the drop of a right mouse button is that your hard disk may eventually become cluttered with such items that you do not need. You may collect a number of these items by accident; shortcuts you once used may no longer be necessary. Use the Find facilities to locate these extraneous items every few months. For instance, you should search for all items whose file types are shortcuts to files, applications, and folders. Also, search for items whose names include the word "New," Windows' default name for new items it creates in Desktop/Explorer windows. Examine each item found in these searches, and delete the ones you no longer need.

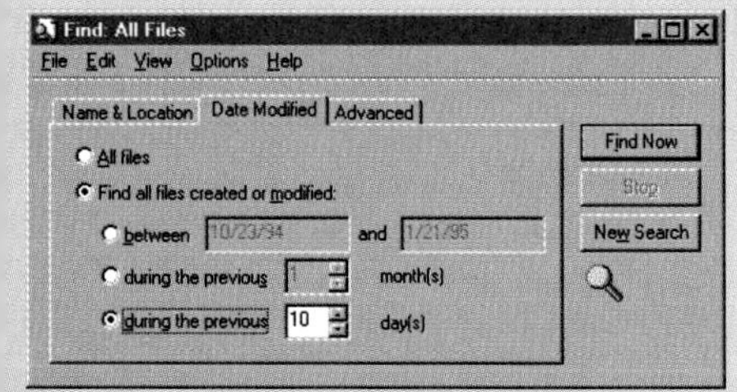

Searching by Date Range

Independent of any entry you make in the Name & Location screen of the Find window, you can ask Windows to locate files (and folders) that meet specific criteria based on the **modified dates** of items. The default setting in the Date Modified panel is All Files, but you can choose from one of three date criteria:

- all items modified **between two dates**
- all items modified within the **past number of months**
- all items modified within the **past number of days**

Remember that if you entered a name or other search criteria in other panels of this window, they apply to the date search criteria set in this panel. Thus, if you entered "Inventory" into the Name & Location panel, and the previous five days in the Date Modified panel, Windows will locate only those files whose name contains "Inventory" and whose modified date is within the previous five days. If you want to locate files based only on the modified date, click the New Search button to clear specifications in all screens.

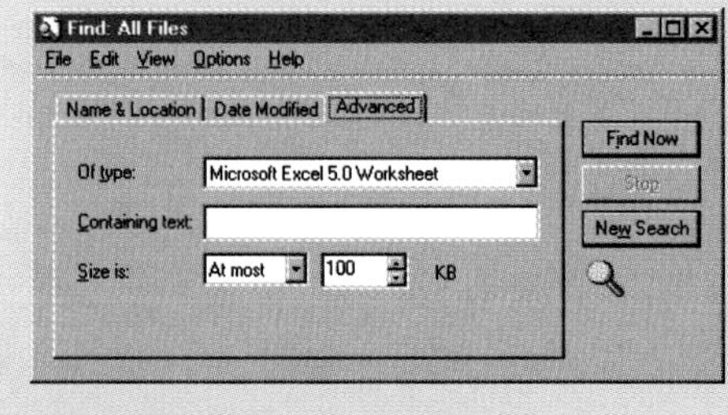

Searching by Type, Size

In the Advanced screen of the Find window are places to enter other search criteria. A pop-up list presents all registered **file types** that your copy of Windows knows about. For example, you can limit searches to all your Excel worksheets.

At the bottom of the panel are two entry areas for specifying a maximum or minimum **size** for files to search for. Either manually enter a kilobyte value, or use the up/down arrow buttons to reach the desired number. This can come in handy if you are copying a bunch of files to floppy disks, and need a file only of no more than a certain size to fit on one of the disks.

Searching by Contents

In the Advanced screen is a field for entry of text that Find can use to explore the **content of files**. This is a much slower process, so it's helpful to narrow the file type on the same screen. While Find performs its job, you can switch to another program, instead of having to wait until it searches the entire disk volume.

Search Scope

While the Windows file searching facility is pretty fast, you can make it even faster if you know that the items you want to find are in a certain folder or nested very deeply along one path. The default scope of a search is My Computer, which could include multiple disk drives or volume partitions. The pop-up list in the Look In field presents a list of all volumes that Windows sees. Choose one to limit search scope to an individual volume.

But you can go further in limiting scope. Click the Browse... button. A hierarchical list just like the left column of Explorer appears in a separate window. Click the plus buttons next to items you wish to open until you see the folder you wish the search to start from. Select that folder and click OK. That folder's path 110 now appears in the Look In field.

Unless instructed otherwise, Windows always drills down through all subfolders of whatever container appears in the Look In field. Uncheck the Include subfolders checkbox if you wish to limit the search to the single folder shown in the Look In field.

One final option that controls the scope of a search is the Case Sensitive menu item in the Options menu. Normally, it's a good idea to ignore case when searching for a file name (or partial file name), because it's easy to forget how you capitalized a file name. But if you think it will help your search, you can turn on case sensitivity by selecting this menu item to toggle it on.

Find Results Display

Search results appear in a bottom extension to the Find window, and the window becomes adjustable in all directions. This part of the Find window behaves like any Desktop window: the View menu lets you choose from the four standard types of display. Because of the amount of screen space taken up by the search criteria of this adjustable window, the Details type of file listing is more useful than the Large or Small Icon view. You also see the beginning of the path, size, file type, and modification date. Columns are resizable by dragging their divider bars. Sort by any column's data by clicking on the column data (or via the View→Arrange Icons menu).

Not only does this part of the window look like a Desktop window, but it also works the same way. All items are active here, so you can double-click to open them, drag them to the Recycle Bin, move or copy, and right-click to get a pop-up menu of common operations for that type of item.

Navigating to a Found Item's Folder

Should you wish to open the folder that contains a found item, Windows can do that for you. Select the item, and choose Open Containing Folder from the File menu. Not only does a Desktop window open to that folder, but the item you selected in the Find window is selected in the newly opened window.

Need a quick peek at the contents of a document file?

Windows 95 includes a facility called **Quick View,** which lets you open a number of different kinds of document files—including graphics, word processing, and spreadsheet files—without opening the program that generated the files. You don't even need to have the application on your computer.

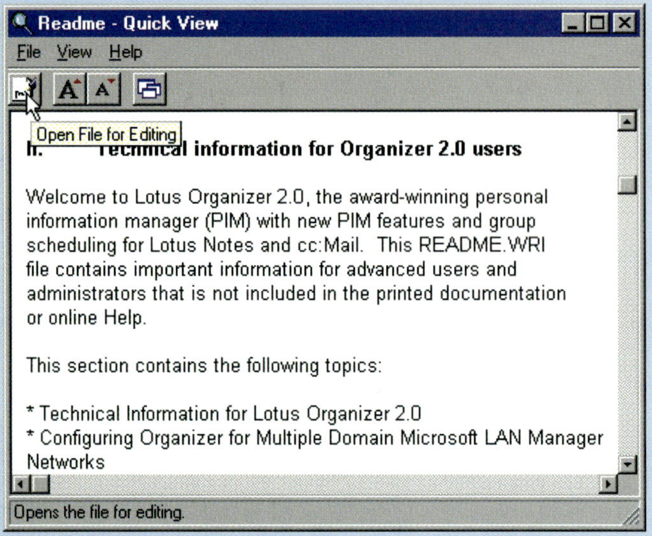

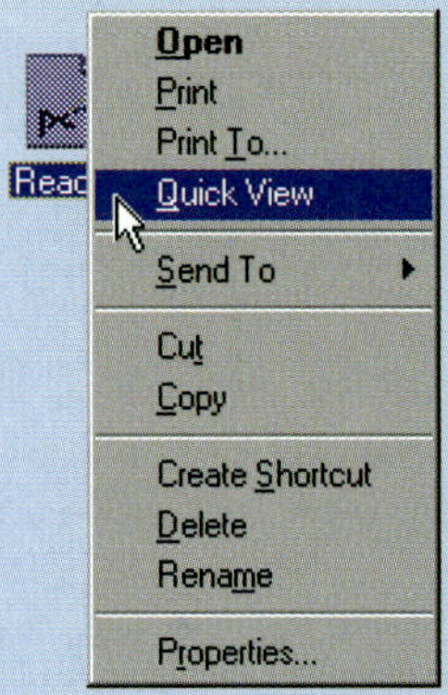

Starting Quick View

When you select a document file in any Desktop/ Explorer window, Windows checks to see if it has a viewer in its library to match the **file type** of the item selected. If a viewer exists, then the `File` menu (or right-click pop-up menu) contains an item called `Quick View`.

Choosing this menu item displays the Quick View window and the contents of the file. In the case of word processing and spreadsheet files, the display does not necessarily include fancy formatting, but does include enough data to read word processed text and identify a spreadsheet file. Some file types activate applicable commands in the `View` menu, such as for rotating a graphics file or selecting a different display font for all of the text. Virtually all types permit viewing in `Page View`, so you can see an entire page scaled to fit the window.

Opening Other Files

One Quick View setting, `Replace Window`, prevents Quick View from opening more than one Quick View window. Should you open another file for quick viewing, the new file replaces the first in the Quick View window.

Some file types may not be registered, but Quick View can open them just the same. Open Quick View with a registered document, and then drag the icon of another file to the window. An alert advises that no viewer file is available, but Quick View will try one of its default viewers, which work on a number of file formats.

Editing a Viewed File

When a file type is registered, a miniature version of the application's icon appears in the **Toolbar**. Click this button to launch the application and load this document. Since the Quick View window is read-only, you will need to open a document in its application to select portions for copying or making any changes to the file.

Quick Viewers

Microsoft includes many viewers in Windows 95. The viewer files are located in the `Windows➜System➜Viewers` folder as .DLL files, all beginning with the letters "Vs." These files allow Quick View to open these standard file types:

.TXT	text/ASCII
.TIF	TIFF
.INF	setup files
.INI	configuration files
.RLE	run-length encoded graphics files
.RTF	rich text format
.BMP	Windows bitmapped graphics
.GIF	graphics
.EPS	encapsulated PostScript

and files from the following programs:

Ami
Ami Pro
Corel Draw
Freelance (Windows)
Lotus 1-2-3, versions 1, 2, 3, 4
Micrographix Draw
Microsoft Excel versions 4, 5
Microsoft Multiplan, versions 3, 4, 4.1
Microsoft PowerPoint, version 4
Microsoft Word (DOS), versions 5, 6
Microsoft Word (Windows), versions 2, 6, 7
Microsoft Works, version 3
Quattro Pro (DOS), versions 1, 5
Quattro Pro (Windows)
Windows Write, version 3.x
WordPerfect, versions 4.2, 5, 6, 6.1, Demo

Windows features a mechanism that associates a file type (based on the MS-DOS file name extension) to one or more applications for actions such as opening or printing.

When you install a new Windows application, this internal file type registration is done for you. But you can change existing associations as well as create new ones for file types unknown to your system. In the same editing area, you can engage Quick View for a file type not currently given that privilege 118.

Checking for Associations

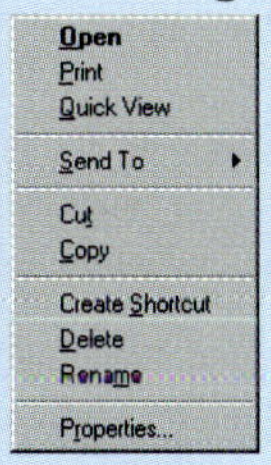

The particular content of the Desktop/Explorer window's File menu when you select different types of files (or right-click on those files) reveals much about their registration settings. Key phrases and their meanings are:

Menu Wording	Meaning
Open With...	No registration. You will be presented with a list of registered file types to choose from. Choosing one automatically registers that file type with Windows for the next time.
Open	Registered to open with an application.
Print	Registered to print with an application (can be different from the application that opens it).
Quick View	Can be opened with Quick View.

Whatever item in the menu is boldfaced is the action that Windows takes with the file if you double-click on the icon.

Easy File Registration

If you know the content and format of a file, and know what application can open it successfully (e.g., a Lotus 1-2-3 file that Excel can open), you can associate that file type with the application by attempting to open the document from the Desktop/Explorer. Double-click on the file (or right-click on it, and choose Open With). A dialog appears listing all the registered applications. Choose from the list or click Browse... to locate an unregistered program. The next time you double-click the icon, it will open the program you assigned to the file (unless you uncheck the Always use this program checkbox—handy when you want a temporary view in a different program).

Editing File Type Registration

From any Desktop/Explorer window, choose Options from the View menu, and activate the File Types screen. The scrolling list displays all file types known by your copy of Windows. Click once on an item to see the extension that Windows uses to make the association, and the name of the application associated with the Open action. Double-click on an item to see all the details in the Edit window.

Type Description

This is the plain language wording that appears in Details Desktop/Explorer views describing what kind of file an item is. Because you can sort lists by these items, you may wish to select wording that places some items near the top or bottom of the list.

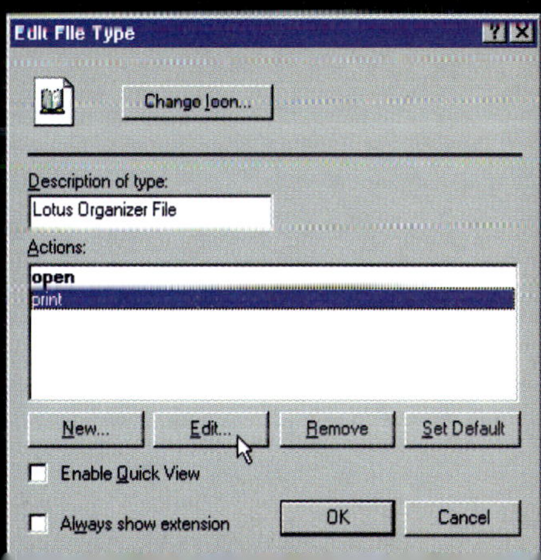

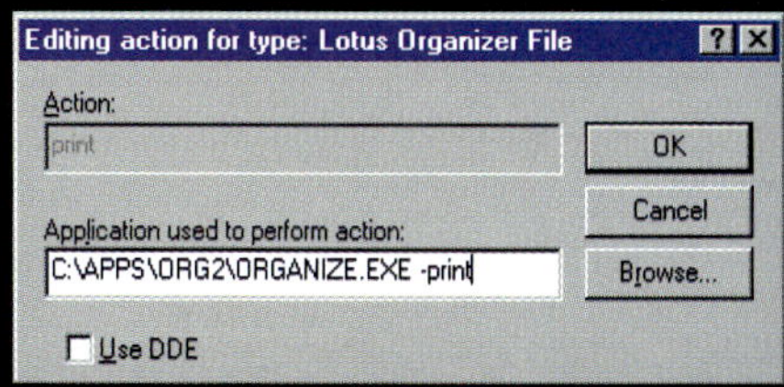

Actions

These are the items that appear at the top of the File menu (or right-click menu) when you select a file in a Desktop/Explorer window. For most document files, the common actions are Open and Print, but other actions may be possible, such as playing a sound or viewing an animation. To make these actions happen, the program must be able to accept extra parameters in its command lines (e.g., "-print"). These extra parameters must be added to the command line associated with the action (click the Edit button to see the command line) to carry out the action when called from the menu. A programs that is DDE-ready may also be scripted for any of its internal commands.

Enable Quick View

Checking this box puts Quick View in the File (or right-click) menu, but does not guarantee that there is a viewer for this file type. You'll discover that fact when you try it the first time.

Set Default

Select an action and click this button to make it the boldfaced entry in the File (or right-click) menu. This will be the action Windows takes when you double-click on the icon.

Registering a New Type

Click the New Type... button in the Options window. A window similar to the Edit window appears, but there is an extra field to type the extensions that will govern how Windows treats all files with that extensions. Be sure you are using the correct extension, and not one already associated with another application.

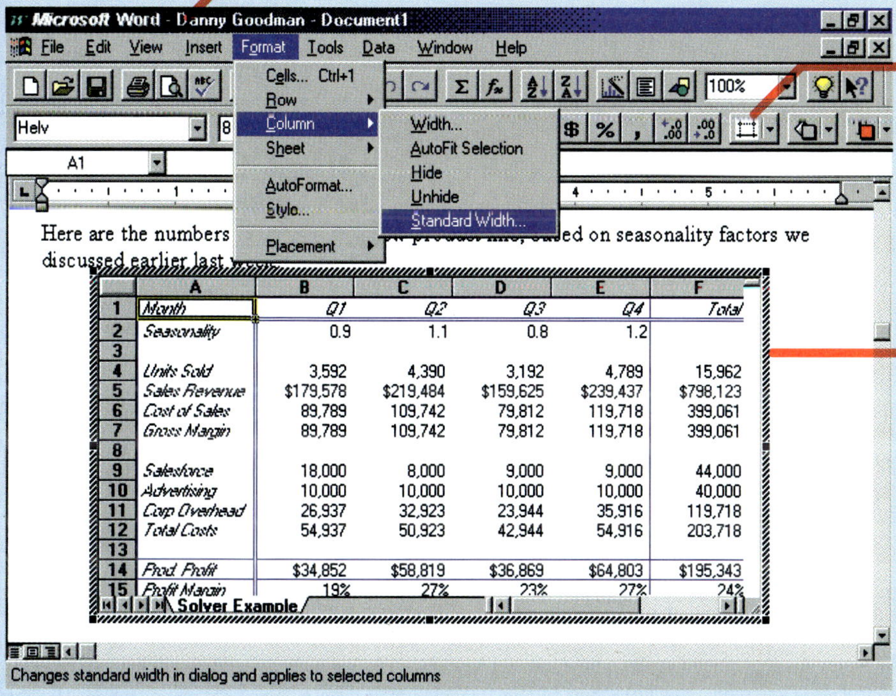
Microsoft Word - Danny Goodman - Document1
File Edit View Insert Format Tools Data Window Help
Cells... Ctrl+1
Row
Column
Sheet
AutoFormat...
Style...
Placement
Width...
AutoFit Selection
Hide
Unhide
Standard Width...
Helv
A1
100%
Here are the numbers ... based on seasonality factors we discussed earlier last ...
Month Q1 Q2 Q3 Q4 Total
Seasonality 0.9 1.1 0.8 1.2
Units Sold 3,592 4,390 3,192 4,789 15,962
Sales Revenue $179,578 $219,484 $159,625 $239,437 $798,123
Cost of Sales 89,789 109,742 79,812 119,718 399,061
Gross Margin 89,789 109,742 79,812 119,718 399,061
Salesforce 18,000 8,000 9,000 9,000 44,000
Advertising 10,000 10,000 10,000 10,000 40,000
Corp Overhead 26,937 32,923 23,944 35,916 119,718
Total Costs 54,937 50,923 42,944 54,916 203,718
Prod. Profit $34,852 $58,819 $36,869 $64,803 $195,343
Profit Margin 19% 27% 23% 27% 24%
Solver Example
Changes standard width in dialog and applies to selected columns

You buy a computer to run applications—the programs that let you capture ideas, create and manage information, communicate with others.

Through the evolution of Microsoft Windows, applications get easier to learn with each new generation, primarily because of increased consistency in basic operations. Once you know how to start and quit one Windows program, you know how to do it for all of them.

Applications interact with operating system software in subtle ways. Being able to run multiple applications at the same time, for example, is a function of the software system.

Applications also seek help from system software to open and save documents—the standard file dialogs are built into the system. And yet, while you are using a program, you almost forget about system software, as you focus on the task inside the program.

Applications and Applets

When you install Windows 95, it places a number of items in a Start menu program grouping called `Accessories`. Here you'll find little programs such as Calculator, HyperTerminal, Paint, and WordPad. Because these programs take up little disk or memory space and provide a minimum of features, they're also known as **applets**.

To Windows, there is little difference between an applet such as Phone Dialer and a giant application such as Microsoft Excel or Aldus PageMaker. They're all launched from executable files (file extensions either .EXE or .COM), and provide some service for users on the computer. There are, however, some differences between these types of programs. As far as users are concerned, for one, Microsoft relies on some of these applets to provide universal services for other programs. If you view a text file from the Microsoft Network online service, for instance, the document is displayed in WordPad on your PC. Another visible difference is that applets generally allow editing of only one document at a time. Closing a document closes the application. Larger programs usually allow multiple documents (each in its own subwindow) to be open within the application window at the same time. In truth, these are subtle differences, and you should treat applets as full citizens of your Windows 95 world.

Installing Applications

Virtually all applications these days include a program named `INSTALL` or `SETUP` that handles the process of copying files from the floppy disk(s) or CD-ROM containing the programs. In fact, the **Add/Remove Programs** control panel offers a feature that looks for installation programs on removable disks, and starts the process for you.

When the application's Setup/Install routines take over, you are sometimes asked to supply information about the setup procedure. Most common is a request for a **folder** (directory) to house the program. The initial suggestion is usually either the **root** (disk) **directory** or the Windows folder. Resist these temptations, and adhere to your organizational scheme 111.

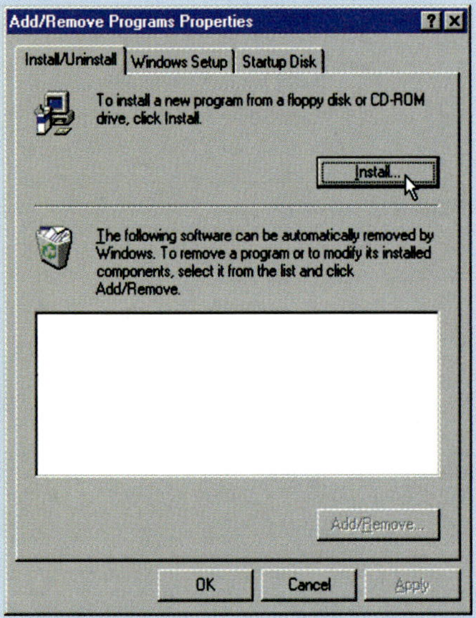

A potential problem for the time when you may wish to remove (uninstall) a program is that the installation procedure copies numerous files to your hard disk, including items that go in folders other than the program's folder. It's not unusual for an installer to copy some files to the `Windows→System` folder or the `Windows→Fonts` folder. Moreover, the installer will try to add a shortcut to the program in a program grouping folder of your Start Menu folder.

Most programs on floppy disks contain one or more compressed files. The primary reason for compressing files is to cram more data on fewer disks to reduce the disk swapping during installation and lower the product's cost. Software publishers have many **compression schemes** to choose from (PKZIP being the most popular), and fortunately, the Setup/Install program handles all decompression for you. However, if a program file should get damaged, you may not be able to copy only that file from the floppy disks without running the Setup/Install program again.

Installing CD-ROM Software

It may seem odd at first to have to run through an installation process for multimedia software that comes on CD-ROM. But if you think that all the software will run from the CD-ROM, think again. Typically, part of the program must be copied to your hard disk so that it runs faster than CD-ROMs allow. The program on your hard disk will access perhaps hundreds of megabytes of data, so you still need the CD-ROM after installation. But some CD-ROMs install a huge quantity of files—sometimes scattered around your folders. When shopping for CD-ROM software, check the packaging carefully for hard disk requirements.

Starting Applications

Windows provides several ways to **start up** (launch) an application. You can combine any of these ways depending on your work habits or other whims. If an application is already running when you attempt any of these procedures, it comes to the foreground. Applets, however, tend to launch additional instances of themselves, which is perfectly fine if you can keep them straight.

Start Menu

If you place a **shortcut** 114 to a program file in the **Start Menu** folder (or simply drag it to the Start button), you can select the program's name from the Start menu to launch the program.

Double-Click Program Icon

If you can see the icon of an program (or its shortcut icon) in any file listing, you can **double-click the icon** to start the program. Double-clicking is the same as selecting the icon (clicking it once) and choosing Open from the File menu (or right-click pop-up menu).

Double-Click Document

Windows maintains a **registry** 119 of document file types and the applications that belong to them. Therefore, if you double-click on a document icon (or a shortcut to a document), Windows locates and launches the application and then opens the document in the program.

Drop Document onto Program Icon

Windows allows you to drag a document icon to an application icon to launch that program and **open the document.** The icons may even be in different windows (clicking and dragging icons in an inactive Desktop window does not activate that window). While it is faster to just double-click a document icon to start the associated application, there are times when the drag is a better option: (1) when the document was not created by the application (but the application can open the document's file type); and (2) when you have multiple versions of an application, and you want to make sure the proper version opens with the document.

Some programs can accept files in formats other than their own. For example, most applications can read a plain text file. Double-clicking on a text file may lead to WordPad. But by dragging the text file to another application icon, you can open that application. An application's icon highlights when you drag any document icon to it, but you may not know if the application can open the document until it tries.

Drop Document into Window

While an application is running, you can open another document by dragging the document's icon (or shortcut) into the application's window or onto the application's button in the **Taskbar.** You won't know whether the application can accept the document until it tries.

Auto-Launch

Newer CD-ROM disks may include a file (AUTORUN.INF) that triggers Windows 95 to run the disk's program when you insert the disk tray or close the door on the drive.

Exiting Applications

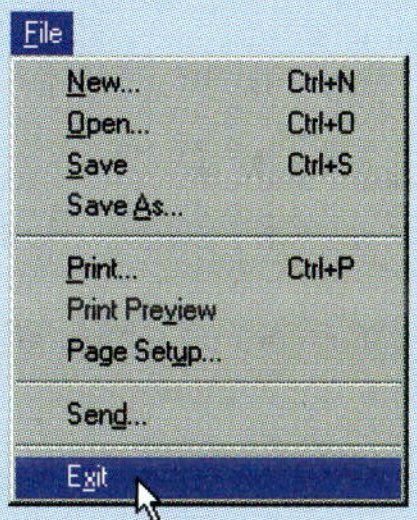

Virtually every application program quits the same way—an Exit option in the File menu. An even faster way is to click the **Close button** (☒) in the upper right corner of the application's window. If you have any open documents whose changes have not yet been saved, the program prompts you about whether you want to save the changes for each one before exiting.

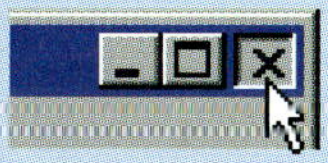

Applets often behave differently. While some include Exit commands in their own menubar, more commonly a click of the window's Close button disposes of the mini program.

A global method of quitting all applications is to issue the Shut Down command in the Start menu. Windows instructs applications to close down as if you had selected the Exit command from their File menus. You'll still be prompted about saving changed documents.

Running Multiple Programs

As long as Windows has the memory resources available, you are encouraged to open as many programs at the same time as you need. To help reduce screen clutter, you can click the **minimize button** in the application window. The application is still running, but hidden from view until you reactivate it by clicking on its button in the Taskbar.

Copy Protection

It's rare these days to encounter a copy-protected application that prevents installation of the program on a hard disk. Entertainment programs frequently had this restriction in the past, but copy protection of this type is rare these days.

Still, a few programs employ copy protection schemes that prevent you from installing multiple copies of the same program on more than one machine connected to a network. These programs have unique **serial numbers** embedded in each copy. As you start the program, it looks in other PCs on the network for any other copy of that software with the same serial number. If it finds a duplicate, it won't let you open the program. The solution is to buy a copy of the software for each user.

Many Application Files

Many of today's programs come not just with a single .EXE or .COM file, but with additional support files (usually of type .DLL) that are essential for the program to run. These application extensions are helpful for programmers to modularize their programs, making it easier, for instance, to prepare a version of the program in a different language. Most extensions are installed in the same folder as the application, but occasionally an installer program places other items in folders nested inside your Windows folder (System and Fonts are common). You won't see these files in Desktop/Explorer windows unless you turn on Show All Files in the Options window (in the View menu). Uninstalling a program may require a lot of detective work, because extra files in folders other than the program's folder are almost impossible to identify unless the software publisher provides a list of them.

Forcing a Program to Exit

If you find that a program has frozen on you, there is a remedy less catastrophic than turning off the computer. Press Control+Alt+Delete. The **Close Program** window appears listing all running processes, with the frozen one usually at the top of the list. Click the End Task button (and confirm in the next dialog) to escape that problem. Other programs and processes should still be OK. More troubleshooting tips begin on 161.

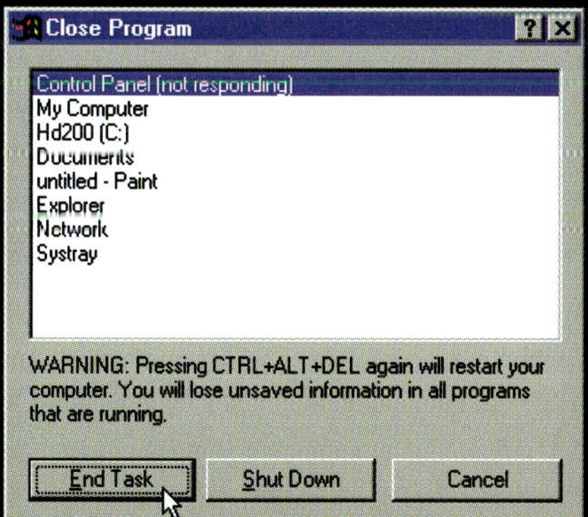

Consistency across a variety of applications makes Windows 95-compatible programs seem easy to use. You won't be frustrated trying to learn and remember a different file saving command for each document—you will know where to look and what to look for in a Save command.

You can count on a number of user interface elements being in virtually every application, from the Desktop to the most esoteric modeling program. Once you understand these items, you're well on your way to being comfortable in almost any Windows 95 software program.

Consistent Menus

Virtually every Windows application displays a window containing a menubar with a basic set of menus. You will probably find a `File`, `Edit`, and `Help` menu in each program.

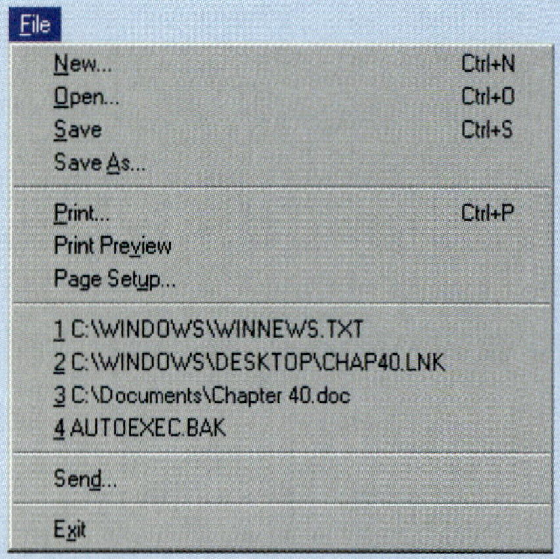

File Menu

Commands you'll almost always find in the `File` menu are those that **open, save, create new** and **print documents.** These menu items tend to have the same Control key equivalents across programs: Control+O, +S, +N, and +P, respectively. You'll also find the `Exit` item in the `File` menu. Many programs adhere to a previous Windows convention of Alt+F4 as a keyboard shortcut for exiting a program.

It is increasingly common to see up to four previously opened documents listed near the bottom of the `File` menu. This lets you quickly open what may be a hot file among your projects.

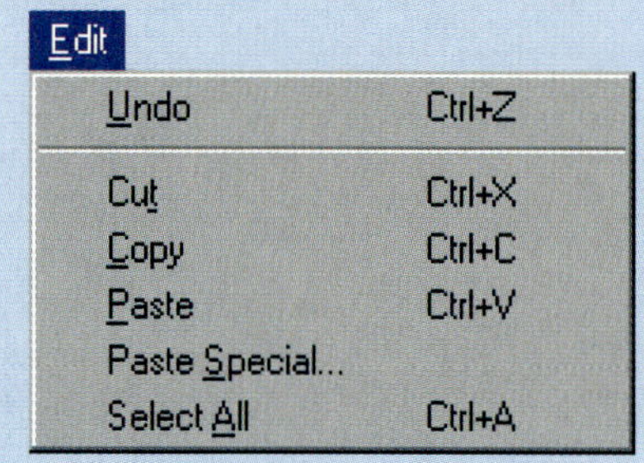

Edit Menu

Required in almost every program are `Edit` menu items for **Undo, Cut, Copy,** and **Paste** (Control+Z, +X, +C, and +V). The exact wording of these items may change in some programs, depending on what kind of information you've selected or have in the **Clipboard**. Moreover, pasting can be empowered to paste different characteristics of the information in some programs. As a result, you may see a `Paste Special` item as well 129.

Application-Specific Menus

Beyond the standard menus and menu items, an application may do anything it pleases to present menus that give you the power to work with information in the program's documents. When exploring a program for the first time, it's a good idea to study the contents of each menu. Select those items with **ellipses** (...) after them to see the resulting dialog boxes. Then cancel each dialog.

Windows

Each program displays an **application window**—all activity using the program takes place within the confines of that window. Additionally, more advanced programs may display **multiple document windows** within the application window. When you start an application, it may either prompt you with an **Open File** dialog 90 to open an existing document or display an empty window, called `Untitled`. The latter assumes that you will create a new document. But if you then open an existing document, you may end up with two windows—your document and the untitled one. Some programs assume that if you open a document with an unused, untitled window showing, the document you're opening should replace the untitled window. There is no consistency to this, so be prepared to see both behaviors.

Editing Text

Text editing is the same throughout the Windows environment. The mouse pointer becomes a **text pointer** whenever the cursor is atop a text editing area. Clicking the pointer in text plants a flashing **text insertion cursor**—signifying the place your next typed character will be inserted. To prepare a chunk of text for an action, you click and drag the text pointer across the characters, words, or paragraphs. The highlighted text is said to be **selected**. You can also select text by planting the text insertion cursor at one end of the selection, and then holding down the Shift key while clicking the pointer at the other end of the text.

Once text is selected, it's usually time to issue some menu or toolbar command that acts on the selection, such as copying it to the Clipboard or changing its font properties. One important property of selected text is that the next character you type replaces all selected text. Thus, to change a word, simply select it (a double-click inside a word selects the entire word), and start typing the replacement—don't bother deleting the old word.

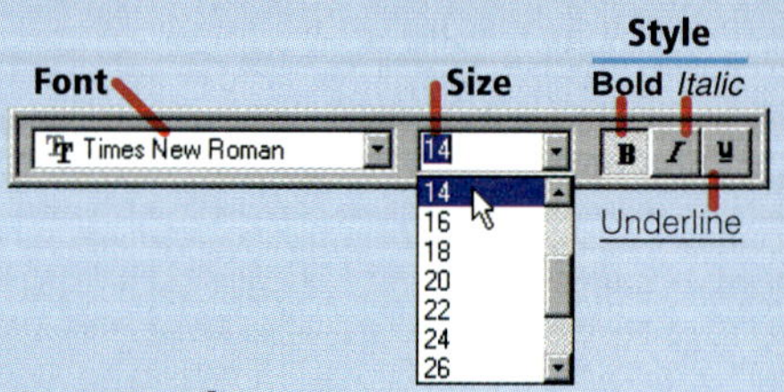

Font Tools

Text-oriented programs provide pop-up lists and buttons to adjust the font, size, and style of selected text. A common location for these tools is in a toolbar or a separate font tool palette.

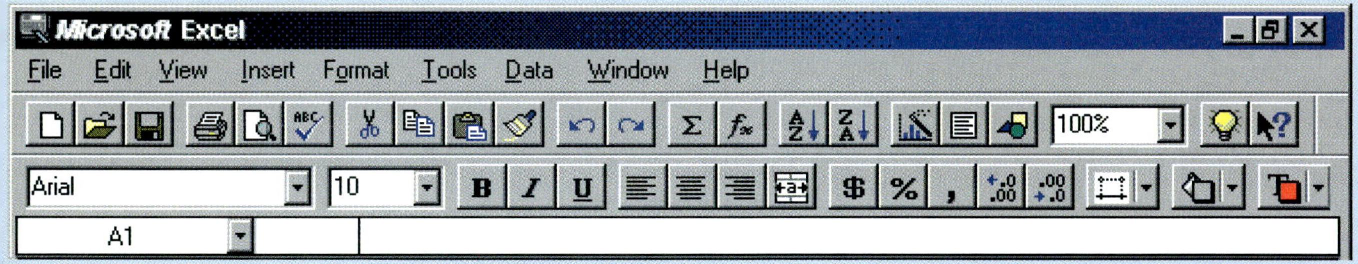

Toolbars

Windows often display one or more horizontal bars of buttons or information. The iconic buttons in these toolbars present **one-click shortcuts** to items normally found in menus or dialog boxes. Many programs let users configure the content of toolbars from a list of all available actions for which the program has a preprogrammed button. At the bottom of some windows are **status bars,** which convey varying types of information—instructions, number of items selected, and so on—depending on what's in the window. Display of toolbars and status bars is usually controlled by toggle menu items in the View menu.

Buttons

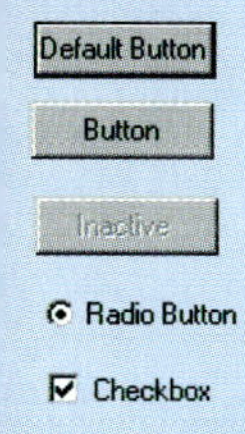

With the mouse being such a large part of a user's interaction with Windows, the profusion of **clickable buttons** is no coincidence. The three most common **button styles** are the **rectangle** (in two or three dimensions), **radio**, and **checkbox**. A rectangle button performs a single action, as designated by its name or icon. When a dark border surrounds such a button, it means that a press of the Enter key acts like clicking the button. Radio buttons come in groups, and are mutually exclusive within the group—only one can be highlighted at a time. Checkbox buttons, on the other hand, let you set or unset whatever the labels indicate. A checkmark in the box means that the setting is enabled or engaged.

Tools

Some programs—usually graphics programs—display palettes of tools. Sometimes a palette can be pulled down from the menubar, and then dragged away from the bar so that the palette remains visible while you work on a document. Click on an icon representing the desired tool. This puts you into a mode that is unique to that tool, whether it be **drawing, filling an area** with a pattern, or **selecting** objects on the screen. The pointer turns into the same shape as the tool you selected. No matter what tool you use, however, as you move the pointer to the menubar, the pointer shape returns to the familiar arrow.

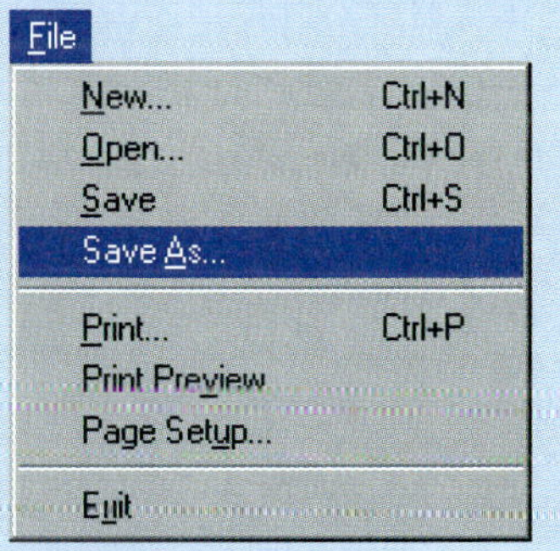

Saving Documents

Most applications that work with documents have two types of Save commands in their File menus: Save and Save As. The first is the one you use when **saving changes** to a document that you've already named and stored on your disk. This version is the one with the convenient Control+S keyboard equivalent, which makes it easy to frequently save your work each time you reach a resting point. The more often you perform intermediate saves, the less work is at the mercy of a power outage or machine failure.

The Save As command, on the other hand, is the command you use to perform the first save of a document. The command leads you to a **Save As** dialog box →91, in which you can **assign a file name** and determine what folder the document should go into. You can also use the Save As command as a way to make a copy of the current document from within the program. Simply issue the command and save the same document to another folder, or assign a different name (perhaps for backup purposes). If you assign a new name, the document window's title bar will bear that new name. Be aware, however, that when you finish with the Save As command, the next Save command you issue will save the document to the last file name and folder specified in the most recent Save As command.

Printing

In the File menu of any program that produces documents is some variation of the Print command (as well as the Page Setup command →140). In programs that allow opening multiple documents, the Print command applies to the active document only. Thanks to the **WYSIWYG** (what you see is what you get) world of Windows, printed output closely resembles the information you see in the window. The Print command leads to a print dialog from which you may select a printer, page range, number of copies to print, and collating order. Click the OK button to send the document to your printer. For more about printing →136-141.

If your PC work is predominantly in graphics programs, then you tend to encounter the alphabet soup of graphics file formats—BMP, GIF, TIFF, EPSF are the most popular.

These formats represent the manner in which graphic information is stored in a disk file. Each one is different and generally incompatible with the others. Fortunately, many graphics programs can save to and open from more than one format.

The file format is distinct, however, from the graphic type: **bitmapped** and **object** graphics. Most graphics programs are one type or the other. Which style you use depends largely on the intended final resting place for the graphic—screen picture, low-resolution printer, high-resolution printer.

Bitmap

A bitmapped graphic consists of a dot map of an image (no object graphics allowed). Each dot can store its own color, but the palette of colors available to each dot depends on the bit depth 30 of the monitor and display adapter being used while creating or editing the graphic. Bitmaps are best used for graphics that appear only on screen, rather than in printed format. Windows recognizes a file as a bitmap when its extension is .BMP.

PCX

The first ultra-popular graphics program on a PC (running under MS-DOS) was PC Paintbrush. A Windows version was bundled with Windows 3.x. Early versions of the program stored bitmapped files in a format called PCX (after the .PCX file extension), which became a popular graphics format. The trend among graphics programs is moving away from PCX (toward .BMP bitmapped format for simple paint programs), but most full-featured graphics programs can open and convert PCX files.

Bitmapped Graphics

Bitmapped graphics are the realm of painting packages, such as the Paint applet that comes with Windows 95. These programs let you work with a graphic on a **pixel-by-pixel** basis, usually in some magnified mode. While the standard granularity of bitmapped programs is approximately 72 pixels per inch, you can find more advanced programs that give you detailed editing abilities up to 300 dots per inch of a laser printer in a highly magnified view.

In paint programs, tools help you set down patterns of dots in squares, circles, and dotted patterns. In color paint programs, you can assign different colors to virtually every pixel (within the color palette of your color video support, 30).

A downside to bitmapped graphics is that once you lay down the pixels, what may appear to be a shape is still nothing more than a collection of dots. If a square you've painted is the wrong size, you'll have to erase and repaint the pixels in the right size. Painting programs let you select a group of pixels (within a selection rectangle or an irregular area). If you drag the selection, you leave white space underneath (or whatever color is currently assigned to be "white" space). If you manipulate the selection, such as by rotating, stretching, or shrinking, the program does its best to maintain the general shape of the original by scaling the dots to a best fit. You'll probably end up with jagged or distorted lines and uneven fill patterns, however.

Still, many Windows artists feel very much at home in bitmapped graphics. When the finished output is to be displayed on a Windows screen, bitmapped graphics produce excellent results. Desktop wallpaper, for instance, is made up of a type of bitmapped graphic 94.

GIF

Developed initially by Unisys, the **Graphics Interchange Format** was adopted by the online service CompuServe as a standard for storing and compressing high-resolution graphics (color or monochrome). Compression is important for reducing the amount of time (and connect charge) for transferring graphics information. Windows includes a Quick viewer for GIF files, and viewers are available on other computing platforms, as well. While GIF is popular now, its future is somewhat in doubt due to patent claims and royalty demands by Unisys on software vendors who supply GIF-based software. CompuServe plans to release its own newer version, called GIF24.

TIFF

An acronym for **Tagged Image File Format, TIFF** (which comes in monochrome, gray-scale, and color versions) is the favorite of high-end bitmapped graphics work. Many scanner software programs offer the TIFF file format as an option. Because TIFF files tend to be at high resolutions, they can get quite large, especially when saved in the gray-scale (256 grays) or color (16.8 million colors) versions. Even at lower resolutions, TIFF files allow for dithering (a method of positioning shaded patterns of black or color together to trick the eye into seeing a color that isn't possible under the existing color constraints). TIFF files can be imported into most page layout programs to produce high-quality photo images inside documents such as newsletters and brochures.

Object Graphics

Object graphics programs, more commonly called **draw** packages, produce graphics in a vastly different way. Instead of specifying, say, the individual pixels along a line, an object line is a **mathematical specification** for a line: two endpoint coordinates and a line of a designated thickness between those two points. Each line, box, circle, polygon, arc, or text chunk is an object that can be individually selected (by just clicking on it), and altered independently of any other object in the document. It's as if each object exists in its own physical layer in the document. Moreover, an object is easy to change. To resize an incorrect square, simply select the object and drag on one of its corners. The program makes note of the new coordinates for that object—the line thickness remains the same.

Due to their mathematical accuracy, object graphics (also called vector graphics) tend to **print smoother shapes** than bitmapped graphics, especially on high-resolution printers. Curves are as smooth as the resolution of the printer can produce.

Data storage requirements for object graphics documents are also less, since there is less information required for most shapes than for bitmaps.

Bitmaps in Object Documents

Most draw programs allow you to paste bitmapped graphics copied from other programs. When you paste the art, however, the bitmap turns into a single, **uneditable** object (there are no pixel editing tools in most draw programs). You can position the art without penalty, but if you try to resize it, the image distorts as the program tries a best fit of pixels to the new orientation.

You'll likely encounter further problems when you try to align a bitmap with object art in the same document. On screen everything may look fine, but when the page prints on a laser printer, the alignment may be off. The problem is that the typically 72-dot-per-inch bitmap is being printed in a 300-dot-per-inch world. Incompatible math makes perfect alignment a gradual, manual fine-tuning process.

Compatibility with Macintosh Graphics

The common bitmapped graphic file formats under Windows are not directly compatible with graphics programs on the Macintosh. The Macintosh world uses other formats (PICT and MacPaint are the most common). Both the Windows and Macintosh worlds, however, work with more advanced graphics formats, such as EPSF and TIFF, which high-end graphics programs can usually generate or read. If you do a lot of graphics work, especially with artists who may use Macintosh computers, you should invest in file format convertor utility programs, which can help you coexist with a number of graphics programs and computing platforms, including Silicon Graphics (SGI) and Sun. One important guideline, however, is that when you start converting formats, you lose image information as you convert to less capable formats (which you may want to do to be compatible with more programs or save disk space). And if a program has a proprietary format, any conversion to standard formats in the **Save As** dialog usually result in some loss of image quality.

EPSF

An **Encapsulated PostScript File** (sometimes just EPS) actually contains two copies of an image. One copy is a PostScript language description of the image (in either ASCII text or a more disk-space-conservative binary format, depending on the graphics program and its options). This is the information that output devices (printers, typesetters, etc.) use to produce the image on paper or film. The second copy is a graphic image that the graphics software uses to produce a comparatively quick representation of the image on the screen. A number of page layout and word processing programs allow you to import or paste EPS graphics just like other graphics. EPS images can be either object or bitmapped graphics, and PostScript does an excellent job of accommodating size and orientation changes to an image.

PostScript Text

Some graphics programs let you save a document entirely as a PostScript description. This is a text document full of PostScript language commands and parameters that PostScript output devices interpret and convert into commands that drive the laser or film imager. Unless you know the PostScript language, you won't be able to edit this kind of file. The advantage, however, is that you can send a text PostScript file to any PostScript device (with a download utility program) without the program you used originally to create and edit the graphic.

Proprietary Formats

It's not uncommon for a graphics program to use as a default file format one that is unique to that program. The primary reason is that the program's designers found ways to store more detailed information about an image than the standard file formats support. It's rare that applications allow translation of other programs' proprietary formats.

Windows programs that support Microsoft's Object Linking and Embedding (OLE—pronounced oh-LAY) offer unique ways of including information from other files in a document.

You can **mix types of data** within a document, even when the main program you're working with doesn't directly support a particular kind of data. For instance, you can place a portion of an Excel spreadsheet into a Word document, and then edit the spreadsheet from within Word. While editing that spreadsheet portion, OLE puts the full power of Excel into your hands, without your having to switch applications.

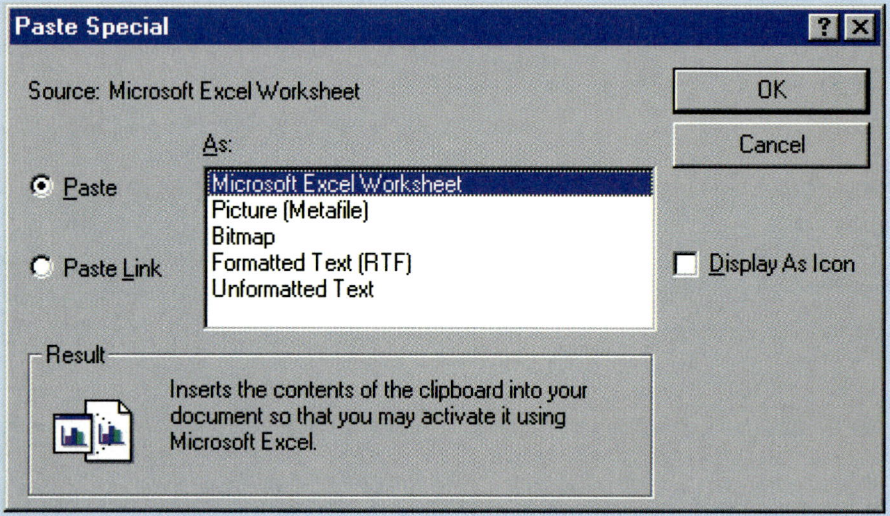

Linking vs. Embedding

While both linking and embedding are part of the OLE name, they are very **different ways of getting data** from one type of document into another. You start either process by selecting and copying to the **Clipboard** information from any kind of document. This **source document** is said to belong to a **server application**.

When you are ready to paste the Clipboard item into the **destination document** (which could be in a different program), you choose `Paste Special` to see what your options are. **Pasting a link** means that you will see the material you're pasting, but the pasted item also maintains a link (or pointer) back to the source document. Each time you open the destination document, it lets Windows know it has a linked item in it; when you open the source document, it, too, tells Windows that it may have linked items out there. Whenever changes are made to the source document (and the source document is saved), Windows passes an updated version to all linked documents are open at the time.

Embedding, on the other hand, places a complete copy of the Clipboard data (which may include some disk-space-intensive data, such as sounds or color graphics) plus a note about the server application that created the data. An embedded object needs this information about the server application: you will use the server app's menus and tools to edit or play the object within the destination document. The big difference, however, is that there is no link back to the server document. Changes made to the server document are not sent to the embedded object.

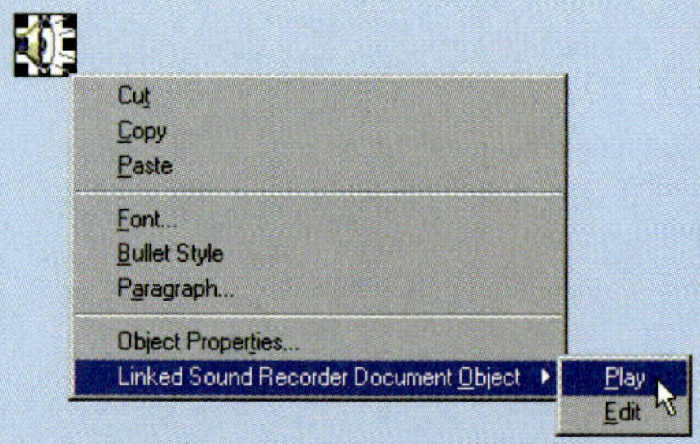

Choosing the Right Data Type

When you choose `Paste Special` in a destination document, a dialog box may present a list of data types currently associated with the data in the Clipboard. Generally speaking, the purpose of pasting a linked or embedded object is to have access to the real data of the source. The item in the listing that appears to be most like an object from the source document is the choice you want (although sometimes a picture will suffice).

Icon or Data?

With many choices in the Paste Special dialog, the `Display As Icon` checkbox is available. For many types of data, such as audio files, you'll get an icon either way. But given a choice, you'll have to determine what works best for the document and its user. **Displaying the data** is the easiest for the document's reader, but it may occupy a lot of screen space if the data is merely background info. Turning **data into an icon** requires the reader to double-click the icon to open the file for viewing or listening. If the document will ultimately be printed, you'll most likely prefer the data in the document, so it will appear in the printout.

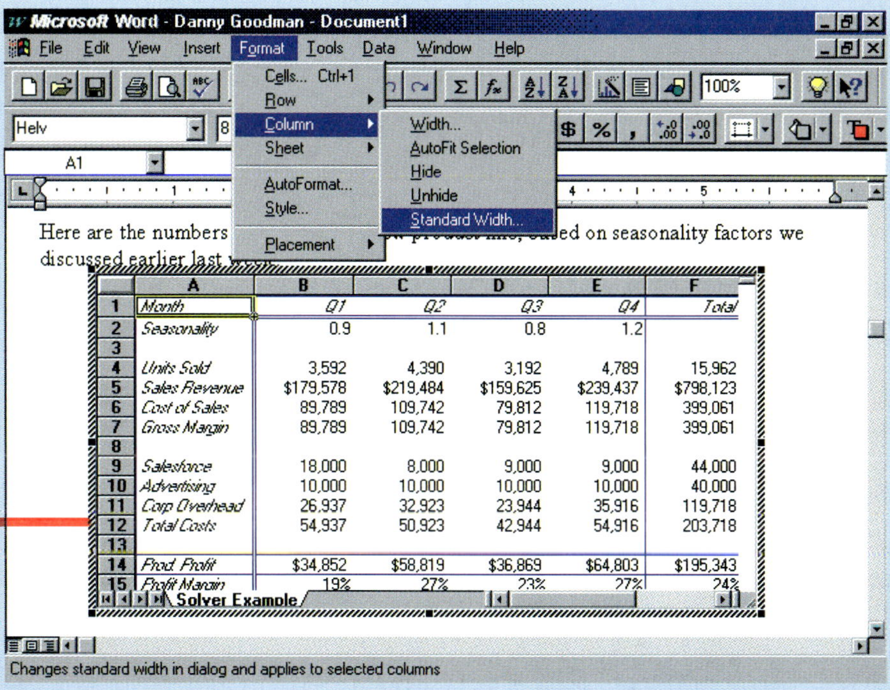

Editing an OLE Object

The user interface for editing objects changes with the amount of OLE support in both the source and destination applications. Good support, as evidenced in Microsoft Office, allows you to use commands and tools from the source application within the destination document. Double-clicking on an embedded object changes its border to wide hashmark lines, while menus and tool bars switch to those of the source program.

For a linked object, it's vital that all changes be made to the actual source document. Thus, the source application launches with the source document in a separate window. Changes appear immediately in the destination document when you switch back.

The best way to see your editing options for any OLE object or icon is to right-click on it. The pop-up menu presents all relevant choices for the type of object and its relation to the original.

When to Link or Embed?

Your choice of OLE method depends a lot on the **availability of the source document.** Because a linked object occupies much less disk space in your destination document than an embedded object, linking makes the best sense when you need copies of the same data in multiple documents. But it also means that the source document must be available to you when you need it, and it cannot move or be renamed. If the source document resides on a network, you won't have that data if the network goes down or you take your PC on the road. In that case, an embedded object would have everything you need—the data and the tools to edit it (provided you also have the OLE server application on your hard disk).

You must also consider the importance of **keeping the pasted data up to date.** If the data is static—a sound file, for instance—then embedding may be the right choice. But if the source document changes all the time (e.g., spreadsheet data recalculated daily to reflect new data), then a link will be vital to keeping all instances of that data current in all documents that use it.

Object Packager

Not every application supports every kind of OLE action, but as long as your client application does, you can still establish links to documents or other objects that don't immediately Paste Special into a document. Windows 95 comes with an **Object Packager** program that supplies missing pieces for OLE whenever it can. For instance, you can select and copy a file icon in a Desktop/Explorer window, and paste it into the Object Packager window. The two panes display the icon that will represent the object in the destination document, as well as the actual content (when possible) of the data. Next, choose `Copy Package` from the `Edit` menu, switch to the destination document, and perform a regular `Paste`. The icon appears in the document, and it is "alive," so that you can double-click it to view or hear the embedded data

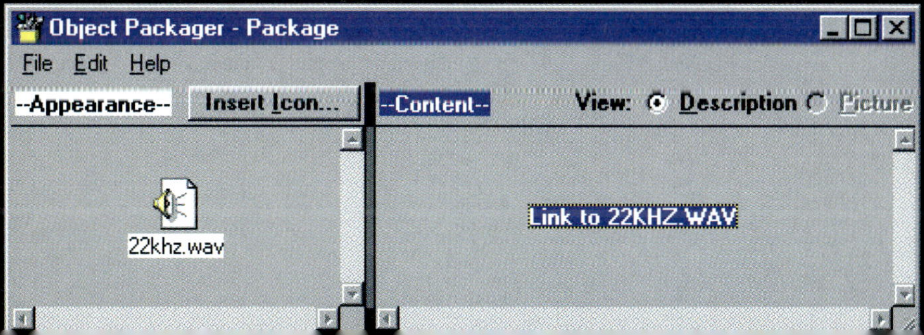

While the future may be Windows, many long-time users of PCs still turn to applications that run only under MS-DOS.

Because Windows 3.x ran atop MS-DOS and a number of veteran PC users still run only MS-DOS, it is not uncommon to find recent software programs in the entertainment and multimedia categories that run on MS-DOS—appealing to the widest possible audience.

Microsoft certainly encourages users of Windows 95 to gravitate toward software that takes advantage of Windows 95 features such as long file names. But acknowledging that many users must run existing MS-DOS programs, the company built in good support for programs that must believe they're running under MS-DOS.

DOS Program Launch Icons

The generic Desktop/Explorer icon for an MS-DOS program launcher looks like a shortcut icon, with the small upward angled arrow in a box at one corner. In fact, the **launcher file** is a special kind of file that DOS programs need. In previous versions of Windows, it was known as a Program Information File. In Windows 95 such files maintain their .PIF file extension, although they are formally called **shortcuts** to MS-DOS programs.

These shortcuts contain far more information about their targets than a typical Windows shortcut. A property sheet for one of these (right-click and choose `Properties` from the pop-up menu) has no fewer than six screens of sometimes complex settings. Many DOS programs released since the popularity of Windows 3.x come with .PIF files, which Windows 95 will pick up and use to fill in the appropriate blanks for the shortcut property sheets.

A Virtual MS-DOS PC

One of the reasons Windows 95 requires an 80386 processor or newer is that these microprocessor chips permit the creation of a **virtual 8086** computer—a section of your PC's memory that is constructed to look just like a standard Intel 8086 microprocessor in which a copy of MS-DOS and your program load and operate. Most MS-DOS programs are designed to operate within the limits of the traditional DOS PC, which means there is a maximum of 640 kilobytes of conventional memory available for the operating system and program, while the remaining portion of the maximum one megabyte is reserved for things like video screen image buffers. With a multiple-megabyte personal computer, there is usually enough room to get at least one MS-DOS session running, totally independent of the Windows 95 workings.

Each time you start an MS-DOS program, Windows sets aside part of available memory for one of these virtual 8086 machines—no two programs share the same virtual PC. At the same time, an MS-DOS program steers clear of your Windows applications, so if there is a crash problem with a DOS program, only that virtual PC is affected.

DOS in a Window

In typical operation, an MS-DOS program operates in a separate window on your Windows desktop. The window is like a separate video monitor for the virtual PC that runs the DOS program. But because it is a Windows 95 window, you can determine how large the window should be, or whether the program should occupy the entire screen without any vestiges of a window (as some game software may require).

DOS-Only Programs

Some MS-DOS programs insist on owning the computer when they run. In other words, they're not about to share hardware resources with Windows or another program. The program requires what is called MS-DOS mode. If you turn this mode on (in the `Program` property sheet panel, Advanced... button), whenever you choose to start the MS-DOS program, Windows (and all running applications) will shut down and *then* the MS-DOS mode program will start. Quitting the program relaunches Windows, as if from a restart.

In most cases, the programs will run without any further adjustments of system settings. But if problems crop up, Windows 95 provides a large array of settings designed to accommodate almost any MS-DOS program.

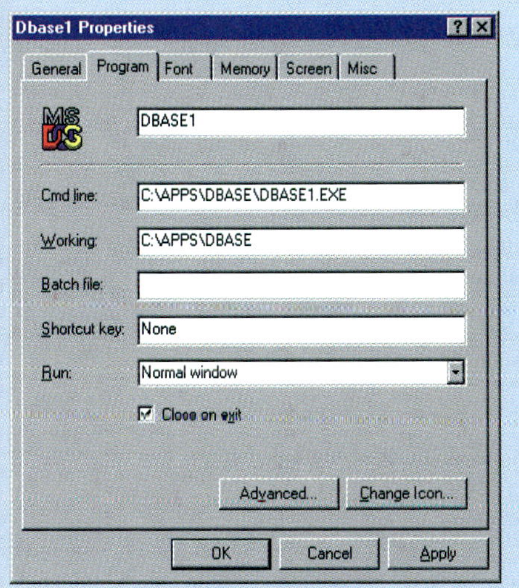

Opening Documents

The rules for associating document files to applications ➔ 119 also hold for MS-DOS programs and their files. But you must make sure that the application is capable of opening a document from its DOS command prompt (usually with the name of the application and the path name to the file). DOS property sheets contain a line of path name information called a **Working Directory** (in the `Program` panel of the property sheet). If this is not filled out correctly (with the path to the folder containing the application), you may receive an error message about an invalid working directory when double-clicking an associated document file.

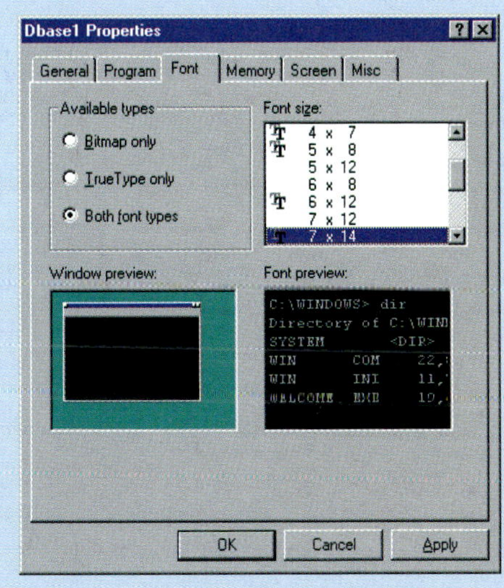

Selecting a Font

The `Font` panel of the property sheet lets you select from a variety of font sizes, each of which defines the size and aspect ratio of the window for the DOS program. It is best to select from both **raster and TrueType** fonts for a wider selection. As you select a font size in the scrolling list, you will see previews below of both the DOS window relative to the entire screen (to indicate its size), and a life-sized view of the font characters. The measurements represent the number of pixels in the horizontal x vertical dimension for each character space. A DOS window that shows the tool bar (recommended; settable in the `Screen` panel of the property sheet) can accommodate fonts up to 16 pixels tall without scrolling, yet allowing the Taskbar to be visible on a 640-by-480 screen. The 7 x 14 TrueType font is also nicely readable, while leaving plenty of breathing room around the DOS window.

MS-DOS Prompt

Automatically installed into the Programs grouping of the Start menu is a shortcut called MS-DOS Prompt. This is actually a shortcut to a COMMAND.COM program that comes with Windows 95. Like any other DOS application, this one runs on a virtual machine, and gives you virtually the same powers that experienced DOS users have at the command line prompt ➔ 132.

Copying and Pasting

A significant advantage to running MS-DOS programs under Windows instead of DOS is that for most programs you can use Windows to copy and paste between applications—something that DOS doesn't do for you. It is best to run DOS windows with the Toolbar showing, because shortcut buttons for marking a selection, copying, and pasting are readily available. In a text-oriented DOS application, here are the steps:

1. Click the Mark button. The cursor turns fat.
2. Use the mouse to drag a rectangular selection of text.
3. Click the Copy button.
4. Switch to a Windows or other DOS window, move the text insertion cursor to the desired location, and paste (via the menu in Windows or the Paste button in DOS). The text (unformatted) pastes into the document.

If you don't have the toolbar showing in the window, click on the icon at the upper left corner of the window to display the window controls. An `Edit` hierarchical menu contains items for `Mark`, `Copy`, and `Paste`. The `Properties` item in this menu displays the multi-panel property sheet for the application.

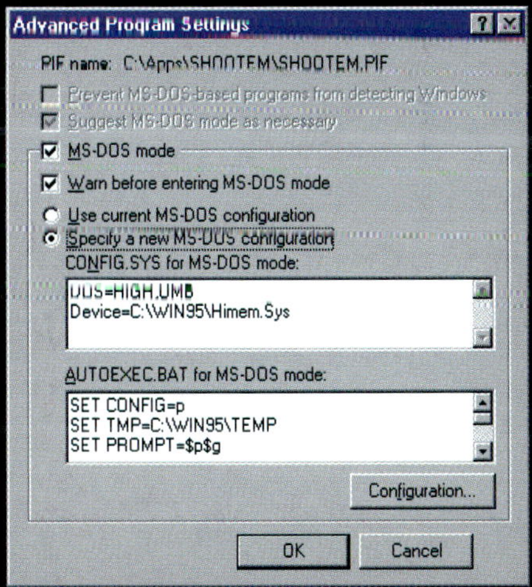

CONFIG.SYS and AUTOEXEC.BAT

When a program runs in MS-DOS mode, Windows 95 essentially turns your PC into a DOS machine. In the property sheet, you can include separate series of commands that would normally be required in a DOS machine's CONFIG.SYS and AUTOEXEC.BAT files to run the program (e.g., it may require that special real-mode drivers be loaded, or a terminate-and-stay-resident (TSR) program be started prior to the main program). The Configure button in this panel leads to a list of common DOS utilities that can be added to both files. It also enters lines commonly found in both files (such as DOS=HIGH, UMB and SET PROMPT=pg).

One of the claims to fame for Windows 95 is that it does away with MS-DOS, incorporating operating system and graphical user interface in one seamless environment.

But for many long-time users of MS-DOS and Windows, old habits die hard. The command-line interface of MS-DOS is a comfortable place for some. Moreover, millions of users have automated a variety of functions by writing batch files (.BAT) that rely on the commands built into MS-DOS.

A Windows 95 installation does not include the DOS directory of Windows 3.x (although if you upgraded, the directory may still exist on your hard disk). Instead, Windows 95 has its own folder of MS-DOS programs that have been optimized to run in Windows 95. These are the commands you control via the MS-DOS Prompt window (selected from the Start→Programs menu).

Internal vs. External Commands

Only users who have studied the contents of the older DOS directory or the new **Command** folder (inside the Windows folder) recognize that not all of the MS-DOS commands have programs listed in these directories. That's because MS-DOS commands are divided into two groups: internal and external.

Internal commands are built into the COMMAND .COM program. Many basic commands, such as dir and mkdir, are part of COMMAND .COM. As such, they are always ready to go whenever you are at the MS-DOS prompt. In fact, you can issue these commands only from the MS-DOS prompt.

External commands are those that trigger small programs in the Command folder. They are .EXE or .COM executable files. As programs, they may be called from within Windows 95, automatically opening an MS-DOS window at the same time. If they do nothing when you try running them, it is probably because the commands require some parameters that you can supply only from a command line (including a command line in a shortcut to the program).

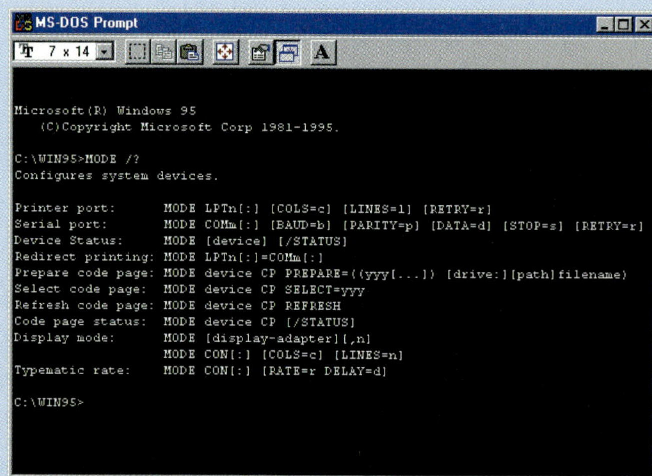

On the screen appears a description of the command, lists of parameters, syntax examples, and other pertinent notes. If the screen scrolls too quickly, issue the command again, and prepare to press the Pause key before information scrolls off the top of the window.

Uncovering Parameters

Unless you're sure about issuing these commands, it's a good idea to see what parameters, if any, a command requires. To get help about that, open the MS-DOS Prompt window, type the command, a space, a slash (/), and a question mark, as in

```
chdir /?
```

MS-DOS Command Editing

Every MS-DOS window you get in Windows 95 automatically has Doskey installed. This utility provides some shortcuts to help active DOS command givers avoid retyping commands. Here are the top shortcuts from Doskey and DOS itself:

Key	Description
F1	Enters previous command one character at a time (so you can change one or two characters when running a series of similar commands)
F3	Enters the entire previous command
F7	Displays a list of all previous commands in the order they were entered
Alt+F7	Emptied the F7 command history
F9	Prompts for command number from F7 list
Up/Down	Cycles through previous commands
Esc	Clears command at prompt line

Using QuickEdit in MS-DOS Windows

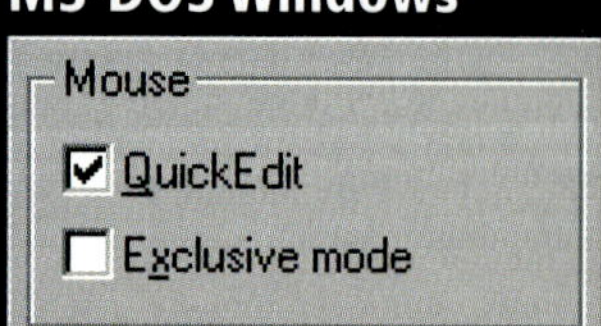

A toolbar in an MS-DOS window includes shortcut buttons for text editing controls, including Mark, Copy, and Paste. But there is an even faster way to copy text to the Clipboard. A feature called QuickEdit can be turned on in the Miscellaneous screen of an MS-DOS program's property sheet.

With QuickEdit engaged, you can use the mouse to click and drag the desired selection. Release the mouse to end the selection. Then click the right mouse button (with the pointer anywhere). The selected text is immediately copied to the Clipboard. Now you can locate the cursor where you like, and choose Paste from the Edit menu (right-click on the titlebar) or click the Paste shortcut button in the toolbar.

Supported MS-DOS Commands

The following list contains all the MS-DOS commands you can issue from the MS-DOS prompt in Windows 95. Some items are best suited for CONFIG.SYS (indicated by *) and AUTOEXEC.BAT (indicated by •) files.

attrib	break	mem	menucolor*
buffers*	call	menudefault*	menuitem*
cd	chcp	mkdir	mode
chdir	chkdsk	more	move
choice•	cls	mscdex	msd
command	copy	net config	net diag
country*	ctty	net help	net init
date	debug	net logoff	net logon
defrag	del	net password	net print
deloldos	deltree	net start	net stop
device*	device_high*	net time	net use
dir	diskcopy	net ver	net view
display.sys*	dos*	nlsfunc	numlock*
doskey	driver.sys*	path	pause
drivparm*	drvspace	prompt	rd
echo	edit	rem	ren
emm386	erase	rename	rmdir
exit	expand	scandisk	set
fc	fcbs*	setver	shell*
fdisk	files*	shift•	martdrv
find	for	sort	stacks*
format	goto•	start/W	submenu*
himem.sys*	if•	subst	switches*
include*	install*	sys	time
keyb	keyboard*	type	ver
label	lastdrive*	verify	vol
lh	loadfix	xcopy	
loadhigh	md		

MS-DOS Commands Missing from Windows 95

Many commands from earlier versions of MS-DOS are not supported in Windows 95, mostly because they are redundant or replaced by more modern equivalents.

append	assign
backup	comp
diskcomp	dosshell
edlin	ega.sys
fasthelp	fastopen
graftabl	graphics
help	interlink
intersvr	join
memcard	memmaker
mirror	msav
msbackup	power
print	printer.sys
qbasic	recover
replace	restore
ramdrive.sys	romdrive.sys
share	smartmon
tree	undelete
unformat	vsafe

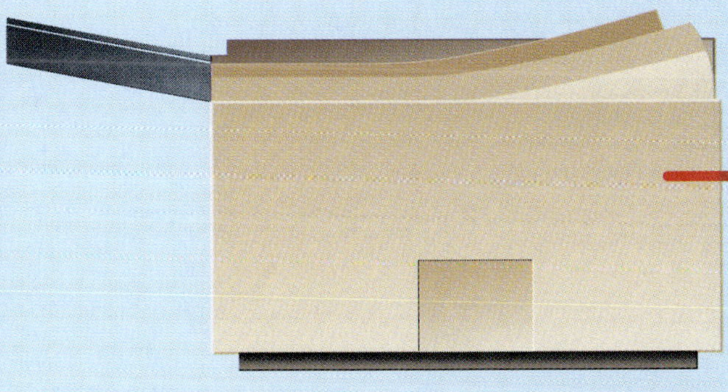

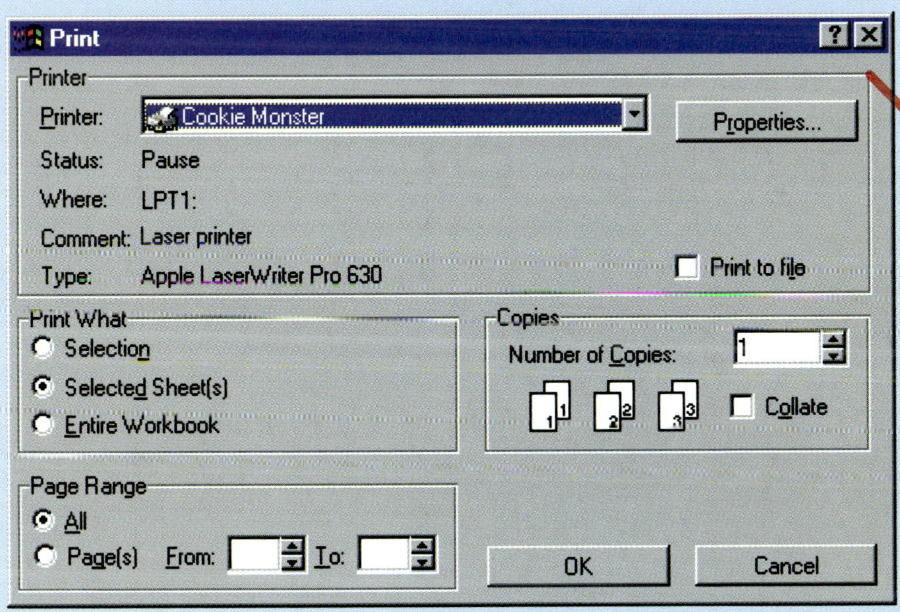
Print
Printer
Printer: Cookie Monster
Properties...
Status: Pause
Where: LPT1:
Comment: Laser printer
Type: Apple LaserWriter Pro 630
Print to file
Print What
Selection
Selected Sheet(s)
Entire Workbook
Copies
Number of Copies: 1
Collate
Page Range
All
Page(s) From: To:
OK
Cancel

Once you establish a routine for printing documents, the process goes smoothly—barring hardware snafus like paper jams. But getting into that routine can be difficult at first because it often entails complex steps and unusual terminology.

Windows printing is a joint effort linking elements from applications programs, system software, and the printer into a printing team. In the case of PostScript-equipped printers, the printer itself is a powerful computer, sometimes more powerful than the PC to which it is connected.

Despite the differences among printers you can use with Windows, the basic printing process is similar across the board. You must go through the same basic steps for all. After that, you're only a Control+P (Print command) away from sending a document to the printer.

Printing System Software

Add Printer

Getting Windows to communicate with your printer requires one or more files (usually hidden) in the Windows→System folder. One of these files allows Windows to talk to a broad class of printers (e.g., non-PostScript printers), while the others are printer drivers for individual printer models. When you install Windows 95, it asks you to select your printer model(s) from a list of all printers it knows about. The setup program then copies all necessary printer drivers to the Windows→System folder. After installation, your printer appears as an icon in the special **Printers** folder, visible in My Computer and in the Control Panels window. You can always add other printers to your selections.

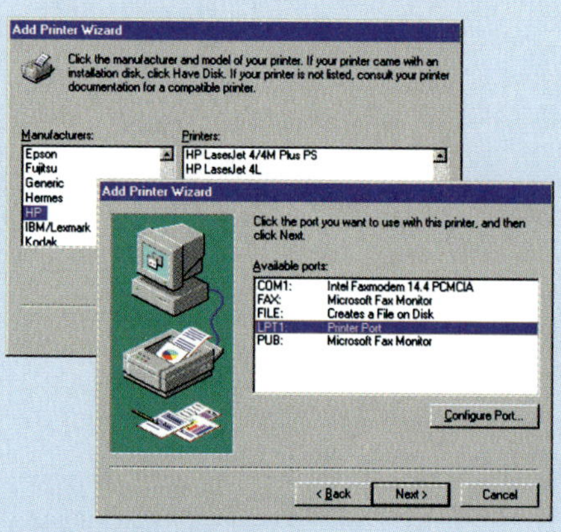

Installing a Printer

Windows 95 includes a printer installation wizard, named **Add Printer** (in the Printers folder). The installation disks and CD-ROM for Windows 95 come with printer drivers for over 800 printer models from at least 40 brands. These include models ranging from inexpensive dot-matrix printers to professional imagesetting machines used for production of high-quality printing films. Unless you have a very old printer or one that is newer than Windows 95, there is a good chance that Windows 95 has a driver for it. Even if not, your printer may emulate a more popular or generic printer included in Windows 95 listings.

You should always perform printer installation with the printer connected and turned on (new printers adhering to the Plug and Play standard install themselves automatically). In any case, the kind of information you will need to specify during installation of a traditional printer is:

- Brand name and model number
- Whether it is accessed via a network or connected directly to your PC
- If a networked printer, the name of the server to which it is connected
- For a local printer, where you want output to go (port number or file)
- A name assigned to the printer's icon in the Printers window.

To finish the installation, Windows loads various files from the installation disks or CD-ROM, so you'll need these items handy as well. If Windows does not have a driver for your (non–Plug and Play) printer, you will need the installer disk that came with your printer. It contains the driver(s) that Windows will need.

Printer Ports

Choices for printer ports during installation depend on the ports recognized by the **Window Device Manager** (in the System control panel). COM1 and COM2 (there may be more on your PC) are serial ports. More commonly, printers are connected to the LPT1 port, which is a parallel connection. Printing to a file causes Windows to assemble the data that normally goes to the printer into a file on your hard disk. You can send it to the printer later (via a DOS COPY command), but there is another way to defer printing in the Printer's property window.

Printing Speed

How fast a printer produces pages is largely controlled by the mechanics of the printer—how fast the print head slides from side to side or how quickly the laser writes to the printer's rotating drum. By and large, your PC works faster than most printers it connects to. When, for example, a PostScript printer must print a large bitmap, the printer circuitry takes a while to convert the graphics to PostScript. Scaling graphics can also take extra time. It's not unusual for complex graphics pages to take many minutes per page, while straight text in a single font can come out at 8 pages per minute on most laser printers.

Printer Properties

Included in the information in each printer's driver is a property sheet tailored to the features of the printer. Right-click on the printer icon (in the Printers folder), and choose Properties. See 138 for more details.

Setting a Default Printer

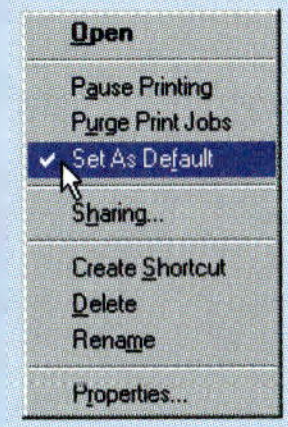

If you have more than one printer driver installed on your PC, you must instruct Windows about which one is the default printer—the one to which it will send stuff to print when you aren't given a chance to select a printer. To make this selection, right-click on the desired printer, and choose `Set As Default`. Right-click again to make sure this menu item is checked, meaning that this printer is the default.

Page Setup

If you intend to make changes to any Page Setup settings ➜140, do so before working on the document, because these changes often affect how a program defines page breaks, margins, and other settings.

Printing Sideways (Landscape)

If you want the document to print sideways on the page, you can change the page orientation setting in the Page Setup dialog. Click the Landscape button. Then be sure the page breaks and margins are set in your document to accommodate the different orientation.

Previewing

Whenever a program offers a `Print Preview` option in the `File` menu, it's a good idea to try it at least the first time you attempt to print a document. You save paper in checking for improper settings.

The Print Dialog Box

The last step before sending a document to the printer is to acknowledge settings in the Print dialog box ➜141. Details of this dialog change with the selected printer.

Printing a Screen

While earlier versions of Windows allowed users to print the current screen directly to some printers, that is no longer the case. All users can **print any screen,** however. Simply press the PrtScrn key to save a picture of the screen to the **Clipboard.** Then paste from the Clipboard into your favorite program capable of holding bitmapped graphics, including Paint. Choose `Print` from the program's `File` menu to send the screen to the printer.

Printing a Window Picture

You can limit screen capture to the active window by holding down the Alt key while pressing the PrtScrn key. Again, this is a bitmapped image of the window as you see it. To print the contents of a Desktop folder, see below.

Printing Documents from Applications

Every program that creates documents has one or more Print commands in its `File` menu. The commands usually refer to the document in the active window. A Print dialog box appears ➜141. Double-check that the correct printer is selected before printing. A pop-up list of all installed printers appears, so you can send some documents to a local printer and others to a networked printer if they're both connected at the same time.

Printing Documents from the Desktop/Explorer

You don't have to open an application to print documents created with that application. In the Desktop/Explorer, you may select one or more documents (even from different programs) and choose the `Print` command in the `File` menu (or right-click pop-up menu). Windows automatically launches each document's program, opens the document, and sends documents directly to the default printer—no Print dialog appears for any document. When Windows finishes queuing the spool files, the program quits.

Another method of printing is to drag documents to either your printer's icon (or a shortcut to it on the Desktop) or to the printer's open print job window.

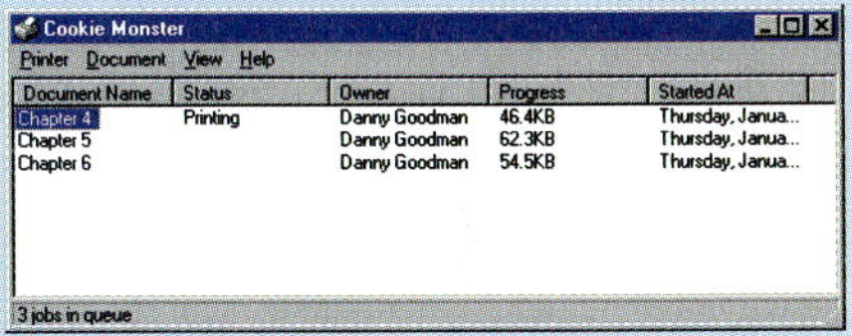

Print Spooling

Whenever you print a document, Windows quietly and relatively quickly saves the print information to a **spool** file ➜106. Each file to be printed is called a print job. If you double-click the printer icon, you'll see all **pending print jobs** in the order that they'll print. Entirely in the background, Windows monitors activity of print job queues, and parcels out information to printers as they are ready to accept it. While Windows is doing this, you are free to work on other tasks. You don't need to open the printer to view the queue unless you're interested in observing progress or need to alter the queue.

Managing Print Jobs

If you want to get all your print jobs in the queue before printing (perhaps you're using a laptop away from your printer), right-click on your printer's icon, and turn on `Pause Printing`. Print your documents as you normally would. When you later connect to the printer, turn off Pause Printing.

If an item is in the print queue, you can remove it by right-clicking on it and choosing `Cancel Printing`. Choosing `Purge Print Jobs` from the Printer menu (or right-click on the printer's icon) empties the entire queue. One or more pages may have already been sent to the printer's built-in memory, so even if you purge or cancel printing on the PC, the printer may continue for a little while.

Printing File Directories

Windows 95 has no built-in capabilities to print the entire contents of a folder. You can, however, create a pair of files that will help automate the process via DOS commands. First, make a copy of the AUTOEXEC.BAT file in your root directory, and rename it as WRITEDIR.BAT. Right-click on it, and choose `Edit`. Delete all text in the file, and enter the one-line command:

```
dir %1 >c:\windows\desktop\Directry.txt
```

Save the file. Next, create a new shortcut on the Desktop. Name it Print Directory, and right-click on the icon to choose Properties. In the Cmd Line field of the Program panel, enter the following:

```
writedir.bat %1
```

Click the Change Icon button if you'd like to assign an icon of your choice. You can now drop any folder from a Directory/Explorer window onto the Print Directory shortcut. The shortcut (via the batch file) generates a text file on the Desktop of the DOS directory listing for the folder. Print it with any text editor.

Today's personal computer printers are loaded with features. Nothing demonstrates that more clearly than the variety of settings in the Windows property sheet for any printer.

For advanced printers, especially color or PostScript laser printers, it is not uncommon for a property sheet to contain eight fully packed screens, some with further subwindows of even more detailed settings. Before straying from the default settings of a printer's property sheet, you should fully understand the printer's features as outlined in the printer manual. Property sheets are usually well informed about a printer's options (e.g., optional sheet or envelope feeders, extra RAM capacity), so you may see choices that apply to options you don't have installed on your printer.

When experimenting with settings, it doesn't hurt to try a sample page from a document. At most you'll waste a sheet of paper (which you can reuse to test printing on the other side); or you'll receive an error message that some setting does not apply. Above all, take time to find the settings that work best for the kinds of documents you print on a regular basis.

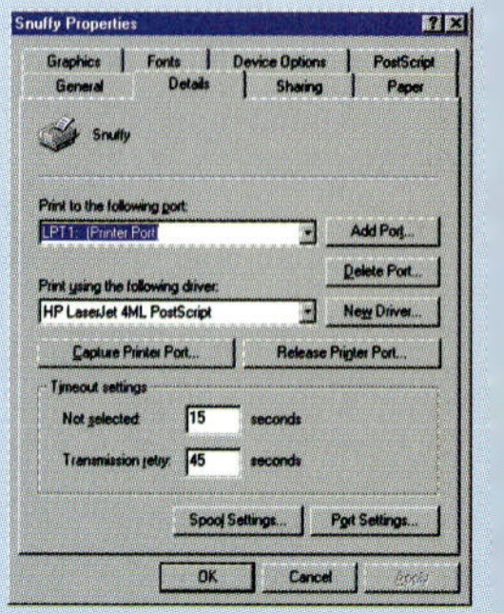

Details

Information that you fill in during printer installation about the printer port or the printer's network location appears here, along with the name of the driver associated with this printer. Avoid changing the driver unless you receive a more recent version. **Timeout settings** in this panel are different from PostScript timeout settings, pertaining, instead, to simple communications with the printer. The Spool Settings... button leads to choices that influence how much disk space is used for spooling; spool file format is also specified in this subwindow (see below).

Restoring Default Settings

On virtually every screen of a printer property sheet is a button that lets you return the screen's settings to the default ones prescribed when you first installed the printer. Default settings usually accommodate the lowest common denominator of requirements for users of the printer.

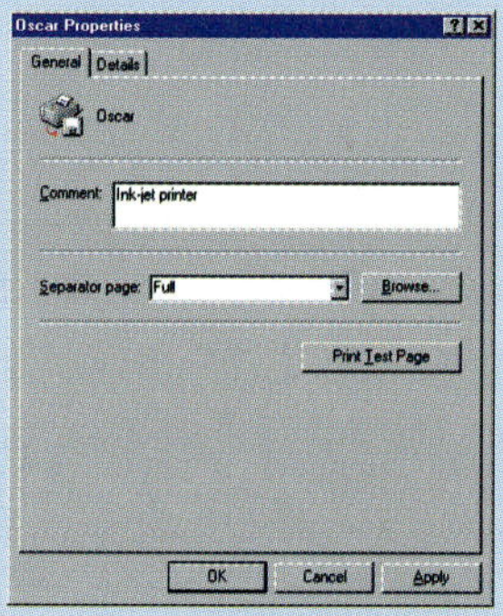

General

Text from the user-editable `Comment` field appears in the **Print** dialog 141 when you print a document. This information is useful primarily for networked printers or when you want to remind yourself about the characteristics of a particular printer before you send a job on its way. Also for **networked printers** or personal printing of multiple documents, you can specify that Windows print a sheet between print jobs. A full separator page is a fancy, large type sheet naming the sender, file name, and GMT time 100 actual printing began; a simple page has the same information but in standard Courier type; a custom separator page can also be specified. The disk and arrow in the printer icon indicate that this printer is set (in another panel) to print to a disk file rather than to a printer port.

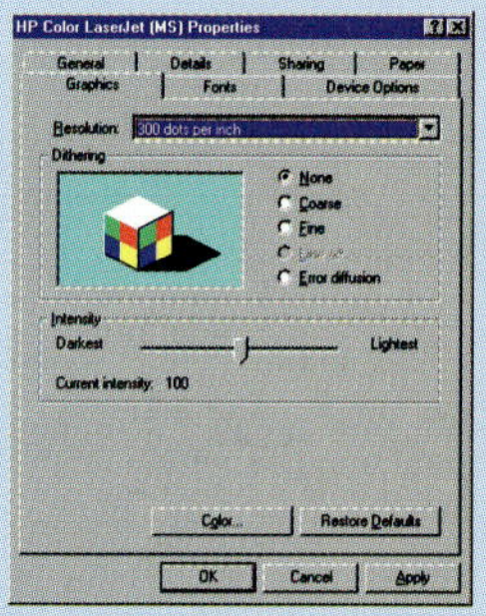

Graphics

Settings in the `Graphics` screen usually affect the **density** (resolution) of points being printed on the page. In dot-matrix printers, the numbers are often measured in the number of pixels per inch in the vertical and horizontal direction (if they're different). Higher resolution devices provide selections in **dots per inch** (dpi) consistent with the resolutions available with the printer. **Dithering** in this context is a printer's way of either blending colors (on a color printer) or making fine adjustments to black dots (on a monochrome printer) to display blended colors or shades of gray. Some monochrome printers call this effect halftoning, and offer you a variety of settings. If these settings are available for your printer, use a graphics file to experiment with each one and see which choices suit your desired output. On many color printers, there are additional color-specific settings either on this screen or on a subwindow visible at the click of a button.

Accessing Properties

Windows 95's designers planned for just about every instance in which you might need access to a printer's property sheet. There are many ways to reach it:

- Right-click on the printer icon in the `Printers` folder, and choose `Properties` from the pop-up menu.
- Select the printer icon and choose `Properties` from the `File` menu.
- From a **Page Setup** dialog, click the Printer or Printer Properties button, if available.
- From the **Print** dialog, click the Properties button.
- From the print job window that opens when you double-click the printer icon, choose `Properties` from the `Printer` menu.

Once in the property sheet, you will see any number of tabs for the screens within the sheet. Click the tab to bring the desired screen forward. Illustrations on these pages come from various printers to demonstrate the types of settings you may encounter.

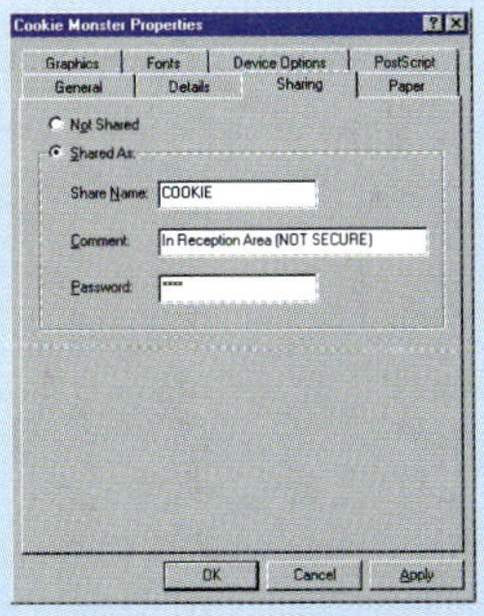

Sharing

If your PC is connected to a network, you can elect to make your printer available to others by engaging the `Shared As` radio button. Add a **comment** that helps users know where the printer is located. Assign a **password** so only users to whom you supply the password can access your printer.

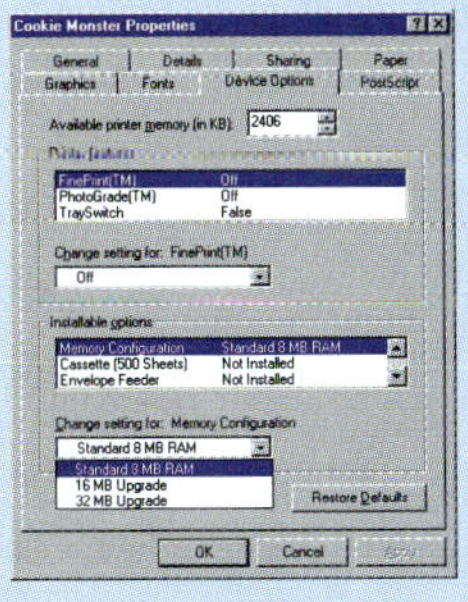

Device Options

Additional printer-specific features appear in the `Device Options` screen. Items such as print quality, printer memory configurations, and switchable software features appear here. Compare the terminology and settings against descriptions of these items in the printer's manual.

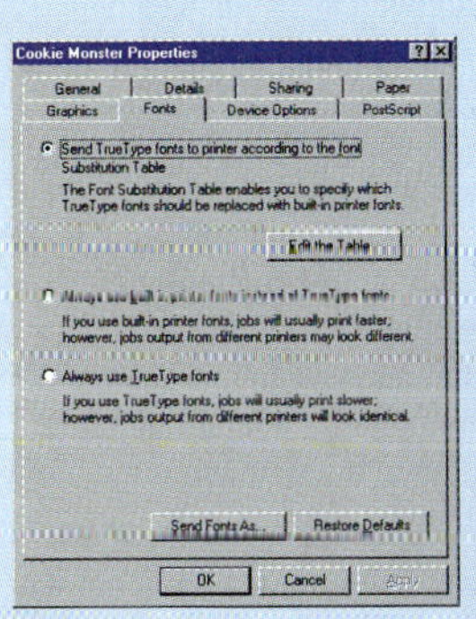

Fonts

Printing and fonts 104 are forever intertwined, and it seems that each printer brand or class of printer has its own scheme for using Windows to control fonts. At one end of the spectrum are the simple printers that have no built-in fonts, and rely on Windows' TrueType font generation to **create nice-looking text** (and don't have a `Fonts` tab in the property sheet). At the other end are PostScript printers, whose internal fonts can at times conflict with TrueType fonts—or at least produce slightly different results. Here, the balance is between what you see on the screen (which could be a mixture of TrueType and PostScript fonts) and what is ultimately printed. PostScript fonts will generally look best, but you should check the final output against what is on the screen if precise layouts are involved.

A number of other printers offer **plug-in cartridge fonts.** The `Fonts` screen of the printer's property sheet lets you select the desired font cartridge (although without a corresponding screen font, you won't be operating in a WYSIWYG world) and add a new cartridge's font to the list of available cartridges.

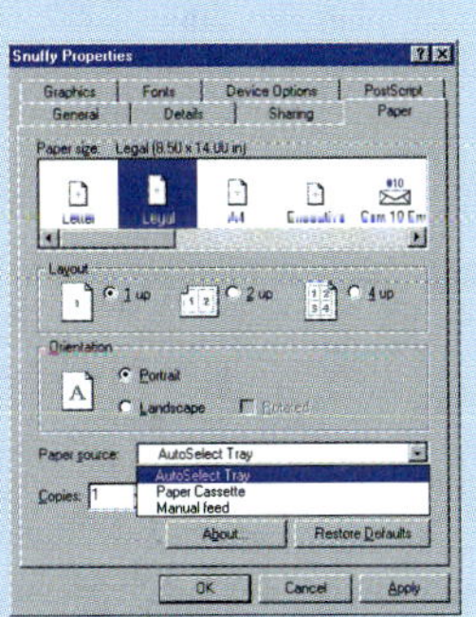

Paper

Choices in the `Paper` screen vary widely among printer models. Paper sizes often depend on `Paper Source` options (e.g., tractor, standard paper tray, envelope feeder). When a `Custom` size is offered, another window appears in which you enter the dimensions of a page in inches or millimeters. Some printers require additional controls for the type of paper (or transparency) being fed into the printer. The orientation (portrait or landscape) setting in this panel can be overridden in the Page Setup dialog prior to printing any document. The setting here establishes the default for new documents.

Multiple Printer Setups

Printers that have complex property sheets can be difficult to reconfigure each time you wish to print according to different settings. You can, however, use the `Add Printer` wizard to install another copy of the same printer in your copy of Windows. Simply assign the two copies different names (as you would rename different versions of the same file), perhaps one for tray feed, the other for manual feed. Make all necessary settings in the property sheet. Then, when you're ready to print, simply select the desired printer from the Print dialog in the application.

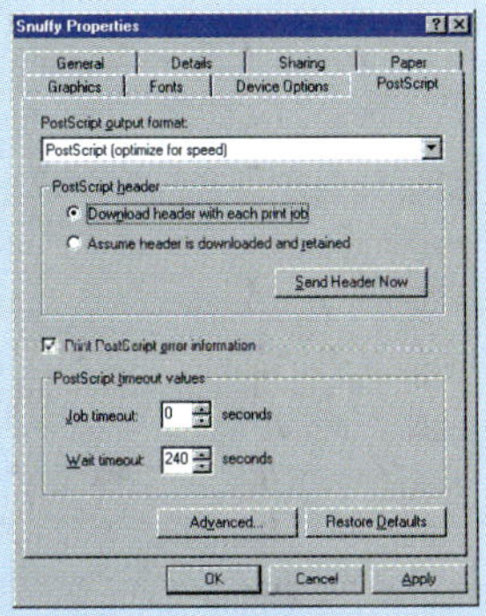

PostScript

For PostScript printers, many advanced settings should be adjusted only if you fully understand the impact of the changes. One important setting, the `PostScript Output Format`, lets you specify sending the output not directly to a printer, but to a file as an **Encapsulated PostScript** (EPS) file. To accomplish this, you must also change the `Print To` setting in the `Details` screen to a disk file, rather than one of the ports. Outputting a job as an EPS file may make sense if you must share the final output with other users whose machines do not run Windows but normally send their output to PostScript printers.

If you find that you receive many PostScript timeout error messages, you might consider increasing the timeout values in this panel. Typically, however, after one timeout, Windows automatically retries the command after five seconds, and the print job will continue normally.

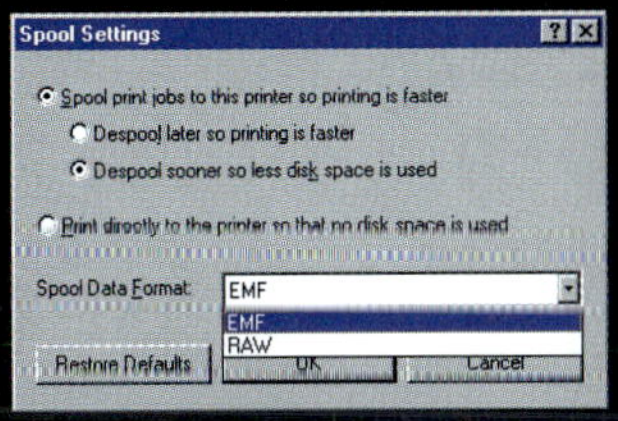

Spooled File Formats

Non-PostScript printers normally have their spooled data written as what is called an Enhanced Metafile (EMF). PostScript printers, on the other hand, tend to write their spool files in "raw" format. If you experience problems printing to a non-PostScript printer, try changing the spool format from EMF to RAW (click the Spool Settings button in the Details screen of the printer's property sheet). For other printing troubleshooting tips, see 176, 177.

The Page Setup dialog is a catchall place to make adjustments to the way text and images meet the sheet of paper.

Most importantly, this is where you designate the size or type of paper going through the printer, and whether images should be printed in **portrait** (tall) or **landscape** (sideways) mode. Each program has its own variation on the Page Setup dialog—some simple, some several screens long. Page Setup settings are saved with each document.

Select Printer Early

From the **Page Setup** dialog in some programs, you can click the Printer button to reach a version of the **Print** dialog 141 that allows you to select a printer. Because the printer model affects the `Page Setup` choices available to you, select a printer for the document before entering other data.

Set Up Pages Early

For many programs, Page Setup dialog settings significantly affect the document page size and orientation on the screen. Most documents use the default settings, so you only have to change settings for nonstandard documents. If you are producing a document that you intend to print, it is important to make Page Setup dialog choices before you start entering information into a new document.

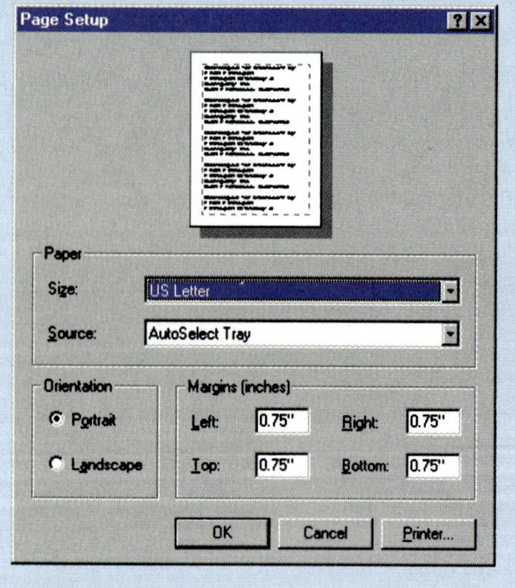

Paper Size

Each printer model lists its own complement of paper sizes that it can accommodate. All printers handle U.S. **letter and legal sizes**, plus the European A4 page. Some printers have special settings for envelopes, while others can accommodate 15-inch-wide fanfold (greenbar) paper.

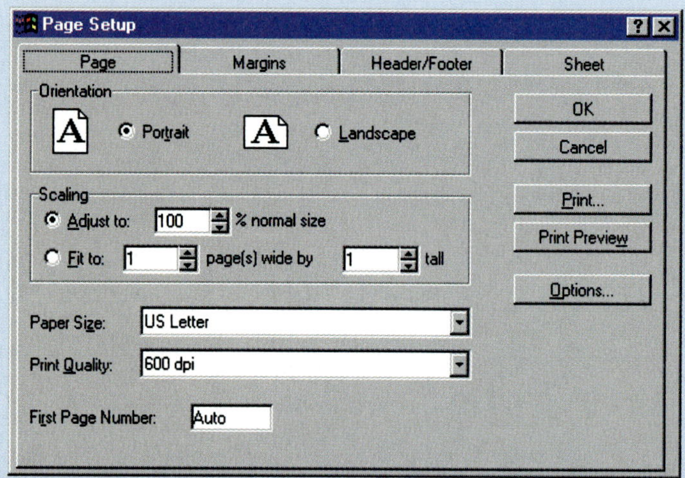

Envelopes

When a printer offers an envelope paper size, it also intends that envelopes be fed in a very specific way. The requirement may be for the envelope to be fed in the center of the paper feed or along one edge. Also critical is whether the envelope should be face up or down. Consult your **printer's manual** for special instructions on envelopes.

Orientation

Two radio buttons (sometimes accompanied by icons) show two page orientations: tall (portrait) and sideways (landscape). In landscape printing the page feeds through the printer like always, but the image is rotated 90 degrees to the right.

Image Size

Each program presents its own possibilities for **reducing** or **enlarging** images. Experiment carefully in selecting scaling factors for non-PostScript printers: only some scaling percentages will come out evenly. PostScript printers, however, can be told to reduce or enlarge in one-percent increments with a good chance of high quality output.

Margins

Programs often allow final adjustments of printed margins in the Page Setup dialog. Be aware that virtually no printer can print to the very edge of the paper (except for the tops and bottoms of tractor fed paper pages). Even the best printers can't print the last one-eighth to one-quarter inch on a side.

Other Settings

As many Microsoft applications reveal, there is no end to the items you may be asked to specify in a Page Setup dialog. In Excel, for instance, headers and footers are added in the Page Setup dialog, because there is no convenient place to enter them in the document (as there is in a word processing program).

Missing Settings

If you find that a particular trait of your printer is missing from the Page Setup dialog, then access the printer's property sheet and make the adjustment(s) there. The new settings become the default values when they're not further adjusted by the program during printing.

What's Print Setup?

Programs that don't quite adhere to the latest user interface plans for Windows 95 may include both `Page Setup` and `Print Setup` items in the `File` menu. In such programs, `Page Setup` covers header, footer, and margins; `Print Setup` has printer selection, paper settings, and orientation buttons. If you feel the Page Setup dialog lacks some settings, look for a companion `Print Setup` menu item.

The Print dialog box is the last dialog you usually see after initiating the printing process.

Items in this dialog tend to be specifications that users are likely to change frequently from printing to printing of a document—printer to use, page range, number of copies, and collating order. Many programs add other items to enhance the choices available for printing the current document.

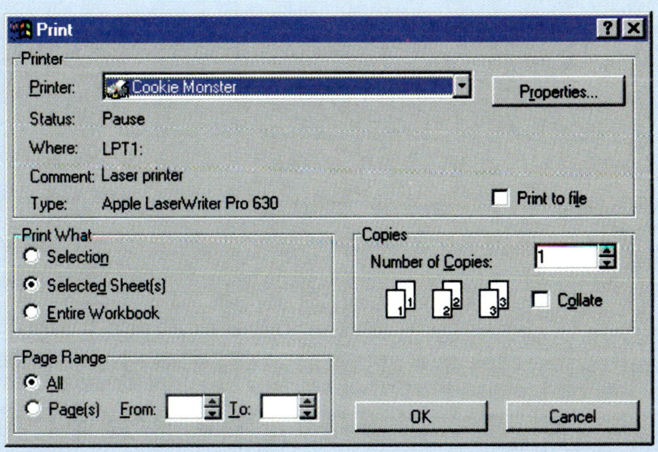

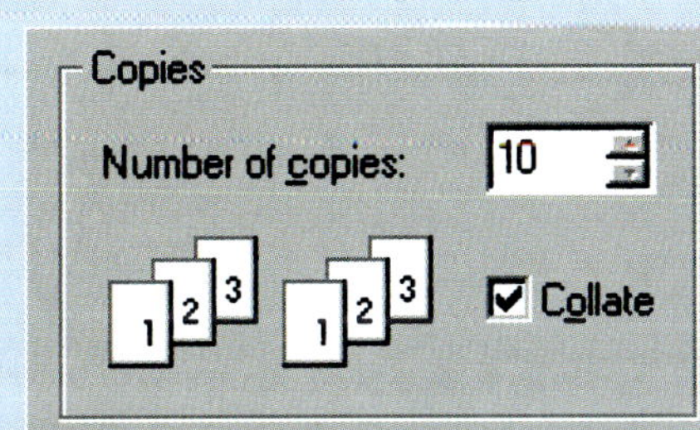

Printer Identification

One advantage of the `Print` dialog is that it gives you one last chance to **select a printer** for the job. This is especially helpful in networked situations, where multiple printers may be available, or when you have the luxury of choosing between a networked laser printer and a personal printer in your office.

Information from the `General` screen of a printer's property sheet appears in this dialog. Notice the `Where` and `Comment` fields. In a multiple-printer environment, these bits of information can help someone choose the right printer for the job.

Page Range

The default setting is to print all pages of a document. But if you need only a specific page or set of pages, you can set the page numbers. Be sure that the radio button attached to the `From/To` fields is highlighted as well. The `All` radio button overrides the page range numbering you enter into those fields. When the program, such as a word processing program, allows you to change the starting page number for the document, use the page numbers as they would appear on the pages for the `From/To` field values.

Print Selection

In some programs, you can select a portion of text or graphic, and tell the program to print only the selection. This would override any page selections made earlier.

Number of Copies

All printers allow you to print **multiple copies** of a document. When the document consists of multiple pages as well, the printer produces multiple copies of each page. Some printer drivers help out with **collating**, offering a choice that prints one copy of the document in order before starting on the next copy. But if a program takes a long time to prepare pages because of heavy graphics or font downloading characteristics, it will probably be faster to let it prepare each page once for any number of copies, rather than making it go through the preparation of each page for each copy of a document.

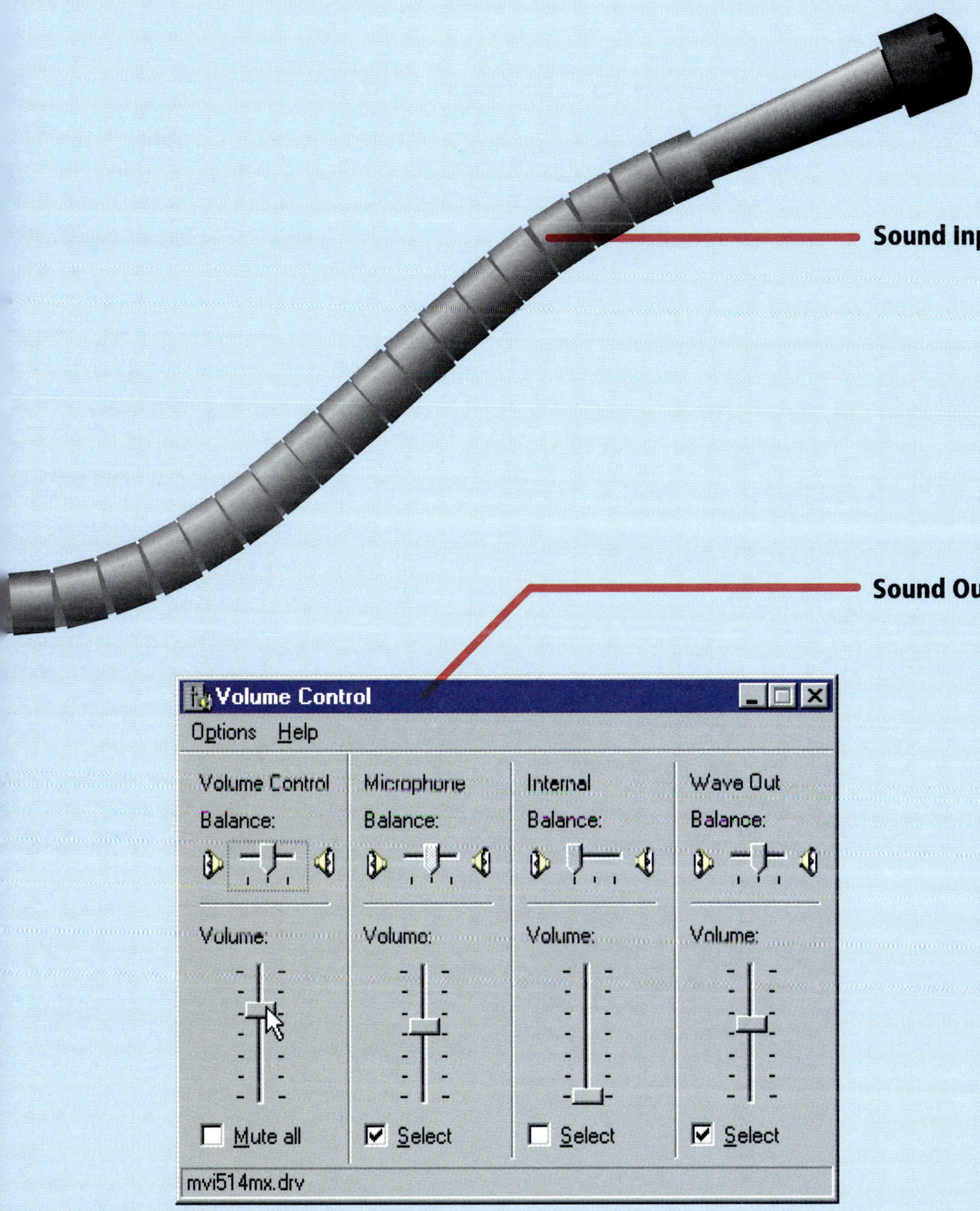

Sound Input, page 144

Sound Output, page 146

Personal computer manufacturers are focusing much attention on the multimedia aspects of computing.

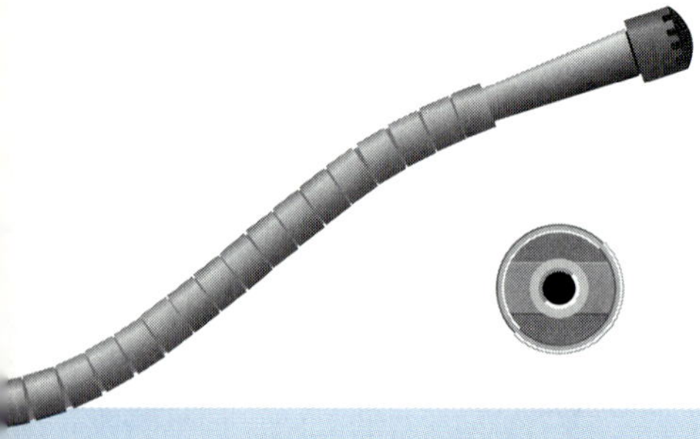

Windows 95 also plays a role by providing system software to support CD-ROM playback and digital sound. Some application programs include features that let you attach a voice annotation to a place in a document. More and more computers arrive from the factory equipped for multimedia, including sound and voice recording—some even including a microphone with the package. Voice annotation, voice mail messages, voice alarms, and custom system sounds are only the beginning of an intriguing future for sound recording on Windows-compatible PCs.

Recording Hardware

Computers that come out of the box equipped for multimedia usually contain ports for audio input, whether from an audio source such as a tape player or from a microphone. Other PCs can be equipped with multimedia upgrade kits, which generally include a sound board capable of capturing sounds through its audio input ports. The electronic components that capture sound are called **digitizers,** because they convert analog audio signals (e.g., your voice) to digital signals that can be manipulated and stored in a computer.

Sound boards (whether built into the computer or added separately) require driver software if Windows and its applications are to work with sounds (other than simple beeps). Windows 95 comes with an array of drivers for all the popular multimedia sound boards. Newer devices will be Plug and Play (i.e., they'll install themselves) or will come with driver software on diskette to install via the `Add New Hardware` wizard 60.

Your choice of **microphone** for voice recording can make a big difference. If your PC came with a microphone, it is already matched for the sound hardware. Otherwise, check the requirements for a microphone's impedance (Z) value (usually rated as high or low), and purchase a microphone that best matches those characteristics.

If your PC (or sound card) is equipped with a line input port, you should use this for connection to line level output connections from audio and video components. These levels are lower than the levels that are fed to speakers. Do not connect speaker or headphone outputs from an audio component (like a CD or cassette player) to a line level input connector—you may damage your sound card.

Sampled Sound

Sound digitizers work by taking distinct snapshots of an analog sound at set intervals (many thousands of times each second). Each snapshot of the sound at an instant is called a **sample.** The sample is assigned a numeric value based on the nature of the sound source at that instant. The Windows startup music, for example, is nothing more than a series of numeric values. When played back through a **digital-to-analog** converter (the reverse of the recording process), the values are converted to analog sound that plays through the speaker—the sound the human ear can hear. This is the process used for digital compact discs.

Sampling Rates

The more often samples of an analog sound are taken, the more likely the digital equivalent will reflect the original sound. This is akin to higher print or video resolutions. The highest **sampling rate** you'll find in software for recording with your PC and sound card is 44.1 kilohertz (44,100 times each second), although your sound card may not be up to the task. A more common high-quality sampling rate is 22 kilohertz (actually 22.05 kHz). While this sampling rate produces excellent quality, it also requires a fair amount memory and disk storage—a minute of monaural sound sampled at 22 kHz occupies more than 1 megabyte of hard disk space without compression.

If you sample less frequently, you can **save memory** and disk space at the cost of quality. For the limited frequency range of the human voice, specifying a smaller sampling rate and monaural sound doesn't do too much damage to intelligibility, but it does greatly reduce the memory requirements. Some sound recording software also allows recording at sampling rates lower than "telephone quality." Memory use is directly proportional to the sampling rate.

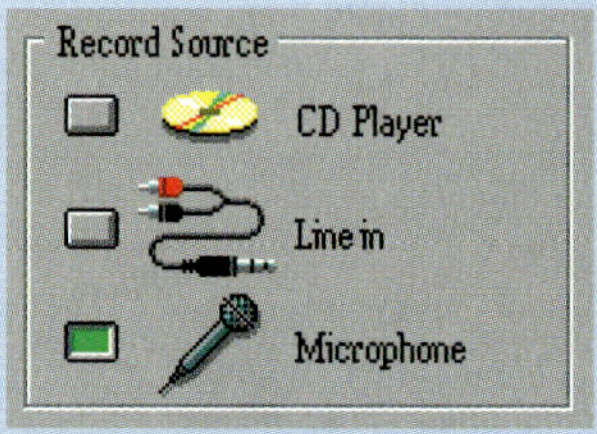

Activating the Microphone

Depending on the sound hardware and software drivers for your PC, you may have to activate the microphone port before recording any sounds. There may be a separate control panel or audio mixer program that controls which audio input port is active and its basic recording level. But if your multimedia hardware and devices are Windows 95-compatible, use the Volume Control program (Sndvol32) to turn on the microphone input. Choose `Properties` from the `Options` menu, and click the `Recording` radio button. Back in the Control window, check the `Select` box under the `Microphone` slider (and uncheck other input sources).

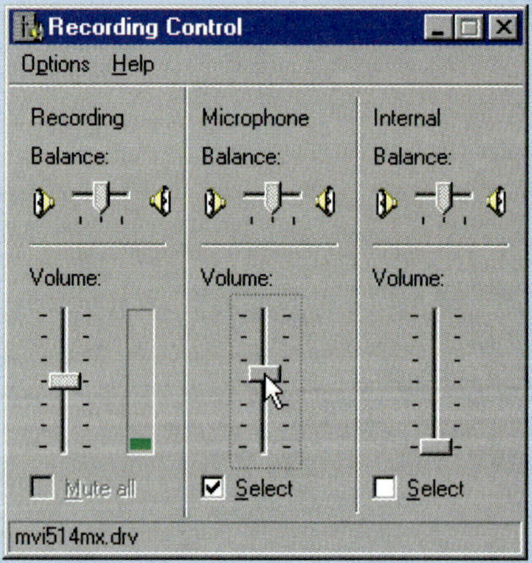

Simple Sound Editing

The Windows 95 Sound Recorder application is hardly a sophisticated sound editing tool, but you can experiment with some aspects of digitized sound with it. You can splice multiple sound files together, mix files (without any balance control, however), and employ a few special effects.

Sound Timer
The slider control shows you how much time has elapsed during the maximum recording time period. A digital readout is shown to the left. It is marked `Position` because it shows how far along the sound timeline the scope view reveals.

Save the Sound
Choose `Save` from the `File` menu to save the sound as a disk file. Another dialog asks you to name the sound. Windows does so as a .WAV file.

Recording Alert Sounds
If you have a sound card and microphone, you can record an alert sound to apply to any of the system actions listed in the Sounds control panel. The program you use to record sound is Sound Recorder, initially installed by Windows in the Start → `Programs` → `Accessories` → `Multimedia` folder.

Starting a New Recording
Choose `New` from the `File` menu. Choose `Audio Properties` in the `Edit` menu. For your first test, choose the `Radio Quality` preset combination from the `Recording Preferred Quality` pop-up list, and click OK.

Record and Stop Buttons
Hold the microphone near your mouth, and click the **Record** (●) button. When the busy pointer disappears, begin speaking into the microphone. Get ready to click the **Stop** (■) button when you finish. You can record up to 60 seconds of sound (depending on available memory). The green line in the scope should create some waves (if not, check the microphone connection and recording volume settings).

Play Button
Before saving the sound, click the **Play** (▶) button to play back the sound. If you want to re-record the sound, click the **Rewind** (◀◀) button, and choose `Delete After Current Position` from the `Edit` menu. Then click the Record button to try again.

Sound Effects
Sound Recorder's `Effects` menu includes two special effects: `Add Echo` and `Reverse`. Both choices affect the entire file. Each time you choose `Add Echo`, the software modifies the current version of the sound with a reverberation effect; multiple applications deepen the effect. `Reverse` plays the sound backwards, and can be undone by choosing `Reverse` again. Speed adjustments in this menu work as they would on a tape player, affecting the pitch of the sound at the same time. More sophisticated sound editing programs (which may be included with your PC or sound card) provide far more in the way of special effects and editing facilities. If you have such a program, use it in place of Microsoft's Sound Recorder.

Trimming Sounds
When you record a sound, there is usually some dead space before and after the solid gold part of the recording. To trim excess sound before a particular location, adjust the slider control to the spot where the sound you want to keep begins (the Ctrl key plus left or right arrows adjusts the slider in .01 second intervals). Then choose `Delete Before Current Position` from the `Edit` menu. You can do the same for deleting anything after a specific point. Because Sound Recorder doesn't let you select a specific range of sound for copying, you can use this method for isolating sounds you may want to insert or mix into other sound files.

Splicing Sounds
At any point along a sound timeline, you can insert another sound file or a sound from the Clipboard. Set the desired position with the slider control, and then choose `Insert File` or `Paste Insert` (depending on the source of the sound) from the `Edit` menu. By setting the slider at the end of a sound, you can string together two sounds.

Mixing Sounds
While the art of sound mixing normally requires great skill, Sound Recorder provides very simple mixing, which overlays one sound file atop another. Set the desired position with the slider control, and then choose `Mix with File` or `Paste Mix` (depending on the source of the sound). When you play back the sound, you'll hear both sound tracks simultaneously. Both sound sources are given equal weight.

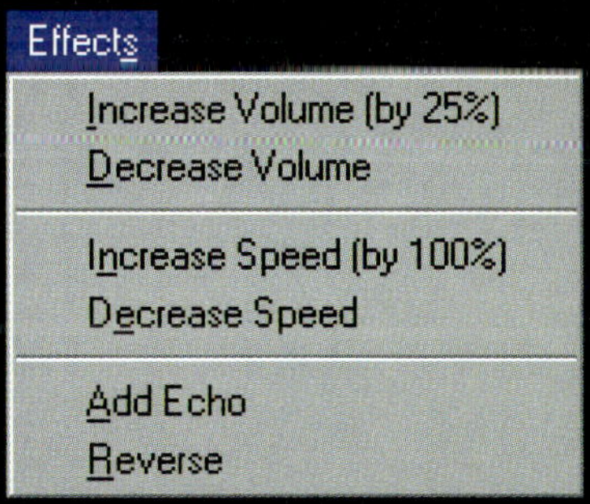

Voice Recognition
Today it is possible to connect third-party devices to respond to spoken commands. Essentially, you teach the software to perform some action (menu command, macro, etc.) in response to a specific voice command you speak into a microphone. You train the software to recognize that voice command by giving it a few samples to use as a comparison.

True voice recognition, in which the computer understands what you are saying (instead of just reacting to a particular speech pattern) is a very complex technology that is still a long way from being practical and affordable. But between voice response and emerging text-to-speech technologies, we will soon be carrying on conversations of a sort with our PCs.

For many years, the typical IBM-compatible PC could sound off with little more than a single beep at varying pitches—simple little tunes at best.

The popular multimedia applications, however, have advanced the basic sound components of most new PCs today so that they can play high-quality recorded digitized sound from CD-ROM programs and other sources.

Windows 95 meets the challenge by supplying system software components that provide basic audio output playback and incorporation of sounds into documents. You can also attach digitized sounds to a variety of actions you and programs take while operating the computer.

Audio Output Hardware

Personal computers equipped for multimedia playback include the **sound card** necessary to drive audio speakers with sound from a variety of computerized sources. All sorts of configurations abound, with speakers sometimes built into the PC system unit or detachable for setup around your computer work area. Older PCs without that capability built in can acquire multimedia upgrade kits that include the sound card and small amplified desktop speakers.

Most PCs that come with CD-ROM drives are capable of playing stereo sound from **compact audio discs** (Windows 95 even includes software that turns the CD-ROM drive into a CD player). Not all multimedia software generates sound in stereo, nor can every sound board record in stereo. But the trend is definitely in that direction. It's not unusual to see a stereo headphone jack on the front panel of a multimedia PC.

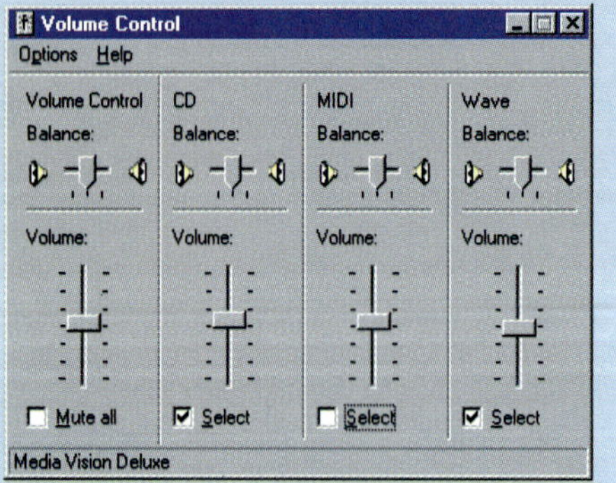

Setting Output Volume

How best to adjust the sound volume depends a lot on your PC hardware. True multimedia PCs these days have all kinds of friendly audio controls on the front panel, including volume. But for control-less PCs, you can control the sound via the Windows 95 **Volume Control** program (located in the Start → Programs → Accessories → Multimedia folder). This master controller includes slider volume and stereo balance controls for a variety of

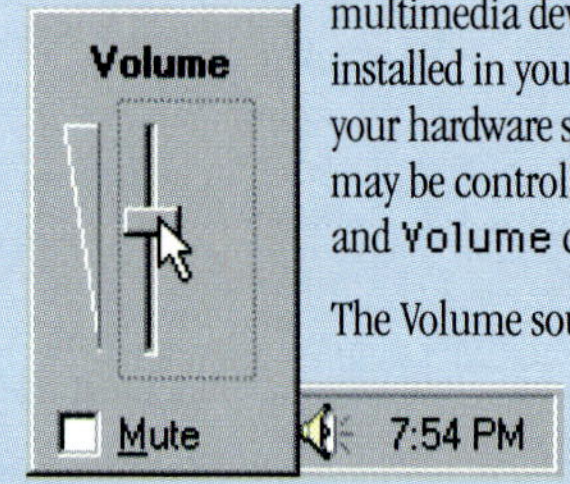

multimedia devices you may have installed in your PC. Depending on your hardware setup, sound volume may be controlled by the Wave and Volume controls.

The Volume sound control is also located in the **Multimedia** control panel (Audio screen), but labeled Playback Volume. A key element of this control panel is a checkbox to indicate that a button to a pop-up volume slider control should always be displayed on the Taskbar. This is a good alternative to the manual volume control.

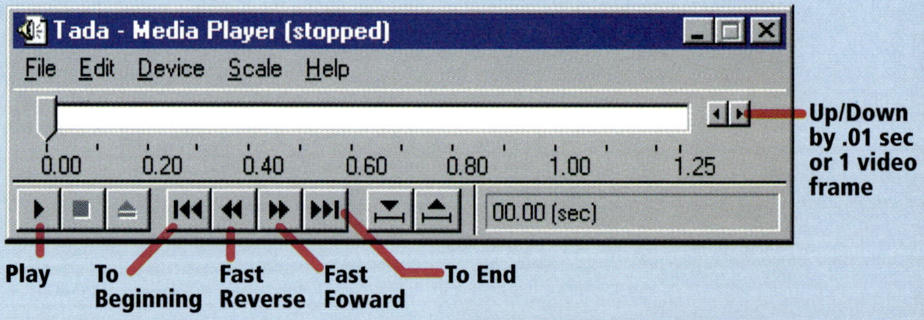

Checking Out Sound Files

While there are several ways to hear a sound file in Windows, two are particularly useful. The simplest is to locate a sound file, right-click on it, and choose Play. This launches the **Sound Recorder** program 144, plays through the sound, and quits the program. The second method uses the universal **Media Player** program (Mplayer) supplied with Windows (in the Start → Programs → Accessories → Multimedia folder). This program lets you play back sound (.WAV), video (.AVI), and MIDI (.MID or .RMI) musical instrument files. Here are the steps you use to play back sounds in the Media Player:

1. Choose Sound from the Device menu.
2. In thOpen file dialog, select a sound file, and click Open.
3. Click the Play (▶) button in the Media Player window.

Media Player is a playback-only program. Any editing must be performed in a sound editing program, such as **Sound Recorder** 144 or programs that come with your multimedia-equipped PC.

Playing Video and MIDI Clips

Media Player is a versatile tool for viewing video clips and hearing both sound and MIDI files. While you can preview any of these files from the Desktop/ Explorer (right-click→Play; or right-click→Properties→ Preview), the Media Player lets you examine any of these time-based media in more detail. For instance, while viewing a video clip, you can advance the video one frame at a time. Or you can replay sections of a MIDI music file over and over.

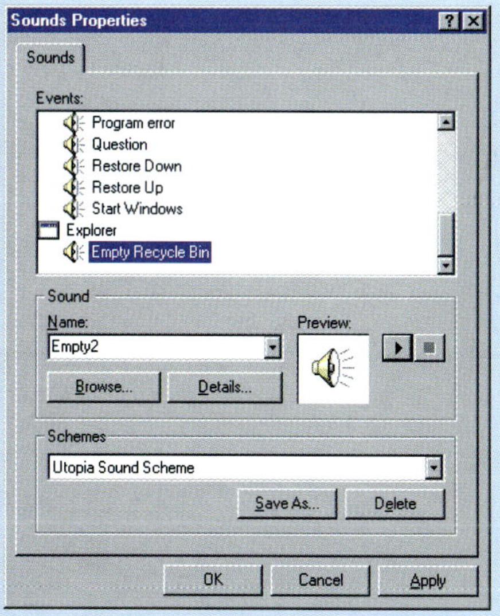

Customizing Event Sounds

Windows 95 identifies more than a dozen user and program actions (called events) to which you may assign sounds. For example, with the basic installation of Windows 95 you hear a sound attached to the Start Windows event just as the Desktop appears on the screen. Any sound file (.WAV) that you have on your hard disk or record 144 can be assigned to events defined in the Sounds control panel. Events named Asterisk, Exclamation, and Question refer to the icons displayed in the three types of system alert boxes that appear when errors or other user notifications are needed.

Let's say you've recorded the word "empty" with an echo effect, and wish to attach it to the `Empty Recycle Bin` event. Here are the steps:

1. Open the Sounds control panel.
2. Scroll the `Events` list until you locate `Empty Recycle Bin`. Click on that item.
3. In the `Name` pop-up list are all the sounds located in the `Windows`→`Media` folder. If you've saved the "empty" sound to that folder, select the sound from the list; otherwise, click the Browse... button to locate the file. A sound icon appears in the `Events` list next to `Empty Recycle Bin`.
4. Click the Play ( ) button in the `Preview` area to hear the sound.

If you make separate sets of sounds for different environments (say, home and office), you can save each set (or scheme) at the bottom of the `Sounds` control panel. To change schemes, simply open the control panel and select the one you want from the bottom pop-up list. Windows comes with a few preset schemes from which to choose.

Removing an Event Sound

Sometimes sounds are neat when you put them in, but wear with familiarity. To remove a sound from an event, open the Sounds control panel and locate the event you'd like to silence. Then choose `(None)` from the `Name` pop-up list.

Sound Files

Windows comes with a number of prerecorded sounds, but you can acquire libraries of sounds from a variety of sources. Windows-oriented bulletin boards or sections on commercial services (CompuServe, America Online, and Microsoft Network) will offer you choices from among hundreds of sounds. Such public domain or shareware collections are also often gathered together on low-cost CD-ROMs available from mail order software outlets and user groups. Snippets from virtually every popular television show and movie are out there for your private use.

Incorporating Media into Documents

Once you have a media file, you can link or embed it into any document of an OLE-compatible program 128. Here are the basic steps:

1. Select the file in the Desktop/Explorer.
2. Right-click on it, and choose `Copy` from the pop-up menu.
3. Switch to your document window, locate an insertion point, and choose `Paste Special` from the `Edit` menu.
4. In the `Paste Special` dialog, choose whether you wish to embed the media file or just create a link to it 128.
5. Check the `Display As Icon` box if you want the item to appear in the document merely as an icon to double-click (recommended for video clips, which would otherwise display the first frame of the clip in the document).

For some applications, you may have to paste the media object into the **OLE Packager** program 128 and then copy that package into your document.

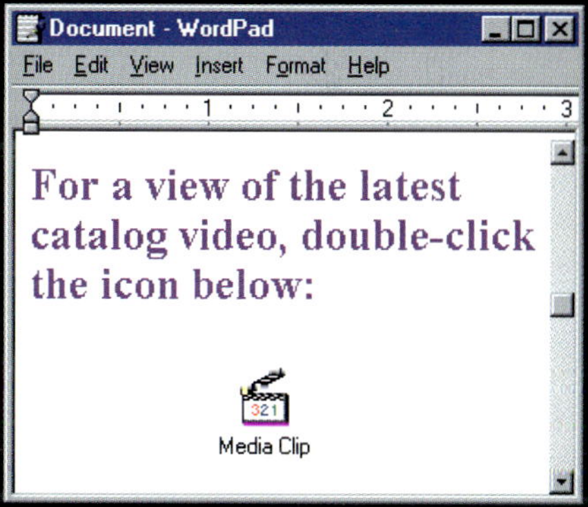

Prior to copying and embedding or linking a media file into a document, you may wish to check some OLE attributes about the file from within **Media Player.** Open the file in Media Player, and choose `Options` from the `Edit` menu. In the dialog you can assign a more friendly name as the caption of the icon to appear in the document, as well as whether the item should display a control bar (e.g., Play and Stop buttons) during playback in the document, and so on. These settings are saved with the media file.

Direct Cable Connection, page 150

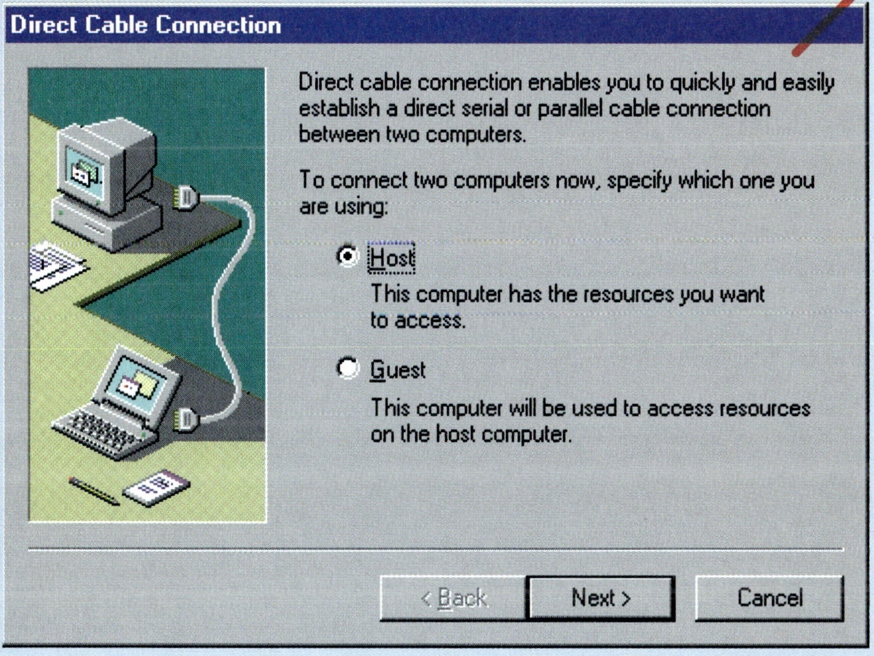

Connecting to the Outside World, page 144

File and Printer Sharing, page 144

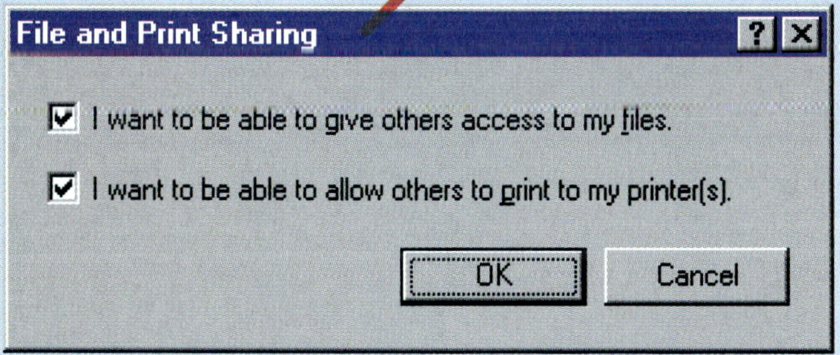

Direct Cable Connection

Windows 95 includes software that allows you to connect two PCs together without the hassle of networking cards or complex cabling.

There are a number of applications for this feature. For example, if you have both a desktop and laptop PC, you can link the two together to quickly exchange files and programs between them. Or, a two-computer office can allow both computer users to share the same printer or mass storage device without an elaborate network installation.

Preparing the two computers for connection takes a bit of work, but once they're set up as desired, you simply run the Direct Cable Connection program on both computers to link up.

The Cable Connection

You may use parallel or serial ports to connect the two machines. The only requirement is that the same style of port be used on both machines: While you cannot connect to a parallel port on one PC and to a serial port on the other, you can use COM1 on one PC and COM2 on the other, if necessary.

Regardless of port, the cable you need is a **straight-through** style (i.e., no wires are crossed). For serial port connection, the connectors on both ends of the cable will be female style (usually **DB-9** 7).

Software Component

Direct Cable Connection (directcc.exe) is the program that makes the direct linkup possible. If you don't see the program listed in the Start menu's Accessories group, then use the Add/Remove Programs → Communications control panel to install the software in both machines you want to connect to each other.

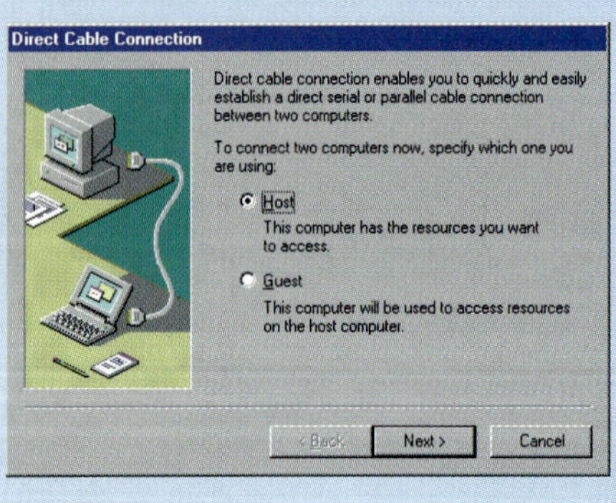

Host vs. Guest

Before setting up the link, you must decide which of the two computers will be the host—the one containing resources that the other will want to use. In a laptop-desktop PC connection, the desktop machine will most likely be the host, because it probably contains file archives and has one or more printers connected to it. In the direct cable connection, one computer must be designated the host, while the other is the guest.

Setting Up a Host

Here are the steps to establish one computer as the host:

1. Open Start → Programs → Accessories → Direct Cable Connection.
2. Click the Host radio button and Next >.
3. Click on the port you are using for the connection and Next >.
4. If you have any reason to worry about unauthorized access, setup a **password.** Click Finish.

A window appears with a message stating that the host is now waiting for a guest to connect via the selected port. The animated icon simulates data movement, even if the connection is not yet established.

You can minimize this window, but if you close it, you will break any connection that exists with the guest computer. The next time you start this program, a window lets you either wait for a connection or change the direct connect status of this PC.

Setting Up a Guest

Here are the steps to establish one computer as the guest:

1. Open Start → Programs → Accessories → Direct Cable Connection.
2. Click the Guest radio button and Next >.
3. Click on the port you are using for the connection and Next >.
4. Click Finish.

A window appears with a message stating that the guest is now trying to connect with a host via the selected port. The animated icon simulates data movement, even if the connection is not yet established.

You can minimize this window, but if you close it, you will break any connection that exists with the host computer. The next time you start this program, a window lets you connect with a host or change the direct connect status of this PC.

Establishing a Link

The guest computer may be prompted for the name of the host computer. This name is available in the **Network** control panel of the host computer, and must be entered letter-for-letter as it appears in the control panel. This **host name** then becomes part of the pathname that the guest computer uses to access disks and files on the host.

Drive Mapping Strategies

If you frequently connect to the same host computer and its shared devices, you can automate the drive mapping process a bit. When mapping the drive, click the Reconnect at Logon checkbox. The next time you restart your PC, the drive icons (with a red X through the network cable indication) will appear in My Computer, even if you are not yet logged onto the host computer. When you start Direct Cable Connection (or whatever network connectivity you used to link with the devices in the first place), the icons will become active, and you can access them from file dialogs, the Desktop, and Explorer.

Deciding what letters to assign is a matter of personal taste. Some users prefer to keep their drive letters in order, assigning the first unused letter after the internal hard disk to the first remote disk. Others prefer to assign letters to remote devices from the end of the alphabet. You can also use mnemonics if they fit your device scheme, such as drive letter M for the Microsoft Mail server shared folder on a local area network. If you connect to multiple host systems at different times (via direct connect, dial-up, or formal network), you should be careful to assign unique letters to each remote item so you don't accidentally store a file in the wrong destination.

Once the host computer is identified, a window opens on the guest computer listing all items (disks, folders, printers, etc.) that are designated as shared items on the host. If you close this window, you can view it again by clicking the View Host button in the Direct Cable Connect window.

Sharing Folders, Disks, and Printers

While Windows 95 includes the system software required to engage file and resource sharing among computers (whether connected directly, over the telephone for remote access, or via a formal network), there are several software components that must be installed for sharing to work at all. See 152 for details on installing the proper software components for sharing.

Once the host PC is setup to allow file and/or printer sharing, the host computer user determines which items are to be shared. Right-clicking on disk, folder, and printer icons on the Desktop or Explorer displays a pop-up menu containing a `Sharing` item. With **sharing** turned on (see 152 for settings details), the item's icon in Desktop and Explorer windows changes to include a hand "serving" the item to authorized users.

Mapping Drives

Shared disks and folders that appear in the Direct Connect window on the Desktop are not truly part of the guest computer. These items are resources available to the guest computer, but they do not appear as storage areas in **Open** or **Save As** dialog boxes 90.

To make them part of the guest computer, each item must be **mapped**—assigned a drive letter that is valid on the guest computer. For example, if the host computer shares its C: drive, it cannot appear on the guest's computer also as a C: drive, because the guest computer most likely has its own C: drive as part of its computer hardware. Mapping lets you assign a drive letter that is meaningful to the computer depicted in the `My Computer` icon on the Desktop.

In the case of a shared folder from the host, it must be assigned a separate drive letter on the guest PC, even though the folder may be on the same physical hard disk drive on the host PC as another shared folder.

To map a remote disk or folder to a local drive letter:

1. Right-click on its icon in the host computer's Desktop window (visible on the guest computer).

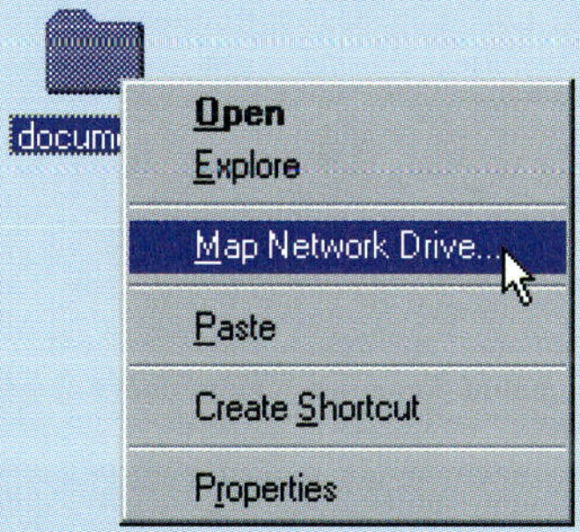

2. Choose `Map Network Drive` from the pop-up menu.

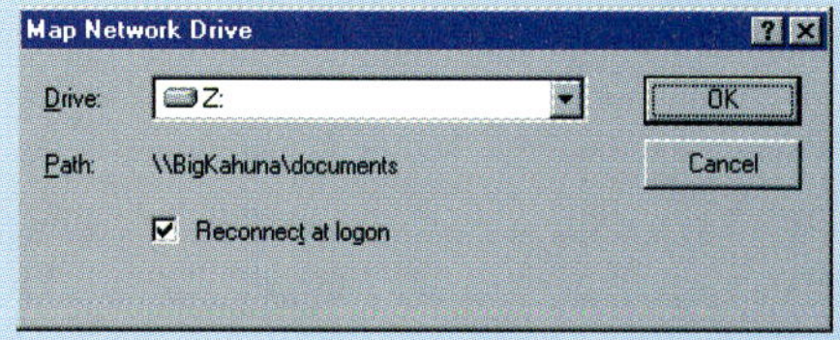

3. Select a drive letter from the pop-up list in the dialog box.

The mapped drive will appear in the `My Computer` window with a special icon denoting the fact that the drive is connected via a network or other linkup.

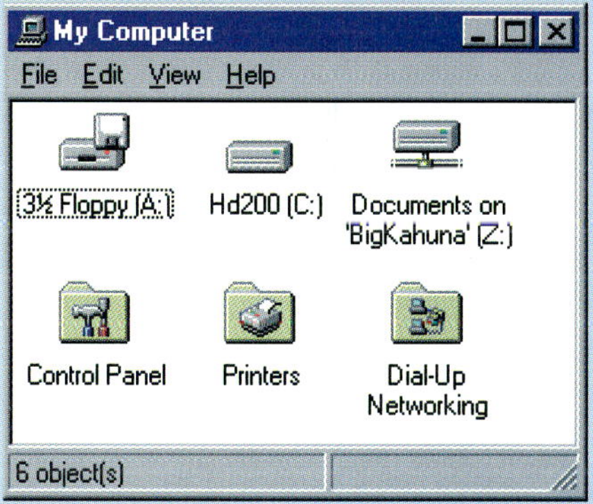

Removing Icons

If you start Windows and see an icon in the My Computer window with a red X on it, it means that the remote drive or folder is not connected. If you don't plan to connect to it again, you can remove the icon by right-clicking on it, and choosing Disconnect from the pop-up menu.

Printing Offline

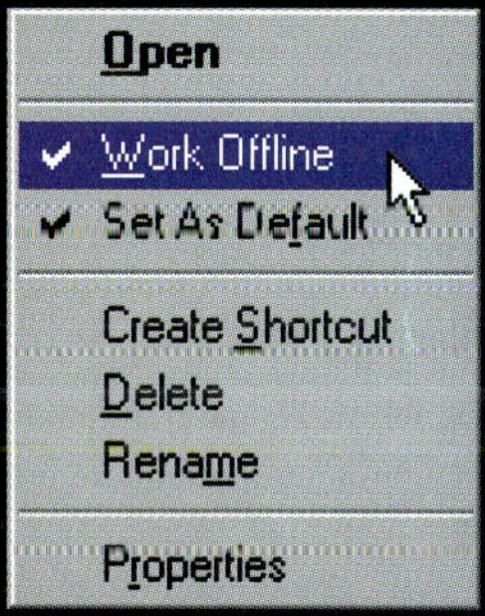

With a shared printer installed on a guest computer, the guest PC can queue up print jobs to be printed once the guest is connected to the host. Right-click the printer icon, and choose `Work Offline` from the pop-up menu. The printer's window contains a message about user intervention required: connecting to the networked printer when you're ready to do so. Issue Print commands in programs as you normally would. Documents are spooled 136. When connected to the host, uncheck the Work Offline item in the pop-up menu to start the printing process.

Installing a Shared Printer

Before you can print to a shared printer attached to a host (or host network), you must install applicable drivers in the guest PC. Windows facilitates this through the network connection:

1. Right-click on the printer icon in the host computer's window.
2. Choose `Install Printer` from the pop-up menu.

Because all drivers are on the host PC, Windows copies all necessary files from the host to the guest PC. The printer's icon (in a special networked version) appears in the guest PC's Printers folder. When the guest computer is not connected to the host, the icon is shaded.

Serial Port Speed

If you use COM ports for direct connection, both ports must be set to the same communications speed. While there are settings adjustable in the `System→Device Manager` control panel (open the Ports item, double-click on the COM port, and click the `Port Settings` tab), your PC may not respond to the speed settings, even though Windows appears to accept the changes. If your PC comes with its own hardware setup program (it may be a DOS program), you must use this software to adjust the port speed.

Because important information for a workgroup may be located on a variety of PCs, the concept of a central file server isn't always practical or appropriate.

It is common today for users on a network to make portions of their storage areas and printers available to one or more users on the network. Multiple users may also want to access a copy of a CD-ROM disc located in one user's PC.

Because the communication is directly between PCs, the common term is peer-to-peer networking. Direct cable connection and remote dial-up access are also in this classification.

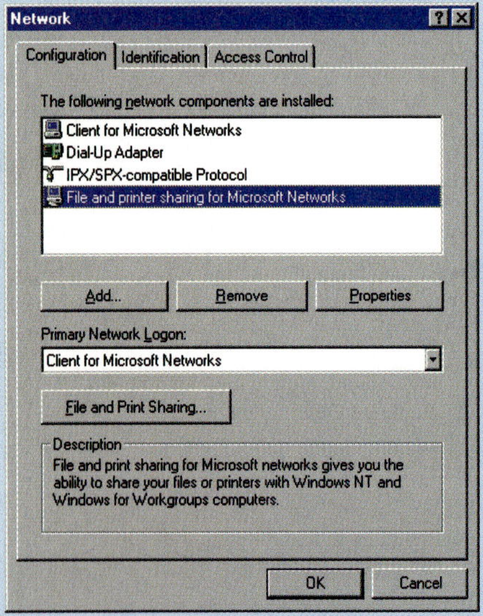

Required Software

If your PC is part of a local area network, the **network administrator** is responsible for making sure your computer has all proper driver software and connectivity hardware installed so you can participate in e-mail and other network services. For direct cable connection 150 and dial-up networking from a remote computer (e.g., a laptop connected via telephone), make sure that the basic connection works before setting up resource sharing. You should be able to log on or connect successfully before digging deeper into sharing.

Windows 95 resource sharing requires Client for Microsoft Networks be installed (or Client for Netware Networks if you are connected to a Novel NetWare network). This software appears in a list in the `Network→Configuration` control panel.

You must also see in that control panel a `File and Printer Sharing` component listed with the other installed items. If not, do the following:

1. Click Add...
2. Click on the `Service` item in the list, and click Add...
3. Click the Microsoft item in the left column, and the item in the right column that matches the type of network you have. If you're not sure, select Microsoft Networks.
4. Click OK

Engaging Global Sharing

Windows 95 includes a kind of master switch that controls all remote access to files and printer resources. In the `Network→Configuration` control panel, click the File and Print Sharing button.

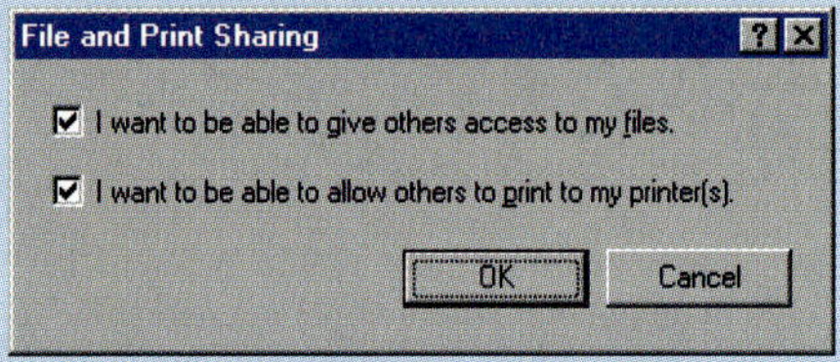

Two checkboxes in the **File and Print Sharing** dialog box let you engage or disengage sharing for each category of resource. Checking either box does not automatically make your resources eligible for sharing: you must make additional, specific settings for that to happen. If you allow many people to access your system but for any reason want to prevent all access for a time (perhaps you're about to back up your hard disk), open this dialog box, and uncheck the desired settings.

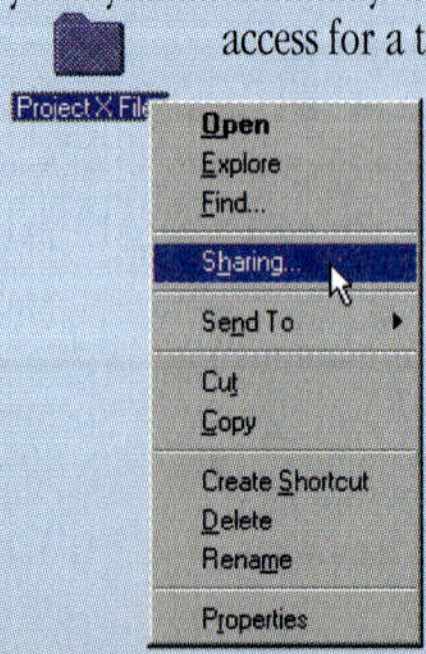

Changes you make to the checkbox settings in this dialog box require a restart of your PC for the changes to take effect.

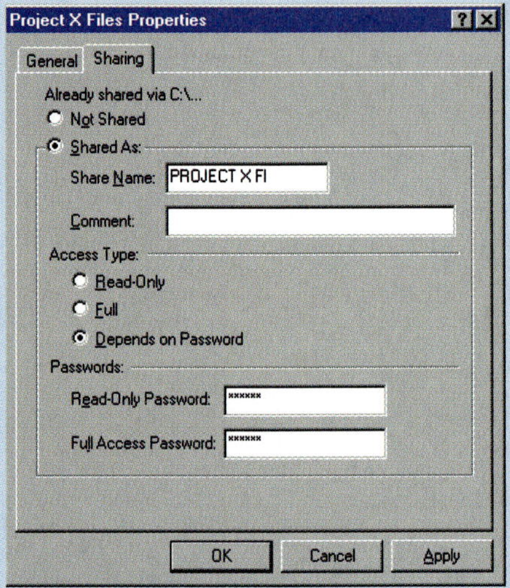

Sharing a Folder or Disk

When global file sharing is turned on, you can right-click any folder or disk icon in the Desktop/Explorer, where the pop-up menu will contain an item named `Sharing`. Choosing this menu item leads to the `Sharing` property sheet for the container (folder or disk). If the `Not Shared` radio button is selected, no other PC can access the container, unless a container higher up the hierarchy is being shared. If a disk drive is being shared, then all items in that drive are shared, even if their property sheets don't indicate specifically that they are shared.

To allow one or more other computer users on the network (or via direct connect or dial-up) to access a disk or folder, click the `Shared As` radio button. Several fields and additional buttons become active. The `Share Name` field is how this item will appear in lists of shared items (e.g., Network Neighborhood). By default Windows suggests the name of the item (the host computer's drive letter for a disk; the first 12 characters of a folder name for a folder). Change the name if you believe it will helpful for others on the network to identify the item.

Windows 95's terminology for this is **file sharing** and **printer sharing**. The "files" are actually containers (folders or disks). For any such resource on your PC, you are in full charge over who has access, but the settings are somewhat complicated to establish the first time.

A Network Neighborhood listing in the Explorer window (the easiest way to work with the Network Neighborhood) displays a hierarchy of all computers with resources to share on the network. Nested within each computer will be a list of all resources (disks, folders, and printers) available from that computer. Assign names to your computer (in the Network control panel) and shared folders that will help any user on the network identify your machine and its shared items.

The `Comment` field is optional, and does not help others identify a particular shared folder.

Setting Up Printer Sharing

Cookie Monster

Right-click on a printer icon you wish to share, and choose Sharing from the pop-up menu (if there is no Sharing item in the menu, then the printer or device cannot be shared). The `Sharing` screen of the printer's property sheet appears. The default setting is `Not Shared`.

Click the `Shared As` radio button to activate fields to help you label the printer for others to select remotely. By default, Windows 95 inserts the name you've assigned to it for yourself (usually just the first word for multi-worded names). While you might use a cute name for own printer, others on the network may not know whether it's the kind of printer they need to borrow, so set the shared name others can recognize.

Accessing Shared Folders

Whether you connect via network, dial-up, or a direct cable, you should map the remote folder to a drive letter that is unique to your own computer. **Drive mapping** is described 150.

Accessing Shared Printers

Before you can use another person's printer, your PC must contain the drivers for that printer model. For information on installing networked printer drivers on your PC 150.

Access Privileges

When sharing a folder or disk, you can assign one of three access privilege levels to remote users: read-only, full, or both depending on the password entered by the remote user. **Read-only** access means that remote users whom you authorize can open any file or folder nested within the shared one. It also means that such users can copy items to their own PCs. But remote users may not modify any files in a read-only folder. Nor can they copy items to the folder.

Full access is precisely that: the ability to modify and delete files or folders contained within the shared folder.

In cases where you may wish some users to have read-only access while others (such as yourself in a dial-up connection) have full access, you can let the remote user's password determine which access privilege level is provided.

Passwords

Managing resource sharing passwords is one of the trickiest parts of implementing sharing among networked users. All passwords are **set by the user** who shares his or her items with others.

In a small workgroup, it may not be necessary to assign passwords at all. By sharing only those items for which security is not a concern, you can leave the password fields empty in the `Sharing` property sheet. Anyone who can see your computer and folder on the network will have the access you specify in the property sheet. If your PC is available to any dial-up access (either directly to your computer or via a dial-in access point on a local area network), you should protect your computer's contents by assigning passwords to any shared item.

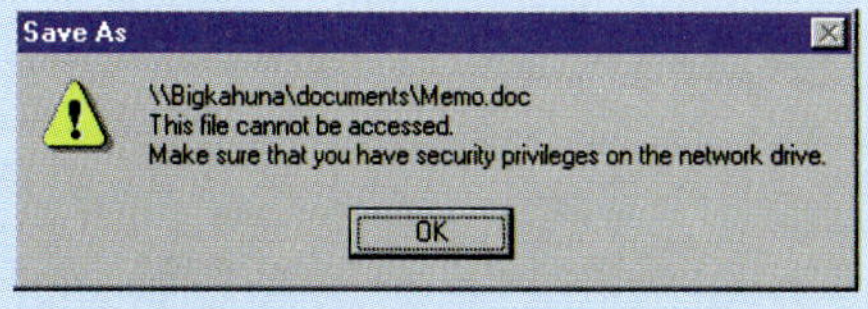

Assigning two **different passwords** for read-only and full access allows you to distinguish among two classes of users you wish to access your resources. You may, for instance, prefer to reserve full access only for yourself, and not reveal the full access password to anyone else.

For any password you assign to items to be shared by other users, you must advise those users of the password for each shared item. You are free to use the same password for all items, if you like. But if privacy and security are serious concerns for your computer, then you should probably not participate in resource sharing on your network, and instead, rely on a central file server and its access privilege management for publishing files others can use.

Passwords should always be kept private. This can be difficult in a workgroup whose users assign multiple passwords. The mistake many users make with passwords is leaving a "cheat sheet" in the open for unauthorized users to see.

Multiple Users—One File

Many applications are designed for multi-user access across a network and manage the reconciliation (or locking) of files when more than one person on the network tries to work with a single file. But other, less-sophisticated programs may allow multiple users to open the same file at once. Should all users have full access to the file's container, it is conceivable that changes saved by one user will wipe out changes made only moments ago by another user. Moreover, it is possible two users could try to save their changes at the same time. In this event, the error message you receive (e.g., File not available) may not help you understand the nature of the problem.

Nested Folders and Access Privileges

Windows 95 is smart about managing access privilege levels even when shared folders may overlap in coverage. For example, if you set up your C: drive for full access with a password that only you know, you can also set up a Documents folder on that drive for read-only access to everyone (no password) or to those who know the read-only password for that folder. When you access the C: drive with your password, you will have full access to everything on that drive, including the Documents folder. But those with read-only access to the folder will be limited to their actions in that same folder (and won't be able to see the rest of your C: drive, because they don't have your secret password). Therefore, you can set up a variety of shared folders for a variety of access privileges for different groups, while maintaining full access to the entire computer just for you.

If John Donne were writing today, he might say instead, "No computer is an island." Beyond linking a PC to others on a local area network, many users have the need to connect to, or share information with, other computers.

The addition of a **telephone modem hardware device** opens a powerful pathway to the information and communities that inhabit commercial on-line services and the Internet. Windows 95 comes with communications software (HyperTerminal) that allows you to connect to local bulletin board services or directly to other computers to transfer files over thousands of miles with the click of a few buttons.

Even without a modem, you can exchange document files with users of Windows or Macintosh computers by swapping 3-1/2-inch diskettes containing files that both types of computers can read.

What's a Modem?

The term modem is a combination of the words **modulator** and **demodulator.** As a modulator, a modem converts the zero and one bit representations of computer information into audible sounds that can travel over regular telephone lines. At the other end, the modem demodulates the signals back into the zeros and ones that the receiving computer understands. External modems connect to one of your PC's COM ports. Newer laptop computers also have PC Card slots, which accept a wide range of commercially available modem cards, including those that can use a cellular telephone as the carrier instead of the regular telephone line.

Of Baud and bps

Modems are often interchangeably rated in two units of measure, called **baud** (pronounced bawd, and named after French communications pioneer J.M.E. Baudot) and **bits per second** (bps). In practice these terms do not refer to the same amount of information per second, so consider the values merely as relative speed indicators.

Common modem speeds these days are 9600 and 14,400 bps for data (the latter also referred to as 14.4 kbps). Fax modems typically send at a minimum speed of 9600 bps, although with an entirely different audio signaling scheme (protocol) than regular data modems. Most commercial on-line services are implementing modem access through regular phone lines at speeds up to 28.8 kbps, but you need an exceptionally clear connection to communicate at that speed.

On-line Services

The Microsoft Network

There is an extensive world of information and community available at the other end of the telephone line when your PC is equipped with a modem and the necessary communications software. Your choice of on-line activity can range from the commercial services, such as Microsoft Network, CompuServe, America Online, and Prodigy (the major services with large followings of PC users) to local bulletin boards and the Internet.

America Online

Sophisticated commercial services generally require special software designed to work only with a particular service. The software programs present point-and-click user interfaces to what used to be confusing arrays of menus and commands.

CompuServe

You can elect to install Microsoft Network into Windows 95 (either during installation or later via the Add/Remove Programs control panel), or try any of the other services by installing software from trial disks frequently included with computer magazine subscriptions or available from those services for the asking.

Mosaic WWW Browser

Once connected to a service, you are assigned an electronic mail box address, to which anyone on any commercial or Internet service can send you private messages. Most commercial services also provide on-line access to product support, discussion groups for practically every imaginable hobby and professional interest, and loads of free and low-cost software programs you can try for free.

On-line services also give you access to many services on the global Internet, including the popular world wide web of linked information screens. These electronic "pages" include text and graphics, frequently with highlighted text on which you click the pointer to branch to information that may be located in a computer on a different continent.

PC-to-PC File Transfer (HyperTerminal)

Hypertrm

Windows 95 comes with a bare-bones telecommunications terminal program, called HyperTerminal. Unlike a full-function program, HyperTerminal only allows you to **dial out** to another computer (i.e., it cannot answer a call from another computer). To do so, you set up a new connection, which include specifications for the number you're calling and communications settings (which must be the same between both computers). You can use HyperTerminal to exchange files between any computer—from PC to mainframe—that can answer a data call (another PC user must have different communications software).

If you are **exchanging files** with another person at his or her computer, the one sending the file should issue the `Send File` command from the appropriate menu. A **file** dialog box 90 opens to select the file to send. If given a choice of error correction protocols, choose ZMODEM, which provides the most efficient and accurate transfer. With ZMODEM, the recipient usually doesn't have to do anything else, because the software will recognize an incoming file and begin file transfer. Both users see progress dialogs during the process. When finished, both users issue the `Disconnect` command from the menu.

It's not uncommon for first attempts at making the initial connection to fail. It may take a few tries of double-checking the software settings and restarting the modem to connect successfully.

Windows-to-Windows Transfer (MS Exchange)

Windows 95's faxing software (which is linked closely to the Microsoft Exchange universal mailbox setup) performs special magic when sending data from one Windows 95 user to another. If you create a fax message consisting of any file attachment (and indicate in the dialog that the document is editable), the fax is sent to any other computer running Windows 95 and the Microsoft Exchange fax receiving software, the file is sent as a binary file (i.e., like a file transfer), rather than as a rendered document to be viewed or printed like a regular fax.

File Compression

To reduce the time it takes to transfer a file from one computer to another, it is advisable to compress the file. A number of shareware, and free utility programs are available from user groups, bulletin boards, and on-line services. **A file compression** program creates a scrunched version of the file (or group of files), which can then be transmitted like any file. At the receiving end, the file can often be double-clicked to automatically expand to its original form; for other compressed formats, a matching decompression utility (usually available freely on-line) restores the original files.

When browsing through libraries of files on bulletin boards and on-line services, you often see files with the .ZIP extension. The most popular program that compresses files into the .ZIP format is called **PKZIP**. Its compressed files are said to be "packed." A shareware Windows program, WINZIP, is much easier to use, and it can also unpack files created with PKZIP. Otherwise, the expansion program, UNZIP, works under MS-DOS to expand packed files.

On Internet libraries, files are often in a format that is best suited to the Unix computers typically storing these files. Such files have the .HQX extension, and require a utility program to decode this "binhex" format.

Depending on the type of original file, file compression can reduce the size of a file by one-half or more. If you are using a commercial service or long distance for file transfer, file compression can be a money saver, even though you must go through extra steps on both ends of the transfer while off-line.

File Formats

Not every PC owner has the same set of applications programs you do. Therefore, if you are preparing document files that others are expected to read or edit, you need to pay attention to the format of the file (which you may upload to an on-line library or transfer to a friend). When preparing a document for wide distribution, you should consider the lowest possible common denominator.

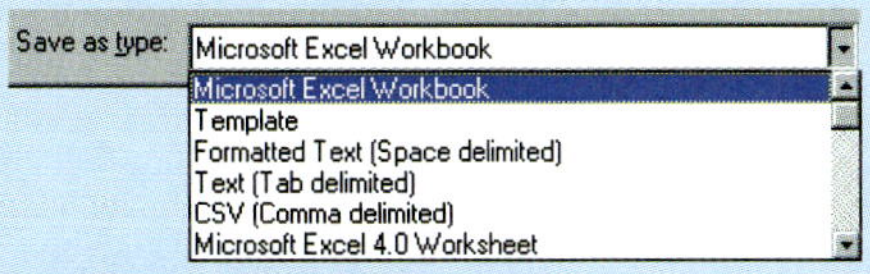

Plain text files (usually file names with the .TXT extension) are one common file type that virtually every personal computer can open with one or more programs on that computer. Many Windows programs, for example, offer options in the **Save As** dialog 91 to save the file as text only. Other programs, such as database programs, provide export facilities to save their information as text files. Another term for a text file an **ASCII** (ASS-kee) file, a reference to a standard coding scheme that assigns numeric values to each letter, numeral, and punctuation mark of the American English language. Every personal computer knows that the ASCII code for the capital letter A is 65.

Windows-to-Macintosh

Once totally incompatible, save for intermediate ASCII files, computers based on Windows and the Macintosh operating system can now work relatively smoothly together. Popular productivity programs have corresponding versions for both systems, and these program's data files are either completely interchangeable or easily converted in the Open and Save As dialog boxes on both computers.

Since the advent of System 7.5 on the Macintosh, Mac owners can insert 1.44MB IBM PC-formatted floppy disks into their disk drives, and work with files as if they were Macintosh files on their Desktop. For example, you can save a newly created document in Microsoft Word in Windows to a floppy disk, insert that disk into a Macintosh, and have the Mac version of Microsoft Windows open that same file directly.

A potential problem with ASCII files, however, is that word processing document style parameters (e.g., bold text, center alignment, tab settings) are not saved with the ASCII characters. To facilitate the bridge between incompatible word processing file formats is a common one called **rich text format** (RTF). Many word processing programs on different computing systems open and save their documents in these formats.

Text versions of **database** and **spreadsheet programs** also adhere to another convention that help other programs use the information. Each database field or spreadsheet cell needs to be distinguished from information in adjacent field or cell, each database record and spreadsheet row needs to be distinguished from its neighbors. The most common way of making these distinctions is with unique delimiter characters. The tab character (ASCII value 9) separates fields and cells from each other; the return character (ASCII value 13) separates records and spreadsheet rows. This format is called a tab-delimited file. Most Windows spreadsheets and databases can read and save information in this format, usually as a method of transferring information between normally incompatible programs.

A comma-delimited file (a fixture from the once popular dBase program) places commas between fields, but the same return character between records.

Recognizing the importance of coexisting with other programs and computers in the workplace, many productivity programs today include provisions for either reading or writing files in formats from even competitive programs. Check the "type" list in **Open** and **Save As** dialogs of your favorite programs to see how cosmopolitan your programs are.

When transferring a file directly via modem between a Windows PC and a Macintosh, the Macintosh user must make a change to the communications software settings. Macs typically transfer files in what is called **MacBinary** format. This must be turned off in the file transfer protocol preferences windows for the transfer to work successfully.

No Messages, page 158

Alert Dialog Messages, page 164

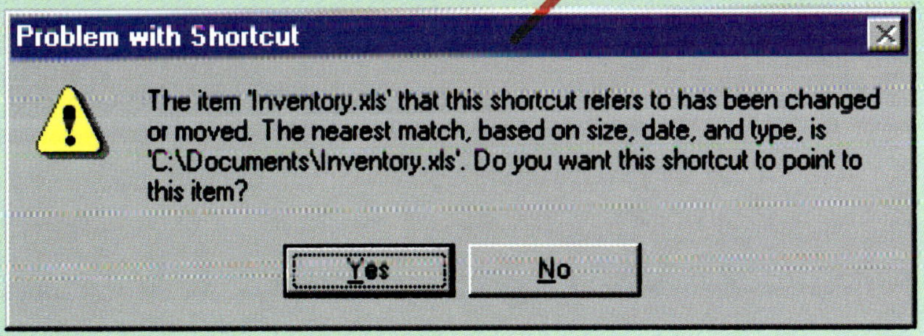

Windows 95 demonstrates a big improvement over Windows 3.x in the area of alerting you to problems and providing tips about how to fix or avoid them.

The Windows help system is somewhat interactive, often providing buttons in the help windows that open control panels or other parts of Windows 95 to guide you through a series of steps. In a few cases, Windows includes some troubleshooting wizards, which walk you through detailed sequences for working out such problems as hardware device conflicts.

Not every problem comes with on-screen instructions. The most frustrating difficulties that Windows users have is when something goes wrong while trying to start the computer or Windows. Rarely are there friendly messages to help. Armed with a bit of troubleshooting knowledge, however, you can work through almost any software-related problem.

Nothing happens when you turn on the PC

Explanation: On a desktop computer, the machine is not getting power; on a laptop PC, either the battery has been removed or it is completely discharged.

Solution: For desktop PCs, check to make sure that the **power cord** is securely connected to the PC and to the **power outlet.** Be sure the outlet, itself, has power. Perhaps the outlet is connected to a wall switch or is part of a switched power strip. Plug another electrical device into the outlet to verify that power is at least reaching the outlet. If the outlet is OK, try another power cord (virtually every PC and peripheral power cord is of the same type). If another power cord still doesn't get your PC going, the problem lies inside the PC, and requires a technician to repair.

For laptops, make sure the battery is inserted properly. Connect the AC charger to the wall power outlet and wait about 15 minutes. If the machine still fails to start, the unit needs repair.

The PC starts, but nothing appears on the video monitor

Explanation: The video monitor is not getting any video signal or electrical power.

Solution: Check first that the monitor is getting electricity. Usually, a **pilot light indicator** on the front panel goes on when the monitor is turned on. If that light isn't lit, check the monitor's own power switch (which you can usually leave in the On position) and the power cable running between it and the PC's rear panel (for those PCs with an extra outlet for the monitor).

If the pilot light is on but you see no video, be sure the brightness and contrast controls of the monitor (if any) are adjusted properly. Also check the security of the connecting video cable between your PC and monitor—tighten any connector screws provided. Jiggle the mouse or press a few keyboard keys to wake up any energy saving circuitry built into your PC. Some monitors have circuitry built in that shuts down the monitor when **operating temperatures** get too high. Turn off the monitor for 15 minutes and try again later. Unless your PC has video support built into the motherboard, it is possible that the video display adapter is not properly seated in the expansion slot. Turn off the PC, remove it's cover, and make sure the card is secure.

LCD panels of laptop computers can experience the same heat-related problems as monitors. It is sometimes necessary to turn off the laptop for several minutes while components cool to comfortable operating temperatures. Some laptops also have a nearly hidden switch that turns off the screen when the lid closes. Make sure nothing is pressing that switch (usually near the hinge).

"Non-system disk or disk error Replace and strike any key when ready" message upon system startup

Explanation: All PCs look first to the floppy disk drive for a disk containing the essential boot files. If there is no disk in the drive, the PC then looks for an internal hard disk. But if there is a disk in the drive and it doesn't have the system files, the PC halts the startup process right there with the DOS-like message on the screen.

Solution: The purpose of this alert is to let you change floppies with one that contains system files, if you like (e.g., for starting from an **emergency boot disk** 70). If you instead want to boot from the hard disk, eject the diskette. Whatever disk choice you make, press any keyboard key to let the PC try to boot again. If there is no diskette in the floppy drive, and the non-system disk is an indication from your hard disk, see the "No hard disk starts up" troubleshooting problem.

An external storage device doesn't appear in My Computer

Explanation: Assuming that the device is working and connected properly, the root cause likely has to do with **device drivers.** Some older devices, which ran under Windows 3.x by virtue of their real-mode drivers, cannot use the corresponding Windows 95 protected mode drivers because the devices incorporate functions not supported by the Windows 95 drivers (e.g., data encryption, disk mirroring, data compression other than DriveSpace-compatible compression). Another possibility is that the device was not properly detected during Windows 95 setup or by the `Add New Hardware` wizard.

Solution: It's important to understand that real mode drivers listed (and not commented out) in CONFIG.SYS are normally unloaded and replaced by the Windows 95 counterparts as Windows starts up. Windows 95 compares all installed real mode drivers against a list maintained in the file IOS.INI (in the Windows folder). If the real mode driver is listed here, Windows 95 is "aware" of it and substitutes its protected mode version. If you don't want the protected mode driver to replace the real mode one (because your device employs functions not covered by the protected mode driver), you must remove the real mode driver name from the IOS.INI list (it may be listed more than once, so use a text processor to search).

For the simpler situation, in which Windows 95 Setup fails to recognize your device, make sure the device is turned on and has some media inserted (in the case of removable media devices) prior to turning on your PC, starting Windows, and running the `Add New Hardware` wizard.

No hard disk starts up

Explanation: The core problem is that your PC is not recognizing your hard disk. The causes can range from something as simple as an external hard disk not being turned on to a complete internal hard disk crash.

Solution: Because there are so many reasons your PC doesn't recognize your hard disk, here is a range of things to look into:

1. Try restarting your PC a couple of times: once by pressing **Ctrl+Alt+Del**; once by completely turning off the PC, waiting about 30 seconds, and turning it on.
2. Start your PC with the emergency boot diskette, and see if you can read the directory of the hard disk (by typing **dir c:** at the A:> prompt). If you see the directory on screen, that's a good sign that your disk is probably still readable.
3. For an external hard disk, be sure all connecting cables are secured prior to turning on the PC. Turn on external drives before turning on the PC.
4. If you have many SCSI devices chained to your PC, disconnect all but the hard disk. Be sure it is terminated per the manufacturer's recommendations and SCSI discussions on 55.
5. Be sure the SCSI ID of an external device is other than zero, seven, or any number used by another device in the SCSI chain.
6. Try another cable for an external SCSI hard disk.
7. For an internal hard disk (SCSI or IDE), make sure all cables connecting the disk to the system board are firmly attached.
8. If you can read the directory of your C drive after booting from the emergency diskette, re-copy the system files to the hard disk by typing **sys c:** at the A> prompt.
9. From the emergency boot disk, use the **ScanDisk** program to examine the integrity of your hard disk. From the A> prompt, type **scandisk c:**, and let it perform all tests, including a surface scan of the disk. If this utility program finds any disk errors, follow its recommendations about fixing problems. Run ScanDisk again to verify that all problems were located and fixed.
10. If you don't have a recent backup of your hard disk, but can see its directory, use the DOS Copy command to copy vital documents from the hard disk to floppy disks in preparation for a reformatting of your hard disk—a next-to-last resort for getting your hard disk back. Then use the FDISK program on the emergency boot disk to reformat the drive.
11. If formatting fails, or you cannot activate your hard disk even with the help of emergency utilities such as Norton Utilities, your hard disk may be damaged beyond anything you can do to fix it. If there is valuable data on the disk that you don't have backed up, you can often retrieve the files with the help of a disk drive recovery service. Such companies generally charge according to the amount of data they can recover from the disk. If you can remember the directory structure of your disk and know where the important files are, this can help reduce the otherwise hefty expense of file recovery.
12. Most disk drives have long warranties (on the order of 5 years), so you can probably send the drive back to the seller for repair. Typically, the company will verify that the drive is bad and supply you with a refurbished drive of the same model and size. They usually do not perform any data recovery from the bad drive. With a fresh drive, you can restore the old drive's original contents from a backup if you made one.

Diagnosing Windows startup woes can be a headache particularly if you have upgraded to Windows 95 from earlier Windows versions and you use a number of older hardware devices.

Most problems occur due to conflicts between devices or their drivers and the more modern Windows 95 environment. Recognizing the possibility for problems, Microsoft includes a number of Windows 95 startup options to help you uncover the sources of trouble. Of these startup options, Safe Mode is the most valuable in checking the Windows startup process for potential problems.

Windows startup freezes or displays errors

Explanation: The startup process of Windows 95 is quite complicated internally, even though a successful startup doesn't seem like much to a user. In an effort to maintain compatibility with the past, Windows 95 dutifully works its way through traditional DOS files such as AUTOEXEC.BAT and CONFIG.SYS, which were used in MS-DOS to load device drivers, adjust memory partitions, and start background processes (the terminate-and-stay-resident, TSR, kinds of programs). Windows 95 users who upgrade from earlier versions may carry a lot of baggage in their startup files. While Windows knows how to handle the majority of them (either commenting out their lines or knowingly overriding their entries later in the Windows startup process), there are still many instances when problems occur during the startup process. Examples include missing driver files and conflicts between real mode commands or programs and the protected mode world of Windows 95.

Solution: Once you successfully start Windows 95, a number of troubleshooting tools help resolve problems such as device conflicts. But until you get there, you are on your own. Your brain and experience will be the primary diagnostic tools while Windows helps you slow down the startup process so you can see step-by-step what's going on. You can also elect to bypass one or more of those steps to help you narrow down problem areas.

1. Restart your PC (Ctrl+Alt+Del).
2. When you see the text message on the screen "Starting Windows 95," immediately press the F8 function key. A special startup menu appears on the screen, offering eight choices. (You may also see this startup menu if your last session of Windows crashed during startup or critical parts of the system Registry are damaged.)
3. Type 5 and Enter.

Step-by-step confirmation presents on the screen each line of booting commands with a prompt for whether you want your PC to execute those lines. The ones to be particularly careful about are the ones in the CONFIG.SYS and AUTOEXEC.BAT files. Look for any error messages that may appear regarding missing driver files or loading failures. More importantly, you should study each line carefully to see if you believe it may not be needed because Windows 95 has protected mode drivers built in.

Ideally, you should gradually work toward eliminating (by erasing or commenting out with a leading REM statement) every line of both the CONFIG.SYS and AUTOEXEC.BAT files unless they contain vital instructions (especially for older or rare hardware) for which Windows 95 has no equivalent. In fact, you might try bypassing running of both files (type N in response to the queries during step-by-step confirmation startup) and see if Windows 95 can handle your hardware and older software.

To make changes to CONFIG.SYS or AUTOEXEC.BAT files (or to other files indicated by error messages during step-by-step startup), you can instruct Windows to start in a special mode that doesn't load any real mode drivers and loads just enough Windows 95 drivers to make the basic computer function with a graphical user interface. This mode is called **Safe Mode.** The quickest way to start in this mode is to restart the PC (Ctrl+Alt+Del) and press F5 while the "Starting Windows 95..." message appears on the screen.

When Safe Mode is in effect, you not only receive an alert message about it before the Desktop appears, but the words "Safe Mode" appear in each of the screen's four corners. Many peripheral devices, such as CD-ROM drives and modems will not be enabled in Safe Mode. The purpose of this mode is to let you start SysEdit.exe (system file editor), adjust control panels, or perform some file maintenance in the friendly graphical environment.

Safe Mode normally does not provide any access to a network. If you need network access while in Safe Mode, press F6 instead of F5 during the Windows 95 Startup message. Not all network services may be available, because only basic networking facilities are loaded in this version of Safe Mode.

After making any changes to system files and/or control panels, restart your PC (via the Shut Down command in the Start menu). You may have to repeat this whole process more than once if multiple driver problems afflict your system.

In theory, 32-bit applications should operate entirely in their own memory spaces, and not affect any other process should there be a problem in one of them. In truth, each application is not necessarily completely shielded from the rest of the system. Knowing how to deal with program or process freezes is important when you rely on Windows day to day.

"Damaged Registry" message during Windows startup

Explanation: The **Registry** is the heart and soul of the Windows startup process, containing a great deal of information about the hardware, drivers, and user interface settings for you. If any part of it is damaged or missing, Windows won't start except in Safe Mode.

Solution: The Registry consists of two files, SYSTEM.DAT and USER.DAT. Windows automatically creates a backup copy of both files with the extension .DA0. If Windows detects that one of the files is missing or bad, it tries to copy its own backup, changing the extension name to the expected .DAT. But if both the .DAT and .DA0 versions of either file should be damaged, Windows won't be able to attempt restoration of the Registry by itself. You'll have to copy the files from a recent backup copy of the system that you made.

Windows or an application freezes

Explanation: Except for cosmetic differences (e.g., MS-DOS programs running in a DOS window; file dialogs in 16-bit applications that don't provide long filename support), you may think of a running program just like any other running program in the Windows 95 environment. Inside Windows, however, it's a different situation. As described (42), how gracefully Windows handles the failure of a given program depends largely on whether it is an MS-DOS, 16-bit, or 32-bit program. A 16-bit program crash, in particular, can bring down all other running 16-bit tasks running at that time, making it impossible to save changes in any program. But if a 32-bit program fails, there is a better chance you can preserve unsaved changes in other programs.

Solution: The first step in extricating yourself from a freeze is knowing for sure that a process or task has indeed frozen. It's not uncommon for Windows to get into trouble and chug along while either waiting for a timeout or other indication from the system that something is wrong. If you suspect that a program has frozen (it does not respond to mouse clicks, for example), wait about 30 seconds. Then see if mouse clicks work again.

If you still think something's fouled up, press Ctrl+Alt+Del. Instead of rebooting your PC, this key sequence displays the **Close Program** window in Windows 95 (123). In this window are listed all running processes and open Desktop windows. Some items you see may be background processes, whose names you don't recognize or readily understand. But you will probably see words in parentheses next to one or more items (e.g., "not responding"), indicating which task is hung up. To give Windows the best chance of keeping the rest of the programs running, select an item labeled as not responding, and click the End Task button. Confirm in the succeeding dialog that you want to end the task.

Desktop windows for an ended task will close, and any changes to documents or settings in that task will be lost. Assuming that you are able to regain control of the other processes, it would be a good idea to save all changed documents in other programs at this point: if the problem is more severe, there is a chance that the other tasks are at risk of failure.

Sometimes you will end a task and see the Desktop disappear momentarily. This will certainly happen if the Explorer task is listed as the one not responding. Whenever you see this happen, close all programs (saving where necessary), and restart Windows via the Shut Down item in the Start menu.

In rare instances, the Close Program window itself will be frozen. At that point, you have little choice but to press Ctrl+Alt+Del again to restart your PC. All unsaved changes will be lost.

Blue screen error message

Explanation: When the Windows system encounters a serious hardware-related problem, it can display a distinctive, MS-DOS-like full screen message. Immediately recognizable by its MS-DOS blue background and plain white text, these messages often contain highly technical information that may be of value to software or hardware vendors in their quest to debug problems.

Solution: Despite their ominous appearance, these blue screen messages usually provide a means of returning to Windows (usually the press of any keyboard key). Sometimes repeating the previous command will work the second time through, even if the task was as risky as saving data to a disk. When a blue screen message appears, **write down the particulars** on the screen. Both Microsoft and the supplier of any hardware or software indicated in the message would be interested in hearing about the problem.

Reporting bugs

Explanation: Unfortunately, the presence of bugs is a fact of life in personal computing. But as long as the publisher or manufacturer of a computer product is in business, it wants to hear about problems and bugs that users encounter. Whether or not you like being a tester for a vendor, your bug reports can help the next version of the product be better for all...provided you know how to supply a meaningful bug report.

Solution: If you've never done any programming before, you won't realize that bug reporting requires some skill to help the programmers find out what your problem is to fix it. The worst kind of report is the one that says "so-and-so doesn't work." That supplies no information whatsoever.

To fix a bug, a programmer must be able to recreate it on his or her own machine. That means that you must supply enough information for a programmer to replicate your PC's configuration and the steps you went through to cause the bug. Configuration information is spread across many system files on your PC. For example, Windows beta testers had to submit copies of many files to help the Microsoft engineers investigate every single bug. But since many of those files helped track Windows setup bugs, you can limit the scope to the following files:

c:\autoexec.bat

c:\autoexec.dos

c:\bootlog.prv

c:\bootlog.txt

c:\config.dos

c:\config.sys

c:\dblspace.ini

c:\msdos.sys

c:\windows\protocol.ini

c:\windows\system.dat

c:\windows\system.ini

c:\windows\win.ini

Be prepared to surrender copies of any of these files to vendors as part of a bug report.

Next, list the steps in detail that led to the problem. Be very specific about which menu you chose or button you clicked. If you entered text in the process, supply the exact text you typed. Describe fully the content of any error messages you saw. In other words, teach the programmer how to make the program fail.

Preventing problems

Explanation: Most problems that occur once you have successfully set up Windows are introduced when you add a new hardware device or software program (especially system-related software). Application programs seldom cause problems on their own, but a newly installed program can react negatively to an existing driver or other piece of system software.

Solution: A key trick in diagnosing problems is restoring your system (hardware and software) to a known, working point. That may mean uninstalling a device driver (even if it must be done in the **Device Manager** 60 via Safe Mode) or restoring previous versions of key system files such as the Registry or CONFIG.SYS and SYSTEM.INI for real-mode applications.

The worst possible scenario for a troubleshooter is diagnosing a problem after installing several new things without checking each installation for success. Computer problem diagnosis relies on techniques similar to the Scientific Method, whereby you have a control (the original working version) and a change of a single factor (e.g., installation of one device). Unfortunately, a common tendency is to acquire a few new items at once and rush to install them in one sitting. This is dangerous. Instead, install one new item and try it out for a day or so before installing the next item. For a hardware device, restart Windows a couple times to make sure Windows recognizes the device and its drivers are in order. After you're satisfied that the new addition is working properly, back up key system files, particularly files in the root directory and all items in the Windows folder (including the contents of nested folders). Thus, if the next item causes a problem, you can revert to a known working system and try to recreate the problem.

For the rest of this Troubleshooting section, we focus on errors and other messages that appear from time to time. Many of these messages include clues about how to fix the problem, but we'll supplement the clues with additional information that may not be intuitive upon first reading. Messages are shown in **alphabetical order**, accompanied by their associated icon (if any).

Alert messages often substitute specific names of documents, applications, folders, and so on as part of the message—all to help you better understand the context of the message. Since each message of this type has different names for objects, the listings below adhere to a convention name an object as "My" plus the type of object: MyDoc is any document; MyFolder is a folder; and so on. Thus, when you encounter an alert message that begins with the name of a document, folder, printer, or disk, look under the M's in the listing below. Also, if the error message displays a number, we substitute the # symbol in our versions here.

A filename cannot contain any of the following characters:

/ \ : , * ? " < > |

Explanation: Windows (and MS-DOS) reserves several characters for internal use, such as the backslash, which delimits folder levels, and the * and ? wildcard symbols. Any other character, including numbers and spaces, can be used in long filenames, but if you try to insert a space before the name, Windows automatically deletes it. For compatibility with PCs not yet running long filenames, Windows compresses multiple-word names into unspaced names, truncating long names to fit in the "eight-dot-three" format 113.

A printer name cannot contain the characters '=', '\', ';', or ','. Specify a new printer name.

Explanation: It's a good idea to assign a highly recognizable name to any printer that appears in the **Printers** folder so you know which it is (especially in a multiple-printer networked environment). But several characters are not allowed. Multiple words are allowed.

A:\ is not accessible. The device is not ready.

Explanation: Windows tried to read the directory of a device (e.g., when you double-clicked its icon in `My Computer` or chose `Refresh` from the drive's Explorer window) but it couldn't get any information back from the device. For removable media, it usually means that the media has been ejected. It may also mean that the device has been turned off or disconnected (intentionally or by accident). External devices usually don't show up in `My Computer` or Explorer unless they were turned on and functioning when Windows started. In the case of ejected media, re-insert the disk or tape and click the error message window's Retry button. If the device has been turned off or disconnected, you'll probably have to restart Windows before Windows will recognize the device again.

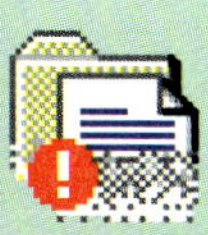

Are you sure you want to delete 'MyFile'?

Explanation: As the icon indicates, agreeing to this message means that the file (or multiple items if designated) will be permanently deleted from your disk directory. This is different from moving something to the **Recycle Bin**: you get this message when you empty the **Recycle Bin**. You also see this message when you delete (or drag to the **Recycle Bin**) any item from a removable medium device: such items do not go into the **Recycle Bin**, but are completely deleted if you click the Yes button of this confirmation dialog.

The bottom checkbox in the Recycle Bin property sheet is not for this alert, but rather for the alert you see when you select an item and choose **Delete** from the **File** menu (or right-click pop-up menu).

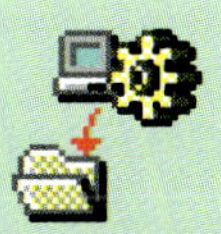

Are you sure you want to move the system file/folder 'MyFile/MyFolder'?

Explanation: Windows 95 keeps track of several root-level system files plus other items scattered around your hard disk. Because Windows relies on these items being in specific places (such as the root directory), it wants to know for sure that you know what you're doing by moving them. It is best not to move any item that generates this alert message. Instead, create a shortcut or copy in another location if necessary.

Are you sure you want to rename the system file 'MyFile1.sys' to 'MyFile2.sys'?

Explanation: Windows requires that some key root-level files be named a certain way or there will be problems with Windows starting up. If you attempt to rename any of these items, this alert message asks for confirmation. Unless you know that there is some significant benefit from renaming such files, always click the No button to avoid grief the next time you start Windows 95.

Are you sure you want to send 'MyFile' to the Recycle Bin?

Explanation: The display of this alert is the default behavior of the Delete menu command (including right-click pop-up menu) for any Desktop/Explorer item. The icon reminds you that the deleted item will be going into the Recycle Bin, rather than into oblivion. You must still empty the Recycle Bin to get rid of the item.

You can eliminate this message each time you delete an item. Right-click on the Recycle Bin icon, choose Properties, and uncheck the bottom checkbox in the property sheet. This does not affect the confirmation alert when you empty the Recycle Bin (that message always appears).

Cannot connect to this network printer. Make sure your network is working properly and the network share you are connected to exists.

Explanation: The printer selected in the Print dialog or to which you've dragged a document was located on the network when you originally installed it. For any number of reasons, that printer is not available on the network at the moment. If the printer is a shared resource from another person's computer on the network, it is possible that the computer is not turned on or not currently connected to the network. Check the Network Neighborhood for the existence of that printer on the network. If it's not there, you will have to specify (and perhaps install drivers for) another shared printer.

Cannot create or replace 'MyFile': The disk is write-protected.

Remove the write-protection or use another disk.

Explanation: You tried to copy or move file to a locked floppy disk. It means that Windows found a disk in the drive, but its locking tab is open. Eject the disk, slide the locking tab, and reinsert the disk. You'll have to perform the copy operation again. Another version of this error message includes the phrase "Access denied." Moreover, this other version is not so specific about what's wrong: it could be a locked disk, a read-only medium, or there is no room on the disk for the copied item.

Cannot create or replace 'MyFile': There is not enough free disk space.

Delete one or more files to free disk space, and then try again.

Explanation: This message appears when copying a file to a disk and the size of the file is larger than the available space on the disk. Windows' suggestion is to delete files to make room for the copied file. That is not always practical. For removable media (e.g., floppy disk) you'll probably want to eject the current disk and insert one with more available space. A different message appears if the file is too large for the medium, even when the destination disk is empty. A different message also appears if you are copying multiple files, and there is room on the destination disk for only some of the files.

If there are items still in the `Recycle Bin` that, if removed, could make space for the new copy, you will see another message window appear atop this one.

Cannot display the Help information. The file WINHELP.EXE may be missing or damaged.

Explanation: WINHELP.EXE is the engine that makes all of Windows 95 help work. If this core program file is corrupted or missing, then you won't be able to use on-line help. To repair the situation, run Windows Setup again, using the **Verify** mode to let it re-install the missing Help system files.

Cannot find MyProgram. Windows needs this file to run MyFilePathName.

Explanation: The details in this alert message can be misleading as to the cause of the interruption. You see this message if you try to open a document and expect its associated application to launch in the process. If the name of the program's .EXE file appears in the message, then you know that Windows has lost track of the program (probably due to you renaming, changing, or moving the path to the folder containing the program files). But you may also see a reference to an application extension file (typically .DLL) that is related to the application. That file may be missing or misplaced on your hard disk. For example, if you move an application file but not its supporting files, the program may not be able to start, and shows this alert message, because it can't locate the supporting files.

Cannot find the file 'MyPath' (or one of its components). Make sure the path and filename are correct and that all required libraries are available.

Explanation: This message usually means that you tried to launch an executable (program) file and either the main file or one of its supporting files is either not on the disk or is in a folder the program doesn't know about. This can happen sometimes if you move a program after installation and its supporting files are not in standard locations, such as the same folder as the application or in a folder nested within the Windows folder. If you cannot figure out which file(s) are the troublemakers, you will have to reinstall the program. The downside of doing this blindly is that you will end up with duplicates of some support files, one set of which is unnecessarily occupying disk space.

Cannot find the 'MyFile.hlp' file. Do you want to try to find this file yourself?

Explanation: New programs for Windows 95 should be centralizing its help files in the **Help** folder inside the Windows folder. You'll see this message when you try to summon help from within an application, and the associated help file is not where the program expects it to be. If you can locate the help file, try putting it into the Help folder or in the same folder as the program. Otherwise, you will have to reinstall the program.

Cannot move 'MyLongLongFileName'.

The filename you specified is invalid or too long. Specify a different filename.

Explanation: The 256-character limit to a long filename is deceiving, because Windows inflicts a more stringent limit of 260 characters for any pathname. Normally, Windows 95 prevents you from renaming a file so that its current path would exceed the 260 character limit. But if you try to copy or move a file with a very long name to another folder, whose combined pathname would exceed 260 characters, you see this alert message and are prevented from finishing the task. The only alternative is to shorten the file's name or move it to a less-nested folder.

Cannot move 'MyFile': The specified file is being used by Windows.

Explanation: You have tried to move an application extension from one of Windows special folder locations, such as the **System** folder. You may be able to move some of these special files in **Safe Mode** (if Windows doesn't use them in Safe Mode), but more than likely, if you must move or delete one of these files (and you had better know what you're doing while you're at it), you will have to start your PC in command prompt only mode (at the Starting Windows 95... startup message, press F8, and choose option six) so you can perform a DOS Move or Erase command action on the desired file.

Couldn't open port.

Explanation: A program tried to dial the telephone modem, but could not even begin conversing with the COM port. The root cause is that the program is looking for a modem to be connected to a particular COM port, but the port either is not installed properly or is turned off at the hardware level.

The first step to perform is to check the **Device Manager** (System control panel) to see that the COM port you use for modem communications is installed and is working properly. Even this can be difficult to determine on some PCs via the Device Manager. A trip to the computer's hardware setup program (sometimes a DOS program) will let you turn on one or more COM ports. And if you are using a PC Card modem (which usually expects port COM1), you may have to try various enabled/disabled settings for all ports in the hardware setup program before Windows 95 assigns COM1 to the PC Card modem.

Next, check the **Modems** control panel. Be sure the modem is assigned to one of the COM ports available on your PC. Then adjust the communications preferences settings on your communications or dialer program to make sure it sends its commands to the same COM port being used by your modem.

If you change a filename extension, the file may become unusable.

Are you sure you want to change it?

Explanation: Windows 95 keeps a watchful eye on registered filename extensions. It knows that when an extension is associated with a particular application or system operation (e.g., .BAT, .DLL, .SYS), any change to the extension will likely destroy its link to an application or Windows itself. The chance of seeing this message is greatly reduced if you choose to let Windows hide filename extensions to registered types (in the Desktop/Explorer's View menu, choose Options, click the View tab, and check the bottom checkbox). With registered extensions normally hidden from view, there is little chance you will attempt to change (intentionally or otherwise) the extension (adding what appears to be an extension to one of these names doesn't truly affect the extension). For simplicity's sake, it's best to keep registered extensions hidden, because it makes saving files in Save As dialogs much easier (you don't have to enter extensions as part of the filename).

MyFile

Unable to register document.

The document may already be open.

Explanation: A message such as this one that appears in WordPad indicates that you tried to open a file that is open in a second instance of WordPad. If the document were opened by another program, a different alert message says so, but doesn't tell you which program has the document.

MyFilePathName

This file already exists.

Replace existing file?

Explanation: You are trying to save a new version of a document over the previous version (or another copy somewhere else in another folder). If you agree to do this, remember that the previous version won't be available any longer. To keep track of versions, you should Save each version with a slightly different name, perhaps with an incrementing serial number.

MyFilePathName

This file exists and is read-only.

To save your changes, use a different filename.

Explanation: You opened a file whose read-only attribute is set to true (i.e., the Read-only checkbox in its property sheet is checked). Windows will not let you overwrite the original file as long as that property is checked. Your choices are:

1. Save the changed document with a different name or with the same name in a different folder location.
2. Change the Read-only property of the file. You can do this from the Save As dialog by right-clicking on the file, choosing Properties from the pop-up menu, and adjusting the setting. After you change the property, you will see a different kind of message asking you to confirm the replacement of the old file with the new one you're trying to save.

MyPrinter printer has # job(s).

To start printing these jobs, click Yes. To pause printing, click No. To delete these jobs, click Cancel.

Explanation: Windows 95 constantly looks for the presence of files in the spool folder so it can automatically send **spooled documents** to the printer. If you start Windows and see this message, it means that one or more printing jobs from the last time you used Windows did not finish printing. Perhaps the printer you wanted wasn't available on the network, or you were in a hurry to shut down and didn't want to wait for the printed output. You also see this message if you had paused printing in your last session.

The behavior of this alert message is different from others you may encounter. Upon Windows startup, it is usually the first window that appears on the Desktop. It is then covered by any other open windows that appear on the Desktop. But after a few seconds, the alert window's button in the Taskbar (labeled `Printers Folder`) starts flashing to call your attention to it.

A spooled document knows which printer was originally assigned the task of printing. If you ask Windows to do the job from this alert message, it will attempt to do so with the printer you assigned in the document's **Print** dialog. If the printer you wanted to use is still not available or you are connected to a printer (e.g., you're using your laptop and have spooled documents hanging around for the next time you connect to a printer), click the No button to continue the paused printing setting. Be very careful with the Cancel button, however. Unlike the Cancel button of other alert windows that safely gets you out of a hazardous situation, this one purges all print jobs from the spool folder. To reassign a print job to another printer, you will have to purge all print jobs and go through the print process again (either from the application or by dragging the document icon to the desired printer icon).

Some files were used only for this printer and are no longer needed. Would you like to delete these files now?

Explanation: You see this message whenever you remove a printer from your system by dragging its icon to the `Recycle Bin` or delete it by menu from the Printers window. The message reminds you that printers come with a set of driver files. If you delete these files and later re-install the same printer model, you will have to go through a typical printer setup involving the Windows setup disks or CD-ROM. On the other hand, if you leave these files intact, you will be able to reinstall the printer later just by selecting it from a list in the `Add Printer` wizard.

The 'MyFile' file cannot start. Check the file to determine the problem.

Explanation: Often referring to a **.DLL** file, the suggestion to check the file is of little help. Frequently one .DLL will look for another .DLL with an unrelated name. Looking into the property sheet of the .DLL shown in this message won't give you any clue about what else it needs. If the name of the .DLL doesn't include any plain language words you can recognize, here are some clues about the first few characters of a .DLL filename: "aw" stands for "At Work," meaning Microsoft At Work, primarily fax related in Windows 95; "cs" is for CompuServe files that are needed by Microsoft Exchange; "hp" are for Hewlett-Packard printer files; "mm" is for multimedia items; "mos" and "msn" are for Microsoft Network files; "net" indicates network facilities; "ole" and "ole2" are for Object Linking and Embedding library files. This still won't tell you what's missing, but you may be able to identify the problem area to see if it affects the work you need to do on your PC. You should later go through Windows 95 Setup again in **Verify** mode to make sure all support files are where they should be.

The Backup/Disk Defragmenter program is not installed on your computer. To install it, double-click the Add/Remove Programs icon in the Control Panel, click the Windows Setup tab, and then follow the instructions on your screen.

Explanation: You receive either of these messages when you try to activate the respective programs from the `Tools` screen of a hard disk property sheet. If the desired program was not installed onto your hard disk during Windows setup, or you removed them since then, you receive these instructions about how to get the desired program onto your PC. Both programs are part of Windows 95, but you can elect not to install them if you are short of disk space.

The destination does not support long file names. Please enter a name for this file.

Explanation: Just because your Windows 95 PC may have long file names turned on doesn't mean that every other Windows PC or network server in the world supports such names. The eight-dot-three naming scheme will persevere in many networked situations for some time to come, so don't be alarmed by this message if you try to save a file to a server or shared PC that is not up to long file names. Instead, supply an eight-character file name (the program will probably supply the extension) for the file.

The disk in drive A is not formatted.

Do you want to format now?

Explanation: You have instigated an action that attempts to read or write to a floppy disk when the disk in the drive is not formatted for a PC. It is possible that the disk is either completely blank, or is from another computer system, such as the Macintosh. If you agree to go ahead and format, be sure the disk is not from another computer and does not have any valuable data files on it: Once you format the disk for Windows, all previous data on the disk will be erased.

More trouble, however, is apparent if you believe that the diskette is not only formatted, but may contain data files. For any number of reasons, Windows thinks that this disk is a dud, and does not see any data files on it. If you think the disk should still be good, save all documents to the hard disk, exit the programs, and restart Windows. Sometimes a restart of Windows makes floppy disk problems go away (until the next time). The same goes for failed disk formatting; restart Windows and try again before throwing away the disk as a bad one.

The disk in the destination drive is full.

Insert a new disk to continue.

Explanation: When you are copying multiple files to another disk or medium, Windows does not check to see that the destination drive has sufficient space for the entire set of files. Instead, Windows starts copying the files, one by one, to the destination drive. When there is no more space on the disk for the next file, you see this alert message. You are instructed to replace the full disk with one with sufficient space to continue. For many megabytes of files, this process could continue for several disks. On the other hand, if you are trying to cram a set of files onto a single disk, you'll have to do the math manually before copying. Using a compression program, such as **PKZIP,** could help you stuff more files onto a single floppy disk.

The file being copied is too large for the destination drive.

If possible, insert a higher-capacity disk.

Explanation: One size measurement that Windows makes prior to copying to another drive is whether the item being copied is larger than any blank medium. For instance, if you are copying a 60MB rendered image file to a 44MB Syquest cartridge, you will get this message. Replacing the 44MB cartridge with an 80MB cartridge, you will have no trouble copying the file. But every medium has its limits. You can't, for example, insert anything larger than a 1.44MB diskette into the standard floppy disk drive. If you get this message for copying to a floppy, consider a file compression utility.

The item 'MyFile' that this shortcut refers to has been changed or moved. The nearest match, based on size, date, and type is 'MyFile2PathName'. Do you want this shortcut to point to this item?

Explanation: A shortcut maintains a link to its original primarily by the pathname of the original item at the time you created the shortcut. But a shortcut also keeps a lot more information about the original item. Therefore, if you move, rename, or delete the original item, the shortcut will do its darndest to locate the item. The shortcut has a number of tricks up its sleeve to locate the original file if you've moved it, such as searching quickly in folders nested within the original folder.

But if the shortcut can't find the original file, it does its best to locate a file that has characteristics similar to the original, based on file size, creation date, and type of file. The alert message shows the full pathname to the suspect, giving you chance to confirm that it found the desired file. The search is not always 100 per cent accurate. It is possible, for instance, for Windows to suspect a file is the original when, in fact, the original has been deleted from the disk. If you know the original file is there, perhaps under a different name, use Windows' Find powers to help you locate the file (also specify the file type to help narrow the search), and then create a new shortcut to it.

The printer name you specified is too long. The name must contain less that 32 characters. Specify a new printer name.

Explanation: A printer's name can be no more than 31 characters long. This should be sufficient for you to assign a printer name that will be meaningful to you or anyone on the network who may intend to share the printer. When you click OK in this alert, the too-long name you entered is selected, ready for overtyping; or you can press Esc to revert to the previous printer name (Undo does not work here).

The printer settings have been changed, but not saved. Printing a test page may not give the desired results until you save these changes. Do you want to print a test page anyway?

Explanation: Like many settings dialog boxes in Windows, a printer's property sheet features an Apply button that essentially saves the current settings without closing the dialog box. If you attempt to print a test page after making changes but before clicking the Apply button, you receive this alert message. In all likelihood, you should click No to give yourself a chance to apply the changes prior to printing a test page.

The program has performed an illegal operation and will be shut down. If the problem persists, contact the program vendor.

Explanation: This is a serious message, usually indicating that there is a software bug looming somewhere, either in the application signified in the alert window's titlebar or in Windows 95. Most likely, the problem is in the application (or the application doesn't work around a known Windows bug). In any case, the programmer of the software will probably be interested in the contents of the `Details` part of the window, which you can view by clicking the Details >> button. Select and copy the contents of the window; paste the text into any text processor window and submit it to the program's publisher or technical support group.

In some cases, when you close this window the program will continue to function normally. But beware that if the program encounters an error serious enough to trigger this message, there is no guarantee as to the integrity of data manipulation for any further actions you take in a document. The safest steps to take are to save the current document(s) to new filenames and exit the program. Restart the program and see if you can recreate the problem. A recurring problem is a definite bug, while an intermittent problem will be difficult for the programmers to locate and fix.

There are no active mixer devices available. You may install or activate mixer devices from the Control Panel.

This application will now exit.

Explanation: You tried to open the `Volume Control` or other sound-oriented facility in Windows. The report that no active mixer devices are available may indicate that none were installed (as suggested in this message) or that some other sound or multimedia-oriented file (usually a .DLL) failed to load during Windows startup. This will be difficult to track down, and may require a reinstallation of Windows (using **Verify** mode) to properly install all multimedia files.

There are no viewers registered for this type of file. Would you like to try the default viewers?

Explanation: You have dragged a file to an open **Quick View** window but that file type is not identifiable as belonging to one of the applications for which Windows 95 has a viewer. Quick View will try to use one of its more generic viewers (usually plain text) to display the contents of the file. This is a good and fast way to examine (but not edit) some system files in the root level (e.g., CONFIG.SYS) or from within the various Windows system folders (such as .INI and .INF files). If you then click the Edit button in the Quick View window, you will see the dialog that lets you register the file's extension with one of the registered applications you have installed. Uncheck the bottom checkbox if you just want a one-time edit of this file type with a particular program.

There is no default printer. To install and select a default printer, click the Start button, point to Settings, click Printers, and then double-click Add Printer.

Explanation: You have set up Windows but have not yet installed a printer. If only one printer is installed, it becomes the default printer automatically. When more than one printer is installed in your system, you can choose which is the default. A default printer is the one that Windows uses when you select a file in the Desktop/Explorer, and choose `Print` from the `File` or right-click pop-up menu.

There is not enough (free) memory to .... Quit one or more programs, and then try again.

Explanation: Despite Windows 95's distribution of typical memory resources among RAM and virtual memory on a hard disk, it is still possible to run out of resources for Windows to carry out an operation such as opening an application or working with a control panel. Behavior of Windows 95 in these circumstances varies. Consider yourself fortunate when you receive a message like this one. In other situations, you may get no message at all when you try to open a new process: the launch fails but you have no indication other than the fact that nothing changes on the screen. You may also receive a message about problems with system files (like RUNDLL32). The files may be in fine shape, but the low memory situation has temporarily confused Windows.

The advice in this message to quit programs you don't need is a good one. If you can pare down your requirements, Windows is smart enough to free up resources as programs quit, leaving room for new processes. But if you find yourself in low memory situations frequently, you should consider adding RAM to your PC, especially if you need to have several high-power applications running at the same time to work efficiently.

There is still mail in your Outbox: exit anyway?

Explanation: You can close Microsoft Exchange without having transmitted any messages in the Outbox. This is particularly helpful if you are a laptop user and wish to load up your Outbox with various fax and email messages to be sent the next time you can connect to a phone line. There is no penalty for leaving items in the Outbox. This message is just a reminder that items are there, in case you forget to check the Outbox while in Microsoft Exchange.

There was an error writing to LPT1: for the printer 'MyPrinter': There was a problem sending your document to the printer. Make sure the printer cable is connected and that the printer is on-line.

Explanation: The printing task entails a two-way conversation between Windows 95 on your PC and the printer. Regardless of the connection path (parallel port, serial port, or network), Windows sends a bunch of data to be printed, waits to hear back from the printer that it's ready for more, and pushes more data down the cable. Occasionally, the printer may send back other messages, such as one about the paper tray being empty. Whatever the content of the conversation, if Windows detects no life from the printer, you will see a message like this one.

Diagnosing printing problems can be tedious at times. Despite the lengthy process involved, it's best to start the diagnosis from a known point: shutting down both your PC and the printer, turning on the printer, and then starting your PC and Windows. This gives Windows a chance to recognize the printer during startup.

Next, open the printer's property sheet and try to print a test page. A helpful dialog box appears after the test page is sent to the printer. If the page fails to print, the dialog box will lead you to Windows own printing troubleshooting sequence, which covers the basics fairly well. Many impact printers have On-line buttons which can be accidentally bumped (the light goes out) so that the printer won't communicate with any computer. Printer cables can easily become loose on both the PC and printer ends—make sure all connectors are secure. As a last resort, de-install the printer (agreeing to the removal of all associated files), and reinstall it via the `Add Printer` wizard in the Printers folder (you'll need your Windows Setup disks or CD-ROM).

This change may impact one or more registered programs. Do you want to continue?

Explanation: You have tried to move or delete a folder or file that contains Windows system-level information. Some of that information helps Windows track the associations between file types and applications. If you continue with the change, it is possible that you won't be able to launch an application by double-clicking its document files. When you see this message, it's risky business to accept the change unless you know very specifically what change you're making and how it will affect your application setup. If you go through with the change, it may be necessary to re-establish the link for one or more file types. For a more drastic change, such as messing with the System folder inside the Windows folder, you may have to reinstall your applications.

This file is too large for Notepad to open. Would you like to use WordPad to read this file?

Explanation: The **Notepad** application, an updated version of an accessory that has been in Windows since the earliest times, is not meant to be a heavy-duty text processing program. Instead, it is intended for quick reading and writing of simple and short text files, such as typical ReadMe files that accompany software programs. But if you have the .TXT file type associated with Notepad, Windows will use Notepad to open any .TXT file you receive on-line or from other sources. Since Notepad can handle only small files, you will receive this message when the document is larger than about 32KB.

This folder already contains a file called 'MyFile'.

Would you like to replace the existing file 'MyFile' with this one?

Explanation: The button choices in this alert message vary with the number of items you are trying to copy to a destination folder. When you copy one item (by dragging or otherwise), Windows compares its name against all items in the destination folder. If an item is already there with the same name (even if it is of a different file type), Windows presents this alert with a simple choice of Yes or No.

But when you copy a bunch of items to a folder, the button choices increase to include Yes to All and Cancel. If you simply click the Yes or No button, Windows continues to copy items until it finds another duplicate item, at which point it displays this alert message again. Clicking the Yes to All button is efficient, but dangerous. It's efficient, because Windows won't bother asking you about duplicate file names for the rest of the items in the group. It's dangerous for the same reason: if you don't know for sure that you want to replace every item, you will be telling Windows to do it without asking you. Choose this button only when you know for sure you want to overwrite any existing files in the destination folder.

For multiple-item copying, the Cancel button lets you halt the process prior to any overwriting. Be aware, however, that this cancellation acts more like an abort command, meaning that any other items already copied to the destination will be there.

This folder already contains a folder called 'MyFolder.'

If the files in the existing folder have the same name as files in the folder you are moving, do you want to replace the existing files?

Explanation: You are attempting to copy one folder into a container that already has a folder of the same name. Windows wants to know how to handle the replacement issues. Specifically, it asks whether it should essentially do a file-by-file copy to the destination folder, overwriting files that have the same name in both folders. Think long and hard about the ramifications of this move if the presence of the alert message surprises you. If you weren't aware that a folder of the same name existed in the destination container, then you may not want to perform the copy at all, but rather rename the original before copying it.

This program is not responding. It may be busy, waiting for a response from you, or it may have stopped running.

- Click Cancel to ignore and return to Windows.

- To close this program immediately, click End Task. You will lose any unsaved information in this program.

- To give the program 20 seconds to finish what it is doing, click Wait, and then try to close the program again.

Explanation: Check the name in the titlebar of this alert message. It points to the program that doesn't seem to be doing what you had asked in a previous command or action. When this alert appears, it's usually a signal that the program is either frozen or wants your attention to take care of another alert box. In approaching this message, try the Cancel button first to see if you can activate the program and attend to whatever user input it may require. If you can tell that the program is not waiting for you (if it is the only program whose window appears on the Desktop), give it the 20 seconds instead. Repeated appearance of this message means that the program is frozen, and you should end the task (losing any unsaved changes in the process unfortunately). This is the same as pressing Ctrl+Alt+Del in a program.

This will clear your current search.

Explanation: In the Find dialog box is a button named New Search. When you click the button, you see this message, which reminds you that all settings of all three tabs of this window will revert to their default, empty states if you agree. Since you may create complex search criteria that include definitions on two or more tabs of this window, you must be sure you don't want to preserve any of those settings for your next search. If you just want to adjust a couple items, do so in the current search, rather than clearing all criteria and starting over.

Too many other files are currently in use by 16-bit programs. Quit one or more 16-bit programs, or increase the value of the FILES command in your CONFIG.SYS file.

Explanation: If you were a Windows user back in the Windows 3.x days, you probably recall that various software installations modified the FILES line of the CONFIG.SYS file. This command regulates the maximum number of files that can be opened at one time. Because of the way Windows treats 16-bit Windows applications (all within one memory segment), you may have to make similar adjustments to the CONFIG.SYS file if you use a lot of file-hungry 16-bit Windows applications. As you gradually upgrade to 32-bit applications, this will become less of an issue for you.

Unable to browse the network.

The network is not accessible.

Explanation: You will see this message if you attempt to open the `Entire Network` icon in the **Network Neighborhood** when you are not connected to an active network. The message directs you to the **Network Troubleshooter** part of the Windows 95 Help system, but except for simple problems, such as a loose network cable or an intuitive Network control panel setting, you will probably have to get help from the network administrator in your office or school.

Unable to open the file 'MyFile'.

Explanation: If you see this message, you'll have to put on your detective cap to understand the problem. Not all programs supply enough details to direct you to the problem. Things to look for include:

1. The file is in use by another program.
2. The file is of a type that cannot be opened by the program you're using (possible if you select "All Files" as the file type in the Open file dialog box).
3. The file is a shortcut to a file that resides on a network, but the file is not available because there is a network problem, you don't have access privileges to the file, or the file sharing setup is not active at the moment.

Unable to set the attributes for 'MyFile'.

Explanation: The most common cause of this problem is that the medium on which the file resides is a read-only medium, such as a CD-ROM. Files on locked media cannot be altered in any way.

User Intervention Required

Explanation: This message doesn't appear in a dialog box, but rather appears in the titlebar of a window for a printer that is unable to print. The severity of this message can be misleading, because in a networked printer environment, it is natural for this message to appear in the window when you are intentionally working off-line. The printer will require user intervention only when you're ready to send data to the printer on-line.

Warning - The default printer has been deleted. The new default printer is 'MyPrinter'.

Explanation: This message appears if you delete the printer that Windows recognizes as the default printer. Even if you leave the driver files intact but delete the printer icon, you'll see this message. As long as another printer (or printer equivalent, such as Microsoft Fax) is installed in the Printers folder, Windows will automatically assign the honor of being default printer to another machine.

Warning - The default printer has been deleted. There are no printers set up on your computer.

Explanation: You see this message only if you delete the last printer (or printer equivalent) from the Printers window. If there is another printer installed when you delete the default printer, Windows automatically makes one of the other printers the default printer (and alerts you to its intentions).

Windows cannot format this disk because it is write protected. If you are sure you want to continue, remove or move the write-protect tab, reinsert the disk, and then click Retry.

Explanation: You tried to format a removable media disk or cartridge whose locking tab is set to the locked position. While this alert message appears, you can manually eject the medium (if the drive supports manual ejection), change the locking tab, reinsert the medium, and click the Retry button to carry on with the formatting.

Windows cannot locate the ScanDisk program. The program file may be corrupt or may have been deleted from your computer. To reinstall ScanDisk, run Windows Setup again.

Explanation: You have tried to run ScanDisk from the property sheet of a disk volume. Like some other Windows 95 disk utilities, this program may not have been installed during Windows setup. If you want to use this program (it's a good idea to run it on your boot disk about once a month), you'll need to install it from the Windows setup disks or CD-ROM. Check the Windows Setup screen of the Add/Remove Software wizard control panel. Select Disk Tools and click the Details button to see if ScanDisk is listed. If so, check it, and let the wizard install it for you. If the program is not listed, go through the Windows setup procedure again in **Verify** mode.

Windows is running in safe mode.

This special diagnostic mode of Windows enables you to fix the problem that is keeping you from starting Windows normally. ... .

Explanation: Safe mode 160 is an important startup mode for Windows when hardware device or networking problems prevent Windows from starting up normally. You see this message when you intentionally start Windows in safe mode, but Windows may also start up in safe mode under other circumstances when it senses you had severe problems with the last time you tried to start. Because safe mode bypasses a number of configuration steps, not all peripherals or advanced hardware features of your PC may be active. The intent of safe mode is to let you modify system files and drivers.

Windows is searching for 'MyFile'. To locate the file yourself, click Browse.

Explanation: You see this alert only when Windows is having trouble locating the original file of a shortcut. The icon animates with the flashlight searching through folders. If you know where the file is (perhaps you've renamed it or moved it to some vastly different folder), you can click the Browse... button to bring up an Open file dialog box. If you don't elect to browse yourself, there is the possibility that Windows will find the wrong file. No matter what it finds, it prompts you with another alert message, showing you the full pathname to the one it thinks the shortcut belongs to.

You are at the top level and cannot go up to another level. To see the desktop, minimize any open windows.

Explanation: This message appears only in the My Computer window, not in the Explorer window. It appears when you click on the toolbar icon that takes the view up one level. Rather than displaying contents of the Desktop (as this button does in the Explorer), Windows displays this alert message instead, recommending that you look at the screen Desktop to view items at that level. Oddly enough, if you open the pop-up list in the toolbar and select the Desktop, you can see the Desktop's items in the window. This is an inconsistency, but is there just the same.

You cannot drag an item onto a button on the Taskbar.

However, if you do this without releasing the mouse button, the window will open and you can then drag the item into the window.

Explanation: When an application is minimized, it may be tempting to drag a document to the application's Taskbar button. In the least, the expectation would be that the document should open in the program, even if you then had to click on the button to bring the program into view. But, as this message clearly states, Windows doesn't work that way (although you can drop items onto the Start button to get them into the Start menu). The trick, it turns out, is to drag the document icon to the button, but keep the mouse button pressed for a couple of seconds. At that point, the program's window restores its display, and (still holding down the mouse button), you can drag the document into the program's window. If the file types don't match, however, you may get an embedded object in the existing document, rather than a new document.

You have print jobs that have not completed and may be lost if you shut down Windows. To shut down, click OK.

Explanation: You are trying to shut down or restart your PC while one or more print jobs are in the queue. The warning about print jobs being lost applies primarily to any print job that is in progress at the time you click OK. Other print jobs will probably still be OK, and you can print them when you restart your PC for the next session (you'll be alerted about pending print jobs). If you must shut down while printing is in progress, open the printer and choose Pause Printing from the Printer menu. Wait about 30 seconds for any pending pages to print. Then shut down.

You have run out of disk space on drive X:\.

There is #MB worth of files in the Recycle Bin on this drive.

Would you like to open the Recycle Bin or empty files in the Recycle Bin from this drive?

Explanation: You have tried to copy or save a file to a disk that no longer has free space on the disk. But Windows noticed that some items remain in the `Recycle Bin`. If these items were emptied from the Bin, there would be room to complete the operation.

Your choices here include one to open the **Recycle Bin** for manual selection of items to delete. A second option is to let Windows go ahead and empty the Bin in its entirety. The third button, Cancel, halts the operation you just tried to perform, giving you a second chance to figure out how to work around the tight disk space arrangements. If you ever see this message, you are running dangerously low of disk space, and should investigate backing up your disk and compressing it, or buying a larger hard disk.

You must restart your computer before the new settings will take effect.

Do you want to restart your computer now?

Explanation: You have made some control panel or device adjustments that won't take effect until the next time you start Windows 95. You don't have to restart right at this point, especially if you want to make some other adjustments or you need to finish a document you're working on from an application. It's safe to work without restarting as long as you don't need the powers enabled with the new settings.

As mentioned earlier in this Troubleshooting section, it's best to make as few device changes as possible in one sitting so you can better test and isolate potential problems. It may seem to take longer to restart Windows after each setting change, but the time will be saved if you have to diagnose a problem that crept in after making three changes without restarting.

24-bit color 30, 34
Video capability to display over 16 million colors at one time on the screen. Requires display adapter or video support with sufficient video RAM to support the colors for a given pixel grid of a monitor.

32-bit addressing 42
Communication channel to RAM available that allows higher maximum RAM capacity, virtual memory, and faster program execution when the program is designed for this feature.

80386 > See CPU

80486 > See CPU

8086, virtual > see virtual machine

8mm tape 54, 59
Consumer videotape format used in tape backup devices for personal computers.

About box 85, 102
Dialog window that displays the full name, author, publisher, and version information about a program. Accessible by choosing About from the Help menu.

AC power > see power (AC) cord

accelerator 31
Add-in board that speeds processing of the computer (with a faster CPU chip) or video refresh when viewing millions of colors.

Accessories 92, 122
An arbitrary grouping of small programs in the **Start** menu. Microsoft's Windows 95 applets appear in this part of the Start menu, but they may be listed anywhere in the Start menu you like.

accent characters > see keyboard character

access time 51
The time, in milliseconds, it takes a disk or tape drive to locate a particular piece of data from the storage medium.

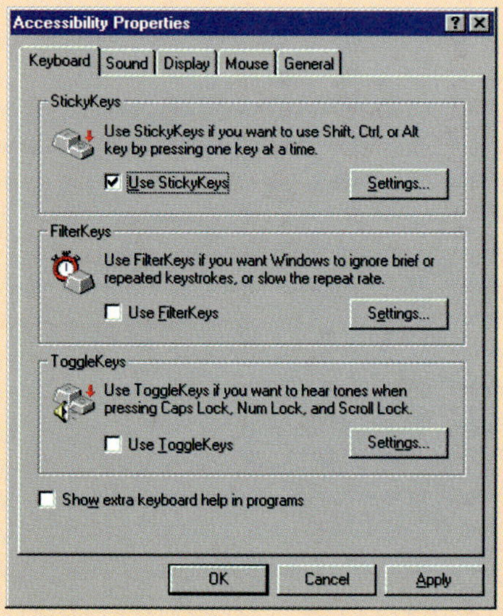

Accessibility Options 24, 33, 100
Control panel that offers many choices for physically challenged users to operate Windows without the benefit of mouse, keyboard, or clear vision of a video display.

active window 15, 35, 85, 86-87
The topmost document window, usually recognizable by the title bar's dark color and white text window name. Only one window may be active at a time.

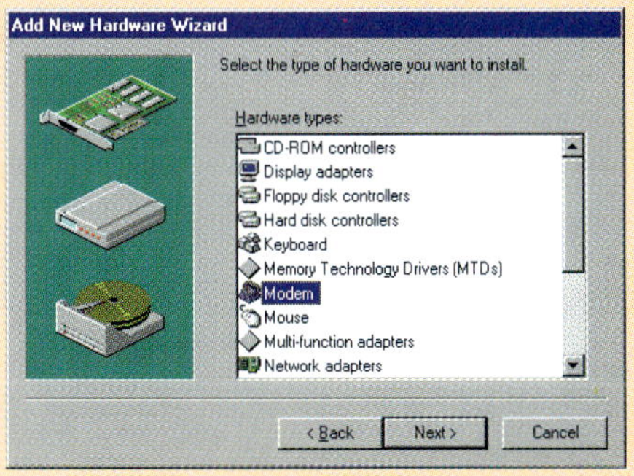

Add New Hardware wizard 55, 60, 100, 144, 159
Control panel for the hardware installation wizard that leads you through installing a new hardware device so that Windows recognizes it.

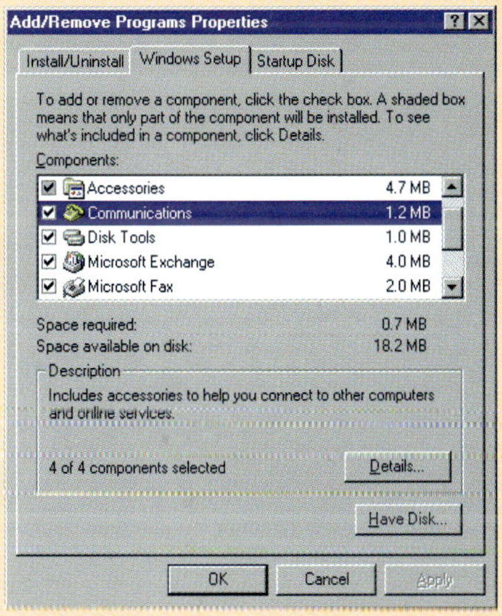

Add/Remove Programs 69, 70, 95, 100, 122, 172
Control panel for the software installation wizard that leads you through installing and uninstalling application programs or optional components of the Windows environment.

address 41, 61
Location in RAM (or ROM), like an address of a house on a street, usually known by a hexadecimal value. Programmers use memory maps to help them visualize the available addresses of a computer system.

Adobe > see PostScript

Adobe Type Manager > see ATM

air flow > see ventilation

airline travel 53
Try to have hard disks and laptop computers hand inspected at security checkpoints.

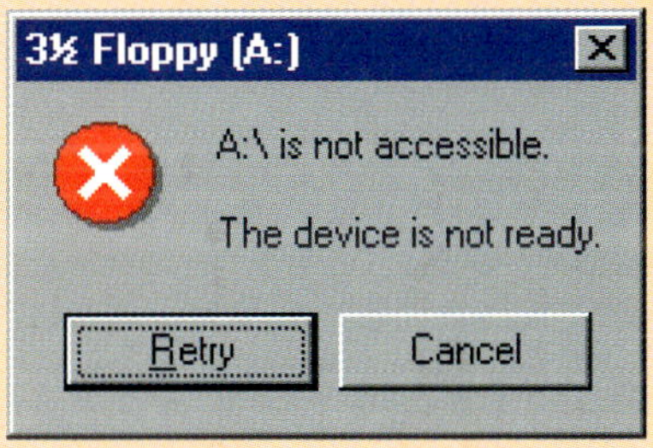

alert box 88, 91, 93
Window that interrupts your action to advise you of important system information or potential danger.

Alt **key** 14, 17, 84, 88
Keyboard **modifier key** often used in conjunction with another key as a shortcut to menu or other commands. Also used with the numeric keypad to enter foreign language symbols and characters.

animated cursor 79
Series of cursors that give the illusion of animation.

applet 122
Program that generally performs a limited function with a minimum of disk space or memory. Windows Setup loads several in the **Accessories** grouping in the Start menu, including Character Map, Paint, and WordPad.

application 67, 71, 82, 90, 107, 112, 122, 123, 130-131
Program written to help users accomplish a task, such as word processing, creating spreadsheets, and so on.

application extension > see dynamic-link library

applications, removing > see uninstalling applications

Arrange Icons 87, 96
Menu command that leads to submenu of choices for organizing icons or lists of files and folders in a Desktop/Explorer window.

arrow keys > see cursor keys

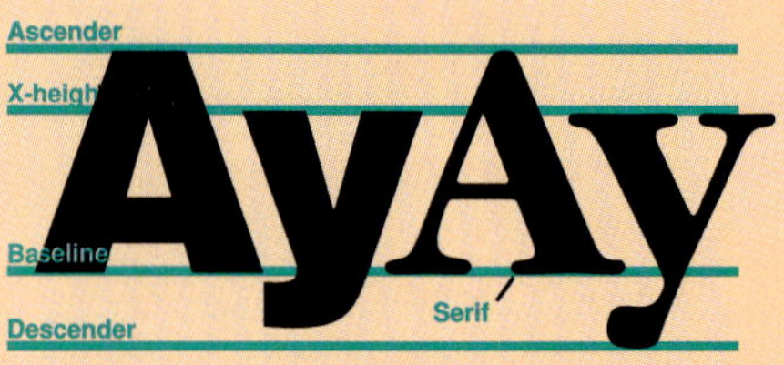

ascender 104
Topmost point of the tallest letter of a typeface.

ASCII 155
American **S**tandard **C**ode for **I**nformation **I**nterchange, a standard that assigns a numeric value between zero and 127 to each letter, numeral, and punctuation mark in American English. Additional values represent control codes for printer and communications devices. **> see ASCII Table on page 189**

assigning drive letters > see mapping a network drive

associate 80, 81, 97, 118, 119, 177
To **link** a document file type (based on file name extension) to an application. When you double-click an associated (or registered) file, the linked application starts up and opens the document.

Asterisk 147
Descriptive name for the type of alert box that displayed an asterisk-style icon in pre-release versions of Windows 95 (now assigned a bubble "i" icon). Generally used to communicate a message from the system to the user.

AT-style keyboard 15
Keyboard designed after the IBM PC model AT keyboard. This has remained the standard desktop computer keyboard arrangement.

ATM 104
Adobe Type Manager allows Adobe font owners to display all sizes of fonts on the screen without requiring dedicated screen fonts.

attributes > see property sheet

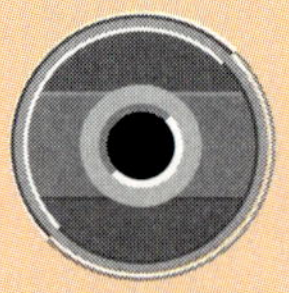

audio input port 9, 144
Rear panel connector for microphone or line level input found on multimedia-equipped PCs or add-in sound cards.

audio output port 9, 146
Rear panel connector for stereo headphones or amplified speakers. Plugging into this port disconnects the internal speakers, if any. Some PCs have front-panel headphone jacks.

AUTOEXEC.BAT 66, 131, 160
Disk file that executes when your PC begins loading Windows 95. You can also direct MS-DOS programs launched from Windows to run their AUTOEXEC.BAT and CONFIG.SYS files prior to starting up so that system parameters required by those programs are set correctly. Any file ending in .BAT is called a batch file.

ASCII Table

ASCII		Character Name	ASCII		Character Name	ASCII		Character Name
0	NUL	Null	43	+	Plus	86	V	
1	SOH	Start of Heading	44	,	Comma	87	W	
2	STX	Start of text	45	-	Hyphen	88	X	
3	ETX	End of Text	46	.	Period	89	Y	
4	EOT	End of Transmission	47	/	Slant	90	Z	
5	ENQ	Enquiry	48	0	Zero	91	[	Open Bracket
6	ACK	Acknowledge	49	1		92	\	Reverse Slant
7	BEL	Bell	50	2		93	]	Close Bracket
8	BS	Backspace	51	3		94	ˆ	Circumflex
9	HT	Horzontal Tab	52	4		95	_	Underline
10	LF	Line Feed	53	5		96	´	Grave Accent
11	VF	Vertical Tab	54	6		97	a	
12	FF	Form Feed	55	7		98	b	
13	CR	Carraige Return	56	8		99	c	
14	SO	Shift Out	57	9		100	d	
15	SI	Shift In	58	:	Colon	101	e	
16	DLE	Data Link Escape	59	;	Semicolon	102	f	
17	DC1	Device Control 1	60	<	Less Than	103	g	
18	DC2	Device Control 2	61	=	Equals	104	h	
19	DC3	Device Control 3	62	>	Greater Than	105	i	
20	DC4	Device Control 4	63	?	Question Mark	106	j	
21	NAK	Negative Acknowledge	64	@	Commercial At	107	k	
22	SYN	Synchronous Idle	65	A		108	l	
23	ETB	End of Transmission Block	66	B		109	m	
24	CAN	Cancel	67	C		110	n	
25	EM	End of Medium	68	D		111	o	
26	SUB	Substittute	69	E		112	p	
27	ESC	Escape	70	F		113	q	
28	FS	File Separator	71	G		114	r	
29	GS	Group Separator	72	H		115	s	
30	RS	Record Separator	73	I		116	t	
31	US	Unit Separator	74	J		117	u	
32	SP	Space	75	K		118	v	
33	!	Exclamation Point	76	L		119	w	
34	"	Quotation Marks	77	M		120	x	
35	#	Number Sign	78	N		121	y	
36	$	Dollar Sign	79	O		122	z	
37	%	Percent	80	P		123	{	Open Brace
38	&	Ampersand	81	Q		124	|	Vertical Line
39	'	Apostrophe	82	R		125	}	Close Brace
40	(	Open Parenthesis	83	S		126	˜	Tilde
41	)	Close Parenthesis	84	T		127	DEL	Delete
42	*	Asterisk	85	U				

Autorun 123
Optional feature of CD-ROM software that launches the program when the disk is inserted.

auto-scroll 80
Process of scrolling a window's contents when you drag an object beyond the viewable area of the window. Available in all Desktop/Explorer windows and in some document windows.

background, screen > see Desktop

background printing 106, 137
Allows Windows to process printing jobs as a secondary task while you continue work on an application. Also called print spooling.

Backspace **key** 14
Keyboard key with a left-facing arrow, which, when pressed, deletes the character to the left of the text insertion cursor.

back up > see disk, backing up

Backup 53, 54, 69, 172
Applet supplied with Windows 95 for basic backup operations.

baseline 104
Imaginary horizontal line on which characters of a typeface rest. Any piece of a character extending below the baseline is called a **descender. > see ascender**

batch file or program 132
Unformatted text file (file name extension .BAT) containing MS-DOS commands, usually designed to automate an MS-DOS file management process. Rarely used with Windows 95.

battery (in standby power supply) 6
Powers your equipment for a brief time if the AC power is disrupted. The battery is kept charged while AC power is connected.

battery, backup
Small lithium battery that keeps the clock and other system settings intact while the PC is turned off.

baud > see bps

beep sound > see Sounds control panel

bit 30, 40
Smallest piece of computer information, either on or off, 1 or 0, white or black. Eight bits in a bunch are called a byte. The more bits in a bunch, the more information the bunch can hold (e.g., 24-bit color).

bitmap graphic 95, 126-127
Image consisting entirely of pixels (some of which may be gray levels or colors). Can produce jagged diagonal lines on printout, compared to object graphics. Resizing a bitmap graphic tends to distort the image.

bitmapped font > see raster font

blank disk > see floppy disk

blink speed of cursor 16, 79
Setting in Keyboard control panel for how quickly the text insertion cursor blinks in a document or field.

boot disk 58, 70, 74, 158
Any disk or diskette containing the minimum of system software that will finish the computer's booting process to reach a command prompt.

booting 10, 49
Starting up a PC to reach an operating system display. Short for "bootstrapping."

bps **154**
Bits per second, usually the measure of data transfer between two computers along a wire or via wireless communications. A similar term, **baud,** is sometimes incorrectly used interchangeably.

breathing room **5, 37**
Space around a computer and video monitor to allow for convective air circulation.

Briefcase **76**
Desktop icon designed to assist in maintaining duplicate copies of files between two computers, usually a desktop and a laptop computer.

brightness **5, 28**
Amount of light energy emitted by a video monitor. Should be adjusted by user according to surrounding light.

bulletin board service (BBS) **154**
Communication service on a computer that allows other users to leave messages and share files. Requires a modem and communications software. Some services are community-based, while a number of commercial services are accessible worldwide.

burn-in, video **36**
Discoloration of the phosphor inside the video monitor. Long exposures of white may make the image visible even when the computer is turned off. Turning down the brightness or using a screen saver can reduce burn-in.

bus **9**
Convention that specifies what signals are on each wire of a connector or pathway between components. Busses can be internal (between microprocessors and integrated circuits) or external (cables between computers and hard disks).

button **35, 81, 82, 86-87, 88-89, 125**
On-screen visual element that you activate by moving the pointer atop it and pressing the mouse button—as if you were pressing the screen button with your finger. A button with an ellipsis (. . .) leads to a dialog box. Other buttons may be icons.

byte **40**
Group of 8 bits. One byte is required to represent an alphanumeric character, defined by its own combination of 8 on-and-off bits.

cable **7, 150**
Wire that connects two devices. Cables may range from a single conductor to dozens inside the insulation.

cable, shielded **7**
Wire that has a braided wrapping around the main, interior wire(s). The braid is connected to the metal cabinets of devices on either end via the outer metal housing of the connectors. Shielded cable can reduce radio-frequency emissions that cause radio and television interference.

cable switcher **9**
External box that connects to a serial port. A switch on the panel lets you attach any of several devices to the single serial port.

cables, changing **8, 53, 55**
Always turn off all devices before changing PC cables, especially SCSI cables.

cache **10**
Portion of RAM or memory built into a microprocessor that holds frequently required information handy. Usually enhances the speed of a computer or device.

CAD > see computer-aided design

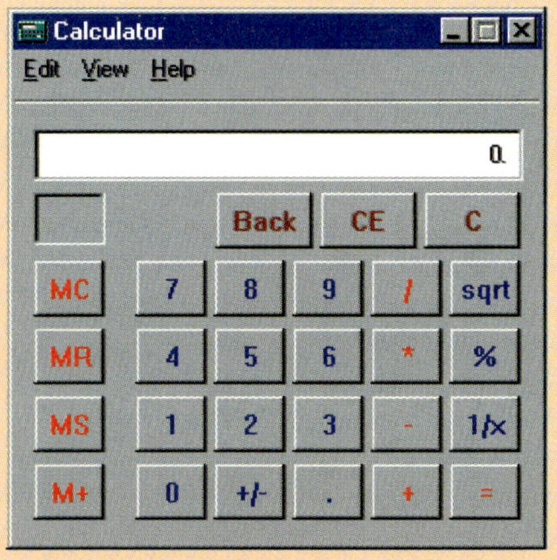

Calculator accessory **122**
Simple scientific calculator applet installed into the Accessories program grouping. You can use your keyboard's numeric keypad to enter values.

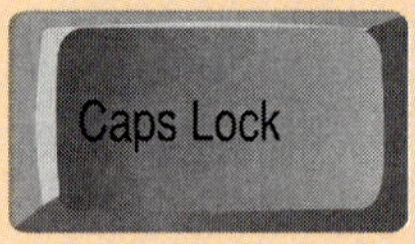

Caps Lock **key** **14**
Push-on/push-off key that locks all alphabet keys in their uppercase characters. Does not affect numbers or punctuation keys.

capturing screen image > see screen shot

cartridge disk drive **59, 93**
Removable hard disk capable of storing 40 to 88 megabytes of information using a single disk drive external device. Practical for backing up high-capacity hard disks.

cartridge font **105, 139**
Plug-in typeface designed for some printer models. Must be installed into Windows via the `Font Installation` wizard (in Fonts folder).

cascading **75, 87**
For windows, method of displaying multiple windows in an overlapping, stair-stepped arrangement. Right-click on the Taskbar to choose `Cascade` from the pop-up menu to cascade all open windows. Also used to describe hierarchical menus.

CD-ROM **9, 59, 60, 80, 101 122, 123, 146**
Compact Disc-Read Only Memory; looks just like a compact audio disc, but stores up to 550 megabytes of computer information. To the PC, a CD-ROM looks like a very large locked disk. Used frequently to publish large amounts of text and graphic information.

Centronics **7, 55**
Early PC printer manufacturer that defined a connection standard for printers still used today. It assumes a connection to the PC's parallel port (LPT1). Centronics printer cables have a male DB-25 on the PC end, and a large 25-pin clip-on connector for the printer end.

CGA **29**
Color Graphics Adapter, an early standard for color video display on an IBM-compatible PC. Displays insufficient resolution for Windows 95 (VGA minimum).

chair height **4**
Distance between the top of the chair seat and the floor. Should be adjusted to let your feet rest squarely on the floor or footrest.

Character Map **17, 18, 69**
Applet supplied with Windows 95 to let you select characters beyond the standard ASCII 128 characters.

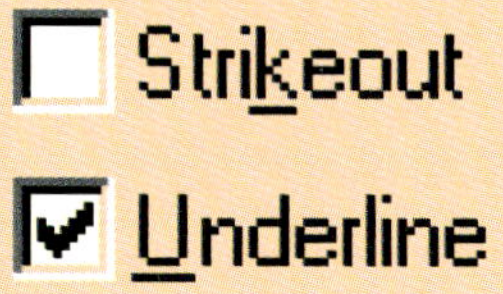

checkbox **88, 125**
Screen button style consisting of a square whose contents (an X or checkmark) indicate whether the labeled item is engaged. Clicking such a button toggles between on and off settings.

choosing > see selecting

clamping voltage **6**
Voltage level at which a surge suppressor prevents current from passing to devices plugged into it.
computers comply with Class B, as do most office PCs.

click **20**
To press the mouse button while the screen pointer is atop an object or between text characters.

client application **128**
In OLE, the program that displays a document containing an OLE linked or embedded object.

Clipboard **33, 69, 92, 103, 128, 131**
Temporary memory space that holds any information an application lets you select and issue the `Copy` command for. Clipboard information is lost when the PC is turned off or restarted.

clock, setting > see Date/Time control panel

close button **75, 87, 89, 123**
Upper right square of many window styles. Clicking the box closes the window.

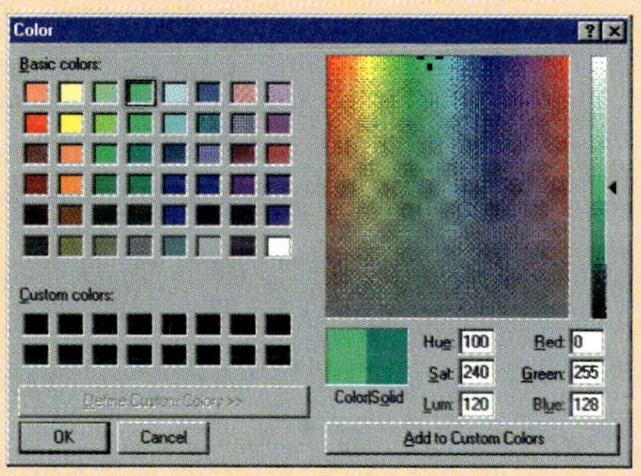

color **30, 34, 94, 101, 138**
With a color monitor, the Windows offers much flexibility with color displays in both the Desktop/Explorer and documents.

color selection **34-35, 94**
A Color dialog box allows you to choose from as many colors as your video monitor circuitry allows. Features a spectrum of available colors and brightness control, as well as entry of RGB and HSV values.

COM1, COM2, etc. **8, 60, 150, 154, 169**
Operating system identifiers for serial port(s) on a PC. Windows modem settings assign the modem to a specific serial port based on these names.

COMMAND.COM **49, 70, 131, 132**
MS-DOS operating system program. Required in the root directory of a disk for booting an MS-DOS computer.

command-line interface **70, 132**
A user interface that produces an on-screen prompt at which the user types commands to carry out file maintenance and program loading. The MS-DOS prompt is a command-line interface.

compressed drive > see DriveSpace

computer-aided design (CAD) **23**
Using a computer as a drawing and modeling tool. Often places great demands on processing and video display power.

CONFIG.SYS 60, 66, 131, 160, 179
A text file containing MS-DOS instructions for working with hardware devices. Generally not required for Windows 95 unless your PC or peripherals are not supported by Windows 95 drivers.

conflict, hardware 60-61, 67, 102
Occurs when two or more devices attempt to use the same hardware resources of the PC, such as IRQs or I/O addresses. Reconcilable through the Add New Hardware wizard.

connector 7, 8
Joint between hardware box and cable. Every connector has a gender—male or female. A male connector attaches only to a female connector and vice versa.

contrast 28
Difference between the lightest and darkest possible pixels of a video monitor. The higher the contrast, the more readable the display.

control 89
User interface element that lets a user adjust some setting or property. Often, consists of an on-screen metaphor for a real-world switch, lever, or meter.

Control (Ctrl) **key** 14, 92
Modifier key on the keyboard used in conjunction with one or more other keys. Used with many common menu commands in Windows 95. Such keyboard combinations show the name of the key to be pressed with the Control key (e.g., Ctrl+C).

control panel 74, 100-102, 184
Small application that lets you adjust settings of the system or external device via software. Control panel settings are remembered after you turn off your PC. Windows groups all control panels in the **Control Panel** folder.

Control Panel

Control Panel folder 100-102
Special folder designated in the Windows folder for all control panels.

convergence 31
Ability of the three phosphor beams in a color monitor to excite the same spot on the monitor.

copy protection 123
Software-based guard against making a copy of files from one disk to another. Not used much these days, except in network protection schemes.

copy to Clipboard 92, 103, 113, 131
Selecting information and issuing the Copy command in an application. A duplicate of that information goes into the Clipboard for pasting in another location later.

copying disk > see disk, copying

CPU 40, 42, 67, 130
Central Processing Unit, the main (microprocessor) chip that controls all electronic activity in a PC. Windows 95 requires Intel brand CPUs of the 80386, 80486, or Pentium models (or compatible chips by other manufacturers).

crash, disk > see hard disk recovery

“curly” "straight"

curly characters 18, 19
Typesetting characters for quote and apostrophe marks which are more rounded than the straight quote and apostrophe marks of typical fonts. Consult the **Character Map** applet for access to these characters in different fonts.

currency format 102
Symbols and decimal separator characters for various countries' money systems. Settable in the Regional Settings control panel.

cursor **79, 124**
Flashing screen indicator showing where the next typed character is to appear. Different from a **pointer,** which is controlled by the mouse.

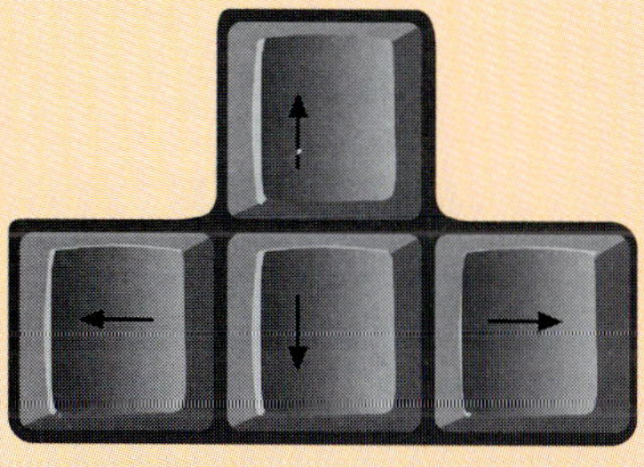

cursor **keys** **14, 84**
Four arrow keys on the keyboard that usually control a text insertion pointer's location within a document. In some programs and documents, may also control screen navigation.

cut to Clipboard **92, 103, 113**
Selecting information and issuing the Cut command in an application. The selected information is deleted from the document, but a copy goes into the Clipboard for pasting in another location later.

daisy chaining **51, 55**
Method of connecting similar device types in series, such that only one device connects directly to the computer. Each device has two connectors so that it can be placed anywhere in the series. Many **SCSI** devices may be chained together. Also called chaining.

DAT **59**
Digital Audio Tape format, used as a tape backup format.

data bus > see bus

date **100**
Maintained as part of the PC internal clock, the date may be set via the Date/Time control panel.

Date/Time control panel **100**
Windows 95 program that allows you to set your PC's internal clock to the correct time and date. Also contains setting for your time zone to help networked PCs in different parts of the world identify when certain network requests (e.g., printing) were made.

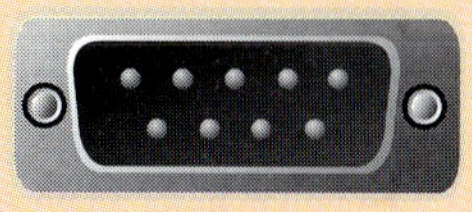

DB-9 connector **7, 8, 150**
Standard 9-pin connector style formerly used for serial port connectors on PCs.

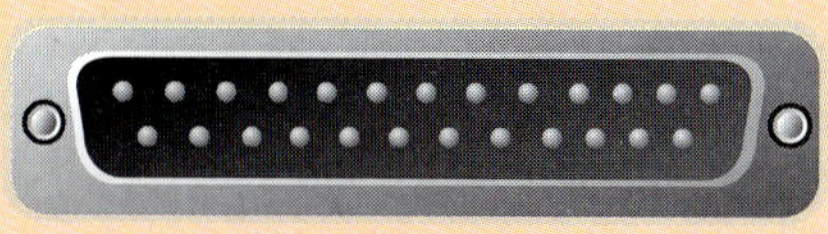

DB-25 connector **7, 8, 55**
Standard 25-pin connector style used for the printer port on most PC rear panels and on many external serial devices.

DDE > see dynamic data exchange

decimal format **102**
Designation of separator character between groups of number digits. Settable in the **Regional Settings** control panel.

default **94, 119, 138**
Setting or value established at the factory, such as control panel settings or software program settings. Also, settings the user controls to influence the regular behavior of a program or its documents.

default printer **137, 176, 181**
Printer to which Windows 95 automatically sends data or documents for printing when no Print dialog appears for the user to select a different printer.

Del **key > see** Delete **key**

delay repeat > see repeat delay

Delete 93, 113
File menu (also right-click pop-up menu) command that removes the currently selected item(s) in the Desktop/Explorer window. Does not transfer selected items to the Recycle Bin.

Delete **key** 14
Deletes the character to the *right* of the text insertion pointer or any selection in a document.

descender 104
Part of a font character (e.g., g, y, q) that extends below the baseline. **> see ascender**

desk accessory 122
Program that uses little memory, and is usually invoked from the Accessories program grouping in the Start Menu.

Desktop 11, 32, 34, 66, 74, 77, 80, 86, 94-97, 110, 113
Primary work area on the Windows screen, including the background space behind windows.

Desktop/Explorer 66, 74, 76-77, 80, 84, 86, 110
Term used in this book to encompass both Desktop windows that display file items and the Explorer program, which performs the same job in a slightly different way.

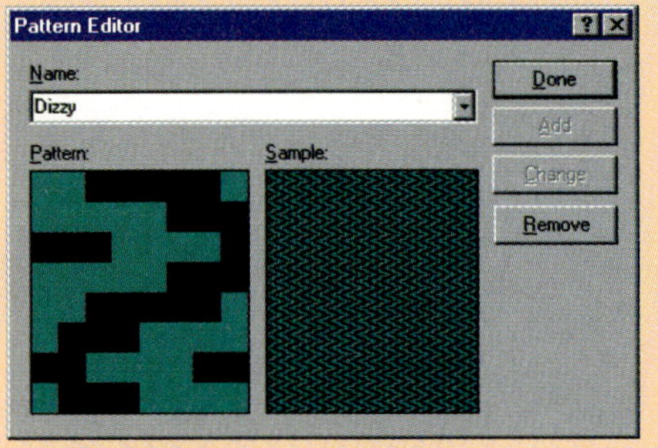

desktop pattern 94, 101
Array of dots and colors in the very background of the Desktop. Can be modified with the **Display** control panel. Mutually exclusive with wallpaper.

desktop picture > see wallpaper

destination document 128
A document file that contains an OLE linked or embedded object.

detail > see property

device driver > see driver

Device Manager 60, 102, 163, 169
Screen in the **System** control panel that lets you view all hardware connected to your PC and recognized by Windows. Also where hardware conflicts are resolved.

Dial-Up Networking folder 80
Contains specifications for each type of dial-up network connection for the computer.

Dialer > see Phone Dialer

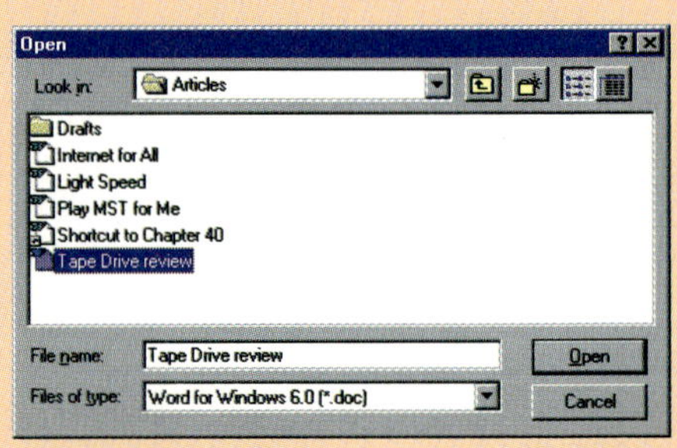

dialog, Open file 90, 110, 113
Standard dialog box that lets you open a document file from within an application. May be augmented by the program's author to let you open a variety of file types or preview a document before opening it.

dialog, Save As file 91, 110, 113, 170
Standard dialog box that lets you name a document and save it in any volume and folder available on the Desktop. May be augmented by the program's author to let you save the document in a variety of file formats.

dialog box 84, 87, 88-89, 90-91
Window that offers you choices, settings, and editable text fields to enter information normally hidden from view.

dialog box, modal 88
Dialog box that takes over your Windows screen, preventing you from working in any window other than the current dialog.

dialog box, modeless 88
Dialog box that allows you to drag it around the screen and work with information in other windows.

digitizing tablet > see graphics tablet

dimmed item 84, 89
An object or text that is grayed out or displayed in a muted color to show that it cannot be activated by the mouse or keyboard. Dimmed menu items can often be activated by selecting document text or objects.

DIN connector 7, 9
Round connector body with numerous pins inside. Commonly used in European audio and video gear.

Direct Cable Connection 150-151
Applet that establishes the software communications between two computers linked together via parallel or serial ports. Applet must be running on both machines, with one set up as the host, the other as the guest.

directory 93
Common MS-DOS name for a container that holds files and other directories. In Windows 95, it is known primarily as a folder.

disk, backing up 50, 52, 54, 59, 67
Process of making duplicate copy of files on another disk. Different backup types are available. Backup is possible to floppy disks, cartridge disks, a tape drive, or hard disk.

disk, copying 50
Process of duplicating a disk, usually floppy disk to floppy disk.

disk, floppy > see floppy disk

disk, optical > see CD-ROM; erasable optical disk; WORM

disk cache 10
Portion of memory set aside to hold a copy of the last information read from or to a hard disk. Speeds some operations when unchanged information is required of the disk file.

disk crash > see hard disk recovery

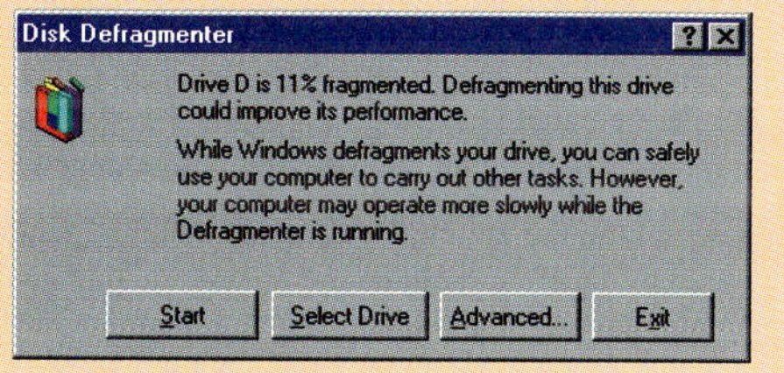

Disk Defragmenter 52, 57, 172
Applet that rewrites files on your hard disk so that all pieces of the file are in contiguous areas on the disk; also organizes contents of the disk so that most frequently accessed files are on the part of the disk with the best access performance.

disk space 50
Available in every disk's property sheet, the combined values of used and free space on the disk.

diskette > see floppy disk

display adapter 9, 28, 30, 32
Plug-in expansion card that acts as the hardware interface between your computer and an external video monitor. Video RAM and other circuitry on the display adapter determine how large a monitor the computer can accommodate and how many colors it can display.

Display

Display control panel 32, 94-95, 101
Small program that lets you adjust screen background colors and patterns, screen saver settings, window object colors, and color palette for your video monitor.

distortion, video 29
Occurs when the rectangular active area of a video monitor is not rectangular—sides bow in, corners bow out.

dithering 138
Method of making two adjacent colors trick the eye into seeing a third color. A common video display and low-resolution color printing technique.

DLL > see dynamic-link library

docking 4, 61
Connecting a laptop computer to a desktop component, which may consist of hard disk, video monitor, keyboard, and multimedia devices. Connection is usually through a dedicated multi-pin connector or SCSI port. Performing a docking maneuver while the laptop and desktop components are turned on is called hot-docking.

document window 122-123, 124
Window style consisting of a title bar, close box, minimize box, maximize box, and scroll bars. Most common window for displaying documents inside an application. Also used by Windows for its Desktop windows.

Documents 83
Start menu item that lists the fifteen most recently used document files, regardless of application. Also the name of the special folder that contains the shortcuts to those files.

DOS 66
Disk Operating System, although not unique to IBM PC-compatible computers, is a common reference to MS-DOS.

dot pitch 28
Distance between two dots on a video monitor. Recommended dot pitch for Windows 95-compatible monitors is a minimum of .28 millimeters.

double-click 21, 89, 122
To press the mouse button twice in rapid succession without moving the pointer. Usually opens an object on the screen.

double-click speed 21, 100
Setting in the **Mouse** control panel that establishes how quickly the mouse button must be pressed to signify a double-click on a screen object.

download 155
To transfer a file from another computer (usually a mainframe or BBS) to a local computer.

dpi 138
Dots per inch, a measure of resolution for printed output and displays.

drag 20, 76, 80-81, 86, 93, 112-113, 124, 165

Process of clicking on an object and moving the mouse while holding the mouse button down.

drag and drop 123

Process of dragging an on-screen object, and releasing the mouse button when the object is atop another object that can act on the dragged object. Dragging and dropping a document file icon atop a printer icon causes Windows to print the document.

drive letter 56, 150-151

Letter from A to Z assigned to a disk drive or other storage device. May also be assigned (mapped) to shared folders on other computers to which you have access.

driver 32, 60, 67, 131, 136, 159

Special file that instructs Windows how to communicate with a specific internal or external device, such as a printer, server, or hard disk. Drivers must be compatible with the system software version you're running.

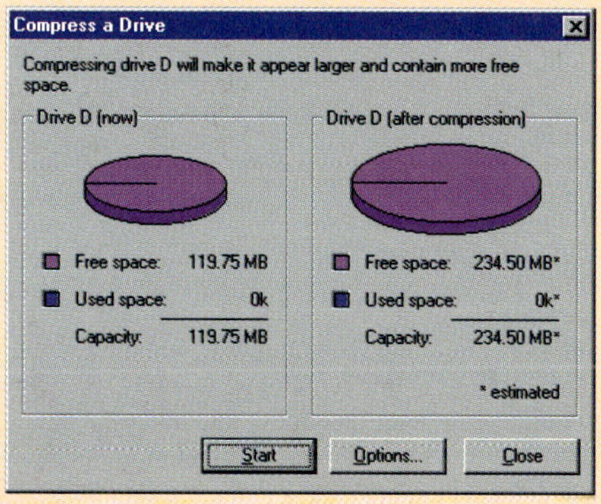

DriveSpace 56, 70

Windows utility program that compresses data on a storage device, often doubling the device's effective capacity.

drop > see drag and drop

dual boot setup 69

Installing Windows 95 so that it does not replace Windows 3.x and MS-DOS. You can boot Windows 3.x instead of Windows 95 by interrupting the Windows 95 startup with the F4 key, then selecting the desired startup sequence from the on-screen menu.

duplicate, file > see file, copying

dynamic data exchange (DDE) 119

Method whereby documents in two Windows programs can exchange information. Largely superseded by OLE.

dynamic-link library (DLL) 80, 118, 123, 167, 172

A portion of a program that exists as a separate file (extension .DLL, and listed in Windows 95 as an Application Extension). The program summons the powers of the DLL when they're needed as the program runs.

earthquake proofing 5

Securing computer and monitor to the desk to prevent the items from creeping off the desk during the shaking of an earthquake.

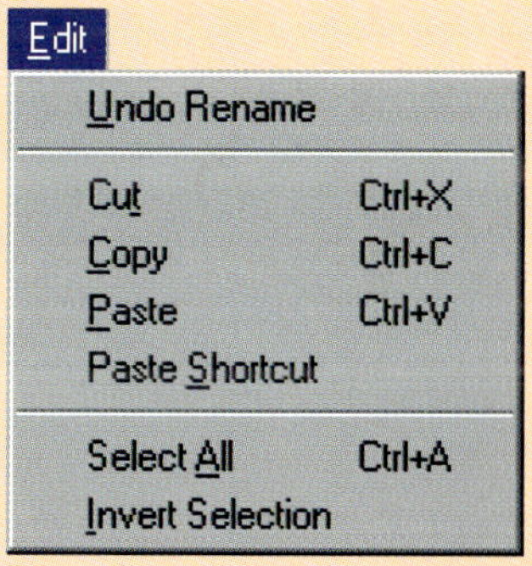

Edit menu 85, 103, 113, 124

Common user interface element in all applications, includes commands to control **Clipboard** contents (Cut, Copy, Paste).

EGA 29
Enhanced Graphics Adapter, a video display standard that was popular between the CGA and VGA eras. Insufficiently powerful to work with Windows 95.

ejecting disks > see floppy disk, ejecting

electrical safety 6
Proper way to protect your computer equipment from large variations in electrical current and voltage.

electromagnetic force (EMF) 29, 36
Invisible force generated by magnetic coils in a video monitor (and, to a lesser extent, electric motors). Adequate distance between an EMF source and humans is recommended.

electronic still camera 31
Single-frame camera that stores the image as an electronic file on a small diskette. Image may be played back on a video monitor or saved as a file with the aid of extra hardware called a frame grabber or video digitizer.

ellipsis 84, 89, 124
Three closely spaced periods, used in menu items and buttons to indicate that their selection leads to another window.

em-dash 19
Typesetter's term for a long dash.

embedding > see Object Linking and Embedding

Empty Recycle Bin 93
Special menu command that empties the contents of Desktop Recycle Bin. Right-click on the bin's icon to see its pop-up menu.

en-dash 19
Typesetter's term for a short dash.

enclosing folder > see parent folder

End **key** 15
Key on the AT keyboard that often positions the text insertion pointer at the end of the screen or document. Must be programmed by the application's author.

Energy Star 29, 36
Industry standard mechanism for reducing energy consumption for video monitors.

Enter **key** 14, 89, 111, 113
Key above the right Shift key and in the numeric keypad of all AT-style keyboards. In dialog boxes, performs the same action as clicking on the item with **focus.**

EPSF 127, 139
Encapsulated PostScript File format, used to store graphics and text information for printing on a PostScript printer or typesetter.

erasable optical disk 59
High-capacity disk storage that uses a laser beam to read and write information on a metal coated disk.

erasing disks > see floppy disk, formatting

ergonomics 4
Branch of knowledge pertaining to the study of people at work and the work environment, used very often to describe human-to-machine interaction.

Escape key 14, 89
Keyboard key used in most programs to cancel operations, close dialog boxes, or backtrack through a series of steps.

event 97, 147
Action user or Windows performs on Desktop or application objects. Different sounds can be assigned to each event via the Sounds control panel.

.EXE 80, 122, 132, 167
Executable file; a program that runs if you double-click it in a Desktop window is an .EXE file. You cannot tell if a program is an MS-DOS or Windows program until you open it.

expanded memory specification (EMS) 43, 45
Operating system method of allowing MS-DOS programs to use more than the traditional one-megabyte address space of original IBM PCs.

expansion card 9
Optional extra circuit board that plugs into a socket on a PC system unit motherboard. Card connectors must match specifications of the motherboard connectors. Not all PCs have the same connector styles or the same number of slots available for expansion cards.

expansion slot 9
Connector on a PC motherboard that accepts an expansion card. Common slot standards include ISA, EISA, Micro Channel, and PCI, the last gradually replacing the others.

Explore 76
Right-click pop-up menu option for containers, leading to Windows Explorer display of that container's contents.

Explorer > see Windows Explorer

extension 91, 96, 169
The last three characters of an MS-DOS file name (preceded by a period). Often hidden from view in Windows 95 display of long file names, the extension is the identifier that Windows uses to classify a file type and to associate documents to their applications.

extended memory specification (XMS) 43, 45, 66
Operating system memory management method that allows Windows 95 to treat multiple megabytes of memory as contiguous RAM address space. Windows 95 automatically invokes XMS when it starts.

fax modem 60, 155
Hardware device that allows users to send documents directly from the PC to a fax machine over the telephone. Some units also capture incoming faxes and turn them into Windows document files.

feature upgrade 66
New version of software that includes one or more enhancements to features or additional features over and above the previous version.

female connector 7
One of a connector pair recognizable for holes that accept the pins of a matching male connector.

field 89, 90-91
Rectangular area in a window for entering text information. Click on a field to display the text insertion cursor for typing. Pressing the Tab key advances activation through items such as fields and buttons in a window.

file 74, 90-91, 112-113, 179, 180
Any entity, other than a disk volume or folder, that appears in a Desktop/Explorer window. A file is a collection of information, whether it be an application (containing program code) or document (containing your data).

file association > see associate

file compression 59, 155
Method of squeezing a file to a smaller size for efficient transfer over telephone lines or networks, or for disk space efficiency. Requires decompression to use the file. PKZIP and PKUNZIP (decompression component) are popular among PC users.

File Manager **66, 77**
In Windows 3.x, the primary user interface to manipulating files and directories. While available as an option in Windows 95 for those who prefer that interface, it has been supplanted by the Desktop/Explorer interface.

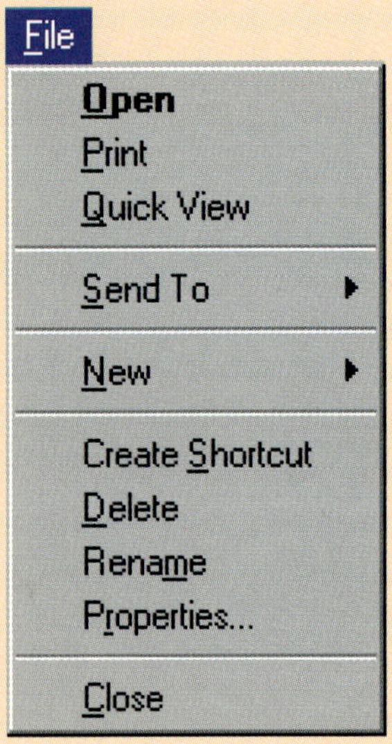

`File` **menu** **85, 110, 113, 118, 119, 124**
Standard user interface item containing commands to open, close, and save files, as well as quit an application.

file name **66, 81, 91, 97, 112, 164, 165, 168**
Identifying name attached to every document, program, or utility file stored on disk or tape. A file name may be up to 256 characters long, but some symbols may not be used in the name.

file server **59, 152**
Shared disk volume on a network. A dedicated file server is a PC and hard disk on a network devoted entirely to the job of acting as a server in conjunction with network server software.

file sharing **101, 150, 152-153**
Technique that allows individual users on a network to open disk drives or folders for access by other individuals on the network.

file transfer **150**
Moving a file from one computer to another, usually via a network or telephone connection.

file type **96, 117, 118, 119, 123, 155**
In Desktop/Explorer window listings, the plain language description of the nature of the file. The description is associated with a particular MS-DOS file name extension, which you normally don't see in Windows file listings.

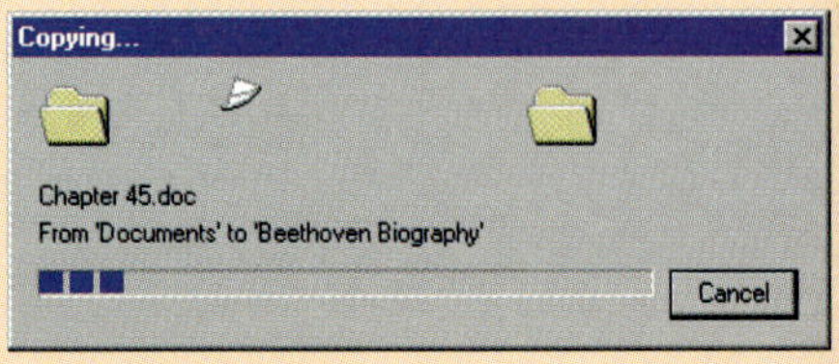

files, copying **103, 113, 173, 178**
Right-click and drag a file's icon to its destination container (folder, disk, or open window), then choose `Copy Here` from the pop-up menu.

files, finding **116-117, 179**
The `Find` command in the Start menu locates stored files that match numerous search criteria. You can perform a simple search on a name or a more defined search on many different characteristics of files.

files, hidden **70, 77, 96, 116**
Windows 95 tries to reduce folder clutter by hiding from view files used primarily by programs rather than users (application extensions, device drivers, and some system files). To see these items in listings, choose `Options` from any Desktop/Explorer `View` menu, then click the `View` tab and the `Show all files` radio button.

files, locking **113**
Checking Read-only in the file's property sheet prevents any program from altering the file. Does not affect the file's deletability.

FilterKeys 23-24
Accessibility Options control panel option that instructs Windows to ignore accidental keystrokes.

finding files > see files, finding

fixed-sized font > see raster font

flicker 28
Interaction between the screen refresh rate of a video monitor and the refresh rate of surrounding fluorescent lighting. The more difference between the refresh rates of the monitor and lighting, the less flicker.

floppy disk 48-50, 58, 60, 70, 93, 155
Storage device capable of 360KB, 720KB, 1.2MB, or 1.44MB of storage, depending on the disk type and formatting. Current standards use 3.5" diameter, plastic-encased floppy disks for 1.44MB high-density application.

floppy disk, ejecting 50
PC floppy disk drives require manual ejection, usually be pressing an eject button on the face of the disk drive. Insertion or removal of a floppy disk does not alter the contents of a Desktop/Explorer window open to the floppy disk drive.

floppy disk, formatting 49, 173, 181
Laying down the parking spaces on a floppy disk for information. All disks must be formatted before they may store information. You can purchase diskettes preformatted for IBM-compatible computers.

floppy disk, locking 48, 58, 70, 166
Preventing a disk from being overwritten. On 3.5" disks, requires the locking tab to be in the open (see through) position. Also prevents viruses from being written to a diskette.

focus 88-89
In dialog boxes, the selection of an object (button, field) that can receive keyboard control.

folder 66, 71, 74, 83, 110-111, 178
Collection of files or other folders, just like a paper folder. A folder may be shared among users on a network.

folder name 81, 111
Identifying name attached to every folder. A folder name can be 256 characters long, but some symbols may not be used in the name.

font 97, 104-105, 124, 131, 139
In personal computer parlance, a particular typeface, regardless of size or style (bold, italic, etc.). Different from typesetting terminology, in which a font is a typeface of a particular style and size.

font file 104-105
File that contains information about a typeface. May be a single bitmapped font size or a TrueType file, which contains specifications about all sizes of a typeface. Font files must be installed with the `Font Installation` wizard to be recognized by applications.

font substitution 105, 139
A table of matchups between Windows fonts and built-in printer fonts. You see the Windows font on the screen, but the printer font is substituted in the final output.

fonts, installation 105
For raster and TrueType fonts, use the Font Installation wizard in the Fonts folder. For PostScript fonts, use ATM.

fonts, PostScript > see PostScript

fonts, TrueType > see TrueType

Fonts folder 104-105
Location on hard disk for all raster and TrueType font files.

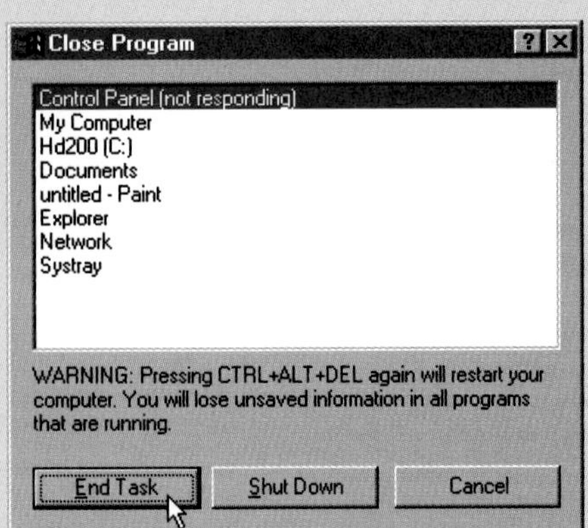

force quit 11, 123
Typing Ctrl+Alt+Del displays a window of all running tasks. Select the one you want to close, and click the 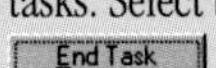 button.

foreign language characters > see keyboard character

formatted capacity 48
Actual amount of empty space available on a disk after the disk has been initialized (formatted). Invisible control information takes up some of the disk's raw storage capacity.

formatting disks > see floppy disk, formatting; hard disk, formatting

fragmentation 52, 57, 67
On hard disks, pieces of a file may be stored on many discontiguous parts of the platter(s), increasing the total access time in reading and writing the file. Remedied by running **Disk Defragmenter.**

frame grabber 31
External hardware (or plug-in expansion board) that connects to a video source and with the help of compatible software, captures a video frame, converting it to information that can be stored in a file. The image may also be modified by graphics software to produce unusual effects.

free space 50, 67, 167
Amount of storage available on a disk. For hard disks, open `My Computer`, and click on the hard disk icon to see free space in the status bar at the window bottom.

freeware > see shareware

freeze 160, 161
Condition in which the PC is unresponsive to mouse clicks or keystrokes.

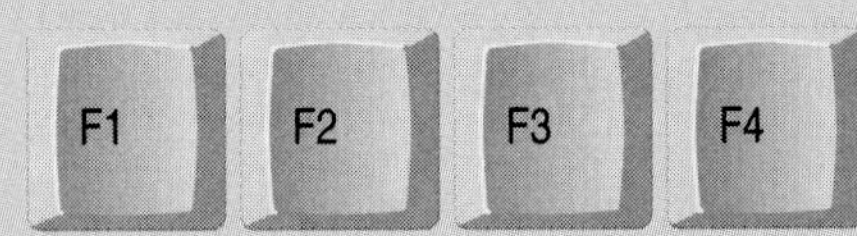

function keys 14, 85
Twelve to fifteen keys along the top of the desktop keyboard that are usually programmed by application authors to carry out a long series of mouse and keyboard motions.

fuse 6
Capsule-sized device placed in a power line to break the circuit when too much current is flowing through the line. An open (blown) fuse may indicate a failure of a piece of electronic equipment that was about to draw more current than normal operation allows. Often built into surge suppressors or power strips.

game port 9
Rear panel connector on many PCs for a joystick or other game controller.

genlock 31
Special external hardware that synchronizes the refresh rate of a PC video monitor with that of a video camera that is recording the PC screen. Prevents the slowly creeping line in the recorded screen.

GIF 126
Graphics Interchange Format, a commonly used graphics file format for storing and exchanging detailed pictures.

gigabyte 51, 59
One billion bytes.

glare 5, 29
Reflection of surrounding objects and light off the glass of a video monitor. Can cause headaches and eyestrain if intense.

graphical user interface (GUI) 74, 78
Sometimes pronounced as GOO-ee. Method of interaction between a computer and its user in which commands are carried out by clicking and pointing with a mouse, rather than typing commands. Files and directories appear as metaphors of real-world objects. In Windows 3.x, the user interface is a layer atop an existing MS-DOS operating system, while Windows 95 (like the Apple Macintosh) combines the operating system and user interface into one software entity.

graphics file format 126-127
Any of several methods of storing graphic data in a file. Common formats today are .BMP, GIF, EPSF, and TIFF.

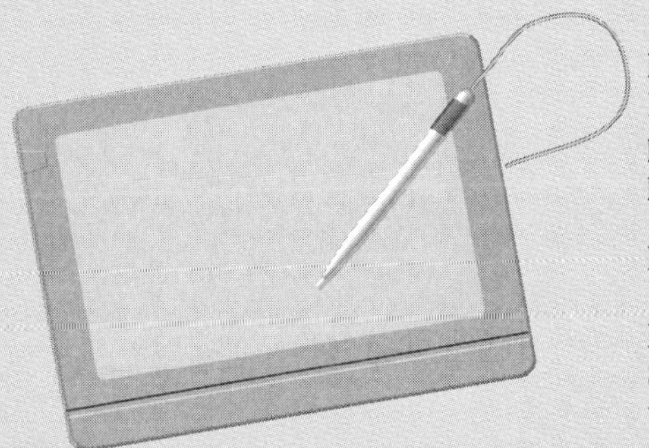

graphics tablet 23
Flat pad that lets you move an on-screen pointer by drawing with a pen that is connected to the pad. Supplements a keyboard in intensely graphic work, such as design drawing, letting you work with a more comfortable pointing and drawing device.

gray-scale 30
Capability of displaying varying intensity of gray at each pixel location. At 256 levels of gray, a monitor is capable of displaying photorealistic images.

ground 6
Electric potential of the earth. Grounding an object means matching its potential with that of the earth. Most electrical outlets are grounded, and the third, round pin of a power cord is usually connected to ground.

GUI > see graphical user interface

handicapped mousing 21, 24
Performing mouse operations without the mouse. Requires **Accessibility Options** control panel.

handicapped typing 23-24
Performing typing operations with a single stylus or pointer. Requires **Accessibility Options** control panel.

hang > see freeze

hard disk 9, 51-53, 54, 55, 59, 60, 184
Storage device capable of storing hundreds or thousands of megabytes of information, usually offering fast access to that information.

hard disk, formatting 52, 58, 159
Laying down the parking spaces (tracks and sectors) on a disk platter. Formatting a hard disk completely erases all previous information on that disk.

hard disk partition 53, 59
Portion of a hard disk that has been assigned (by partitioning software) as a separate disk volume when viewed on the Desktop.

hard disk recovery **54, 58**
Repair of a hard disk that is not immediately readable when the PC starts up. May entail several different techniques and a few attempts.

headphones **9, 146**
Same as Walkman-style stereo headphones for listening to multimedia audio through the audio output port. Provides improved fidelity over the internal speaker, which it disables.

heat **5, 53**
Number One enemy of computers. Allow for good ventilation around the system unit and monitor.

Help menu **78, 85**
Rightmost menu in a window. Programs may add more help items to the menu.

hidden files > see files, hidden

hierarchical menu > see menu, hierarchical

High Contrast **24, 33**
Accessibility Options control panel screen that sets Windows screen colors and fonts for easier reading for the sight-impaired user.

Home key **15**
Keyboard key used in document navigation. Must be programmed by the application's author.

hot spot, monitor **5**
Bright spot caused by glare from external light source. Can be minimized with an adjustable monitor stand.

hot spot, pointer **79**
Single pixel on a pointer that must be atop a button or other object to effect action with the mouse button.

hue, lightness, saturation (HLS) **34**
Three-value system of defining a color. Available as an option for selecting a color in the **Color** selection dialog window.

HyperTerminal **69, 101, 122, 154**
Applet that provides simple telecommunications software for accessing text-based on-line services. Provides terminal emulation for standard communications access and file transfer.

icon, desktop **66, 74, 80-81, 115, 122**
Representation for disks, folders, documents, and other files presented by the Desktop/Explorer.

IDE **51, 59**
Integrated Drive Electronics, a hardware standard for connecting a hard disk to a motherboard. Being challenged by the SCSI device standard.

imagesetter **136**
Expensive device that transfers text and graphics files to photographic film, usually at very high resolutions. Film output is used in the production of printer material. A familiar brand name is Linotronic, which offers devices capable of 2540 dpi.

inactive window **35, 87**
Window that is not the current window, often covered by another window on the screen. Discernible by its lack of color in the menubar.

indicator lights, keyboard **15**
AT keyboard lights above the numeric keypad that show the status of Num Lock, Caps Lock, and Scroll Lock. Num Lock and Scroll Lock features have to be programmed into an application by the author. Caps Lock works all the time.

.INI files 60, 66, 67, 95
Initialization files required for Windows 3.x and Windows applications. In Windows 95, the function is covered by the built in Registry.

initializing diskette > see floppy disk, formatting

initializing hard disk > see hard disk, formatting

input/output (I/O) 61
Refers to any computer item (hardware device, software program) related to moving data into or out of the CPU.

Insert **key** 14
A carryover from early days of PCs, when software sometimes required the user to invoke an insert mode to insert characters in a line of text. Rarely used today except for keyboard combinations with modifier keys.

insertion point > see text insertion cursor

installing applications 69, 122
Entails copying files from the distribution diskettes to the hard disk. Sometimes includes an installer program (named SETUP.EXE or INSTALL.EXE) to move files to their proper places, including inside the Windows folder when necessary.

installing Windows 95 68-69
Requires the Windows Setup program on the Windows 95 installation diskettes or CD-ROM. You must use Windows Setup to upgrade from Windows 3.x.

Intel 61
Primary manufacturer of microprocessors in PCs capable of running Windows 95.

interference, electromagnetic 29
Invisible fields that interfere with video displays, causing wobbly screen images. Requires that the source of interference be separated from your video monitor.

interference, radio and TV 7
Radio frequency signals generated by electronic equipment and cables. Can cause noise in radio and television signals.

internal clock > see Date/Time control panel

international characters > see Character Map

Internet 154-155
A global communications network that connects millions of individuals via corporate, university, government, and commercial computer systems.

Interrupt Request Line (IRQ) 61
A numbered connection that hardware devices can use to get the CPU's attention when they must process information. Each device must be assigned its own IRQ (of 15 possible).

Invert Selection 81
Edit menu command that changes the selected status of all items in the window: selected items become unselected, and vice versa.

invisible files > see files, hidden

I/O > see input/output

joystick 9
Controller that consists of a vertical stick that gives the user 360-degree control over a pointer or action figure on the computer screen. Used primarily for game software.

jumpiness, video 29
Sign of either an unstable video circuitry or electromagnetic interference.

K, KB > see kilobyte

key repeat rate **16**
Keyboard control panel setting to adjust how fast a keyboard key repeats itself once it begins repeating.

keyboard, AT **15**
Larger keyboard patterned after the IBM PC AT model keyboard. Includes 15 function keys, document navigation keys, cursor keys in an inverted "T" arrangement, and indicator lights in addition to a numeric keypad.

keyboard, laptop **15**
A smaller version of the AT keyboard, it usually includes all the keys, but often with some keys scaled down and other shaving double functions with the addition of a special Fn key.

keyboard character **18-19**
Any alphanumeric character or symbol created with the keyboard. Not all fonts in a language have the same characters. Use **Character Map** applet to see what characters each font contains.

keyboard connection **9**
A five-pin round DIN connector, usually on the rear panel of the PC.

Keyboard

Keyboard control panel **16, 100**
Control panel for setting the key repeat delay, repeat frequency, and alternate language keyboard.

keyboard equivalent > see menu, keyboard equivalent

keyboard height **4**
Distance between the floor and the surface on which the keyboard rests. For most people this should be less than standard 29" desk height.

keyboard macro **23**
One-key command (or Command-key sequence) that performs a series of mouse and keyboard actions as trained once by the user. Provides shortcuts for repetitive operations.

keyboard shortcuts **88, 92, 124**
Convenient ways to perform specific mouse or menu actions from the keyboard. Not every shortcut equivalent is displayed in menus. In the tables below are the most practical shortcuts for various parts of Windows 95.**> see keyboard shortcuts on page 209**

keyboards, foreign language **17, 100**
Keyboards for other languages have different character layouts. The **Keyboard** control panel lets you alert Windows as to the keyboard style you are using.

keypad, numeric **17**
Grouping of keys at the right edge of the AT keyboard (or integrated into letter keys of a laptop keyboard) dedicated to entering numbers and simple arithmetic symbols. Replicates adding machine layout for rapid entry of many numbers.

Keyboard Shortcuts

Desktop and Taskbar

Shortcut	Action
F1	Start Windows Help
Shift+F10	Show context menu for Taskbar
Ctrl+Esc	Show Startup menu (use arrow keys)
Alt+Tab	Switch to next task or item shown in Taskbar
Ctrl+Esc, Esc	Switch focus to Taskbar
Alt+M	Minimize all windows (from focus on Taskbar)

Desktop/Explorer Windows

Shortcut	Action
F3	Show Windows Find dialog
F4	Show popup list in toolbar
F5	Refresh window
Ctrl+A	Select All command (Edit menu)
Ctrl+Z	Undo previous action(s)
Backspace	Show parent folder window or listing

Windows Explorer

Shortcut	Action
Ctrl+G	Go To command (Tools menu)
+ (numeric)	Expand tree selection
- (numeric)	Collapse tree selection
* (numeric)	Expand entire tree under selection
Up Arrow	Select next visible item higher in tree
Down Arrow	Select next visible item lower in tree
Right Arrow	Select next visible child or expand tree selection
Left Arrow	Select next visible parent or collapse tree selection
Ctrl+Arrow	Scroll tree without moving selection

Selected Desktop/Explorer Object

Shortcut	Action
F2	Rename command (File menu)
Ctrl+X	Cut command (Edit menu)
Ctrl+C	Copy command (Edit menu)
Ctrl+Y	Paste command (Edit menu)
Del	Move object to Recycle Bin
Shift+Del	Delete object immediately
Alt+Enter	Show property sheet
Alt+double-click	Show property sheet
Shift+double-click	Show Explorer (for folder in Details view)

File Dialogs

Shortcut	Action
F4	Show and activate Look In popup list
F5	Refresh view
Backspace	Up One Level (when focus is on file list field)
Esc	Close (cancel) dialog, no action
Arrow	Select adjacent item in file list field
Enter	Open selected item in list field

kilobyte (K, KB) **40, 48, 112**
One thousand bytes: more accurately 1024 (210) bytes, based on the binary arithmetic of the computer worl.

LAN > see local area network

landscape printing **137, 140**
Rotating the printed image 90 degrees to the right so that a wide image is printed on the page sideways. May be selected for all printers and documents in the **Page Setup** dialog.

laptop computer **4, 11, 17, 23, 32, 37, 40 42, 53, 61, 84, 137**
Self-contained, battery-operated computer usually weighing between 4 and 8 pounds. Also called a notebook computer because its size resembles a notebook.

Large Icons **96**
View menu choice that displays items in Desktop/ Explorer windows in the largest icon size supported by Windows.

laser printer **104, 136**
High-resolution printer that utilizes a low-power laser light to attract microscopic toner particles to a passing sheet of paper. Consumer models print at resolutions up to 600 dpi.

launch **83, 107, 122**
Process of starting an application.

LCD **21, 37, 158**
Liquid Crystal Display, a low-power flat panel display technology used in portable computers. Uses one of several technologies to display either gray-scale or color. A backlight is usually required for high contrast.

leading **104**
Line spacing between baselines of adjacent lines of text.

left-handed mouse **21**
Mouse in which behavior of the two mouse buttons has been switched using the **Mouse** control panel.

license, software
Written contract user agrees to by opening a software package. Grants user limited rights with virtually no warranty from the software publisher.

lighting **5, 29**
Surrounding light sources have a big impact on monitor viewing comfort and fatigue.

lightning precautions **6**
Strong spikes by nearby and direct lightning strikes can damage a computer unless it is protected by a surge protector.

Line Up Icons 87, 96
View menu choice that instructs Windows to adjust location of all icons in the window to their nearest grid locations.

linking > see object linking and embedding

List 96
View menu choice that instructs Windows to display Desktop/Explorer items with small icons in a list.

list box 85, 88, 90-91, 110
In a dialog box, a scrollable field containing textual lists of items. Select an item by clicking once; initiate action on the item by double-clicking on it.

local area network (LAN) 60, 152
Collection of computers and shared devices linked together, usually by cable. Network operating system software (including some facilities built into Windows 95) controls the flow of data among devices. A local area network can be as simple as two computers or as extensive as an entire building full of computers, printers, and other shared devices.

local printer 136
A printer connected directly to a PC, usually via the parallel (LPT) port.

localization 123
Process of tailoring software for a particular country's language and other cultural facets. Often simplified by editing DLLs for menus, dialog boxes, and text strings.

locking floppy disk > see floppy disk, locking

logic board > see motherboard

long file names 66, 77, 81, 90, 97, 110, 113, 164, 172
Feature of Windows 95 that allows users to assign names to files and folders up to 256 characters long. In contrast to MS-DOS file naming convention of eight characters, a period, and three more characters (extension). Windows maintains an MS-DOS compatible file name for every long file name it creates.

LPT1 8, 60, 136, 177
Line Printer port number 1, an MS-DOS designation for the parallel port on most PCs. Some settings in Windows 95 also refer to the LPT1 port.

MacOS 66, 155
Shorthand for Macintosh Operating System, referring more specifically to the system software (System and Finder) in comparison to MS-DOS, Windows, and other operating systems or graphical user interfaces.

macro > see keyboard macro

maintenance upgrade 66
Update to software that fixes bugs or adds compatibility for a new operating system version. No new features included.

male connector 7
One of a connector pair recognizable for pins that go into the holes of a matching female connector.

mapping a network drive 85, 150-151
In some network connections, you must assign a remote computer's contents to a drive letter on your PC for programs to open and/or save documents there. You can assign any unused letter.

maximize 87
To command a window to occupy the entire screen. Click the middle button of the grouping at the upper right corner of a window to maximize the window. Click the button again to restore it to its previous size.

Media Player 69, 146-147
Windows 95 applet that allows playback of sound (.WAV), video clip (.AVI), and MIDI (.MID or .RMI) files, provided a PC has sufficient sound hardware.

megabyte (M, MB) 40, 42, 48
One million bytes, or more accurately, 1,048,576 bytes. The unit of measure for RAM and hard disk capacity.

memory, computer > see RAM

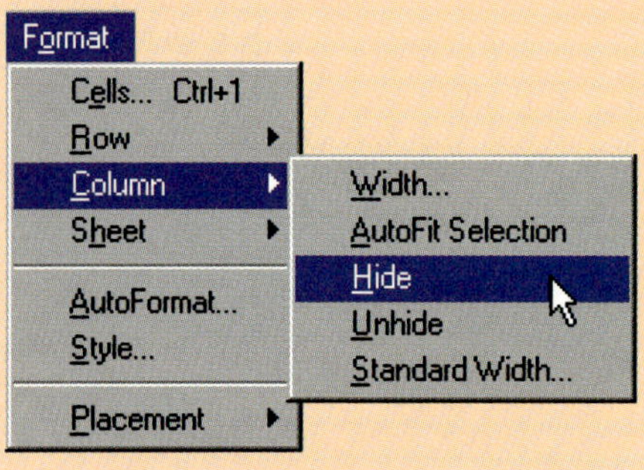

menu, hierarchical 71, 82-83, 84
Drop-down menu in which an item has a right-pointing arrow that leads to a submenu for that item. Also called cascading menu.

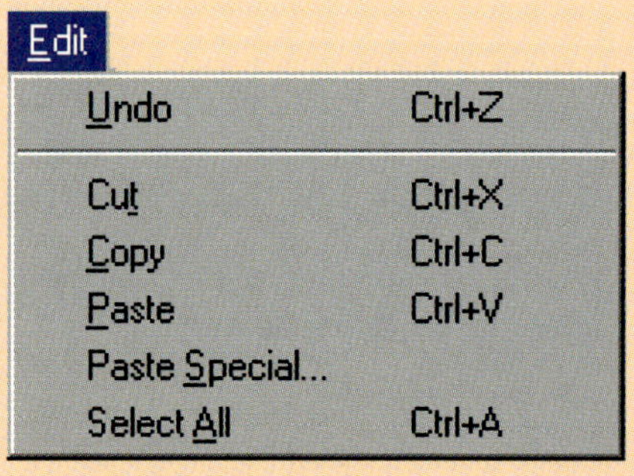

menu, keyboard equivalent 84, 92, 124
One or more keyboard keys that perform the same action as a pull-down menu command. A keyboard equivalent (if any) appears to the right of a drop-down menu item.

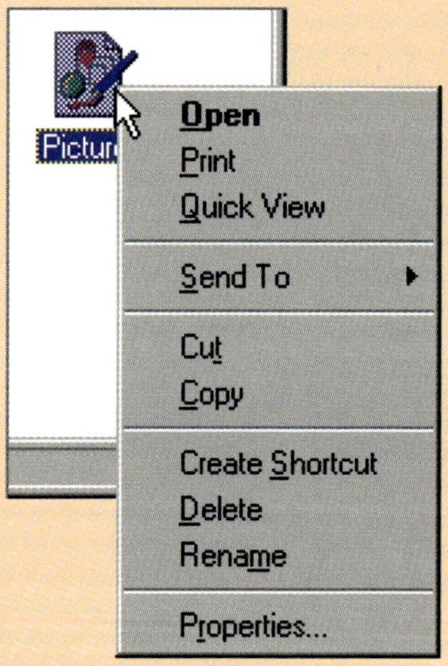

menu, pop-up 85, 113
Menu style normally used to let you choose from a pre-set list of choices to fill in a preferences setting. Common with right-clicking on Desktop/Explorer objects.

menu, drop-down 35, 84, 124
Menu of commands which you access by clicking a menu title in the menubar. The menu drops down, allowing you to either click on or drag the mouse to the desired command.

menubar 35, 84, 86, 124
Bar beneath a window's titlebar that contains titles of drop-down menus.

microprocessor > see CPU

Microsoft Exchange 66, 69, 176
Desktop icon representing a universal mailbox for Microsoft Mail or other linked mail systems.

Microsoft Network (MSN) 69, 101, 154
Commercial on-line service sponsored by Microsoft for its Windows 95 and other users. On-line registration software comes with Windows 95. Service offers on-line support, plus meeting places for a variety of non-computer interests and hobbies.

MIDI 9, 101, 146-147
Musical Instrument Digital Interface, an industry standard for connecting electronic musical instruments to computers for recording and playback. Windows 95 includes support for playing back files containing MIDI music.

mini DIN-8 connector 7, 9
Smaller version of a round DIN connector, used for mouse ports.

minimize 86-87, 123
To command a window to hide itself, but remain open. Click the window's button in the Taskbar to show the window.

modal dialog > see dialog box, modal

modeless dialog > see dialog bpx, modeless

modem 60, 101, 154
Hardware device that converts the computer's electrical signals into audible tones for transmission across telephone wires or radio waves, and reconverts received audio into computer signals.

modem cable 7, 8, 154
Cable configured to connect a PC serial port and modem. Most modems are standard enough to allow a generic cable to work.

Modems control panel 101, 169
Small program that assists in installing Windows 95 driver software for modems.

modifier key 14, 85
Any of several non-character keys pressed in concert with one or more other keys to modify their normal behavior. The modifier keys are Shift, Control, Alt, and Caps Lock.

money > see currency format

monitor stand 4, 29
Allows for adjustment of monitor in many directions to avoid glare and hot spots from surrounding light sources.

monochrome 28
Monitor that displays a single color against its black background. This is distinct from gray-scale, which requires different video monitor driving circuitry.

motherboard 40, 51
Main circuit board inside the PC that holds the CPU, RAM, and other primary board components. Also called the logic board.

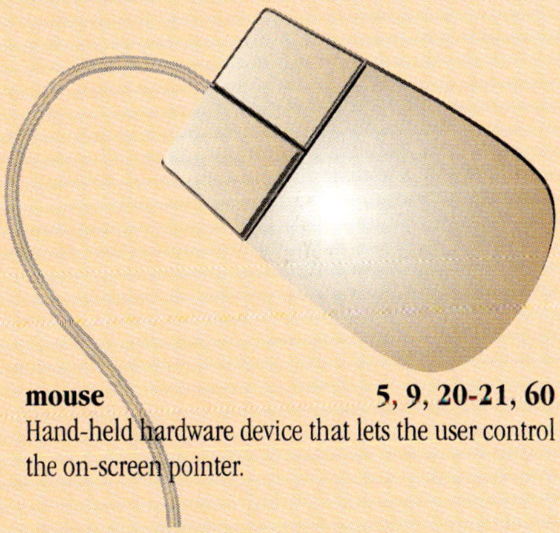

mouse 5, 9, 20-21, 60
Hand-held hardware device that lets the user control the on-screen pointer.

Mouse control panel 20-21, 100
Control panel for adjusting button behavior, pointer art, double-click speed, and tracking speed of a mouse.

Mouse Keys 21, 24
Accessibility Options setting that lets you use the numeric keypad as a substitute for the mouse.

mouse pad 5
Rubber or plastic slab on which you roll the mouse when traction on the desk surface is not sufficient.

mouse tracking 21
Speed at which the screen pointer responds to rapid movement of the mouse. Adjustable in the **Mouse** control panel, it may be set between completely linear and very fast (to allow coverage of large screens with a minimum of mouse motion).

mouse trail 21
Images of the pointer along the path is just traveled as you move the mouse. Helpful to see in some LCD displays, and adjustable in the **Mouse** control panel.

move > see drag

MPC 9
Multimedia Personal Computer, a minimum hardware standard for using multimedia software. Later updated to MPC II to accommodate better sound and video with more RAM and larger hard disks.

MS-DOS 45, 66, 130-133
Microsoft's Disk Operating System, first released with the original IBM Personal Computer in 1981. Revised many times, it was still the operating system foundation for Windows 3.x. With Windows 95, the functionality of MS-DOS is incorporated into Windows. Programs (and users) requiring MS-DOS can access simulated MS-DOS from Windows.

MS-DOS commands 43, 77, 132-133
Commands that you can type into the MS-DOS prompt window from Windows 95.

multimedia 9, 60, 101, 144-147
Combination of static (text, graphics) and time-based (sound, video, animation) information in a single software program or presentation. Multimedia that invites responses and involvement from the user is called interactive multimedia.

multiple files or folders > see selecting

multitasking 43, 67
Ability of a computer to carry on (or appear to carry on) multiple jobs at the same time. While the CPU can perform only one task at a time, multitasking operating system software schedules tasks so that all pending tasks share processing time.

multithreading 43, 67
Multitasking one better, allowing more than one process within a single application to take place (or appear to take place) at the same time, such as downloading one file from a communications service while making other requests of the service at the same time.

My Computer

My Computer 66, 75, 80, 159
Windows 95 default name for the Desktop icon that represents all the storage devices and features of your own PC, separate from any networked devices.

name 81, 86, 91, 97, 112, 115, 125
Identifying name for any disk, folder, or file. In Windows 95, file and folder names may be up to 256 characters long. On a network, each PC must also have a name, set in its Network control panel in the Identification screen.

nanosecond (ns) 40
One-billionth of a second, the unit of measure of RAM chip refresh and access speeds. Faster PC models require faster RAM chips.

network > see local area network, wide area network

Network control panel 152
Control panel that lets you adjust your PC for use on a network by adding network driver software, turn on file and print sharing, assign a network name for your computer, and control who has access to your PC via the network.

Network Neighborhood 75, 153, 166, 180
Representation on the Windows 95 Desktop of all items available to your PC via a network.

New 110
Desktop/Explorer File menu choice (also in right-click pop-up menu) for creating a new folder or registered file type without first opening the application.

non-PostScript printer 105-136
Printer (local or network) that does not have Adobe's PostScript technology built into it. Relies on TrueType or other internal fonts for character generation on paper.

notebook computer > see laptop computer

Notepad 95
Small text editing applet for opening and editing plain ASCII text files.

ns > see nanosecond

Num Lock 15
AT-style keyboard key that some programs have programmed to toggle a keypad between a numeric keypad and a navigation keypad.

object 67, 80, 85, 103, 128-129
In the Windows 95 world, any selected chunk of information that can be linked to or embedded into another program's document. See also object linking and embedding.

object graphics 126-127
Images defined by mathematical representations, such as a line with endpoint coordinates and a line thickness. An object requires less disk storage than the bitmapped equivalent, and can be resized without distortion.

Object Linking and Embedding (OLE) 128-129, 147
Microsoft technology that allows documents to share information, and users to edit disparate types of data within one program by displaying menus and other commands from the source application. A link is a pointer to the original file; an embedded object contains the object's entire set of data, and can be transported to another computer location without the source object.

Object Packager 129, 147
Program that works with OLE to provide OLE-like functionality for source documents or objects that don't support OLE.

OCR > see optical character recognition

OLE > see object linking and embedding

open file dialog > see dialog, open file

Open With **119**
File menu (or right-click pop-up menu) command for opening an unregistered document file type with a program installed on your PC. Performing this operation associates the file and other files of its type (file name extension) with the application in the future.

operating system **66**
Combination of ROM and disk-based software that turns the assemblage of chips and components into a functioning computer.

optical character recognition (OCR) **22**
Method of converting printed text to editable text characters in a document. Requires scanner hardware and OCR software.

optical disk > see CD-ROM; WORM; erasable optical disk

orientation > see landscape printing; portrait

outlet > see connector

outline font **104**
Font specification that defines a character's appearance by mathematical calculations of points along the outline of that character. TrueType and PostScript fonts are outline fonts.

package **129, 147**
Icon in a document that represents a linked or embedded object. Double-clicking the icon opens the object (e.g., views a text file, plays a sound file, shows a video clip).

Page Down **key** **15**
AT-style keyboard key usually programmed to mimic the action of clicking in the Page Down area of a scroll bar in a document window.

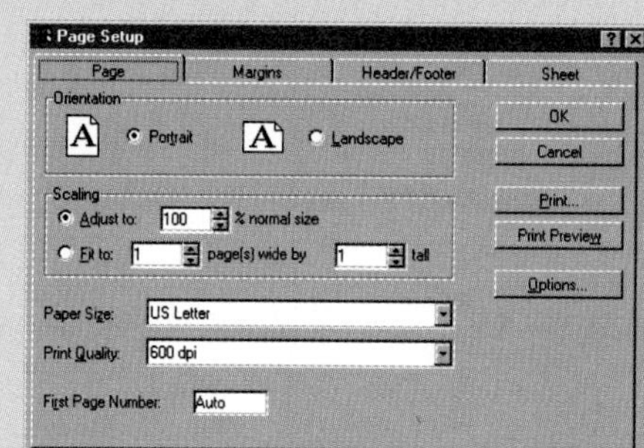

Page Setup dialog **137, 140**
Presents choices affecting appearance of a document on the page, such as paper size and orientation. Settings are saved with the document.

Page Up **key** **15**
AT-style keyboard key usually programmed to mimic the action of clicking in the Page Up area of a scroll bar in a document window.

Paint **79, 95, 137**
Applet supplied with Windows 95 to provide basic paint program functionality.

paint program **126, 137**
Application that lets you create graphic images by setting individual pixels to white, black, or colors. See also bitmap graphic.

palette > see tool palette

palette, color **33, 34-35, 126**
Collection of colors from which the video display selects colors for individual pixels. The greater the bit depth of the monitor and display adapter, the larger the palette of colors.

pane **54, 76-77, 86**
Separate rectangular area of a window whose content area is divided into two or more distinct sections.

parallel printer **8, 60**
Printer that communicates with a computer through a cable along eight simultaneous data lines. On PCs, connects through the parallel (LPT1) port.

parent folder 90, 112, 117
The folder that contains the folder being viewed at any given moment. An item can have only one parent folder; a folder may contain many children. Also known by the term enclosing folder.

parity RAM 40
Memory that includes one extra error-checking bit for each byte (8 bits) of data memory. Frequently demanded in specifications for government computers, most PCs today do not require memory modules in this configuration.

partition > see hard disk partition

password 11, 153
Series of characters user must enter into a dialog box field to gain access to a protected portion of a PC or a network. Passwords are intended to prevent unauthorized access to computer information or equipment, so keep passwords private.

Passwords control panel 101
Centralized place in Windows 95 to register and store passwords for Windows and some network access.

paste from Clipboard 92, 103, 131
Edit menu command places a copy of the Clipboard contents at the location of the text insertion cursor or selection in a document.

Paste Link 128
Extra Paste command in some programs for pasting an OLE link from the Clipboard into the current document.

Paste Special 92, 103, 124, 128, 147
Extra Paste command in some programs for pasting certain attributes of a complex information item in the Clipboard (e.g., just the formulas from spreadsheet cells in the Clipboard). Also used to place a linked or embedded OLE object.

path name 96, 110, 114, 116, 168, 183
Notation for specifying a file's location on a disk volume, consisting of volume letter and all intervening folders, each separated by a backslash.

pattern > see desktop pattern

Pause **key** 15
Keyboard key that pauses rapidly scrolling display of MS-DOS information to a screen. Not used in Windows 95.

PC Card 51, 61, 101, 169
New name for Personal Computer Memory Card International Association (PCMCIA) standard for the design of credit card–sized plug-in additions for PCs. Typical PC Card applications are memory, modems, network adapters, and hard drives. Slots are most commonly built into laptop and handheld computers.

PC Card control panel 101
Small program that lets you set various properties of the PC Card socket in your PC (usually laptops only).

PCMCIA > see PC Card

peer-to-peer 152
Local area network connection scheme that links multiple PCs without a centralized file server.

peripheral 8, 60-61
Device that connects to the PC via one of its front or rear panel ports.

Phone Dialer 69, 101, 122
Applet that provides automated phone dialing for voice calls when your PC is telephony equipped. Includes speed dial buttons for eight common calls.

phosphor 30
Coating inside the face of video tube. When a phosphor spot is touched by an electron beam, it illuminates.

phototypesetter > see imagesetter

picture element > see pixel

Picture file > see screen shot

PIF files 45, 130
Program Information File data that Windows uses to prepare a virtual machine for running an MS-DOS program.

pincushioning > see distortion, video

pinout > see connector

pixel 28, 94, 126-127
Picture element, the smallest graphical unit on a video display. Depending on the monitor, may be black, white, a gray level, or any color within the video monitor's circuitry capability.

pixel density > see resolution, video

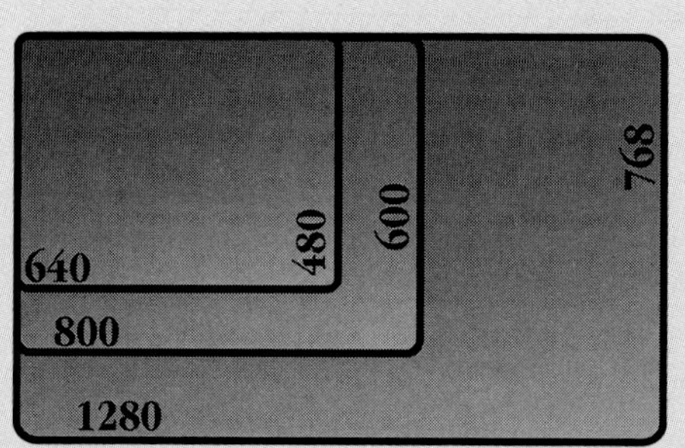

pixel grid 28
Count of pixels horizontal by pixels vertical on a video display. Not to be confused with video resolution, which indicates how densely pixels are drawn on the screen.

PKUNZIP > see PKZIP

PKZIP 122, 155, 173
Popular program that compresses PC disk files to allow more information to be delivered on diskettes or transmitted over phone lines. Zipped files can be uncompressed with the free PKUNZIP program, usually included on disks containing files compressed with PKZIP.

plug > see connector

Plug and Play (PnP) 60-61, 67
Peripheral hardware standard devised by Intel and Microsoft to allow Windows 95 to automatically recognize and install new hardware components on a PC. The computer must be built to accommodate Plug and Play for expansion cards, but Plug and Play components connected via PC Card sockets in non-Plug and Play computers are recognized by Windows.

plug-in board > see expansion card

PnP > see Plug and Play

point 104
1/72 of an inch, a typesetter's measure. Also the unit of measure of computer font sizes and line spacing.

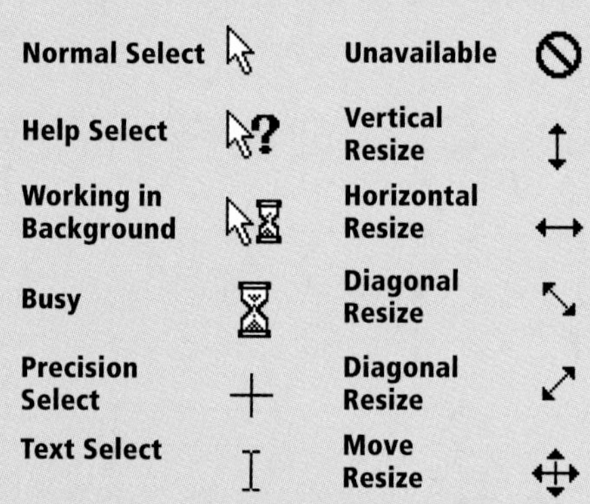

pointer 21, 24, 67, 77, 79, 84, 125
On-screen representation of the action spot controlled by the mouse. A pointer's art changes depending on what action it is performing at any instant. Some art is user changeable in the **Mouse** control panel.

pop-up menu > see menu, pop-up

port 8, 154
Front or rear panel connector to which cables are attached.

portrait 140
Page orientation that is taller than it is wide.

PostScript 104-105, 127
Page description language by Adobe Systems that uses outline definitions of font characters to product smooth characters in any size and rotation. Built into most laser printers, responds to PostScript commands sent by the computer to describe and print each page.

power (AC) cord 6, 8, 158
Grounded cable between computer system unit and AC power outlet.

power outlets 6, 158
Some offices are equipped with special power outlets with built-in surge suppressers.

power strip 6, 158
AC power extension featuring multiple power outlets for plugging in several electrical devices. Fused power strips offer better protection.

power switch 10
Located in varying places on the system unit, depending on manufacturer and model, this switch turns the computer on and off.

print dialog 106, 137, 141, 171
Final dialog before document goes to the printer, where you can select choices that affect the print job—number of copies, page range, etc.

print job 106, 137, 171
Printing task generated by a program's Print command. Most commonly the printing of a document, but can also be a selection of pages as designated in the Print dialog box.

print monitor 106, 137
Small application that runs in the background to handle print spooling. It watches for any spool files pending, and opens the conversation between Windows and the printer to carry out the job.

Print Screen **key** 15, 137
Pressing this key captures a bitmap of the current screen in the Clipboard (it does not print). Holding down the Alt key while pressing this key captures a bitmap of only the active window on the screen. Print screens by pasting from the Clipboard into a graphics program, and printing from there.

print sharing 139, 150, 153
Ability in Windows to let people on a local area network use a local printer connected to a PC.

print spooling 106, 137
Saving the printed version of a document as a temporary file, which is gradually sent to the printer, while the user is free to return to work on other documents or applications.

printer, choosing 141
Essential part of opening the communication between Windows and printer. Select the printer for a particular print job from a pop-up list in the **Print** dialog.

printer driver > see driver

printer font 105, 139
Font definitions either permanently stored in a printer or added by plugging in a software cartridge. Corresponding screen font files for Windows are required to display the font on the screen as it will appear in the printed page.

printer port 8, 136
Rear panel connector, usually the parallel port marked LPT1, most commonly used for printers.

Printers folder 106, 137, 171
Special folder containing icons representing printers installed on the PC.

printing 106, 125, 136-141, 151, 153, 166, 171, 174, 177, 181, 183

Converting screen images to paper via a printer. Each printer requires a driver.

processor > see CPU

profile 71, 82

Specifications about a user's Desktop arrangement, Start menu contents, and other customizable settings. Loaded into Windows when a user enters a name and password (if asked) upon startup. Allows multiple people to use the same PC, each using a personalized setup.

program > see application

Program Manager 66, 71, 77, 83

One part of the Windows 3.x user interface. Functionality is now built into the `Programs` menu in the Start button.

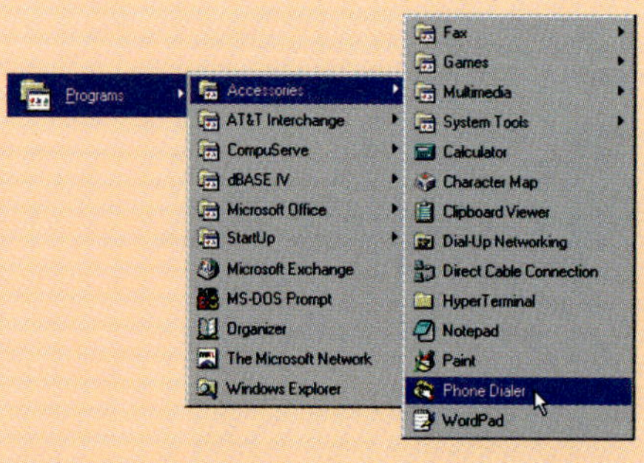

Programs menu 71, 83

Menu item in the Start menu that leads to entries representing applications and subgroupings of applications. A selection of any item in the menu or submenu launches that program.

prompt 70, 131

In MS-DOS, the on-screen signal that the computer is ready for the user to type a command. A common format for an MS-DOS prompt is the letter of the currently selected disk drive, plus any directory path where the next command typed will be sent.

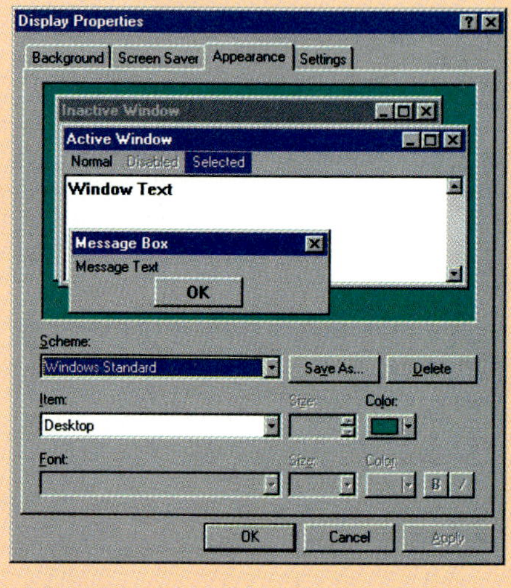

property 67, 112, 138-139

Attribute of an object, such as its name, size, location on the hard disk, and so on. Viewed and changed by way of property sheets.

property sheet 45, 60-61, 67, 75, 112, 130, 138-139

Window that lets a user view and/or modify individual properties of an object. Usually accessible quickly by right-clicking on an object and choosing Properties from the pop-up menu.

protocol 154

Agreed-upon standard for exchange of data between computers.

public domain software 154
Applications, system utilities, and data files widely distributed by user groups, dealers, on-line services, and bulletin boards. Such programs are copyrighted by their authors, but are free. See also shareware.

pull-down menu > see menu, drop-down

queue 106, 137, 151
List of print jobs waiting to be printed. Double-click a printer icon to see if any jobs are queued for that particular printer.

quick format 49
A choice for formatting diskettes that simply overwrites the disk directory with an empty one, but does not completely erase the files previously on the disk.

Quick View 67, 69, 118, 119, 175
Right-click pop-up menu choice for document files of registered file types. When Windows has a viewer adapter for the file type, this displays the file in a read-only window without having to start the application that created the file

radiation 36
Electromagnetic field (EMF) forces generated by high-voltage electronic devices such as video monitors.

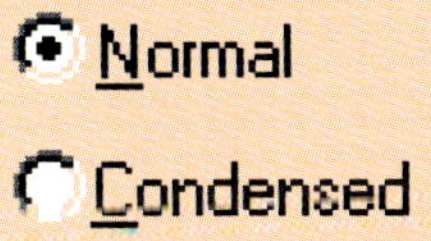

radio button 89, 125
User interface element found in groups of two or more to specify a setting or preference. Click once to activate an item; all other items in the group turn off (like a car radio station preset button).

radio interference > see interference, radio and TV

RAM 40-45, 176
Random Access Memory, temporary storage of programs and documents while you use them. Except for laptop computers with sleep capability, contents of main RAM are erased when you turn off or restart the PC.

RAM, video 30, 41
Memory devoted to holding a copy of information displayed on the video screen. May be built into the motherboard of some PCs, or may be on a video display adapter card.

RAM chip > see SIMM

RAM disk 42
Section of RAM reserved to act as a separate disk volume on the desktop. With items such as programs copied to RAM disk, performance improves substantially. Except on laptop computers with sleep capability, contents disappear on shut down or restart.

random access memory > see RAM

raster font 104-105, 131
Font file that contains the pixel map for each character of a typeface in a particular size. Can be used for screen display, but provide less attractive printout compared to TrueType or PostScript fonts.

RCA phone jack 9
Common audio stereo jack used for audio input and output ports. When a plug is inserted into the audio output port, the internal speaker is disabled.

read-only memory > see ROM

read/write optical disk > see erasable-optical disks

reboot 10-11, 82
Restarting the computer.

recovering damaged disk > see hard disk recovery

Recycle Bin 75, 80, 93, 165, 166, 184
Temporary holder of files and folders for deletion. Dragging items to the bin stores them temporarily (for possible recall) until the bin is emptied or its capacity (determined by its property sheet) is exceeded.

refresh rate 28
Number of times each second that the video screen has its phosphor repainted by the electron beam inside the tube. The higher the refresh rate, the less likely you'll experience flicker as interference with fluorescent lighting.

Regional Settings

Regional Settings control panel 102
Small application for setting the formatting for items that may differ from country to country, such as date and time formats, currency symbols, and number groupings.

registration > see file type

Registry 60, 66, 80, 82, 118, 161
Normally hidden Windows files that contain configuration information for Windows, PC hardware, and programs. Largely replaces .INI file mechanism in Windows 3.x.

Registry Editor 70
Program for experienced users to view and change the contents of the Windows Registry.

remote access 152
Ability to connect a personal computer to a local area network or desktop PC via telephone modem. Setup process is in the Dial-Up Networking applet.

removing applications > see uninstalling applications

Rename 81, 111, 112, 115
`File` menu (or right-click pop-up menu) command that prepares a Desktop/Explorer icon's name for editing. Clicking twice slowly on the name does the same.

repeat delay 16
Keyboard control panel setting that determines how long you must hold down a key before it starts repetitively typing the same character.

repetitive strain injury (RSI) 4
Muscular disease that can be caused by extensive keyboarding without proper support, adjustment, and rest periods.

resize 76, 86
Adjust the dimensions of a screen window by clicking and dragging any window border or corner.

resolution, video 28
Density of pixels per inch on the video screen. The higher the resolution, the smaller recognizable items, such as menubars and icons, appear.

resources 42
Those parts of a computing system—RAM, hard disk space, etc.—that are occupied when Windows 95 and applications run.

response time 6
Amount of time required for a surge suppressor to kick in after receiving a jolt above the clamping voltage.

restart 10, 107, 159-161, 184
Shut down and turn on the computer without completely shutting down power to the system. Far less jarring to the circuitry than turning the machine completely off and turning it back on.

RGB (red, green, blue) 30, 35
Common method of specifying a color by its red, green, and blue components. Color Picker offers fields for direct entry of RGB values, if known. An RGB monitor is one that receives signals for each of the three colors, as opposed to a composite video signal.

right-click 67, 75, 85, 93, 112-113, 137
Placing the pointer atop an object and clicking the right button (i.e., the button other than the primary button).

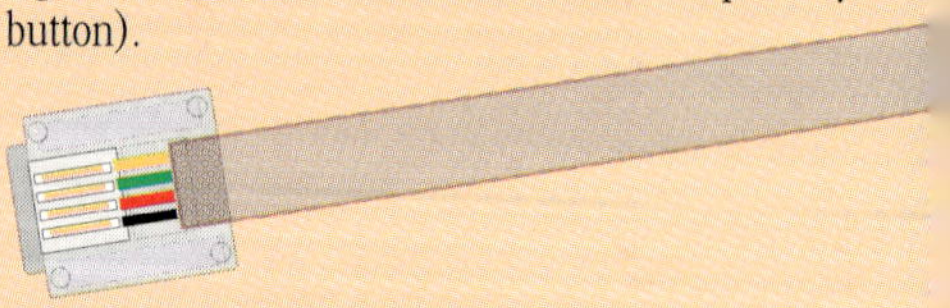

RJ-11 8
Standard modular telephone jack style. Commonly used as a port in a modem for connection to a telephone and the telephone wall jack (which is also an RJ-11 in most home installations).

ROM 10, 40
Read-Only Memory chip containing information built in at the factory. Its contents cannot be changed by the user or a program. In PCs, ROM contains basic instructions that direct the computer to load the operating system from a floppy or hard disk.

root directory 75
Topmost level of a disk volume—the window you see when you double-click a disk icon in `My Computer`.

RSI > see repetitive strain injury

Run 82
Start menu command that lets you start any executable file. The same as double-clicking on an executable item's icon.

Safe mode

safe mode startup 160, 163, 169, 182
Method of starting up Windows 95 so that no device drivers load or Startup programs run, allowing you a chance to run Windows and adjust hardware or software conflicts. Accessible by pressing F8 at PC startup (while screen says "Starting Windows 95") and then pressing F5.

sampled sound 144
Electronic representation of real sound, derived by taking many thousands of readings each second and converting those readings to numbers. Sample sounds may then be edited in a sound editing program and saved as a file or resource.

Sans Serif

sans serif 97, 104
Typeface style without any ornamentation on the ends of strokes. Helvetica and Arial are sans serif fonts.

save file dialog > see dialog, Save As

ScanDisk 58, 159, 182
Applet that checks a disk volume for various surface or data integrity errors.

scanner 22
External device that converts a printed page to an electronic image. Companion software saves the image in a variety of graphic file formats for editing in other graphics and desktop publishing programs.

screen capture; screen dump > see screen shot

screen font > see raster font

screen saver 36, 101
Program (usually an extension or control panel) that blanks the video screen or displays random images to prevent burn-in.

screen shot 15, 33, 137
Copy of the video screen. Press the Print Screen key for the entire screen; Alt+PrtScrn for the active window only. The picture is stored in the Clipboard.

scroll bar 33, 35, 86-87
Control on document windows that allows you to adjust the view through the window to the underlying document. A scroll bar features five elements: up arrow, page up area, view, page down area, down arrow. View indicates relative location within the document and how much along that axis you currently see.

Scroll Lock 15
Key that toggles to keep the spreadsheet cursor at the same cell while you scroll around the spreadsheet (instead of moving the active cell with the scroll).

SCSI cable **7, 51, 55**
Wiring that connects Small Computer Systems Interface standard devices. Comes in a variety of styles and connector versions.

SCSI cabling **55, 159**
Varieties of cabling scenarios are needed to make some combinations of devices work properly.

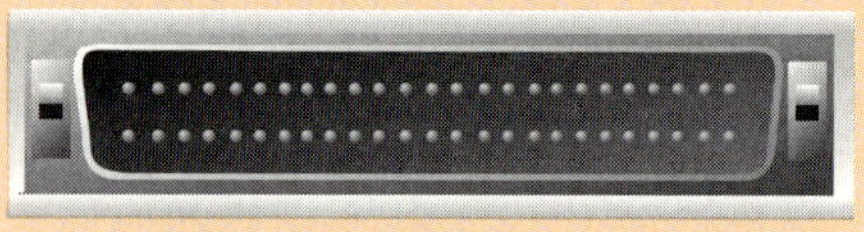

SCSI connector **7, 9, 55**
A Centronics standard 50-pin connector with spring clips on most SCSI peripherals.

SCSI port **9, 55, 59, 60**
Rear panel connector for connecting high-speed peripheral devices, such as hard disks, scanners, and video digitizers.

SCSI terminator > see SCSI cabling

SCSI-2 connector **9, 52, 55**
Small-scale 25-pin connector often found on laptop computers that have built-in SCSI ports and on some peripherals.

search > see files, finding

security > see password

seek time **51**
Amount of time (in milliseconds) it takes a disk drive to find a particular track on a disk.

selecting **80-81, 124**
Process of marking text, graphics, or other objects that will be affected by the next command or action. This usually requires clicking or clicking and dragging on the screen. Selected items are highlighted in various ways: inverse black/white; heavy border around the item; shaded colors; dotted line around the object.

Send To **113**
`File` menu (or right-click pop-up menu) command for directing a copy of the selected item to another container or object on your PC or a network.

separator page **138**
Sheet of paper printed as the first page of a print job, bearing the name of the computer that originated the job and the time the job started printing.

serial port **8, 60, 154**
Rear panel connector for connecting medium-speed peripheral devices, such as telephone modems, audio digitizers, and some printers. Usually labeled COM plus a number.

serial ports, adding **9**
Increasing the number of available serial ports is possible with a cable switcher or expansion boards.

serif **104**
Ornamental stroke at the free ends of a character. Times New Roman is a serif font.

server application **128**
In OLE, the program that created a source document and that will be called upon to provide menus and tools for editing a linked object in another program.

shareware **155**
Software freely distributed by its author, who asks users to try the software for free, but pay a modest licensing fee for continued use.

sharing a folder/disk **150, 152**
Setting up a folder or disk for others on the network to access files in the shared container.

shortcut **71, 75, 83, 111, 114-115, 130, 174, 182**
Tiny file that stands in for any file, folder, or disk. Leave the original file where you like it, and create shortcuts for places where you'd like another copy of the original's icon, such as in the Start menu or Desktop.

shortcuts, keyboard > see keyboard shortcuts

shut down 10, 82, 123, 183
Preparing to turn off your PC via the Shut Down command in the Start menu. Properly closes all applications before instructing you to turn off the PC's power.

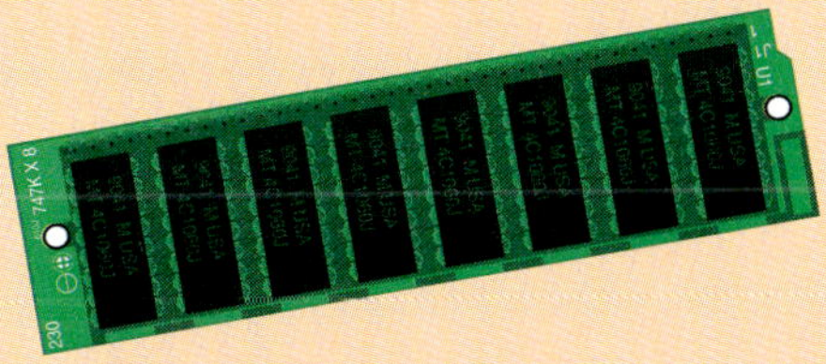

SIMM 40
Single In-line Memory Module, a small circuit board consisting of RAM chips for simplified memory enhancement of personal computers. SIMMs install into matching SIMM sockets on the system board. SIMMs come in a variety of configurations and sizes.

sleep 11, 43
Battery-saving mode of laptop computers. All activity ceases, but contents of RAM are maintained on low current-drain RAM chips.

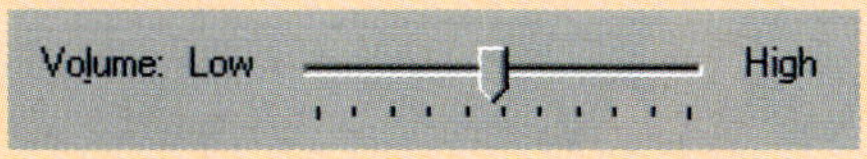

slider control 89, 144, 146
Screen metaphor for a variable setting that you drag with the pointer. Used for volume setting in Volume Control applet.

Small Icons 96
View menu choice that displays Desktop/Explorer items with small icons, in a predominantly horizontal arrangement.

sound file 97, 145, 146-147
Data file containing digitized sounds for playback through multimedia PC audio output components. Sound recording programs can save sampled sounds as sound files (extension .WAV).

sound, playback 146-147, 175
Hardware facilities for playing sound files. Usually built into multimedia-ready PCs; otherwise, requires addition of a sound card and speakers.

sound, recording 93, 144-145
Hardware facilities for recording sounds from a microphone or other audio input. Usually built into multimedia-ready PCs; otherwise, requires addition of a sound card.

Sound Recorder 69, 93, 97, 145
Applet that digitizes and stores sounds from sound input hardware. Can also be used to play a previously saved sound. A small amount of editing and mixing is also possible.

Sounds control panel 93, 97, 147
Control panel for assigning sound files to a variety of system and user events. Sound volume is adjustable through the Volume Control applet.

source document 128
Document file that contains the original data pointed to by OLE links in other documents.

speaker, amplified 9
Connecting to the audio output port, an external speaker that significantly enhances sound quality coming from a sound card.

speaker, internal 146
Built-in speaker in all PCs. Computers without multimedia enhancements can generate simple tones; others can play any digitized sound.

speech, recording > see sound, recording

spike 6
Instantaneous high voltage, usually generated by the electrical power utility. Can be dangerous to electronic equipment that is not protected by a surge protector.

spool 106, 139, 171
Process of allowing simultaneous background communication with a peripheral while foreground activity continues as normal.

standby power supply 6
External device inserted between PC and power outlet. If AC power stops, the internal battery of the power supply furnishes enough power for you to save open documents before shutting down.

Start menu 71, 82-83, 115, 122, 183
Leftmost button of the Taskbar where you can find applications and other Windows 95 commands.

Startup folder 45, 107
Special system folder item that contains programs, documents, or shortcuts (to programs, documents, and servers) that are automatically loaded as Windows starts up.

static electricity 6
Charge stored on the body, especially in low-humidity environments, that can damage chips and other components when touched.

status bar 77, 86, 125
At the bottom of many windows, a strip that displays information about the window's contents or items selected in the window. Usually controlled by a listing in the window's View menu.

stop printing 137
Halt printing by right-clicking on the printer icon and choosing either Pause Printing or Purge Print Jobs from the pop-up menu. Pages already sent to a printer will continue to print.

subdirectory 110
A folder nested inside another folder.

submenu > see menu, hierarchical

surge 6
Instantaneous burst of voltage coming through the power line. Can be damaging to electronic equipment that is not protected by a surge protector.

surge protector 6
Power line device inserted between power outlet and PC to filter extraneous surges and spikes in the AC power.

SYSEDIT.EXE 160
System file editor program (in Windows) for editing the text files for AUTOEXEC.BAT, CONFIG.SYS, and .INI files that may need tweaking to work with Windows 95.

swap file 144
Normally hidden file in the Windows folder that serves as the disk file for virtual memory activities.

Symbol font 105
TrueType font that contains various scientific and math symbols (including many Greek letters).

Syquest 59
Maker of cartridge disk drive mechanisms employed by many disk drive brands. Such cartridges are capable of storing 40, 88, and 230 megabytes.

System control panel 42, 44, 56, 60, 102
Control panel that contains four screens of information about the Windows environment on the current machine and hardware system as recognized by Windows. Hardware conflicts can be resolved and virtual memory settings made here.

System folder
Folder inside the Windows folder that contains many system-wide utility files, rarely accessed directly by users.

system numbering **66**
Conventions used in assigning numbers to system software versions.

system version > see system numbering

tablet > see graphics tablet

tagged image file format > see TIFF

tape drive **8, 54, 59**
External device using removable tape cartridges, primarily for hard disk backup.

target **114-115**
File or container object to which a shortcut points. A button on a shortcut property sheet locates the target item for you.

task **11, 88, 161**
In Windows 95, any running program process, including application programs and background actions the system performs periodically.

Taskbar **66, 71, 75, 82-83, 123, 183**
User interface element containing the Start button and buttons for all open windows and programs. May also display controls or settings from variety of control panels or applets, such as time (Date/Time) and sound volume (Media Player). The Taskbar can be dragged to any side of the screen or stretched taller or wider to accommodate lots of buttons.

Telephone Dialer > see Phone Dialer

telephone line port **8**
Connector in a modem to attach a line to a telephone jack. Usually an RJ-11 type connector.

television **31**
Video input and output sources for the PC with the help of external hardware and video software.

television interference > see interference, radio and TV

terminator > see SCSI cabling

test page **136, 174**
Single page you can print from any printer's property sheet to make sure the printer is connected properly and accepting commands as it should.

text file **155, 178**
Lowest-common-denominator computer file, consisting of plain letters, numerals, and punctuation marks without any font or formatting information. Can be opened by every word processing and spreadsheet program.

text insertion cursor **14, 79, 124**
Flashing vertical bar in a text document indicating where the next character typed from the keyboard will appear. Location can be controlled by the mouse or by cursor keys from the keyboard.

third party **67**
Company other than Microsoft that supports Microsoft's products with additional hardware and software.

TIFF **126**
Tagged Image File Format, a graphics file format.

tiling windows **77, 87**
Method of organizing screen windows so that each is of equal size and none overlaps another. Available in horizontal and vertical arrangements by right-clicking a blank area on the Taskbar.

time, setting > see Date/Time control panel

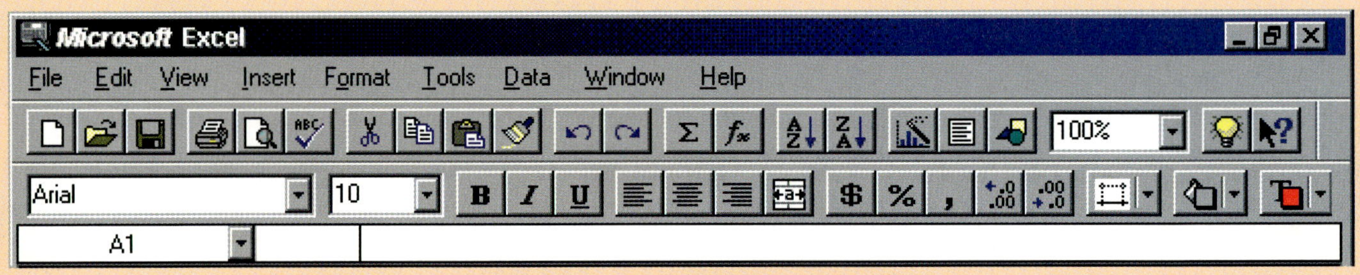

timeout 139
Point at which a software component stops waiting for another software or hardware component to respond to a command or request. Occasionally, the originating software will allow the user to adjust the amount of time to wait for a response; or it may ask the user whether it should try again.

title bar 35, 86
Window element that stretches across the top of the window, featuring the name of the document in the window or the name of the folder whose contents are shown in the window. Color in the title bar indicates an active window; otherwise the window is inactive. At the right end of a title bar are window control buttons.

toggle 84, 125
A switch between two settings, usually On and Off. Some menu items toggle between On and Off, with a checkmark next to the menu item indicating that the feature is turned on.

ToggleKeys 24
Accessibility Options control panel choice that generates a tone whenever a locking key is pressed.

tool bar 77, 86, 118, 125, 131
Across the top of some windows (just below the titlebar), a strip that contains buttons and other settings as shortcuts to complex menu choices. Usually controlled by a listing in the window's View menu.

tool palette 35, 125
Free-standing window or button grouping containing icons representing graphics tools. Clicking on a tool turns the screen pointer into that tool icon, ready to perform whatever action is programmed for that tool.

touch pad 23
Mouse alternative; lets you use your finger on the touchpad as a screen pointer control.

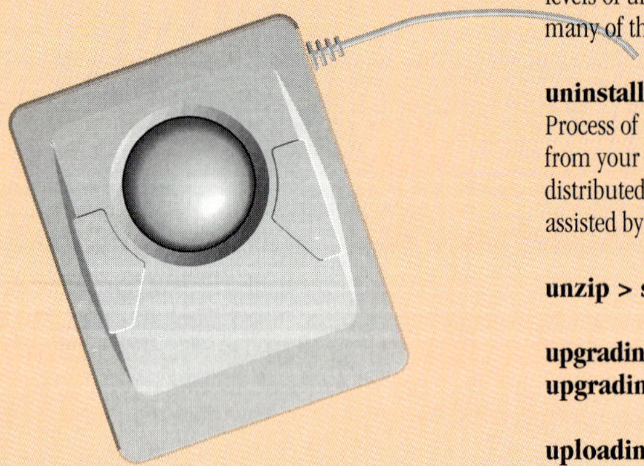

trackball 23
Mouse alternative resembling an inverted mouse, in which you control a roller ball with your fingers or palm.

TrueType 104-105, 131
Font system that uses outline fonts for displaying and printing characters in any font size without scaling of characters.

TSR 67, 131
Terminate-and-stay-resident program which usually loads prior to Windows. TSRs often provide shortcuts or system-level functions that operate in the background.

Undo 85, 113
Edit menu command that reverses the last action taken in a program. Some programs offer multiple levels of undo, whereby the program can take back many of the previous actions, one at a time.

uninstalling applications 69, 70
Process of removing all files belonging to a program from your hard disk. A difficult task when files are distributed throughout many folders, it is sometimes assisted by uninstaller software.

unzip > see PKZIP

upgrading to Windows 95 > see Windows 95, upgrading to

uploading 155
Transferring data from your PC to a larger or more widely available computer, such as a mainframe, network server, or BBS, via a network or telephone modem.

user group 154
Primarily, a local gathering of computer users with similar interests (e.g., Windows 95). Many groups publish newsletters and have manufacturer demonstrations at meetings. Larger user groups also have subgroups, called Special Interest Groups (SIGs), for specialties (e.g., programming, business). User groups are an excellent source for public domain and shareware software as well as help and advice.

user interface 71, 76, 80
The collection of screen elements that acts as a go-between for the computer and human user. An interface that represents the file system and peripherals as icons is called a graphical user interface (GUI, pronounced GOO-ee).

user name 150
The text characters that identify you to a computer. For on-line services, this may also be an electronic mail address. For a network, it is usually your full name.

VCR 31
Video cassette recorder, which can record Windows video with the proper hardware or cable conversions. A VCR can also serve as a video input source for a frame grabber to capture and convert a video image to an electronic file.

vector graphics > see object graphics

ventilation 5, 37
Air flow around and through your system unit and video monitor. Should not be blocked by material on top of units.

VGA video monitor 28, 30, 34, 37
Video Graphics Array, the minimum video display requirement for Windows 95, specified for 640 by 480 pixels at 16 colors. An enhanced version, SVGA (S for Super), allows for larger screens and more colors.

video board > see display adapter

video camera 31
Video input source for a frame grabber.

video clip 147
File containing video information, playable on the computer screen via the Windows 95 Media Player applet and other video-aware multimedia software.

video digitizer 31
External device or expansion board that converts a video signal to electronic images for storage and editing on a PC.

video, local bus 9
Display adapter circuitry built into the system unit, presenting a video port for direct connection to a compatible computer video monitor.

video monitor, AC power 8, 158
Sometimes available through an auxiliary AC power connector on the rear panel of the PC system unit to reduce competition for power outlets.

video monitor setup 5, 158
Physical and cable arrangement of the external video display.

video port 9
Rear panel connector for video monitor, available on some PC models with built-in video support.

View menu 77, 87, 97, 169
Desktop/Explorer window menu that lets you select method of displaying files and folders inside windows.

viewing angle 4
Angle between the eyes and the center of the video display. A viewing angle parallel to the floor can cause fatigue.

virtual machine 130
A portion of RAM that Windows sets aside to appear to an MS-DOS program as if there is a standard 8086-style computer operating. Allows most MS-DOS programs to function at the same time as Windows programs.

virtual memory 43, 44
Capability built into Windows 95 that assigns empty hard disk space to behave as temporary extra RAM. Performance is less than with real RAM, but additional megabytes of RAM can let you open more applications at one time when needed.

virus 58
Small program that tends to propagate from computer to computer by attaching itself to files transferred among computers. Some viruses are minor nuisances, while others can damage important files. Virus detection programs reduce likelihood of infection.

voice > see sound, playback; sound, recording

voice annotation 144
Voice message that is recorded and attached to a document, spreadsheet cell, or other element. Requires an audio input device, such as a microphone or audio digitizer.

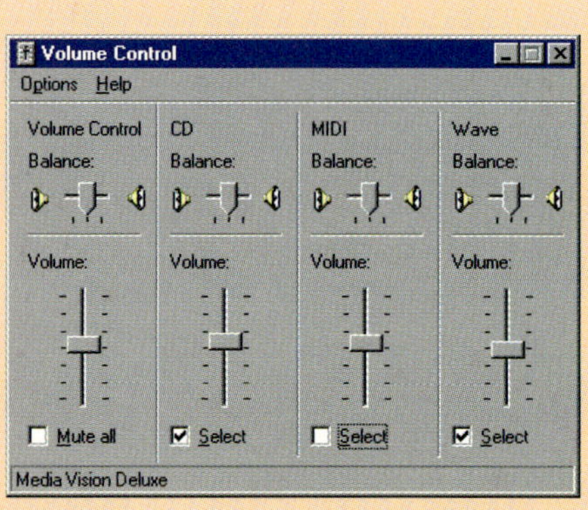

volume **69, 144, 146, 175**
Setting of the sound playback level, adjusted in the Volume Control applet.

wallpaper **94, 95, 101, 124**
Bitmapped graphics that can be assigned to the background of the Desktop view of Windows 95. Adjusted in the Display control panel.

What's This? **78**
Single menu command in a pop-up menu when you right-click on buttons and fields in dialog boxes. Choosing this item presents a pop-up window describing the purpose and operation of that item.

wildcard **90**
Character that represents any character or group of characters. A question mark (?) stands in for a single character; an asterisk (*) stands in for any number of characters that would occupy the same position in a series of characters. Useful in the Find dialog.

Win32 API **43, 67**
Specifications used by programmers to create programs that exploit the features of Windows 95 (and Windows NT).

WIN.INI file **66, 67**
Configuration file for Windows 3.x. Largely unused for Windows 95, but available for older programs that expect the file to be there.

window **35, 79, 86-87, 88, 96, 123, 124, 130**
Screen element that provides a view to a document. When the document is larger than the window, the window usually offers scroll bars to let you move the view to other places in the document.

Windows 95, upgrading to **66-71**
Process of updating your computer from MS-DOS or Windows 3.x to Windows 95.

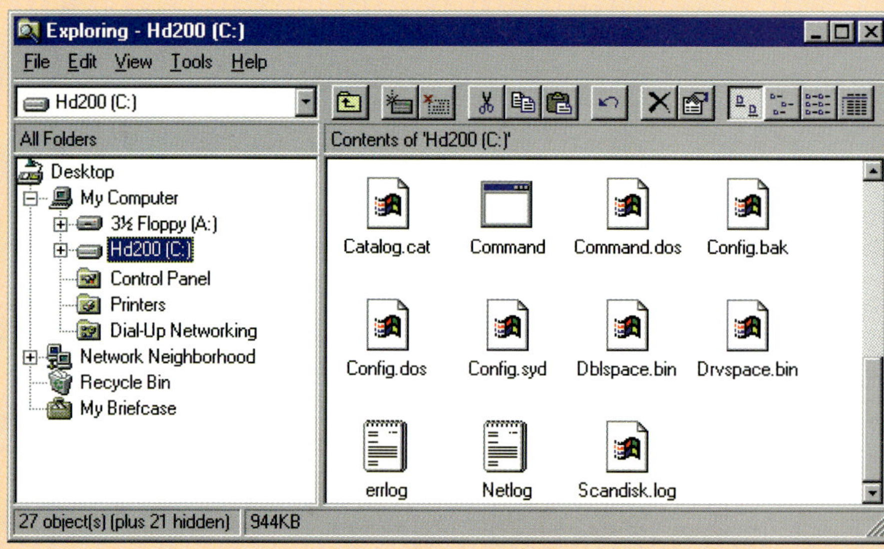

Windows Explorer **66, 74, 76-77, 183**
The primary user interface program for Windows 95 consisting of both the Desktop display and the Explorer window. In this book, "Windows Explorer" refers to the Explorer window only.

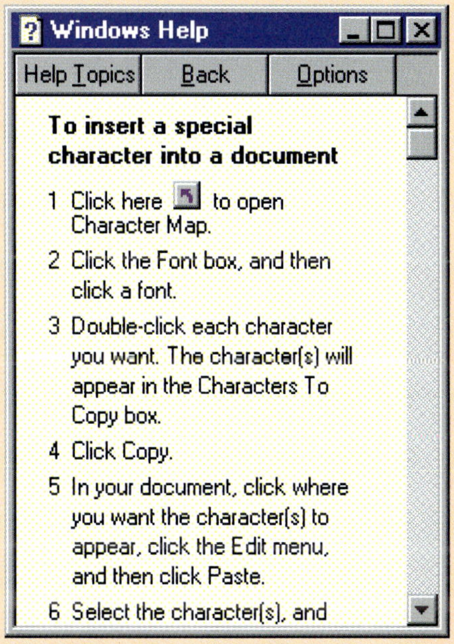

Windows Help 78, 82, 85, 167, 168
On-line help system built into Windows 95. Available by choosing Help from the Start menu. Other Windows programs share the same functionality as the Windows Help windows.

Wingdings font 17, 105
TrueType font that contains a number of symbols useful in desktop publishing.

WordPad 69, 122
Standard text editing applet in Windows 95. Capable of opening and saving Word for Windows 6.0 files and other formats.

WORM 59
Write Once Read Many high capacity optical disk storage. Best used for archival storage.

write protecting a disk > see floppy disk, locking

WYSIWYG 125, 139
What You See Is What You Get, pronounced WIZ-ee-wig. Implies that the layout and quality of images on the screen is exactly what appears in a printout. With TrueType and object graphics, printouts on most printers exceed the quality of the display.

zip > see PKZIP

Zmodem 154
Efficient file transfer protocol that performs error checking after the transfer of each block of the file. When an error is detected, the receiving computer signals the sending computer to re-send the block.

About the Author

Danny Goodman has been an active participant on the editorial side of the personal computer and consumer electronics revolutions since the late 1970s. His articles in the field have appeared in some of the most prestigious general audience publications, such as *Playboy, Science Digest, Chicago* and *Los Angeles* city magazines, and in-flight magazines for United, TWA, and several other airlines. He has written dozens of feature articles for leading computer publications, such as *PC Magazine, PC World, Macworld,* and *MacUser.*

Danny is also the author of twenty-two books on computing and information superhighway technologies. *Living at Light Speed* (Random House, 1995) punctures the myths surrounding the information highway hoopla, while providing a daily-grind's-eye view of how the various technologies will affect the daily lives of everyday folks. Another title, *The Complete HyperCard Handbook,* published by Bantam Books in August 1987, claimed honors as the best selling Macintosh book and fastest selling computer book in the history of the industry. That book is now in its fourth edition and has been translated into more than a half-dozen languages. His *HyperCard Handbook* and *HyperCard Developer's Guide* have both received Best Product-Specific Book awards from the Computer Press Association (1987 and 1988, respectively). *Danny Goodman's Macintosh Handbook* (1993), a radical departure from traditional computer books, won Danny's third CPA award. The book's four-color design, created in collaboration with world-class information architect, Richard Saul Wurman, is the inspiration for *Danny Goodman's Windows 95 Handbook.*

To demonstrate the capabilities of products he was writing about, Danny has also developed commercial software. In November 1987, Activision published his *Focal Point* and *Business Class* programs. These two products (a personal information manager and an international travel resource) received the Software Publishers Association awards for best products in three categories for 1987. Focal Point won the MacGuide Golden Gavel award based on subscribers' write-in ballots for products in 1988. In November 1988, *Focal Point II* shipped under Mediagenic's TENpointO label to critical acclaim. His latest software product, *Apple Guide Starter,* is an authoring tool for the Apple Guide technology of MacOS version 7.5. The program is part of a book/disk package, *Danny Goodman's Apple Guide Starter Kit* (Addison-Wesley, 1995) with co-author Jeremy Joan Hewes.

Danny was born in Chicago, Illinois "in the middle of the century." He earned a B.A. and M.A. in Classical Antiquity from the University of Wisconsin — Madison, and moved to the San Francisco area, where he now alternates views between computer screens and the Pacific Ocean.

About vivid studios

vivid is an innovative online studio that is redefining experiences in human communications. Aiming it's talents at online development, **vivid** leverages it's technological expertise, design savvy, and rigorous testing standards, to create, implement, and manage entertaining, informative online experiences. This expertise consistently earns **vivid** a place among America's best online developers—including *I.D.Magazine's* Top 40 American design firms and *Interactive Age's* top 100 websites.

vivid's approach is to develop superbly designed and structured products whether the medium is print, CD-ROM, or online. It's experience in information design and interaction design is paramount to this approach.

vivid takes an active role in educating others about multimedia. Many **vivids** are on the faculty of San Francisco State University's Multimedia Extension and are frequently invited to speak at industry conferences and events. The company and staff have appeared in *Fortune, Interactive Age, Advertising Age, New Media,* and *Online Design.* **vivid** has up-to-date information about it's products, people, and process on the World Wide Web at: http://www.vivid.com.

Stuart L. Silberman managed the design and production of *Danny Goodman's Windows 95 Handbook.*

John "Zippy" Lehnus,
Steve de Brun, and
André Marschalko assisted with page layout.

Steve de Brun and
Scott Summers
created the illustrations.

Nathan Shedroff and **Richard Saul Wurman** designed *Danny Goodman's Macintosh Handbook,* the prototype for this book.

AnnD Canavan
provided management inspiration.

Henri Poole and
Ken Fromm
initiated this project and made it possible.

vivid thanks
Jennifer Dowling and
Michael Roney
of Random House, Inc.